An Introduction to ERROR-CORRECTING CODES

COMPUTER APPLICATIONS IN ELECTRICAL ENGINEERING SERIES

Franklin F. Kuo, *editor*

Davis *Computer Data Displays*
Jensen & Lieberman *IBM Circuit Analysis Program: Techniques and Applications*
Kuo & Magnuson *Computer Oriented Circuit Design*
Lin *An Introduction to Error-Correcting Codes*
Sifferlen & Vartanian *Digital Electronics with Engineering Applications*

PRENTICE-HALL INTERNATIONAL, INC., *London*
PRENTICE-HALL OF AUSTRALIA PTY. LTD., *Sydney*
PRENTICE-HALL OF CANADA, LTD., *Toronto*
PRENTICE-HALL OF INDIA PRIVATE LTD., *New Delhi*
PRENTICE-HALL OF JAPAN, INC., *Tokyo*

An Introduction to ERROR-CORRECTING CODES

SHU LIN

Department of Electrical Engineering
University of Hawaii

Prentice-Hall, Inc., Englewood Cliffs, New Jersey

Current printing (last digit): 10 9 8 7 6 5 4 3 2 1

13–482810–0

Library of Congress Catalog Card Number: 76–124417

PRINTED IN THE UNITED STATES OF AMERICA

To

Paul E. Pfeiffer

W. Wesley Peterson

and

Tadao Kasami

PREFACE

One of the serious problems in a digital data communication system is the occurrence of errors in the data transmitted over a noisy channel. A major concern to thc communication engineer is the control of these errors such that reliable transmission of data can be obtained. In 1948, Shannon demonstrated that by proper encoding and decoding of the data, errors induced by a noisy channel can be reduced to any desired level without sacrificing the data transmission rate. Since the appearance of this result, a great deal of effort has been expended on the problem of devising efficient encoding and decoding schemes for error control over noisy channels. As a result of this effort, numerous papers and reports on this subject have been published. Most of these papers and reports are generally mathematically sophisticated. So sophisticated, in fact, that most practicing communication engineers find the subject of coding very difficult to understand.

The purpose of this book is to present error-correcting codes and their decoding techniques which show promise for practical applications. Our intention is to bring highly complex material down to a reasonably simple level such that the practicing communication engineer can understand the material with a minimum background in mathematics. This book is also intended for use as a text for senior or first-year graduate students. We have taken a middle ground between mathematical rigor and heuristic reasoning. If a proof does not contribute materially to the understanding of a particular coding technique, the proof is omitted and replaced by working examples.

A brief description of the subject matter follows. Chapter 1 gives a brief introduction to the coding problem. Chapter 2 provides the reader with an elementary knowledge of modern algebra that will aid in the understanding of the material in the following chapters. The treatment is basically descriptive and no attempt is made to be mathematically rigorous. Basic concepts of block codes are introduced in Chapter 3. In Chapter 4, cyclic block codes which form an important subclass of block codes are discussed. Important cyclic block codes and their decoding techniques are presented in Chapters 5, 6, 7, 8, and 9. In Chapter 10, the basic concepts and structures of convolutional codes are introduced. Chapters 11 and 12 give a compilation of important convolutional codes and their decoding techniques. In Chapter

13, a short description of sequential decoding for convolutional codes is given. The decoding techniques discussed in Chapters 4-12 are entirely based on the algebraic structures of the codes. The sequential decoding for convolutional codes presented in Chapter 13 is a probabilistic decoding scheme.

The material covered in Chapters 2, 3, 4, and 10 can be used as a supplementary subject for a course on information theory.

Even though this book is a systematic introduction to error-correcting codes, it uses many concepts and techniques which were developed by people doing research in coding theory. In fact, without my deep involvement in research, this book could not have been written. It is a pleasure to publicly acknowledge the research support of the University of Hawaii, the National Aeronautics and Space Administration, the National Science Foundation, and the Air Force Cambridge Research Laboratory.

I was most fortunate in having the opportunity to study under Professor Paul E. Pfeiffer at the Rice University. My four years of graduate work under his supervision was most stimulating. I have been profoundly influenced by his philosophy of teaching and writing, which places strong emphasis on clarity of exposition. I cannot adequately express the satisfaction and value that I have found in this philosophy.

I am very grateful to Professors W. Wesley Peterson and Tadao Kasami who stimulated my serious work in algebraic coding theory and to whom I owe much of my understanding of the subject. My association with Professors Peterson and Kasami began in 1965, when I came to the University of Hawaii as a research associate under their supervision. Since then, I have been working closely with them and have always found discussions with them fruitful and stimulating. I am particularly indebted to Professor Peterson for his contributions to the writing of Sections 2.1, 6.2, and 6.3. His criticisms and suggestions of the entire draft are invaluable.

To Professor Franklin F. Kuo, I wish to express my sincere gratitude for his suggestion to write this book and his constant encouragement and editorial assistance during the process of writing. I also wish to thank Professor Edward J. Weldon, Jr., who reviewed the entire manuscript and supplied helpful criticisms and suggestions.

My indebtedness to the literature on the subject is as obvious as it is great. I apologize to many authors of significant papers in coding theory whom I neglected to cite either through oversight or ignorance. I tried to list the references that I found useful in the preparation of this book along with references for selected and advanced material.

Anyone who has ever put together a book knows how much an author owes to a patient and capable secretary. Miss Gayle Harimoto more than deserves my gratitude for her efforts to produce a usable manuscript.

Finally, to my parents and wife, I owe a special debt of gratitude. Their affection and encouragement made the writing of this book possible.

Shu Lin

Honolulu, Hawaii
March 12, 1970

CONTENTS

An Introduction to

ERROR-CORRECTING CODES

CHAPTER 1

COMMUNICATION AND CODING

1.1 INTRODUCTION

In recent years, the demand for efficient and reliable digital data transmission systems has been accelerated by the increasing use of automatic data processors and the rising need for long range communications. One of the serious problems in any high speed data transmission system is the occurrence of errors. The problem of how to control these errors is one of basic importance.

In most present digital computers and digital data communication systems, information is handled in binary form; more specifically, information is coded in binary digits "0" or "1." A block diagram of a typical digital data communication system (or an information storage system) is shown in Fig. 1.1. The first element of this system is the *information source*, which

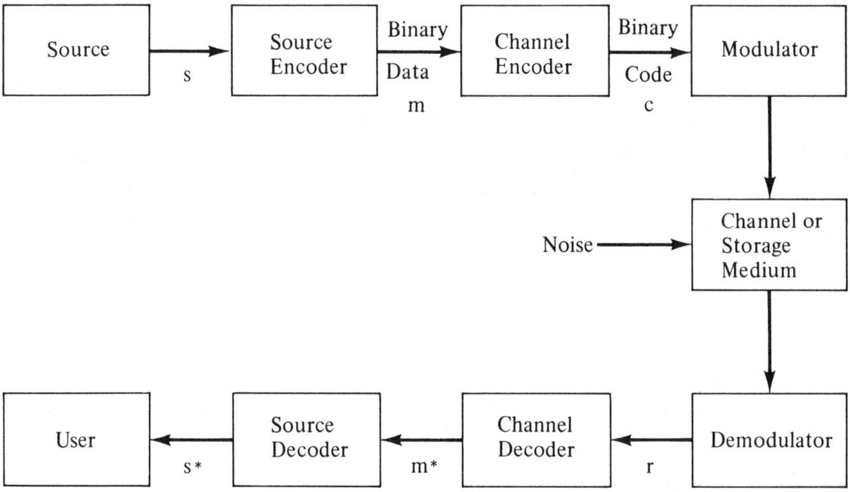

Fig. 1.1. Block diagram of a typical data communication or storage system.

may be a person or a machine (for example, a digital computer). The output of the source may be a continuous waveform or a sequence of discrete symbols (or letters). The *channel* is a medium over which signals containing useful information are transmitted. Typical examples of transmission channels are telephone lines, high frequency radio links, space communication links, and magnetic tape units including writing and reading heads for storage systems. The channel is usually subject to various types of noise disturbances, natural or man-made. For example, on a telephone line, the disturbance may come from thermal noise, lightning, impulse noise, or crosstalk from other lines. On a magnetic tape, tape defects are regarded as a disturbance. The *source encoder* transforms the source output into a sequence **m** of binary symbols, i.e., a sequence of 0's and 1's, which is called the *information sequence.* The transformation should be done in such a way that: (1) the number of binary digits per unit of time required to represent the source output is small; and (2) the reconstruction of the source output from the information sequence **m** is possible. The *channel encoder*, according to some *rules*, transforms the input information sequence **m** into some longer binary sequence **c** which is called the *code word* of **m**. This transformation is referred to as *channel encoding.* The binary digits are not suitable for transmission over the physical channel. The function of the *modulator* is to encode each output digit of the channel encoder into one of two physical waveforms of duration T seconds. For example, a "1" may be encoded into a positive pulse of duration T, and a "0" encoded into a negative pulse (or a blank) of duration T. The output signal of the modulator enters the channel and is disturbed by noise. The *demodulator* makes a decision for each received signal of duration T to determine whether a 1 or 0 was transmitted. Thus, the output of the demodulator is a sequence **r** of binary digits. The sequence **r** is called the *received sequence.* Due to the channel noise disturbance, the received sequence **r** might not match the code word **c**. The places where they differ are called *transmission errors* (or simply errors). For example, if $\mathbf{c} = (1\ 1\ 0\ 0\ 1\ 1\ 0\ 0\ 0\ 1\ 1\ 1\ 0\ 1\ 1)$ is transmitted and $\mathbf{r} = (1\ 1\ 0\ 0\ 0\ 1\ 0\ 0\ 0\ 1\ 0\ 1\ 0\ 1\ 1)$ is received, then errors occur at the 5th and the 11th places. The channel encoder should be designed such that its output code words have the capability of combatting the transmission errors. The *channel decoder*, based on the received sequence **r**, the rules of channel encoding, and the channel characteristics, does the following two things: (1) It attempts to correct the transmission errors in **r** and produces an estimation **c*** of the actual transmitted code word **c**. (2) It transforms **c*** into an information sequence **m*** which is an estimation of the transmitted information sequence **m**. The *source decoder*, based on the rules of source encoding, transforms **m*** into an estimation **s*** of the actual source output **s** and delivers it to the user. If the channel is quiet, **c***, **m***, and **s*** are reproductions of **c**, **m**, and **s** respectively. If the channel is very noisy, **s*** might be quite different from the actual source output.

A major communication engineering problem is to design the channel encoder-decoder pair such that: (1) the binary data can be transmitted over the noisy channel as *fast* as possible; and (2) *reliable reproduction* of the information sequence **m** can be obtained at the output of the channel decoder. The design of the channel encoder-decoder pair is primarily based on the channel characteristics.

1.2 BLOCK CODES AND MAXIMUM LIKELIHOOD DECODING

If we are only concerned with channel encoding and decoding, the system in Fig. 1.1 can be reduced to the form shown in Fig. 1.2, where the source consists of the original source and the source encoder, and where the

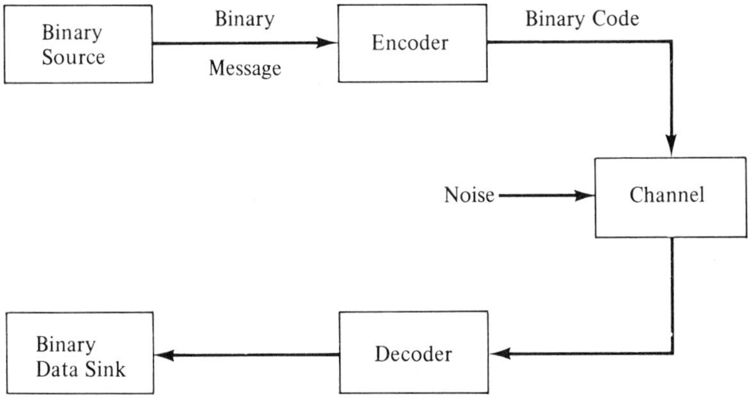

Fig. 1.2. Channel model.

channel consists of the modulator, the original channel, and the demodulator. In this case, the channel accepts binary data and delivers corrupted binary data to the decoder.

One example of an encoding scheme is presented in the following discussion. The output information sequence of the source is first segmented into message blocks; each message block $\mathbf{m}$ consists of k information digits. There are a total of 2^k distinct messages. The encoder transforms each input message $\mathbf{m}$ into a longer binary sequence $\mathbf{c}$ of n digits, which is called a *code word* of $\mathbf{m}$. Therefore, corresponding to 2^k possible input messages, there are 2^k possible code words at the output of the encoder. This set of 2^k code words is called a *block code.* The $n - k$ digits added to each message block by the encoder are called *redundant digits.* These redundant digits carry no new information and their function is to provide the code with the capability of correcting errors made in transmission. How to form these redundant digits such that the code has good error-correcting capability is a major concern in designing the encoder. The ratio $R = k/n$ is called the *code rate*, which is interpreted as the number of information digits entering the encoder per transmitted channel digit.

Suppose that $\mathbf{c} = (c_0, c_1, c_2, \ldots, c_{n-1})$ is the transmitted code word and $\mathbf{r} = (r_0, r_1, r_2, \ldots, r_{n-1})$ is the sequence received at the channel output. The received sequence might differ from the transmitted code word $\mathbf{c}$ because of channel noise disturbance. On the basis of $\mathbf{r}$ and the channel characteristic, a decision is made at the decoder concerning the transmitted code word. This decision process is called *decoding.* An erroneous decoding is committed if the decoder fails to identify (reproduce) the actual transmitted code word. The probability of an erroneous decoding depends on the code used, the channel characteristic, and the decoding strategy employed at the decoder. If all the code words have equal likelihood of being transmitted, the best decoding scheme is as follows. Upon receiving the sequence $\mathbf{r}$, the decoder computes the conditional probability $P(\mathbf{r}|\mathbf{c}_\ell)$ for all 2^k code words. The code word $\mathbf{c}_t$ is identified as the transmitted word if the conditional probability $P(\mathbf{r}|\mathbf{c}_t)$ is the largest. This decoding scheme is known as *maximum likelihood decoding.*

The most important and most striking result on transmission of information over a noisy channel is Shannon's "coding theorem."[21,22] The theorem says that every channel has a definite capacity C, and that for any rate R less than C, there exist codes of rate R which, with maximum likelihood decoding, have an arbitrarily small probability of erroneous decoding $P(\varepsilon)$. More specifically, for any given rate $R < C$ and length n, there exists a block code such that the probability of erroneous decoding

$$P(\varepsilon) \leqslant e^{-nE(R)} \quad , \tag{1.1}$$

where $E(R)$ is a positive function of R for $R < C$ and is specified by channel transition probabilities. Therefore, the probability of decoding error can be made as small as we desire by increasing the code length n and keeping rate R less than the channel capacity C. Shannon's theorem only shows the existence of codes which give arbitrarily small probability of decoding error, but does not indicate how these codes can be constructed. We are thus faced with the problem of how to construct these good codes of large n promised by Shannon.

As shown in Eq. (1.1), the code length n must be large for a code to be effective. If we implement this code with an encoder which stores 2^{nR} $(= 2^k)$ code words and a decoder which performs the maximum likelihood decoding, then both encoder and decoder would be prohibitively complex. As for the decoder, it has to compute 2^{nR} conditional probabilities $P(\mathbf{r}|\mathbf{c}_\ell)$. Therefore, one is faced with the following three problems: (1) to find long good codes; (2) to find a practical method of encoding; and (3) to find a practical method of decoding.

The probability of erroneous decoding for a code depends on the statistical properties of the transmission errors. Theoretical studies almost invariably assume that there is a probability of $q_0 > ½$ that the same symbol as transmitted will be received and probability $p_0 = 1 - q_0$ that the opposite symbol will be received, as shown in Fig. 1.3. It is also assumed that the channel acts on the transmitted symbols independently. A channel satisfying these conditions is called a *binary symmetric channel* (*BSC*). The probability p_0 is called the transition probability. For the binary symmetric channel, the conditional probability $P(\mathbf{r}|\mathbf{c}_\ell)$ can be expressed as follows:

$$P(\mathbf{r}|\mathbf{c}_\ell) = \prod_{i=0}^{n-1} P(r_i|c_{\ell i}) \quad , \tag{1.2}$$

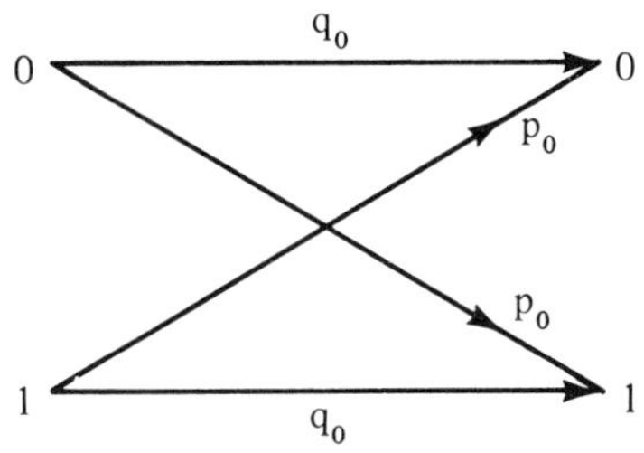

Fig. 1.3. The binary symmetric channel.

where $P(r_i|c_{\ell i}) = q_0$ for $r_i = c_{\ell i}$ and $P(r_i|c_{\ell i}) = p_0$ for $r_i \neq c_{\ell i}$. Let d_ℓ be the number of places where the code word $\mathbf{c}_\ell$ and the received sequence $\mathbf{r}$ differ. Then Eq. (1.2) becomes

$$P(\mathbf{r}|\mathbf{c}_\ell) = q_0^{\,n-d_\ell}\, p_0^{\,d_\ell} \tag{1.3}$$

Since $q_0 > p_0$, $P(\mathbf{r}|\mathbf{c}_\ell)$ decreases monotonically with increasing d_ℓ. Therefore, to find the code word $\mathbf{c}_t$ such that $P(\mathbf{r}|\mathbf{c}_t)$ is maximized is equivalent to finding the code word $\mathbf{c}_t$ that differs from the received sequence $\mathbf{r}$ in the fewest places.

The transmission errors induced on the binary symmetric channel are referred to as *random errors.* The codes devised for combatting this kind of errors are called *random-error-correcting codes.* Unfortunately, very few real channels are like the binary symmetric channel. There is usually serious dependence of errors in successive transmitted symbols. The noise disturbance – a stroke of lightning or a man-made electrical disturbance, for example – frequently affects several adjacent symbols. Defects on magnetic recording devices also usually affect more than one symbol. Thus, errors occur in *bursts*. The observation of this phenomenon led to the development of codes for correcting burst errors. Unfortunately, they do not solve the problem either, because sometimes the bursts come in bursts. A channel may be very good for a long time and then very bad for a while – perhaps a short while, but long enough to make error correction very difficult, if not impossible. For such a channel only limited improvement can be attained with error correction alone, and some combination of error correction with error detection and request for repeat is required (the request signal is transmitted back to the transmitter via a reverse channel). In this book, we are only concerned with various kinds of coding techniques for error correction in digital communication systems with a one-way channel.

1.3 AN EXAMPLE

The following simple example of an error-correcting code illustrates the type of presentation and introduces some terminology.

Suppose we have a message of 12 binary information digits to transmit. The 12 digits of the message might be arranged in a 3×4 rectangular array:

$$\begin{matrix} X_{11} & X_{12} & X_{13} & X_{14} \\ X_{21} & X_{22} & X_{23} & X_{24} \\ X_{31} & X_{32} & X_{33} & X_{34} \end{matrix}$$

Now add to each row and each column one more symbol, chosen to make the number of 1's in each row and column even. Finally, add a symbol at the lower right corner, chosen to make the last row also have an even number of 1's. Now it will turn out that the last column also has an even number of 1's:

$$\begin{matrix} X_{11} & X_{12} & X_{13} & X_{14} & X_{15} \\ X_{21} & X_{22} & X_{23} & X_{24} & X_{25} \\ X_{31} & X_{32} & X_{33} & X_{34} & X_{35} \\ X_{41} & X_{42} & X_{43} & X_{44} & X_{45} \end{matrix}$$

For the information shown, the check symbols would be chosen as shown.

$$\begin{array}{cccc|c} 1 & 1 & 1 & 0 & 1 \\ 1 & 1 & 0 & 0 & 0 \\ 0 & 1 & 0 & 1 & 0 \\ \hline 0 & 1 & 1 & 1 & 1 \end{array}$$

Now if this entire array is transmitted row by row (or column by column) and if along the way a single symbol is changed – i.e., there is a single error – it can be corrected. Correction is done by checking each row and column for even *parity* – an even number of ones. If there is a single error, one column check and one row check will fail, and the error must be at the intersection. It can then be corrected. These 20 transmitted symbols form a code word. This code has a total of $n = 20$ symbols, of which $k = 12$ are information symbols. It is referred to as a (20,12) code. There are $n - k = 20 - 12 = 8$ check symbols. These are the redundant digits added to the message to provide the code word with error-correcting capability.

All the codes described in this book are based on mathematical ideas similar to the ones used for this (20,12) code. The ideas are generally mathematically deeper and lead to better codes. For example, the Hamming codes[15] require the minimum number of check symbols for a single-error-correcting code, significantly fewer than the above code requires.

The distance between two n-symbol code words is the number of positions in which they differ, and the minimum distance for a code is the minimum distance between two code words. The minimum distance for the code in the example is 4 – changing four symbols at the corners of a rectangle changes one code word into another, because then all row and column parity-checks will still hold. For correction of all combinations of t or fewer errors, the minimum distance must be at least $2t + 1$. This assures that if t errors occur, the received sequence will still be closer to the actual transmitted code word than to any other possible code word. In this case, the actual transmitted code word $\mathbf{c}_t$ will give the largest conditional probability $P(\mathbf{r}|\mathbf{c}_t)$. Thus, for correction of single errors, the minimum distance must be at least 3.

In the code given as an example, the minimum distance of 4 assures correction of all single errors. For all double errors, two row checks and/or two column checks will fail, and although the errors are detected, they cannot be located. Combinations of three errors in various locations may show two, four, or six row and column check failures. Generally, triple errors can be detected and distinguished from single errors, but if the three errors happen to lie at the three corners of a rectangle, there will be one column failure and one row failure and the decoder will probably incorrectly interpret this as a single error. Similarly, most combinations of four errors are detected, but four errors at the corners of a rectangle result in a received sequence with no parity failures.

In general, simultaneous correction of all combinations of up to t errors and detection of all combinations of $\ell \geqslant t$ errors requires minimum distance $t+\ell+1$. Furthermore, for any of the codes described in this book, it is possible to limit the correction from the maximum possible t to some smaller value and assure detection of a larger class of errors.

REFERENCES

1. Abramson, N., *Information Theory and Coding,* McGraw-Hill, New York, 1963.

2. Ash, R. B., *Information Theory,* Interscience Publishers, New York, 1965.

3. Berlekamp, E. R., *Algebraic Coding Theory,* McGraw-Hill, New York, 1968.

4. Elias, P., "Error Free Coding," *IRE Trans. on Information Theory,* **IT-4**, pp. 29-37, September, 1954.

5. Elias, P., "Coding for Noisy Channels," *IRE Convention Record,* Part 4, pp. 37-46, 1955.

6. Fano, R.M., *Transmission of Information,* The M.I.T. Press, Cambridge, Massachusetts, and John Wiley, New York, 1961.

7. Feinstein, A., *Foundations of Information Theory,* McGraw-Hill, New York, 1958.

8. Forney, G.D., *Concatenated Codes,* The M.I.T. Press, Cambridge, Massachusetts, 1967.

9. Gallager, R.G., "A Simple Derivation of the Coding Theorem and Some Applications," *IEEE Trans. on Information Theory,* **IT-11**, pp. 3-18, January, 1965.

10. Gallager, R. G., *Information Theory and Reliable Communication*, McGraw-Hill, New York, 1968.

11. Gilbert, E. N., "A Comparison of Signaling Alphabets," *Bell Systems Tech. J.*, **31**, pp. 504-522, 1952.

12. Gilbert, E. N., "Capacity of Burst Noise Channel," *Bell Systems Tech. J.*, **39**, pp. 1253-1256, January, 1960.

13. Golay, M. J. E., "Binary Coding," *IRE Trans. on Information Theory*, **PGIT-4**, pp. 23-28, September, 1954.

14. Jelinek, F., *Probabilistic Information Theory*, McGraw-Hill, New York, 1968.

15. Hamming, R. W., "Error Detecting and Error Correcting Codes," *Bell Systems Tech. J.*, **29**, pp. 147-160, April, 1950.

16. Lucky, R. W., J. Salz, and E. J. Weldon, Jr., *Principles of Data Communication*, McGraw-Hill, New York, 1968.

17. Peterson, W. W., *Error-Correcting Codes*, The M.I.T. Press, Cambridge, Massachusetts, and John Wiley, New York, 1961.

18. Peterson, W. W., "Error-Correcting Codes," *Scientific American*, **206**, pp. 96-108, February, 1962.

19. Peterson, W.W., "Binary Codes for Error Control," *Proc. National Electronics Conference*, **16**, pp. 15-21, October, 1960.

20. Peterson, W. W., and E. J. Weldon, Jr., *Error-Correcting Codes*, 2nd Edition, The M.I.T. Press, Cambridge, Massachusetts, 1970.

21. Shannon, C. E., and W. Weaver, *A Mathematical Theory of Communication*, University of Illinois Press, Urbana, Illinois, 1949. (The first part of this book is a reprint of Shannon's paper, "A Mathematical Theory of Communication," *Bell Systems Tech. J.*, **27**, 1948.)

22. Shannon, C.E., "Certain Results in Coding Theory for Noisy Channels," *Information and Control*, **1**, pp. 6-25, September, 1957.

23. Slepian, D., "A Class of Binary Signaling Alphabets," *Bell Systems Tech. J.*, **35**, pp. 203-234, January, 1956.

24. Slepian, D., "A Note on Two Binary Signaling Alphabets," *IRE Trans. on Information Theory*, **PGIT-2**, pp. 84-86, June, 1956.

25. Wolfowitz, J., *Coding Theorems of Information Theory*, Prentice-Hall, Englewood Cliffs, New Jersey 1961.

26. Wozencraft, J. M., and I. M. Jacobs, *Principles of Communication Engineering*, John Wiley, New York, 1967.

CHAPTER 2

INTRODUCTION TO ALGEBRA

The purpose of this chapter is to provide the reader with an elementary knowledge of algebra that will aid in the understanding of the material in the following chapters. The treatment is basically descriptive and no attempt is made to be mathematically rigorous. There are many good textbooks on algebra. The reader who is interested in more advanced algebraic coding theory is referred to the textbooks listed at the end of this chapter.

2.1 GALOIS FIELD ARITHMETIC

It is possible to define addition and multiplication for a finite number of symbols, *if the number of symbols is a power of a prime number*, in such a way that most of the rules of ordinary arithmetic apply. It is therefore possible to utilize most of the techniques of algebra. In particular, for digital computers and digital data transmission we usually use two symbols, 0 and 1, for which addition and multiplication can be defined as follows:

$0 + 0 = 0$	$0 \cdot 0 = 0$
$0 + 1 = 1$	$0 \cdot 1 = 0$
$1 + 0 = 1$	$1 \cdot 0 = 0$
$1 + 1 = 0$	$1 \cdot 1 = 1$

Table 2.1. Addition and multiplication for an alphabet of two symbols.

The addition and multiplication defined above are called *modulo-2 addition* and *multiplication* respectively. This is actually equivalent to ordinary arithmetic, except that we consider 2 to be equal to 0. Note that since $1 + 1 = 0$, $1 = -1$. The alphabet of two symbols, 0 and 1, together with modulo-2 addition and multiplication is called a *field* of two elements (or a *binary field*), which is usually denoted by $GF(2)$.

To illustrate how the ideas of algebra can be used with the above arithmetic, we consider the following set of equations:

$$\begin{aligned} X + Y \quad\ &= 1 \\ X \quad + Z &= 0 \\ X + Y + Z &= 1 \quad . \end{aligned}$$

These can be solved by subtracting the first equation from the third, giving $Z = 0$. Then from the second equation, if $Z = 0$ and $X + Z = 0$, $X = 0$ also. From the first equation, if $X + Y = 1$ and $X = 0$, then $Y = 1$. We can substitute these solutions back into the original set of equations and verify that they are correct.

Since we were able to solve the equations, they must be linearly independent, and the determinant of the coefficients on the left side must be non-zero. If the determinant is non-zero, it must be 1. This can be verified as follows:

$$\begin{vmatrix} 1 & 1 & 0 \\ 1 & 0 & 1 \\ 1 & 1 & 1 \end{vmatrix} = 1 \cdot \begin{vmatrix} 0 & 1 \\ 1 & 1 \end{vmatrix} - 1 \cdot \begin{vmatrix} 1 & 1 \\ 1 & 1 \end{vmatrix} + 0 \cdot \begin{vmatrix} 1 & 0 \\ 1 & 1 \end{vmatrix}$$

$$= 1 \cdot 1 - 1 \cdot 0 + 0 \cdot 1 = 1 \quad .$$

We could have solved the equations by Cramer's rule:

$$X = \frac{\begin{vmatrix} 1 & 1 & 0 \\ 0 & 0 & 1 \\ 1 & 1 & 1 \end{vmatrix}}{\begin{vmatrix} 1 & 1 & 0 \\ 1 & 0 & 1 \\ 1 & 1 & 1 \end{vmatrix}} = \frac{0}{1} = 0$$

$$Y = \frac{\begin{vmatrix} 1 & 1 & 0 \\ 1 & 0 & 1 \\ 1 & 1 & 1 \end{vmatrix}}{\begin{vmatrix} 1 & 1 & 0 \\ 1 & 0 & 1 \\ 1 & 1 & 1 \end{vmatrix}} = \frac{1}{1} = 1$$

$$Z = \frac{\begin{vmatrix} 1 & 1 & 1 \\ 1 & 0 & 0 \\ 1 & 1 & 1 \end{vmatrix}}{\begin{vmatrix} 1 & 1 & 0 \\ 1 & 0 & 1 \\ 1 & 1 & 1 \end{vmatrix}} = \frac{0}{1} = 0$$

Now we consider computations with polynomials whose coefficients are either 0 or 1. For real numbers, if λ is a *root* of the polynomial $f(X)$ (that is, if $f(\lambda) = 0$), $f(X)$ is divisible by $X - \lambda$. This is still true for $f(X)$ with binary coefficients. Let $f(X) = X^4 + X^3 + X^2 + 1$. Then, $f(1) = 1^4 + 1^3 + 1^2 + 1 = 1 + 1 + 1 + 1 = 0$. Thus, $f(X)$ should be divisible by $X - 1 = X + 1$,

$$\begin{array}{r|l}
 & X^3 \qquad + X \qquad + 1 \\
\cline{2-2}
X + 1 & X^4 + X^3 + X^2 \qquad + 1 \\
 & X^4 + X^3 \\
\cline{2-2}
 & \qquad\qquad X^2 \qquad + 1 \\
 & \qquad\qquad X^2 + X \\
\cline{2-2}
 & \qquad\qquad\qquad X + 1 \\
 & \qquad\qquad\qquad X + 1 \\
\cline{2-2}
 & \qquad\qquad\qquad\qquad 0
\end{array}$$

The only polynomials of degree 1 are X and $X + 1$. The only polynomials of degree 2 are X^2, $X^2 + X$, $X^2 + 1$, and $X^2 + X + 1$. Of these polynomials of degree 2, X^2 and $X^2 + X$ factor in the obvious way. Since $1^2 + 1 = 0$, $X^2 + 1$ must be divisible by $X + 1$ – in fact, $(X + 1)^2 = X^2 + X + X + 1 = X^2 + 1$. However, $X^2 + X + 1$ does not have 0 or 1 as roots and so is not divisible by any polynomial except 1 and itself. A polynomial $p(X)$ of degree m is said to be *irreducible* over the binary field $GF(2)$ if $p(X)$ is not divisible by any polynomial of degree less than m and greater than zero. We can prove that $X^4 + X + 1$ is irreducible by noting that if it is not irreducible, there must be an irreducible factor of degree equal to or less than 2. Since 0 and 1 are not roots, X and $X + 1$ are not factors. The only remaining possibility is $X^2 + X + 1$, and we can verify by long division that $X^4 + X + 1$ is not divisible by $X^2 + X + 1$. Thus, $X^4 + X + 1$ is irreducible.

Fields with 2^m symbols are called *Galois fields*, $GF(2^m)$, and are important in the study of cyclic codes. In particular, they are used in decoding *BCH* codes and as symbols in *Reed-Solomon* codes. An arithmetic with 2^m symbols is derived as follows. First, we start with an arithmetic with two symbols and a polynomial $p(X)$ of degree m. Next we introduce a new symbol, α, and assume that $p(\alpha) = 0$, *just as we may assume that* $2 = 0$ *in an arithmetic with two symbols*. Then a table of powers of α is developed. If we choose $p(X)$ properly, the powers of α up to $2^m - 2$ will be different, $\alpha^{2^m-1} = 1$, and $0, 1, \alpha, \alpha^2, \ldots, \alpha^{2^m-2}$ will be the set of 2^m field elements. Furthermore, each element can be expressed as a sum of the elements $1, \alpha, \alpha^2, \ldots, \alpha^{m-1}$. For example, for $m = 4$, $p(X) = X^4 + X + 1$ gives us the following table:

0

1

α

α^2

α^3

$\alpha^4 = \alpha + 1$

$\alpha^5 = \alpha(\alpha + 1) = \alpha^2 + \alpha$

$$\alpha^6 = \alpha(\alpha^2+\alpha) = \alpha^3+\alpha^2$$

$$\alpha^7 = \alpha(\alpha^3+\alpha^2) = \alpha^4+\alpha^3 = \alpha^3+\alpha+1$$

$$\alpha^8 = \alpha(\alpha^3+\alpha+1) = \alpha^4+\alpha^2+\alpha = \alpha^2+\alpha+\alpha+1 = \alpha^2+1$$

$$\alpha^9 = \alpha(\alpha^2+1) = \alpha^3+\alpha$$

$$\alpha^{10} = \alpha(\alpha^3+\alpha) = \alpha^4+\alpha^2 = \alpha^2+\alpha+1$$

$$\alpha^{11} = \alpha(\alpha^2+\alpha+1) = \alpha^3+\alpha^2+\alpha$$

$$\alpha^{12} = \alpha(\alpha^3+\alpha^2+\alpha) = \alpha^4+\alpha^3+\alpha^2 = \alpha^3+\alpha^2+\alpha+1$$

$$\alpha^{13} = \alpha^4+\alpha^3+\alpha^2+\alpha = \alpha^3+\alpha^2+\alpha+\alpha+1 = \alpha^3+\alpha^2+1$$

$$\alpha^{14} = \alpha^4+\alpha^3+\alpha = \alpha^3+\alpha+\alpha+1 = \alpha^3+1$$

$$\alpha^{15} = \alpha^4+\alpha = \alpha+\alpha+1 = 1$$

Table 2.2. The Galois field of 2^4 elements $(GF(2^4))$ with $p(\alpha)=\alpha^4+\alpha+1=0$ (or $\alpha^4=\alpha+1$).

The element α is called a *primitive element* of the field $GF(2^m)$. In general, any element of $GF(2^m)$ whose powers generate all the non-zero elements of $GF(2^m)$ is said to be primitive. For example, the powers of α^4 of $GF(2^4)$ given in Table 2.2 are

$$(\alpha^4)^0 = 1, \quad (\alpha^4)^1 = \alpha^4, \quad (\alpha^4)^2 = \alpha^8,$$

$$(\alpha^4)^3 = \alpha^{12}, \quad (\alpha^4)^4 = \alpha^{16} = \alpha, \quad (\alpha^4)^5 = \alpha^{20} = \alpha^5,$$

$$(\alpha^4)^6 = \alpha^{24} = \alpha^9, \quad (\alpha^4)^7 = \alpha^{28} = \alpha^{13}, \quad (\alpha^4)^8 = \alpha^{32} = \alpha^2,$$

$$(\alpha^4)^9 = \alpha^{36} = \alpha^6, \quad (\alpha^4)^{10} = \alpha^{40} = \alpha^{10}, \quad (\alpha^4)^{11} = \alpha^{44} = \alpha^{14},$$

$$(\alpha^4)^{12} = \alpha^{48} = \alpha^3, \quad (\alpha^4)^{13} = \alpha^{52} = \alpha^7, \quad (\alpha^4)^{14} = \alpha^{56} = \alpha^{11},$$

which generate all the 15 non-zero elements of $GF(2^4)$. Thus, α^4 is a primitive element of $GF(2^4)$. The element α^3 is not a primitive element of

$GF(2^4)$. A polynomial $p(X)$ of degree m that gives a complete table with 2^m distinct symbols containing 0 and 1 is called *primitive*. Alternatively, an irreducible polynomial $p(X)$ of degree m is said to be primitive if $p(\beta) = 0$, where β is a primitive element of $GF(2^m)$. It has been proved that for each positive integer m there exists at least one primitive polynomial of degree m. It is not easy to recognize a primitive polynomial. However, there are tables of polynomials in which primitive polynomials are indicated. A list of primitive polynomials is given in Table 2.3. For extensive tables, the reader is referred to References 4 and 5.

Now, to multiply two of these symbols, we simply add exponents and use the fact that $\alpha^{15} = 1$ (or in general, $\alpha^{2^m-1} = 1$). For example, $\alpha^5 \cdot \alpha^7 = \alpha^{12}$, and $\alpha^{12} \cdot \alpha^7 = \alpha^{19} = \alpha^4$. Division is similar: $\alpha^{12}/\alpha^5 = \alpha^7$, and $\alpha^4/\alpha^{12} = \alpha^{19}/\alpha^{12} = \alpha^7$. To add two symbols, we use the other form in the table in each case. Thus,

$$\alpha^5 + \alpha^7 = (\alpha^2 + \alpha) + (\alpha^3 + \alpha + 1) = \alpha^3 + \alpha^2 + 1 = \alpha^{13}$$

$$1 + \alpha^5 + \alpha^{10} = 1 + \alpha^2 + \alpha + \alpha^2 + \alpha + 1 = 0 .$$

Note that since $-1 = 1$, subtraction is the same as addition.

Let us perform some example computations. Consider the linear equations

$$\begin{aligned} X + \alpha^7 Y &= \alpha^2 \\ \alpha^{12} X + \alpha^8 Y &= \alpha^4 . \end{aligned} \tag{2.1}$$

Multiplying the second equation by α^3 gives

$$\begin{aligned} X + \alpha^7 Y &= \alpha^2 \\ X + \alpha^{11} Y &= \alpha^7 . \end{aligned}$$

By adding the above two equations, we get

m	Primitive Polynomials
3	$1 + X + X^3$
4	$1 + X + X^4$
5	$1 + X^2 + X^5$
6	$1 + X + X^6$
7	$1 + X^3 + X^7$
8	$1 + X^2 + X^3 + X^4 + X^8$
9	$1 + X^4 + X^9$
10	$1 + X^3 + X^{10}$
11	$1 + X^2 + X^{11}$
12	$1 + X + X^4 + X^6 + X^{12}$
13	$1 + X + X^3 + X^4 + X^{13}$
14	$1 + X + X^6 + X^{10} + X^{14}$
15	$1 + X + X^{15}$
16	$1 + X + X^3 + X^{12} + X^{16}$
17	$1 + X^3 + X^{17}$
18	$1 + X^7 + X^{18}$
19	$1 + X + X^2 + X^5 + X^{19}$
20	$1 + X^3 + X^{20}$
21	$1 + X^2 + X^{21}$
22	$1 + X + X^{22}$
23	$1 + X^5 + X^{23}$
24	$1 + X + X^2 + X^7 + X^{24}$

Table 2.3. A list of primitive polynomials.

$$(\alpha^7 + \alpha^{11})Y = \alpha^2 + \alpha^7$$

$$(\alpha^3 + \alpha + 1 + \alpha^3 + \alpha^2 + \alpha)Y = \alpha^2 + \alpha^3 + \alpha + 1$$

$$(\alpha^2 + 1)Y = \alpha^3 + \alpha^2 + \alpha + 1$$

$$\alpha^8 Y = \alpha^{12}$$

$$Y = \alpha^4 \ .$$

Substituting $Y = \alpha^4$ into the first equation of (2.1), we obtain

$$X + \alpha^7 \cdot \alpha^4 = \alpha^2$$

$$X = \alpha^2 + \alpha^{11} = \alpha^2 + (\alpha^3 + \alpha^2 + \alpha) = \alpha^3 + \alpha = \alpha^9 \ .$$

Thus, the solution for the equations of (2.1) is $X = \alpha^9$ and $Y = \alpha^4$.

Alternatively, the equations of (2.1) could be solved by using Cramer's rule:

$$X = \frac{\begin{vmatrix} \alpha^2 & \alpha^7 \\ \alpha^4 & \alpha^8 \end{vmatrix}}{\begin{vmatrix} 1 & \alpha^7 \\ \alpha^{12} & \alpha^8 \end{vmatrix}} = \frac{\alpha^{10} + \alpha^{11}}{\alpha^8 + \alpha^4} = \frac{\alpha^3 + 1}{\alpha^2 + \alpha} = \frac{\alpha^{14}}{\alpha^5} = \alpha^9$$

$$Y = \frac{\begin{vmatrix} 1 & \alpha^2 \\ \alpha^{12} & \alpha^4 \end{vmatrix}}{\begin{vmatrix} 1 & \alpha^7 \\ \alpha^{12} & \alpha^8 \end{vmatrix}} = \frac{\alpha^4 + \alpha^{14}}{\alpha^8 + \alpha^4} = \frac{\alpha^3 + \alpha}{\alpha^2 + \alpha} = \frac{\alpha^9}{\alpha^5} = \alpha^4 \ .$$

As one more example, suppose that we want to solve the equation

$$f(X) = X^2 + \alpha^7 X + \alpha = 0 \ .$$

The ordinary method will not work because it requires dividing by 2, and in this field, $2 = 0$. If $f(X) = 0$ has any solutions in $GF(2^4)$, the solutions can be found simply by substituting all symbols of Table 2.2 for X. By doing so, we would find that $f(\alpha^6) = 0$ and $f(\alpha^{10}) = 0$, since

$$\begin{aligned} f(\alpha^6) &= (\alpha^6)^2 + \alpha^7 \cdot \alpha^6 + \alpha = \alpha^{12} + \alpha^{13} + \alpha = 0 \\ f(\alpha^{10}) &= (\alpha^{10})^2 + \alpha^7 \cdot \alpha^{10} + \alpha = \alpha^5 + \alpha^2 + \alpha = 0 \end{aligned}$$

and we would find that no other elements give zero as the value of $f(X)$. Thus, $f(X) = (X + \alpha^6)(X + \alpha^{10})$, where α^6 and α^{10} are called the *roots* of $f(X)$.

The above calculations are typical of those required for decoding *BCH* codes, and they can be programmed quite easily on a general-purpose computer. It is also a simple matter to build a computer which can do this kind of arithmetic.

Let $f(X)$ be a polynomial of the following form,

$$f(X) = f_k X^k + f_{k-1} X^{k-1} + \ldots + f_1 X + f_0 \quad ,$$

where f_i is either 0 or 1.

Consider

$$\begin{aligned} f^2(X) &= (f_k X^k + f_{k-1} X^{k-1} + \ldots + f_1 X + f_0)^2 \\ &= (f_k X^k)^2 + 2(f_k X^k)(f_{k-1} X^{k-1} + \ldots + f_1 X + f_0) \\ &\quad + (f_{k-1} X^{k-1} + \ldots + f_1 X + f_0)^2 \end{aligned}$$

(the equality $(b + c)^2 = b^2 + 2bc + c^2$ is used). According to modulo-2 arithmetic, $1 + 1 = 2 = 0$ and $1 \cdot 1 = 1^2 = 0$. Then we have

$$f^2(X) = f_k X^{2k} + (f_{k-1} X^{k-1} + \ldots + f_1 X + f_0)^2 \quad .$$

Expanding the above equation, we obtain

$$\begin{aligned} f^2(X) &= f_k X^{2k} + f_{k-1} X^{2(k-1)} + \ldots + f_1 X^2 + f_0 \\ &= f(X^2) \ . \end{aligned}$$

For example,

$$\begin{aligned} f^2(X) &= (X^4 + X + 1)^2 = X^8 + X^2 + 1 + 2X^5 + 2X^4 + 2X \\ &= X^8 + X^2 + 1 = f(X^2) \ . \end{aligned}$$

It follows that for any positive integer ℓ,

$$[f(X)]^{2^\ell} = f(X^{2^\ell}) \ .$$

Let β be an arbitrary element of the Galois field $GF(2^m)$. The polynomial $m(X)$ of smallest degree with binary coefficients such that $m(\beta) = 0$ is called the *minimum polynomial* of β. The minimum polynomial of β is irreducible. This can be seen as follows. Suppose that $m(X)$ is not irreducible, say $m(X) = m_1(X)\, m_2(X)$, where $m_1(X)$ and $m_2(X)$ are nontrivial. Both $m_1(X)$ and $m_2(X)$ have degree lower than the degree of $m(X)$. Since $m(\beta) = m_1(\beta)\, m_2(\beta) = 0$, then either $m_1(\beta)$ or $m_2(\beta)$ must be zero. This contradicts the hypothesis that $m(X)$ is the polynomial of the smallest degree such that $m(\beta) = 0$. Therefore, $m(X)$ cannot have nontrivial factors and it must be irreducible. It has been proved that every element of $GF(2^m)$ has a minimum polynomial whose degree is m or less. Since $m(\beta) = 0$ and $[m(X)]^{2^\ell} = m(X^{2^\ell})$, then

$$[m(\beta)]^{2^\ell} = m(\beta^{2^\ell}) = 0 \ .$$

This is to say that β^{2^ℓ} is also a root of $m(X)$. Consequently,

$$\beta, \beta^2, \beta^{2^2}, \ldots, \beta^{2^\ell}, \ldots$$

are all roots of $m(X)$. Since $m(X)$ has finite degree, it must have a finite number of roots. Thus, there must be repetition in the above sequence. Let e be the degree of $m(X)$. It can be shown that $\beta, \beta^2, \beta^{2^2}, \ldots, \beta^{2^{e-1}}$ are all the distinct roots of $m(X)$. These elements will repeat in the sequence after $\beta^{2^{e-1}}$.

To find the minimum polynomial of a given element β in $GF(2^m)$ can be best explained by an example. Consider the field $GF(2^4)$ of Table 2.2. Let $\beta = \alpha^3$. We form the following sequence

$$\beta = \alpha^3, \quad \beta^2 = \alpha^6, \quad \beta^{2^2} = \alpha^{12}, \quad \beta^{2^3} = \alpha^{24} = \alpha^9,$$

$$\beta^{2^4} = \alpha^{48} = \alpha^3, \quad \beta^{2^5} = \alpha^{96} = \alpha^6, \ldots .$$

Notice that repetition begins at β^{2^4}. Therefore, the minimum polynomial of α^3 has

$$\alpha^3, \alpha^6, \alpha^9, \alpha^{12}$$

as all its roots. Thus,

$$m(X) = (X + \alpha^3)(X + \alpha^6)(X + \alpha^9)(X + \alpha^{12}) .$$

Multiplying out the right-hand side of the above equation with the aid of Table 2.2, we obtain

$$\begin{aligned} m(X) &= X^4 + (\alpha^3 + \alpha^6 + \alpha^9 + \alpha^{12})X^3 \\ &\quad + (\alpha^9 + \alpha^{12} + \alpha^{15} + \alpha^{15} + \alpha^{18} + \alpha^{21})X^2 \\ &\quad + (\alpha^{18} + \alpha^{21} + \alpha^{24} + \alpha^{27})X + \alpha^{30} \\ &= X^4 + X^3 + X^2 + X + 1 . \end{aligned}$$

Alternative methods of finding the minimum polynomial of a given field element can be found in Albert[1] and Peterson[5].

2.2 VECTOR SPACES

As we discussed in Section 2.1, the alphabet of two symbols, 0 and 1, together with modulo-2 addition and multiplication defined by Table 2.1 is called the binary field $GF(2)$. Now consider an ordered sequence of binary symbols

$$\mathbf{v} = (v_1, v_2, v_3, \ldots, v_n) \tag{2.2}$$

where the ith component v_i is either "0" or "1". This sequence is generally called an *n-tuple over* $GF(2)$. Since there are two choices for each v_i, we can construct 2^n possible distinct n-tuples. Now we introduce an addition operation for any two binary n-tuples as follows:

$$\begin{aligned} \mathbf{v} &= (v_1, v_2, v_3, \ldots, v_n) \\ \mathbf{u} &= (u_1, u_2, u_3, \ldots, u_n) \\ \mathbf{v}+\mathbf{u} &= (v_1+u_1,\ v_2+u_2, \ldots,\ v_n+u_n) \end{aligned} \tag{2.3}$$

where $v_i + u_i$ is modulo-2 addition as defined in Table 2.1. Therefore, $\mathbf{v}+\mathbf{u}$ is also a binary n-tuple with $v_i + u_i$ as its ith component. That is, with the above definition, the addition of two n-tuples yields a third n-tuple. Since $v_i + u_i = u_i + v_i$, it is obvious that

$$\mathbf{v}+\mathbf{u} = \mathbf{u}+\mathbf{v} \; . \tag{2.4}$$

Scalar multiplication of a binary n-tuple by a symbol from $GF(2)$ is defined as

$$\sigma(v_1, v_2, v_3, \ldots, v_n) = (\sigma v_1, \sigma v_2, \ldots, \sigma v_n) \tag{2.5}$$

where the ith component σv_i is either "0" or "1" according to the rules defined in Table 2.1. It is easy to see that in the set of all n-tuples, there is an n-tuple which is all "0":

$$\mathbf{0} = (0, 0, 0, \ldots, 0) \quad . \tag{2.6}$$

The set of all binary n-tuples is called a *vector space over* $GF(2)$ and is denoted as $\mathbf{V}_n$. *Such a vector space plays a central role in coding theory.* The n-tuples of $\mathbf{V}_n$ are usually called *vectors*. An example will illustrate the above concepts.

Example 2.1: Let $n = 4$. The vector space $\mathbf{V}_4$ consists of the following vectors:

$$\begin{array}{ll} (0\ 0\ 0\ 0), & (0\ 0\ 0\ 1) \\ (0\ 0\ 1\ 0), & (0\ 0\ 1\ 1) \\ (0\ 1\ 0\ 0), & (0\ 1\ 0\ 1) \\ (0\ 1\ 1\ 0), & (0\ 1\ 1\ 1) \\ (1\ 0\ 0\ 0), & (1\ 0\ 0\ 1) \\ (1\ 0\ 1\ 0), & (1\ 0\ 1\ 1) \\ (1\ 1\ 0\ 0), & (1\ 1\ 0\ 1) \\ (1\ 1\ 1\ 0), & (1\ 1\ 1\ 1)\ . \end{array}$$

According to the rule for vector addition,

$$\begin{aligned} (0\ 1\ 0\ 1) + (1\ 1\ 1\ 0) &= (0 + 1,\ 1 + 1,\ 0 + 1,\ 1 + 0) \\ &= (1\ 0\ 1\ 1)\ . \end{aligned}$$

According to the rule for scalar multiplication

$$\begin{aligned} 1 \cdot (1\ 0\ 1\ 1) &= (1 \cdot 1,\ 1 \cdot 0,\ 1 \cdot 1,\ 1 \cdot 1) \\ &= (1\ 0\ 1\ 1) \end{aligned}$$

$$0 \cdot (1\ 0\ 1\ 1) = (0 \cdot 1,\ 0 \cdot 0,\ 0 \cdot 1,\ 0 \cdot 1)$$
$$= (0\ 0\ 0\ 0)\ .$$

A subset $\mathbf{S}$ of $\mathbf{V}_n$ is called a *subspace* if (1) the all-zero vector is in $\mathbf{S}$ and (2) if the sum of any two vectors in $\mathbf{S}$ is also in $\mathbf{S}$.

Example 2.2: Consider the following set of vectors

$$\mathbf{v}_0 = (0\ 0\ 0\ 0)$$
$$\mathbf{v}_1 = (0\ 1\ 0\ 1)$$
$$\mathbf{v}_2 = (1\ 0\ 1\ 0)$$
$$\mathbf{v}_3 = (1\ 1\ 1\ 1)$$

which is a subset of the vector space $\mathbf{V}_4$. It contains the all-zero vector and we can easily check that, for any two vectors in $\mathbf{S}$, their sum is also in $\mathbf{S}$. Thus, $\mathbf{S} = \{\mathbf{v}_0, \mathbf{v}_1, \mathbf{v}_2, \mathbf{v}_3\}$ forms a subspace of $\mathbf{V}_4$.

Let $\mathbf{v}_1, \mathbf{v}_2, \ldots, \mathbf{v}_k$ be k vectors of $\mathbf{V}_n$. A *linear combination* of $\mathbf{v}_1, \mathbf{v}_2, \ldots, \mathbf{v}_k$ is a vector of the form

$$\mathbf{u} = c_1\mathbf{v}_1 + c_2\mathbf{v}_2 + \ldots + c_k\mathbf{v}_k \qquad (2.7)$$

where c_i is from $GF(2)$ and is called the *coefficient* of $\mathbf{v}_i$.

Example 2.3: Consider the vector space $\mathbf{V}_4$ given in Example 2.1. Let

$$\mathbf{v}_1 = (0\ 1\ 0\ 0)$$
$$\mathbf{v}_2 = (1\ 0\ 1\ 0)$$
$$\mathbf{v}_3 = (1\ 0\ 1\ 1)$$
$$\mathbf{v}_4 = (1\ 1\ 0\ 0)$$

and $c_1 = 1$, $c_2 = 0$, $c_3 = 1$, and $c_4 = 1$. Then

$$\begin{aligned}\mathbf{u} &= c_1\mathbf{v}_1 + c_2\mathbf{v}_2 + c_3\mathbf{v}_3 + c_4\mathbf{v}_4 \\ &= 1\cdot(0\ 1\ 0\ 0) + 0\cdot(1\ 0\ 1\ 0) + 1\cdot(1\ 0\ 1\ 1) \\ &\qquad + 1\cdot(1\ 1\ 0\ 0) \\ &= (0\ 1\ 0\ 0) + (1\ 0\ 1\ 1) + (1\ 1\ 0\ 0) \\ &= (0\ 0\ 1\ 1)\ .\end{aligned}$$

A set of vectors is said to be *linearly dependent* if and only if there are scalars $c_1, c_2, \ldots, c_n$ from $GF(2)$, not all zero, such that

$$c_1\mathbf{v}_1 + c_2\mathbf{v}_2 + \ldots + c_n\mathbf{v}_n = 0\ .$$

Example 2.4: Consider the following set of vectors:

$$\begin{aligned}\mathbf{v}_1 &= (1\ 1\ 0\ 0) \\ \mathbf{v}_2 &= (1\ 0\ 1\ 0) \\ \mathbf{v}_3 &= (1\ 0\ 1\ 1) \\ \mathbf{v}_4 &= (1\ 1\ 0\ 1)\ .\end{aligned}$$

If we set $c_1 = c_2 = c_3 = c_4 = 1$, then

$$\begin{aligned}\mathbf{u} &= c_1\mathbf{v}_1 + c_2\mathbf{v}_2 + c_3\mathbf{v}_3 + c_4\mathbf{v}_4 \\ &= 1\cdot(1\ 1\ 0\ 0) + 1\cdot(1\ 0\ 1\ 0) + 1\cdot(1\ 0\ 1\ 1) \\ &\qquad + 1\cdot(1\ 1\ 0\ 1) \\ &= (1\ 1\ 0\ 0) + (1\ 0\ 1\ 0) + (1\ 0\ 1\ 1) \\ &\qquad + (1\ 1\ 0\ 1)\end{aligned}$$

$$= (0\ 1\ 1\ 0) + (0\ 1\ 1\ 0)$$

$$= (0\ 0\ 0\ 0)\ .$$

Thus, $\mathbf{v}_1$, $\mathbf{v}_2$, $\mathbf{v}_3$, and $\mathbf{v}_4$ are linearly dependent.

A set of vectors is said to be *linearly independent* if it is not linearly dependent. A set of vectors is said to *span* a vector space if every vector in the vector space is equal to a linear combination of the vectors in the set.

Example 2.5: The following set of vectors

$$\mathbf{v}_1 = (1\ 0\ 0\ 0)$$

$$\mathbf{v}_2 = (0\ 1\ 0\ 0)$$

$$\mathbf{v}_3 = (0\ 0\ 1\ 0)$$

$$\mathbf{v}_4 = (0\ 0\ 0\ 1)$$

are obviously linearly independent. Any vector in $\mathbf{V}_4$ is a linear combination of this set of vectors. Thus, $\mathbf{v}_1$, $\mathbf{v}_2$, $\mathbf{v}_3$, and $\mathbf{v}_4$ span the vector space $\mathbf{V}_4$.

In any vector space or subspace there exists at least one set of linearly independent vectors which spans the space. This set is called a *basis* of the vector space. The number of vectors in a basis is called the *dimension* of the vector space. The vector space $\mathbf{V}_n$ of all binary n-tuples is an *n-dimensional* vector space which is spanned by a basis of n linearly independent vectors. If $k < n$ and $\mathbf{v}_1, \mathbf{v}_2, \ldots, \mathbf{v}_k$ are k linearly independent vectors, then all the linear combinations of $\mathbf{v}_1, \mathbf{v}_2, \ldots, \mathbf{v}_k$ of the form

$$\mathbf{u} = c_1\mathbf{v}_1 + c_2\mathbf{v}_2 + \ldots + c_k\mathbf{v}_k$$

form a k-dimensional subspace $\mathbf{S}$ of $\mathbf{V}_n$. Since each c_i has two possible values, 0 or 1, there are 2^k possible distinct linear combinations of $\mathbf{v}_1$, $\mathbf{v}_2$,

$\ldots, \mathbf{v}_k$. Thus, $\mathbf{S}$ has 2^k distinct vectors and is a k-dimensional subspace of $\mathbf{V}_n$.

2.3 MATRICES

Consider a $k \times n$ rectangular array of k rows and n columns as follows:

$$\mathbf{G} = \begin{bmatrix} g_{11} & g_{12} & \cdots & g_{1n} \\ g_{21} & g_{22} & \cdots & g_{2n} \\ \vdots & \vdots & & \vdots \\ g_{k1} & g_{k2} & \cdots & g_{kn} \end{bmatrix} \tag{2.8}$$

where the element g_{ij} is either "0" or "1". This array $\mathbf{G}$ is called a $k \times n$ *matrix over* $GF(2)$. Each row is a binary n-tuple and each column is a binary k-tuple. If the k rows are k $(k \leqslant n)$ linearly independent n-tuples from $\mathbf{V}_n$, then all linear combinations of rows of $\mathbf{G}$ form a k-dimensional subspace of $\mathbf{V}_n$ which we call the *row space* of $\mathbf{G}$.

Example 2.6: Consider

$$\mathbf{G} = \begin{bmatrix} 1 & 0 & 0 & 1 & 0 & 1 \\ 0 & 1 & 0 & 0 & 1 & 1 \\ 0 & 0 & 1 & 1 & 1 & 0 \end{bmatrix} .$$

This is a 3×6 binary matrix. There are 3 rows and 6 columns. Each row is a 6-tuple and each column is a 3-tuple. We can easily verify that the three rows are linearly independent. The linear combinations of these rows are:

0 0 0 0 0 0

1 0 0 1 0 1

0 1 0 0 1 1

0 0 1 1 1 0

1 1 0 1 1 0

1 0 1 0 1 1

0 1 1 1 0 1

1 1 1 0 0 0 .

This set is a subset of the vector space $\mathbf{V}_6$ which consists of $2^6 = 64$ 6-tuples. Since it satisfies the definition of a subspace and has 2^3 elements, it is a 3-dimensional subspace of $\mathbf{V}_6$.

Consider any two vectors $\mathbf{v} = (v_1, v_2, \ldots, v_n)$ and $\mathbf{u} = (u_1, u_2, \ldots, u_n)$. We define the *inner product* or dot product of $\mathbf{v}$ and $\mathbf{u}$ as

$$\mathbf{v} \cdot \mathbf{u} = v_1 \cdot u_1 + v_2 \cdot u_2 + \ldots + v_n \cdot u_n \qquad (2.9)$$

where the addition and multiplication are modulo-2 operations defined in Table 2.1. If $\mathbf{v} \cdot \mathbf{u} = 0$, $\mathbf{v}$ and $\mathbf{u}$ are said to be *orthogonal*.

For any $k \times n$ matrix $\mathbf{G}$ with k linearly independent rows, there exists an $(n-k) \times n$ matrix $\mathbf{H}$ with $n-k$ rows

$$\mathbf{H} = \begin{bmatrix} \mathbf{h}_1 \\ \mathbf{h}_2 \\ \vdots \\ \mathbf{h}_{n-k} \end{bmatrix} = \begin{bmatrix} h_{11} & h_{12} & \cdots & h_{1n} \\ h_{21} & h_{22} & \cdots & h_{2n} \\ \vdots & \vdots & & \vdots \\ h_{n-k,1} & h_{n-k,2} & \cdots & h_{n-k,n} \end{bmatrix} \qquad (2.10)$$

with $\mathbf{h}_j = (h_{j1}, h_{j2}, \ldots, h_{jn})$ such that $n - k$ rows are linearly independent and any vector $\mathbf{v}$ in the row space of $\mathbf{G}$ is orthogonal to all the rows of $\mathbf{H}$, i.e., the inner product

$$\mathbf{v} \cdot \mathbf{h}_j = 0, \quad \text{for } 1 \leqslant j \leqslant n-k .$$

Since $\mathbf{g}_i$ is a vector in the row space of $\mathbf{G}$, the inner product

$$\mathbf{g}_i \cdot \mathbf{h}_j = 0$$

for $1 \leqslant i \leqslant k$ and $1 \leqslant j \leqslant n-k$. Let $\mathbf{u}$ be a vector in the row space of $\mathbf{H}$. Then $\mathbf{u}$ is a linear combination of rows of $\mathbf{H}$,

$$\mathbf{u} = d_1 \mathbf{h}_1 + d_2 \mathbf{h}_2 + \ldots + d_{n-k} \mathbf{h}_{n-k}$$

where $d_i = 0$ or 1 for $1 \leqslant i \leqslant n-k$. The inner product of $\mathbf{v}$ and $\mathbf{u}$ is

$$\begin{aligned} \mathbf{v} \cdot \mathbf{u} &= \mathbf{v} \cdot (d_1 \mathbf{h}_1 + \ldots + d_{n-k} \mathbf{h}_{n-k}) \\ &= d_1 (\mathbf{v} \cdot \mathbf{h}_1) + \ldots + d_{n-k} (\mathbf{v} \cdot \mathbf{h}_{n-k}) . \end{aligned} \tag{2.11}$$

Since $\mathbf{v} \cdot \mathbf{h}_j = 0$, $\mathbf{v} \cdot \mathbf{u} = 0$. That is, any vector $\mathbf{v}$ in the row space of $\mathbf{G}$ and any vector $\mathbf{u}$ in the row space of $\mathbf{H}$ are orthogonal, $\mathbf{v} \cdot \mathbf{u} = 0$. The row space of $\mathbf{G}$ is called the *null space* of $\mathbf{H}$ or vice versa.

PROBLEMS

2.1. Solve the following simultaneous equations for X, Y, Z, and W with modulo-2 arithmetic.

$$
\begin{aligned}
X + Y + Z + W &= 1 \\
X + Y \qquad + W &= 1 \\
X \qquad + Z + W &= 0 \\
Y + Z + W &= 0
\end{aligned}
$$

2.2. Show that $f(X) = X^3 + X + 1$ is an irreducible polynomial.

2.3. The polynomial $p(X) = X^3 + X^2 + 1$ is a primitive polynomial of degree 3. Assuming that $p(\alpha) = 0$, construct the table of Galois field of 2^3 elements, $GF(2^3)$.

2.4. Use the table which you have constructed in Problem 2.3 to find the roots of $f(X) = X^3 + X + 1$ in $GF(2^3)$.

2.5. Use Table 2.2 to find the roots of $f(X) = X^4 + X^3 + 1$ in $GF(2^4)$.

2.6. Use Table 2.2 to find the roots of $f(X) = X^3 + \alpha^6 X^2 + \alpha^9 X + \alpha^9$ in $GF(2^4)$.

2.7. Construct the vector space $\mathbf{V}_5$ of all binary 5-tuples and find a basis for $\mathbf{V}_5$.

2.8. Construct a 3-dimensional subspace of $\mathbf{V}_5$.

2.9. Given a matrix

$$
\mathbf{G} = \begin{bmatrix} 1 & 0 & 0 & 1 & 1 & 0 & 1 \\ 0 & 1 & 0 & 1 & 1 & 1 & 0 \\ 0 & 0 & 1 & 0 & 1 & 1 & 1 \end{bmatrix}
$$

show that the row space of $\mathbf{G}$ is the null space of

$$H = \begin{bmatrix} 1 & 1 & 0 & 1 & 0 & 0 & 0 \\ 1 & 1 & 1 & 0 & 1 & 0 & 0 \\ 0 & 1 & 1 & 0 & 0 & 1 & 0 \\ 1 & 0 & 1 & 0 & 0 & 0 & 1 \end{bmatrix} .$$

REFERENCES

1. Albert, A. A., *Modern Higher Algebra*, Chicago, The University of Chicago Press, 1937.

2. Birkhoff, G., and S. MacLane, *A Survey of Modern Algebra*, Macmillan, New York, 1953.

3. Carmichael, R. D., *Introduction to the Theory of Groups of Finite Order*, Ginn & Company, Boston, 1937.

4. Marsh, R. W., *Table of Irreducible Polynomials over GF(2) Through Degree* 19, NSA, Washington, D. C., 1957.

5. Peterson, W. W., *Error-Correcting Codes,* The M.I.T. Press, Cambridge, Massachusetts, 1961.

6. Van der Waerden, B. L., *Modern Algebra* (Volumes 1 and 2), Ungar Publishing Company, New York, 1949.

CHAPTER 3

LINEAR BLOCK CODES

In this chapter, some basic concepts of block codes are introduced. For the ease of code synthesis and implementation, we restrict our attention to a subclass, the *linear block codes*.[14,16] In Sections 3.2 and 3.3, matrix descriptions of a linear block code are given and the parity-check equations for a *systematic code* are derived. In Section 3.4, we define the *minimum distance* of a block code and show that the *random-error-correcting capability* and *random-error-detecting capability* of a block code is determined by its minimum distance. In Section 3.5, we discuss the decoding of a block code and introduce a decoding table for a linear block code. The reader who is interested in the theory of linear codes is referred to References 11 and 12 at the end of this chapter.

3.1 DEFINITION

We shall assume that information coming out from the information source is in binary form (a sequence of binary digits). The encoding procedure consists of two basic steps: (1) the information sequence is segmented into message blocks, each block consisting of k successive information digits; (2) the encoder, *according to certain rules*, transforms a message block into a longer block of n $(n > k)$ binary digits (a binary n-tuple) which we call a *code word*. Since each message block consists of k binary digits, there are 2^k possible distinct message blocks. Therefore, corresponding to 2^k possible messages, there are 2^k possible code words at the output of the encoder. This set of 2^k code words is called a *block code*. A code word is frequently called a *code vector* because it is an n-tuple from the vector space $\mathbf{V}_n$ of all n-tuples.

For a block code as defined above, unless it has a certain special structure, the encoding apparatus would be prohibitively complex for large k since it has to store the 2^k code vectors in a dictionary. Therefore, we must restrict our attention to codes which can be mechanized in a practical manner. In the following, we shall consider codes with the structure that the 2^k code vectors of each code form a k-dimensional subspace of all n-tuples.

With this structure in a code, the encoding complexity will be considerably reduced; this will be clear in the sequel.

Definition 3.1: *A set of* 2^k *n-tuples is called a linear code if and only if it is a subspace of the vector space* $\mathbf{V}_n$ *of all n-tuples.*

Example 3.1: Consider an encoder which segments the information sequence from the source into message blocks of three digits and transforms each message block into a code vector of six digits as follows:

Message	Encoder	Code Words
0 0 0	↔	0 0 0 0 0 0
0 0 1	↔	0 0 1 1 0 1
0 1 0	↔	0 1 0 0 1 1
0 1 1	↔	0 1 1 1 1 0
1 0 0	↔	1 0 0 1 1 0
1 0 1	↔	1 0 1 0 1 1
1 1 0	↔	1 1 0 1 0 1
1 1 1	↔	1 1 1 0 0 0 .

Since $k = 3$, there are $2^3 = 8$ possible distinct messages. Each message is transformed into a code word of six digits by the encoder. All code words are distinct. Thus, from a code word, one can tell which message block was transmitted. We can easily see that the set of code words forms a 3-dimensional subspace of the vector space of all 6-tuples. Therefore, it is a linear code.

3.2 GENERATOR MATRIX

For a subspace **S** of $\mathbf{V}_n$, it is possible to find a set of linearly independent n-tuples, say k of them $\mathbf{v}_1, \mathbf{v}_2, \ldots, \mathbf{v}_k$, such that each n-tuple of **S** is a linear combination of $\mathbf{v}_1, \mathbf{v}_2, \ldots, \mathbf{v}_k$ in the following form:

$$\mathbf{u} = m_1\mathbf{v}_1 + m_2\mathbf{v}_2 + \ldots + m_k\mathbf{v}_k \tag{3.1}$$

where $m_i = 0$ or 1 for $i = 1, 2, \ldots, k$. This subspace is a k-dimensional subspace of $\mathbf{V}_n$, and it consists of 2^k n-tuples. From the above facts, we can then describe a linear code of 2^k code vectors by a set of k linearly independent code vectors. Let us arrange these k independent code vectors as rows of a $k \times n$ matrix

$$\mathbf{G} = \begin{bmatrix} \mathbf{v}_1 \\ \mathbf{v}_2 \\ \vdots \\ \mathbf{v}_k \end{bmatrix} = \begin{bmatrix} v_{11} & v_{12} & v_{13} & \cdots & v_{1n} \\ v_{21} & v_{22} & v_{23} & \cdots & v_{2n} \\ \vdots & \vdots & \vdots & & \vdots \\ v_{k1} & v_{k2} & v_{k3} & \cdots & v_{kn} \end{bmatrix} \tag{3.2}$$

where $\mathbf{v}_i = (v_{i1}, v_{i2}, v_{i3}, \ldots, v_{in})$ for $i = 1, 2, \ldots, k$. Let $\mathbf{m} = (m_1, m_2, \ldots, m_k)$ be a message block. Then the corresponding code word can be given as follows:

$$\begin{aligned} \mathbf{u} &= \mathbf{m}\mathbf{G} \\ &= (m_1, m_2, \ldots, m_k) \begin{bmatrix} \mathbf{v}_1 \\ \mathbf{v}_2 \\ \vdots \\ \mathbf{v}_k \end{bmatrix} \\ &= m_1\mathbf{v}_1 + m_2\mathbf{v}_2 + \ldots + m_k\mathbf{v}_k . \end{aligned} \tag{3.3}$$

That is, the code word corresponding to the message $(m_1, m_2, \ldots, m_k)$ is a linear combination of the rows of **G**. Thus, the rows of matrix **G** generate a linear code. We call **G** the *generator matrix* of the code. The linear code described above is called an (n,k) code; that is, a block of k information digits is encoded into a code word of n digits for transmission over the noisy channel. The ratio $R = k/n$ is called the *code rate*. Since a linear code is completely specified by its generator matrix **G**, the storage size of the encoder is greatly reduced. The encoder has only to store the k rows of **G** instead of storing the 2^k code vectors of the code. Besides the storage element, the encoder must have a logic element to perform the linear combinations of the rows of **G**.

Example 3.2: The code given in Example 3.1 is a (6,3) code with the generator matrix

$$\mathbf{G} = \begin{bmatrix} \mathbf{v}_1 \\ \mathbf{v}_2 \\ \mathbf{v}_3 \end{bmatrix} = \begin{bmatrix} 1 & 0 & 0 & 1 & 1 & 0 \\ 0 & 1 & 0 & 0 & 1 & 1 \\ 0 & 0 & 1 & 1 & 0 & 1 \end{bmatrix} .$$

The code word corresponding to message $\mathbf{m} = (1\ 0\ 1)$ is

$$\begin{aligned} \mathbf{u} &= (1\ 0\ 1) \begin{bmatrix} \mathbf{v}_1 \\ \mathbf{v}_2 \\ \mathbf{v}_3 \end{bmatrix} \\ &= 1 \cdot \mathbf{v}_1 + 0 \cdot \mathbf{v}_2 + 1 \cdot \mathbf{v}_3 \\ &= 1 \cdot (1\ 0\ 0\ 1\ 1\ 0) + 0 \cdot (0\ 1\ 0\ 0\ 1\ 1) \\ &\qquad + 1 \cdot (0\ 0\ 1\ 1\ 0\ 1) \\ &= 1\ 0\ 1\ 0\ 1\ 1 \ . \end{aligned}$$

It is possible to encode each message block into a code word in such a way that the first k digits of the code word are exactly the same as the message block and the last $n - k$ digits are *redundant digits* which are functions of information digits as illustrated in Fig. 3.1.

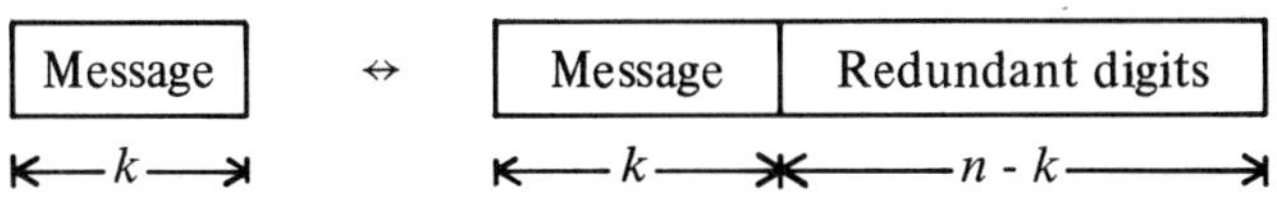

Fig. 3.1

A code of this form is called a *systematic code*. *The redundancy should be such that it has the ability to combat errors introduced during the transmission over a noisy channel, or, in other words, the redundancy should have the capability to protect the message.* Now the encoding problem is to form these redundant digits. A systematic (n,k) linear code can be described by a $k \times n$ generator matrix of the following form:

$$\mathbf{G} = \begin{bmatrix} 1\,0\,0\,0 \ldots 0 & p_{11} & p_{12} & \cdots & p_{1,n-k} \\ 0\,1\,0\,0 \ldots 0 & p_{21} & p_{22} & \cdots & p_{2,n-k} \\ 0\,0\,1\,0 \ldots 0 & p_{31} & p_{32} & \cdots & p_{3,n-k} \\ \vdots \qquad\quad \vdots & \vdots & \vdots & & \vdots \\ 0\,0\,0\,0 \ldots 1 & p_{k1} & p_{k2} & \cdots & p_{k,n-k} \end{bmatrix} \tag{3.4}$$

where $p_{ij} = 0$ or 1. Let $\mathbf{I}_k$ be the $k \times k$ identity matrix and let $\mathbf{P}$ be the $k \times (n-k)$ matrix of p_{ij}. Then the generator matrix of a systematic code can be written in the following form:

$$\mathbf{G} = [\mathbf{I}_k \mathbf{P}] \ .$$

Consider a message block $\mathbf{m} = (m_1, m_2, \ldots, m_k)$. By using the generator matrix of Eq. (3.4), the corresponding code word is

$$\begin{aligned} \mathbf{u} &= (u_1, u_2, u_3, \ldots, u_n) \\ &= (m_1, m_2, \ldots, m_k)\,\mathbf{G} \\ &= (m_1, m_2, \ldots, m_k) \begin{bmatrix} 1\,0\,0\,0 \ldots 0 & p_{11} & p_{12} & \cdots & p_{1,n\text{-}k} \\ 0\,1\,0\,0 \ldots 0 & p_{21} & p_{22} & \cdots & p_{2,n\text{-}k} \\ \vdots & \vdots & \vdots & & \vdots \\ 0\,0\,0\,0 \ldots 1 & p_{k,1} & p_{k,2} & \cdots & p_{k,n\text{-}k} \end{bmatrix}. \end{aligned} \tag{3.5}$$

By matrix multiplication, it can be shown that

$$u_i = m_i \quad \text{for} \quad i = 1, 2, \ldots, k \tag{3.6a}$$

and

$$u_{k+j} = p_{1j}m_1 + p_{2j}m_2 + \ldots + p_{kj}m_k \tag{3.6b}$$

for $j = 1, 2, \ldots, n - k$. From Eqs. (3.6a) and (3.6b), we easily see that the first k digits of the code word are just the information digits to be transmitted; the last $n - k$ digits are linear functions of information digits. We shall call the last $n - k$ redundant digits of $\mathbf{u}$ the *parity-check digits* of the code word. The equations of (3.6b) are called the *parity-check equations* of the code.

Example 3.3: Consider the generator matrix given in Example 3.2. The code word corresponding to a message block $(m_1 m_2 m_3)$ is

$$\mathbf{u} = (u_1, u_2, u_3, u_4, u_5, u_6)$$

$$= (m_1 m_2 m_3) \begin{bmatrix} 1\,0\,0\,1\,1\,0 \\ 0\,1\,0\,0\,1\,1 \\ 0\,0\,1\,1\,0\,1 \end{bmatrix}$$

$$= (m_1, m_2, m_3, m_1 + m_3, m_1 + m_2, m_2 + m_3) \quad .$$

Thus, $u_1 = m_1$, $u_2 = m_2$, $u_3 = m_3$, and

$$\begin{aligned} u_4 &= m_1 + m_3 \\ u_5 &= m_1 + m_2 \\ u_6 &= m_2 + m_3 \quad . \end{aligned}$$

For a linear code in systematic form, the encoding complexity can be further reduced since it has only to store $k \times (n-k)$ digits p_{ij} of the **P** matrix instead of storing $k \times n$ digits of the generator matrix **G**.

3.3 PARITY CHECK MATRIX

As stated in Chapter 2, for each $k \times n$ matrix **G** there exists a $(k-n) \times n$ matrix **H** such that the row space of **G** is orthogonal to **H**; that is, the inner product of a vector in the row space of **G** and a row of **H** is zero. Let

$$\mathbf{H} = \begin{bmatrix} \mathbf{h}_1 \\ \mathbf{h}_2 \\ \vdots \\ \mathbf{h}_{n-k} \end{bmatrix} = \begin{bmatrix} h_{11} & h_{12} & \cdots & h_{1n} \\ h_{21} & h_{22} & \cdots & h_{2n} \\ \vdots & \vdots & & \vdots \\ h_{n-k,1} & h_{n-k,2} & \cdots & h_{n-k,n} \end{bmatrix} \qquad (3.7)$$

and let $\mathbf{u} = (u_1, u_2, \ldots, u_n)$ be a vector in the row space of $\mathbf{G}$. Then

$$\mathbf{u}\,\mathbf{H}^{\mathrm{T}} = (0\,0 \ldots 0) \tag{3.8}$$

or

$$\mathbf{u} \cdot \mathbf{h}_i = u_1 h_{i1} + u_2 h_{i2} + \ldots + u_n h_{in} = 0 \tag{3.9}$$

for $i = 1, 2, \ldots, n-k$. Thus, we can describe the linear code generated by $\mathbf{G}$ in an alternate way as follows: $\mathbf{u}$ *is a code word in the code generated by* $\mathbf{G}$ *if and only if* $\mathbf{u}\,\mathbf{H}^{\mathrm{T}} = \mathbf{0}$. The matrix $\mathbf{H}$ is called the *parity-check matrix* of the code.

If the generator matrix of a systematic code is of the form of Eq. (3.4), then the parity-check matrix of this code is

$$\mathbf{H} = \begin{bmatrix} p_{11} & p_{21} & \cdots & p_{k1} & 1\,0\,0\,0 \ldots 0 \\ p_{12} & p_{22} & \cdots & p_{k2} & 0\,1\,0\,0 \ldots 0 \\ \vdots & \vdots & & \vdots & \vdots \qquad \vdots \\ p_{1,n-k} & p_{2,n-k} & \cdots & p_{k,n-k} & 0\,0\,0\,0 \ldots 1 \end{bmatrix} \tag{3.10}$$

$$= [\mathbf{P}^{\mathrm{T}}\ \mathbf{I}_{n-k}]$$

where $\mathbf{P}^{\mathrm{T}}$ is the transpose of matrix $\mathbf{P}$. The parity-check equations of (3.6b) can also be obtained from $\mathbf{H}$. This can be seen as follows. Let $\mathbf{u} = (u_1, u_2, \ldots, u_n)$ be the code word corresponding to message $\mathbf{m} = (m_1, m_2, \ldots, m_k)$, where $u_i = m_i$ for $i = 1, 2, \ldots, k$. Since

$$\mathbf{u}\,\mathbf{H}^{\mathrm{T}} = \mathbf{0} \;,$$

then we have

$$\begin{aligned} u_{k+j} &= p_{1j}u_1 + p_{2j}u_2 + \ldots + p_{kj}u_k \\ &= p_{1j}m_1 + p_{2j}m_2 + \ldots + p_{kj}m_k \end{aligned} \tag{3.11}$$

for $j = 1, 2, \ldots, n-k$, which is exactly the same set of equations as Eq. (3.6b). At this point, we can make the following remark: A linear code can be uniquely specified either by its generator matrix or by its parity matrix. In designing a linear code, the **P** matrix should be chosen in such a way that the code has the desired error-correcting properties. Constructive procedures for choosing **P** will be discussed in the following chapters.

Consider a linear (n,k) code with generator matrix **G** and parity check matrix **H**. Let **u** be a code vector which was transmitted over a noisy channel. At the receiver, we obtain a corrupted vector **r** which is a vector sum of the original code vector **u** and an error vector **e**, i.e.,

$$\mathbf{r} = \mathbf{u} + \mathbf{e} \ . \tag{3.12}$$

The receiver does not know **u** and **e**. The purpose of the decoder is to recover **u** from **r**. The $(n-k)$ component vector

$$\mathbf{s} = \mathbf{r}\mathbf{H}^{\mathrm{T}} \tag{3.13}$$

is called the *syndrome* of **r**. By Eq. (3.8), the syndrome is zero if **r** is a code vector and is not zero if **r** is not a code vector. The syndrome of a received vector at the channel output will be used for error-detection and correction.

The notions of parity check matrix and syndrome should be clarified by an example.

Example 3.4: Consider the generator matrix given in Example 3.2

$$\mathbf{G} = \begin{bmatrix} 1 & 0 & 0 & 1 & 1 & 0 \\ 0 & 1 & 0 & 0 & 1 & 1 \\ 0 & 0 & 1 & 1 & 0 & 1 \end{bmatrix}$$

According to Eq. (3.10), the parity check matrix is

$$\mathbf{H} = \begin{bmatrix} 1 & 0 & 1 & 1 & 0 & 0 \\ 1 & 1 & 0 & 0 & 1 & 0 \\ 0 & 1 & 1 & 0 & 0 & 1 \end{bmatrix} .$$

The 6-tuple $\mathbf{u} = (1\ 1\ 1\ 0\ 0\ 0)$ is the code vector corresponding to message $(1\ 1\ 1)$. Then

$$\mathbf{s} = \mathbf{u}\mathbf{H}^T = (1\ 1\ 1\ 0\ 0\ 0) \begin{bmatrix} 1 & 1 & 0 \\ 0 & 1 & 1 \\ 1 & 0 & 1 \\ 1 & 0 & 0 \\ 0 & 1 & 0 \\ 0 & 0 & 1 \end{bmatrix}$$

$$= (0\ 0\ 0) .$$

The 6-tuple $(1\ 1\ 1\ 0\ 0\ 1)$ is not a code word. The syndrome of this vector is

$$\mathbf{s} = (1\ 1\ 1\ 0\ 0\ 1) \begin{bmatrix} 1 & 1 & 0 \\ 0 & 1 & 1 \\ 1 & 0 & 1 \\ 1 & 0 & 0 \\ 0 & 1 & 0 \\ 0 & 0 & 1 \end{bmatrix} = (0\ 0\ 1) .$$

3.4 ERROR-CORRECTING CAPABILITY OF A LINEAR CODE

At this point we introduce some of the basic terminology which we will use to define the error-correcting ability of a linear code.

Definition 3.2: *The (Hamming) weight of an n-tuple* **v**, $\omega(\mathbf{v})$, *is defined as the number of non-zero components of* **v**; *i.e., if* **v** = (1 0 0 1 0 1 1 0 0 0 1), $\omega(\mathbf{v}) = 5$.

Let **u** and **v** be two n-tuples.

Definition 3.3: *The (Hamming) distance between* **u** *and* **v**, $d(\mathbf{u},\mathbf{v})$, *is defined as the number of components in which they differ; i.e., if*

$$\mathbf{u} = (1\ 0\ 0\ 1\ 0\ 1\ 1\ 0\ 0\ 0\ 1)$$

$$\mathbf{v} = (1\ 1\ 0\ 0\ 1\ 0\ 1\ 0\ 1\ 0\ 1) \ ,$$

then $d(\mathbf{u},\mathbf{v}) = 5$.

By the definition of modulo-2 addition, it can be easily seen that

$$d(\mathbf{u},\mathbf{v}) = \omega(\mathbf{u}+\mathbf{v}) \ . \qquad (3.14)$$

That is, the distance between **u** and **v** is just equal to the weight of their vector sum, **u** + **v**. Consider the two n-tuples given above,

$$\mathbf{u}+\mathbf{v} = (0\ 1\ 0\ 1\ 1\ 1\ 0\ 0\ 1\ 0\ 0)$$

and $\omega(\mathbf{u}+\mathbf{v}) = 5$, which is just $d(\mathbf{u},\mathbf{v}) = 5$.

Given a linear code, we can calculate the distances between all possible pairs of code words; *the smallest distance is called the minimum distance of the code*, which is denoted as $d_{\min}$. If **u** and **v** are two code vectors of a linear code, then **u** + **v** must also be a code vector since the set of all code vectors is a subspace of all n-tuples. Therefore, by definition, the distance between any two code vectors is equal to the weight of a third code vector. Thus, the minimum distance of a linear code is equal to the *minimum weight* of its non-zero code vectors. The notion of minimum distance or minimum weight is important since it determines the *error-correcting capability* of a linear code.

In certain communication channels, transmission errors occur independently; that is, each transmitted symbol is affected independently by noise. Errors of this kind are called *random errors*. Codes which are designed to combat independent errors are called *random-error-correcting codes*. There are also channels (telephone lines, magnetic-tape storage systems, etc.) on which the disturbances introduce errors of unspecified time duration; that is, errors tend to cluster together in bursts. Codes which are designed to correct this kind of error bursts are called *burst-error-correcting codes*. In the following, the capability of a code for random-error-correction will be discussed. The burst-error-correcting capability of a code will be discussed in a later chapter.

Consider a code that is used for a binary symmetric channel (*BSC*) Let $\mathbf{v} = (v_1, v_2, \ldots, v_n)$ be the transmitted code vector and let $\mathbf{r} = (r_1, r_2, \ldots, r_n)$ be the received vector. Because of the channel disturbance, the received vector $\mathbf{r}$ may be any of the 2^n n-tuples. The difference between $\mathbf{r}$ and $\mathbf{v}$ is

$$\begin{aligned} \mathbf{e} &= (e_1, e_2, \ldots, e_n) \\ &= \mathbf{r} + \mathbf{v} \\ &= (r_1, r_2, \ldots, r_n) + (v_1, v_2, \ldots, v_n) \\ &= (v_1 + r_1,\ v_2 + r_2, \ldots,\ v_n + r_n) \end{aligned}$$

which is the *error pattern* (or *error vector*) caused by the channel disturbance. When $e_i = v_i + r_i = 1$, the ith symbol of the transmitted code vector is corrupted, and we say that there is an *error* at the ith position of $\mathbf{r}$. Since the received vector $\mathbf{r}$ may be any of the 2^n n-tuples, there are 2^n possible error patterns. For binary symmetric channels, an error pattern of fewer errors is more likely to occur than an error pattern with more errors.

At the receiver, the function of the decoder is to identify the actual transmitted code vector from the received vector **r**. For maximum likelihood decoding with *BSC*, the decoder will identify **v** as the transmitted code vector if **v** is the code vector which is closest to **r** in the sense of Hamming distance (i.e., $d(\mathbf{v},\mathbf{r})$ is minimum). If a code with minimum distance d_{min} such that $2t + 2 \geqslant d_{min} \geqslant 2t + 1$ is used for random error correction, the decoder can correct all error patterns of t or fewer errors which may occur in the received vector. This can be justified as follows. Let **v** be the transmitted code vector and **u** be any other code vector. The Hamming distances among **v**, **u**, and **r** satisfy the following inequality:

$$d(\mathbf{v},\mathbf{r}) + d(\mathbf{u},\mathbf{r}) \geqslant d(\mathbf{v},\mathbf{u}) \quad . \tag{3.15}$$

If an error pattern of t' $(t' \leqslant t)$ errors occurs, then the Hamming distance between the transmitted code vector **v** and the received vector **r** is $d(\mathbf{v},\mathbf{r}) = t'$. Since $d(\mathbf{v},\mathbf{u}) \geqslant d_{min} \geqslant 2t + 1$, then, by Eq. (3.15), we obtain

$$\begin{aligned} d(\mathbf{u},\mathbf{r}) &\geqslant 2t + 1 - t' \quad , \\ d(\mathbf{u},\mathbf{r}) &\geqslant t + 1 \quad , \\ d(\mathbf{u},\mathbf{r}) &> t' \quad . \end{aligned} \tag{3.16}$$

The inequality of Eq. (3.16) says that, if an error pattern of t or fewer errors occurs, the received vector **r** is closer to the actual transmitted code vector **v** than to any other code vector **u**. Thus, the decoder will make a correct decoding and the errors will be corrected. On the other hand, with the above code, the decoder cannot correct all the error patterns of ℓ errors, $\ell \geqslant t + 1$, for there is at least one case where an error pattern of ℓ errors results in a received vector which is closer to an incorrect code vector than to the transmitted code vector. In this case, the decoder will make an incorrect decoding. Thus, we say that the above code has error-correcting capability t. In general, a code with minimum distance d_{min} has error-correcting capability

$$t = [(d_{min} - 1)/2] \quad ,$$

where $[(d_{min} - 1)/2]$ denotes the largest integer no greater than $(d_{min} - 1)/2$. A code of error-correcting capability t is generally called a *t-error-correcting code*.

Example 3.5: Consider the code given in Example 3.1. The minimum distance is 3. Its error-correcting capability is 1. Thus, all patterns of a single error are correctable. To show that not all error patterns of double errors are correctable, we transmit the code vector (0 0 0 0 0 0). Suppose that two errors occur at the third and the sixth places. Then the received vector will be (0 0 1 0 0 1), which differs from the transmitted vector in two places, but differs from the code vector (0 0 1 1 0 1) in only one place. It turns out that the code vector (0 0 1 1 0 1) is the closest vector to the received vector. Thus, the received vector will be decoded into (0 0 1 1 0 1) and incorrect decoding will be made by the decoder.

Now we consider the *error-detecting capability* of a code. If a code with minimum distance d_{min} is used for straight error detection, the decoder can detect all error patterns of $d_{min} - 1$ or fewer errors. This is so since no error pattern of $d_{min} - 1$ or fewer errors will alter the transmitted code vector into another code vector. Thus, the decoder will detect the existence of errors. On the other hand, the decoder may not detect an error pattern of ℓ errors for $\ell \geqslant d_{min}$. This can be seen as follows. Suppose that there exists some pair of code vectors **u** and **v** whose Hamming distance $d(\mathbf{u},\mathbf{v})$ is ℓ. Consider the error pattern $\mathbf{e} = \mathbf{u} + \mathbf{v}$ of ℓ errors. This error pattern will alter **u** into **v** and vice versa. Thus, if **u** is the transmitted code vector and **e** is the error pattern, then **v** will be the received vector. Since **v** is a code vector, the decoder will assume that no error has occurred and accept **v** as the transmitted code vector. Thus, the error pattern **e** is not detectable.

Sometimes a code is used for simultaneous correction of all combinations of t or fewer errors and detection of all combinations of $\ell \geqslant t$ errors. For this purpose, the code is required to have minimum distance $t + \ell + 1$. Furthermore, for any of the codes described in this book, it is possible to limit the correction from the maximum possible t to some smaller value than $[(d_{min} - 1)/2]$ and assure detection of a larger class of errors.

From the above discussion, it is obvious that for given n and k, we would like to design an (n,k) code with minimum distance as large as possible (for random error correction). So far, there is no systematic way to do it.

3.5 THE STANDARD ARRAY

Suppose that an (n,k) linear code $\mathbf{C}$ is used for (random or burst) error-correcting purposes. Let $\mathbf{v}_1, \mathbf{v}_2, \ldots, \mathbf{v}_{2^k}$ be the 2^k code vectors. For any code vector which is transmitted over the noisy channel, the received vector $\mathbf{r}$ may be any of the 2^n n-tuples. Any decoding scheme used in the decoder is a rule to partition the 2^n n-tuples into 2^k disjoint subsets $\mathbf{D}_1, \mathbf{D}_2, \ldots, \mathbf{D}_{2^k}$ such that the subset $\mathbf{D}_i$ contains only the code vector $\mathbf{v}_i$. Thus, each subset $\mathbf{D}_i$ is one-to-one correspondence to a code vector $\mathbf{v}_i$. If the received vector $\mathbf{r}$ is found in the subset $\mathbf{D}_i$, then the decoder identifies $\mathbf{v}_i$ as the transmitted code vector. *Correct decoding is made if the received vector* $\mathbf{r}$ *is in the subset* $\mathbf{D}_i$ *which corresponds to the actual transmitted code vector. An incorrect decoding results if the received vector* $\mathbf{r}$ *is in the subset which does not correspond to the actual transmitted code vector.*

A way to partition the 2^n n-tuples is described as follows. The 2^k code vectors are placed in a row with the zero code vector $\mathbf{v}_1 = (0, 0, \ldots, 0)$ as the leftmost element. From the remaining $2^n - 2^k$ n-tuples, an n-tuple $\mathbf{e}_2$ is chosen and is placed under the zero code vector $\mathbf{v}_1$. Then the second row is completed by adding $\mathbf{e}_2$ to each code vector $\mathbf{v}_i$ and placing the sum $\mathbf{e}_2 + \mathbf{v}_i$ under $\mathbf{v}_i$. Having completed the second row, an unused n-tuple $\mathbf{e}_3$ is chosen from the remaining n-tuples and is placed under $\mathbf{v}_1$. Then the third row is completed by adding $\mathbf{e}_3$ to each code vector $\mathbf{v}_i$ and placing the sum $\mathbf{e}_3 + \mathbf{v}_i$ under $\mathbf{v}_i$. We continue this process until all the n-tuples are used. Then we have an array of rows and columns as shown in Fig. 3.2. Each row consists of 2^k n-tuples.

Theorem 3.1: (1) No two n-tuples in the same row of the array are identical. (2) No n-tuple appears in different rows.

Proof: (1) Suppose that two n-tuples in the ℓth row are identical, say $\mathbf{e}_\ell + \mathbf{v}_i = \mathbf{e}_\ell + \mathbf{v}_j$ with $i \neq j$. Then we have $\mathbf{v}_i = \mathbf{v}_j$, which is impossible.

Therefore, no two n-tuples in the same row are identical.

(2) Suppose that an n-tuple appears in both the ℓth row and t^{th} row, say $\ell < t$. Then this n-tuple must be equal to $\mathbf{e}_\ell + \mathbf{v}_i$ for some i and must be equal to $\mathbf{e}_t + \mathbf{v}_j$ for some j. Therefore, $\mathbf{e}_\ell + \mathbf{v}_i = \mathbf{e}_t + \mathbf{v}_j$. From this, we obtain $\mathbf{e}_t = \mathbf{e}_\ell + (\mathbf{v}_i + \mathbf{v}_j)$. Since $\mathbf{v}_i$ and $\mathbf{v}_j$ are two code vectors, $(\mathbf{v}_i + \mathbf{v}_j)$ is also a code vector, say $\mathbf{v}_s$. Then $\mathbf{e}_t = \mathbf{e}_\ell + \mathbf{v}_s$. This implies that the n-tuple $\mathbf{e}_t$ is in the ℓth row, which contradicts the construction rule of the array that $\mathbf{e}_t$, the first element of the tth row, should be unused in the previous rows. We thus conclude that no n-tuple appears in different rows.

Q.E.D.

$$
\begin{array}{lllll}
\mathbf{v}_1 & \mathbf{v}_2 & \cdots\ \mathbf{v}_i & \cdots\ \mathbf{v}_{2^k} \\
\mathbf{e}_2 & \mathbf{e}_2 + \mathbf{v}_2 & \cdots\ \mathbf{e}_2 + \mathbf{v}_i & \cdots\ \mathbf{e}_2 + \mathbf{v}_{2^k} \\
\mathbf{e}_3 & \mathbf{e}_3 + \mathbf{v}_2 & \cdots\ \mathbf{e}_3 + \mathbf{v}_i & \cdots\ \mathbf{e}_3 + \mathbf{v}_{2^k} \\
\vdots & & & \vdots \\
\mathbf{e}_\ell & \mathbf{e}_\ell + \mathbf{v}_2 & \cdots\ \mathbf{e}_\ell + \mathbf{v}_i & \cdots\ \mathbf{e}_\ell + \mathbf{v}_{2^k} \\
\vdots & & & \vdots \\
\mathbf{e}_{2^{n-k}} & \mathbf{e}_{2^{n-k}} + \mathbf{v}_2 & \cdots\ \mathbf{e}_{2^{n-k}} + \mathbf{v}_i & \cdots\ \mathbf{e}_{2^{n-k}} + \mathbf{v}_{2^k}
\end{array}
$$

Fig. 3.2. A standard array for an (n,k) linear code.

From the above theorem, we see that each row of the array consists of 2^k distinct n-tuples and all the rows are disjoint. That is, every n-tuple appears *once and only once* in the array. Therefore, there are $(2^n/2^k) = 2^{n-k}$ disjoint rows. This array is called a *standard array* [14] for the given (n,k) linear code; the 2^{n-k} rows are called *cosets*, and the leftmost n-tuple $\mathbf{e}_\ell$ of each row is called a *coset leader*.

Example 3.6: Consider the (6,3) code whose generator matrix is

$$\mathbf{G} = \begin{bmatrix} 1\,0\,0\,0\,1\,1 \\ 0\,1\,0\,1\,0\,1 \\ 0\,0\,1\,1\,1\,0 \end{bmatrix} .$$

The eight code vectors are

Messages	Code Vectors
$\mathbf{m}_1 = (0\,0\,0)$	$\mathbf{v}_1 = (0\,0\,0\,0\,0\,0)$
$\mathbf{m}_2 = (0\,0\,1)$	$\mathbf{v}_2 = (0\,0\,1\,1\,1\,0)$
$\mathbf{m}_3 = (0\,1\,0)$	$\mathbf{v}_3 = (0\,1\,0\,1\,0\,1)$
$\mathbf{m}_4 = (1\,0\,0)$	$\mathbf{v}_4 = (1\,0\,0\,0\,1\,1)$
$\mathbf{m}_5 = (0\,1\,1)$	$\mathbf{v}_5 = (0\,1\,1\,0\,1\,1)$
$\mathbf{m}_6 = (1\,0\,1)$	$\mathbf{v}_6 = (1\,0\,1\,1\,0\,1)$
$\mathbf{m}_7 = (1\,1\,0)$	$\mathbf{v}_7 = (1\,1\,0\,1\,1\,0)$
$\mathbf{m}_8 = (1\,1\,1)$	$\mathbf{v}_8 = (1\,1\,1\,0\,0\,0)$.

A standard array for this code is shown in Fig. 3.3.

A standard array for an (n,k) code consists of 2^k columns which are disjoint. Each column is a set of 2^{n-k} n-tuples with the topmost n-tuple as a code vector. Denote the jth column as $\mathbf{D}_j$. Then

$$\mathbf{D}_j = \{ \mathbf{v}_j, \mathbf{e}_2 + \mathbf{v}_j, \mathbf{e}_3 + \mathbf{v}_j, \ldots, \mathbf{e}_{2^{n-k}} + \mathbf{v}_i \} \tag{3.17}$$

Coset Leader							
000000	001110	010101	100011	011011	101101	110110	111000
000001	001111	010100	100010	011010	101100	110111	111001
000010	001100	010111	100001	011001	101111	110100	111010
000100	001010	010001	100111	011111	101001	110010	111100
001000	000110	011101	101011	010011	100101	111110	110000
010000	011110	000101	110011	001011	111101	100110	101000
100000	101110	110101	000011	111011	001101	010110	011000
001001	000111	011100	101010	010010	100100	111111	110001

Fig. 3.3. A standard array for the (6,3) code.

where $\mathbf{v}_j$ is the jth code vector and $\mathbf{e}_2, \mathbf{e}_3, \ldots, \mathbf{e}_{2^{n-k}}$ are coset leaders. Therefore, a standard array partitions the 2^n n-tuples into 2^k disjoint subsets $\mathbf{D}_1, \mathbf{D}_2, \ldots, \mathbf{D}_{2^k}$. These 2^k disjoint subsets can then be used for decoding as described in the first paragraph of this section. Suppose that the code vector $\mathbf{v}_i$ is transmitted over a noisy channel. From Eq. (3.17), we can see that the received vector $\mathbf{r}$ is in $\mathbf{D}_i$ if the error pattern caused by the channel is a coset leader. Then the received vector will be decoded correctly into $\mathbf{v}_i$. On the other hand, if the error pattern caused by the channel is not a coset leader, an incorrect decoding will result. This can be seen as follows. The error pattern $\mathbf{w}$ caused by the channel must be in some coset and under some code vector, say in the ℓth coset and under the code vector $\mathbf{v}_j$. Then $\mathbf{w} = \mathbf{e}_\ell + \mathbf{v}_j$ and the received vector $\mathbf{r} = \mathbf{v}_i + \mathbf{w} = \mathbf{e}_\ell + (\mathbf{v}_i + \mathbf{v}_j) = \mathbf{e}_\ell + \mathbf{v}_s$. The received vector is thus in $\mathbf{D}_s$ and is decoded into $\mathbf{v}_s$, which is an incorrect decoding. In summary, *when a standard array is used for decoding, the decoding is correct if and only if the error pattern caused by the channel is a coset leader.* The 2^{n-k} coset leaders are called *correctable error patterns.* In order to minimize the probability of decoding error, *the 2^{n-k} coset leaders are chosen to be the error patterns which are most likely to occur for a given channel.* Let $\mathbf{e}_i$ and $\mathbf{e}_j$ be two error patterns with weights $\omega(\mathbf{e}_i)$ and $\omega(\mathbf{e}_j)$ respectively. For the binary symmetric channel, if $\omega(\mathbf{e}_i) < \omega(\mathbf{e}_j)$, then $\mathbf{e}_i$ is more likely to occur than $\mathbf{e}_j$. Therefore, in each case the coset leader should be chosen as a vector with minimum weight from the remaining available vectors.

A standard array has an important property which can be used to simplify the decoding process. Let $\mathbf{H}$ be the parity check matrix of the given (n,k) code.

Theorem 3.2: (1) All the 2^k n-tuples of a coset have the same syndrome. (2) The syndromes for different cosets are different.

Proof: (1) Consider the ℓth coset whose coset leader is $\mathbf{e}_\ell$. An n-tuple in this coset is equal to $\mathbf{e}_\ell + \mathbf{v}_i$ for some i. The syndrome of this n-tuple is

$$(\mathbf{e}_\ell + \mathbf{v}_i)\,\mathbf{H}^{\mathrm{T}} = \mathbf{e}_\ell\,\mathbf{H}^{\mathrm{T}} + \mathbf{v}_i\,\mathbf{H}^{\mathrm{T}} .$$

Since $\mathbf{v}_i$ is a code vector which is in the null space of $\mathbf{H}$, then $\mathbf{v}_i\,\mathbf{H}^{\mathrm{T}} = 0$. Thus,

$$(\mathbf{e}_\ell + \mathbf{v}_i)\,\mathbf{H}^{\mathrm{T}} = \mathbf{e}_\ell\,\mathbf{H}^{\mathrm{T}} .$$

That is, the syndrome of any n-tuple in a coset is equal to that of the coset leader. Therefore, all the n-tuples of a coset have the same syndrome.

(2) Suppose that the syndromes of the ℓth coset and the tth coset $(\ell < t)$ are equal. From part (1), we have

$$\mathbf{e}_\ell\,\mathbf{H}^{\mathrm{T}} = \mathbf{e}_t\,\mathbf{H}^{\mathrm{T}} .$$

Then $(\mathbf{e}_\ell + \mathbf{e}_t)\mathbf{H}^{\mathrm{T}} = 0$. This implies that the n-tuple $(\mathbf{e}_\ell + \mathbf{e}_t)$ must be a code vector, say $\mathbf{v}_j$. Thus, $\mathbf{e}_t = \mathbf{e}_\ell + \mathbf{v}_j$. That is, $\mathbf{e}_t$ is in the ℓth coset, which contradicts the construction rule of the standard array that the coset leader $\mathbf{e}_t$ should be previously unused. Therefore, we conclude that for $\ell \neq t$, $\mathbf{e}_\ell\,\mathbf{H}^{\mathrm{T}} \neq \mathbf{e}_t\,\mathbf{H}^{\mathrm{T}}$.

Q.E.D.

The syndrome of an n-tuple is an $(n\text{-}k)$-tuple. There are 2^{n-k} distinct $(n\text{-}k)$-tuples. Since there are 2^{n-k} cosets, then, by Theorem 3.2, there is a *one-to-one correspondence between a coset and an* $(n\text{-}k)$*-tuple syndrome*. Or, there is a *one-to-one correspondence between a coset leader* (a *correctable error pattern*) *and a syndrome*. Now we may form a *decoding table* which is simpler than a standard array. The table consists of 2^{n-k} coset leaders (the error pattern to be correctable) and their corresponding syndromes. The decoding of a received vector $\mathbf{r}$ consists of three steps:

(1) Calculate the syndrome $\mathbf{r}\mathbf{H}^T$ of $\mathbf{r}$.

(2) Locate the coset leader $\mathbf{e}_\ell$ whose syndrome is equal to $\mathbf{r}\mathbf{H}^T$. Then $\mathbf{e}_\ell$ is assumed to be the error pattern caused by the noisy channel.

(3) The code vector $\mathbf{v}_i = \mathbf{r} + \mathbf{e}_\ell$ is identified as the transmitted code vector.

Example 3.7: Consider the (6,3) code given in Example 3.6. The parity check matrix is

$$\mathbf{H} = \begin{bmatrix} 0\,1\,1\,1\,0\,0 \\ 1\,0\,1\,0\,1\,0 \\ 1\,1\,0\,0\,0\,1 \end{bmatrix} .$$

The table with coset leaders and their corresponding syndromes is

Syndrome	Coset Leader
0 0 0	0 0 0 0 0 0
0 0 1	0 0 0 0 0 1
0 1 0	0 0 0 0 1 0
1 0 0	0 0 0 1 0 0
1 1 0	0 0 1 0 0 0
1 0 1	0 1 0 0 0 0
0 1 1	1 0 0 0 0 0
1 1 1	0 0 1 0 0 1 .

Suppose that the code vector $\mathbf{v}_8 = (1\ 1\ 1\ 0\ 0\ 0)$ is transmitted and $\mathbf{r} = (1\ 1\ 1\ 0\ 0\ 1)$ is received. For decoding $\mathbf{r}$, we calculate the syndrome of $\mathbf{r}$ which is

$$(1\ 1\ 1\ 0\ 0\ 1)\begin{bmatrix} 0\ 1\ 1 \\ 1\ 0\ 1 \\ 1\ 1\ 0 \\ 1\ 0\ 0 \\ 0\ 1\ 0 \\ 0\ 0\ 1 \end{bmatrix} = (0\ 0\ 1)\ .$$

From the table, we find that $(0\ 0\ 1)$ is the syndrome of coset leader $(0\ 0\ 0\ 0\ 0\ 1)$. Thus, $(0\ 0\ 0\ 0\ 0\ 1)$ is assumed to be the error pattern caused by the channel, and $(1\ 1\ 1\ 0\ 0\ 1) + (0\ 0\ 0\ 0\ 0\ 1) = (1\ 1\ 1\ 0\ 0\ 0)$ is identified as the transmitted code vector. Obviously, the decoding is correct since the error pattern $(0\ 0\ 0\ 0\ 0\ 1)$ is a coset leader in the standard array of Fig. 3.3. Now suppose that $\mathbf{v}_8 = (1\ 1\ 1\ 0\ 0\ 0)$ is transmitted and $\mathbf{r} = (1\ 1\ 1\ 0\ 1\ 1)$ is received. The syndrome of $\mathbf{r}$ is $(0\ 1\ 1)$. The coset leader which has this syndrome is $(1\ 0\ 0\ 0\ 0\ 0)$. Thus, $(1\ 0\ 0\ 0\ 0\ 0)$ is assumed to be the error pattern caused by the channel and $(1\ 1\ 1\ 0\ 1\ 1) + (1\ 0\ 0\ 0\ 0\ 0) = (0\ 1\ 1\ 0\ 1\ 1)$ is identified as the transmitted code vector. This is an incorrect decoding since the error pattern caused by the channel is $(1\ 1\ 1\ 0\ 1\ 1) + (1\ 1\ 1\ 0\ 0\ 0) = (0\ 0\ 0\ 0\ 1\ 1)$, which is not a coset leader in the standard array of Fig. 3.3. Since all error patterns of weight one are coset leaders, this code corrects single errors at any position; it also corrects one error pattern of double errors. Thus, it is a single-error-correcting code.

The decoding described above is called table *look-up decoding*. Step 2 of this decoding can be implemented in the following manner. The decoder generates the syndrome corresponding to each coset leader and then compares it to the syndrome of the received vector $\mathbf{r}$. When the coset leader $\mathbf{e}_\ell$ whose syndrome matches the syndrome of $\mathbf{r}$ is found, it is assumed to be the error pattern caused by the channel noise. In principle, the table look-up decoding can be applied to any linear (n,k) code. But, for large $n-k$, this decoding becomes very impractical since the decoder has to store 2^{n-k} coset leaders and perform a large number of computations in order to find the coset leader whose syndrome matches the syndrome of the received vector. For example, for a (100,70) code, there are $2^{30} \cong 10^9$ coset leaders. If the table look-up decoding were employed, the decoder would be prohibitively complex. Several practical decoding methods which are refinements of the table look-up decoding will be discussed in the following five chapters. Each of these decoding methods requires additional properties in a code other than just the linear property.

For an (n,k) linear code, if it is possible to construct a standard array such that all the error patterns of weight t or less (but not all of weight $t+1$ or more) can be used as coset leaders, then the code is a t-error-correcting code whose minimum distance is at least $2t+1$. On the other hand, if an (n,k) linear code has minimum distance $2t+1$, it is possible to construct a standard array such that all error patterns of weight t or less (but not weight $t+1$ or more) can be used as coset leaders.

PROBLEMS

3.1. Consider a (7,4) code whose generator matrix is

$$\mathbf{G} = \begin{bmatrix} 1\,0\,0\,0\,1\,1\,1 \\ 0\,1\,0\,0\,1\,0\,1 \\ 0\,0\,1\,0\,0\,1\,1 \\ 0\,0\,0\,1\,1\,1\,0 \end{bmatrix}.$$

(a) Find all the code vectors of this code.
(b) Find the parity check matrix $\mathbf{H}$ of this code.

3.2. Consider a systematic (8,4) code whose parity check equations are given below:

$$\begin{aligned} u_5 &= m_1 + m_2 + m_4 \\ u_6 &= m_1 + m_3 + m_4 \\ u_7 &= m_1 + m_2 + m_3 \\ u_8 &= m_2 + m_3 + m_4 \end{aligned}$$

where m_1, m_2, m_3, m_4 are message digits. Find the parity and generator matrices for this code. Show that the minimum weight of this code is 4.

3.3. Construct a standard array for the code given in Problem 3.1.

3.4. Use the standard array which you obtained in Problem 3.3 to construct a decoding table for the code given in Problem 3.1.

3.5. Let **C** be an (n,k) code with minimum weight $d = 2t + 1$. Prove that at least one error pattern of weight $t + 1$ cannot be used as a coset leader.

3.6. Suppose that the minimum weight of an (n,k) code **C** is d. Prove that every combination of $d - 1$ or fewer columns of the parity check matrix **H** of **C** is linearly independent. Also, prove that there exists at least one combination of d columns of **H** which is linearly dependent.

3.7. Let **H** be the parity check matrix for an (n,k) linear code **C** which has odd minimum weight d. Construct a new code $\mathbf{C}_1$ whose parity check matrix is

$$\mathbf{H}_1 = \left[\begin{array}{c|c} \mathbf{H} & \begin{matrix} 0 \\ 0 \\ \vdots \\ 0 \end{matrix} \\ \hline 1\ 1\ \ldots & 1 \end{array}\right]$$

(a) Prove that $\mathbf{C}_1$ is an $(n+1, k)$ code.

(b) Prove that every code vector in $\mathbf{C}_1$ has even weight.

(c) Prove that the minimum weight of $\mathbf{C}_1$ is $d+1$.

3.8. Let $\mathbf{C}$ be a linear (n, k) code with both even weight and odd weight code vectors. Show that the number of even weight code vectors is equal to the number of odd weight code vectors.

REFERENCES

1. Ash, R., *Information Theory*, John Wiley, New York, 1965.
2. Berlekamp, E. R., *Algebraic Coding Theory*, McGraw-Hill, 1968.
3. Dwork, B. M., and R. M. Heller, "Results of a Geometric Approach to the Theory and Construction of Non-Binary, Multiple Error and Failure Correcting Codes," *IRE National Convention Record*, Part 4, pp. 123-129, 1959.
4. Fontaine, A. B., and W. W. Peterson, "Group Code Equivalence and Optimum Codes," *IRE Trans. on Information Theory*, **IT-5**, Special Supplement, pp. 60-70, May, 1959.
5. Gallager, R. G., *Information Theory and Reliable Communication*, John Wiley, 1968.
6. Golay, M. J. E., "Notes on Digital Coding," *Proc. IRE*, **37**, p. 657, June, 1949.
7. Hamming, R. W., "Error Detecting and Error Correcting Codes," *Bell Systems Tech. J.*, **29**, pp. 147-160, April, 1950.
8. Lucky, R. W., J. Salz, and E. J. Weldon, Jr., *Principles of Data Communication*, McGraw-Hill, 1968.

9. MacDonald, J. E., *Constructive Coding Methods for the Binary Symmetric Independent Data Transmission Channel,* M.S. Thesis, Department of Electrical Engineering, Syracuse University, Syracuse, New York, 1958.

10. MacDonald, J. E., "Design Method for Maximum Minimum-Distance Error-Correcting Codes," *IBM J. Research Develop.*, **4**, pp. 43-57, 1960.

11. Peterson, W. W., *Error-Correcting Codes,* The M.I.T. Press, Cambridge, Massachusetts, and John Wiley, New York, 1961.

12. Peterson, W. W., and E. J. Weldon, Jr., *Error-Correcting Codes,* 2nd Edition, The M.I.T. Press, Cambridge, Massachusetts, 1970.

13. Prange, E., "The Use of Coset Equivalence in the Analysis and Decoding of Group Codes," AFCRC-TR-59-164, Air Force Cambridge Research Center, Cambridge, Massachusetts, June, 1959.

14. Slepian, D., "A Class of Binary Signaling Alphabets," *Bell Systems Tech. J.*, **35**, pp. 203-234, January, 1956.

15. Slepian, D., "A Note on Two Binary Signaling Alphabets," *IRE Trans. on Information Theory*, **IT-2**, pp. 84-86, June, 1956.

16. Slepian, D., "Some Further Theory of Group Codes," *Bell Systems Tech. J.*, **39**, pp. 1219-1252, September, 1960.

CHAPTER 4

BINARY CYCLIC CODES

During the past decade, most of the research on block codes has been concentrated on a subclass of linear codes known as *cyclic codes*. Cyclic codes are attractive for two reasons. First, encoding and syndrome calculation of a cyclic code can be implemented easily by employing simple shift registers with feedback connections. Secondly, because they have considerable inherent algebraic structure, it is possible to find various simple and efficient decoding methods.

The algebraic structure of cyclic codes is developed in Section 4.1. Encoding and syndrome calculation of cyclic codes with feedback shift registers are presented in Sections 4.2, 4.3, and 4.4. In Section 4.5, a general decoder for cyclic codes is described. Several practical refinements of this decoder will be discussed in the following chapters.

Cyclic codes were first studied by Prange in 1957.[20] Since then, progress in the study of cyclic codes for both random-error correction and burst-error correction has been spurred by many algebraic coding theorists. References 4, 18, and 19 contain excellent expositions of cyclic codes and their implementations.

4.1 DESCRIPTION OF CYCLIC CODES

Definition 4.1: *An (n,k) linear code* **C** *is called a cyclic code if it has the following property: If an n-tuple*

$$\mathbf{v} = (v_0, v_1, v_2, \ldots, v_{n-1})$$

is a code vector of **C**, *the n-tuple*

$$\mathbf{v}^{(1)} = (v_{n-1}, v_0, v_1, \ldots, v_{n-2}) \tag{4.1}$$

obtained by shifting **v** *cyclically one place to the right is also a code vector of* **C**.

From the definition, it is clear that

$$\mathbf{v}^{(i)} = (v_{n-i}, v_{n-i+1}, \ldots, v_{n-1}, v_0, v_1, \ldots, v_{n-i-1}) \tag{4.2}$$

obtained by shifting **v** to the right cyclically i places is also a code vector. We shall treat the components of a code vector as coefficients of a polynomial as follows:

$$\begin{aligned} \mathbf{v} &= (v_0, v_1, v_2, \ldots, v_{n-1}) \iff \\ \mathbf{v}(X) &= v_0 + v_1 X + v_2 X^2 + \ldots + v_{n-1} X^{n-1} \ . \end{aligned} \tag{4.3}$$

Thus, each code vector corresponds one-to-one to a polynomial of degree n-1 or less. If $v_{n-1} \neq 0$, the degree of $\mathbf{v}(X)$ is $n-1$; if $v_{n-1} = 0$, the degree of $\mathbf{v}(X)$ is less than $n-1$. We shall call $\mathbf{v}(X)$ the *code polynomial* of **v**. Hereafter, *we shall use the terms code vector and code polynomial interchangeably*. The code polynomial which corresponds to the code vector $\mathbf{v}^{(i)}$ is

$$\begin{aligned} \mathbf{v}^{(i)}(X) &= v_{n-i} + v_{n-i+1} X + \ldots + v_{n-1} X^{i-1} + v_0 X^i \\ &\quad + v_1 X^{i+1} + \ldots + v_{n-i-1} X^{n-1} \ . \end{aligned} \tag{4.4}$$

It can be shown easily that $\mathbf{v}^{(i)}(X)$ *is the remainder resulting from dividing* $X^i \mathbf{v}(X)$ *by* $X^n + 1$, i.e.,

$$X^i \mathbf{v}(X) = \mathbf{q}(X)(X^n + 1) + \mathbf{v}^{(i)}(X) \ . \tag{4.5}$$

It is clear that $\mathbf{v}^{(i)}(X) = X^i \mathbf{v}(X)$ if the degree of $X^i \mathbf{v}(X)$ is $n-1$ or less.

With polynomial representation, it is possible to develop some important properties for a cyclic code which make the simple implementation of encoding and syndrome calculation possible. We shall state these properties in a number of basic theorems.[16,18,20,22]

Theorem 4.1: In an (n,k) cyclic code, there exists one and only one code polynomial $\mathbf{g}(X)$ of degree $n-k$,

$$\mathbf{g}(X) = 1 + g_1 X + g_2 X^2 + \ldots + g_{n-k-1} X^{n-k-1} + X^{n-k} \quad . \tag{4.6}$$

Every code polynomial $\mathbf{v}(X)$ is a multiple of $\mathbf{g}(X)$ and every polynomial of degree $n-1$ or less which is a multiple of $\mathbf{g}(X)$ must be a code polynomial.

Proof: Let $\mathbf{g}(X) = g_0 + g_1 X + g_2 X^2 + \ldots + g_{r-1} X^{r-1} + X^r$ be a nonzero code polynomial of *minimum degree* in the (n,k) cyclic code. Due to the cyclic property of the code, $X\mathbf{g}(X), X^2\mathbf{g}(X), \ldots, X^{n-r-1}\mathbf{g}(X)$ are also code polynomials. Since the code is linear, a linear combination of $\mathbf{g}(X), X\mathbf{g}(X), \ldots, X^{n-r-1}\mathbf{g}(X)$,

$$\begin{aligned} \mathbf{v}(X) &= m_0 \mathbf{g}(X) + m_1 X \mathbf{g}(X) + \ldots + m_{n-r-1} X^{n-r-1} \mathbf{g}(X) \\ &= (m_0 + m_1 X + m_2 X^2 + \ldots + m_{n-r-1} X^{n-r-1}) \mathbf{g}(X) \quad , \end{aligned}$$

is also a code polynomial, where m_i is either 0 or 1. Thus, any polynomial of degree $n-1$ or less which is a multiple of $\mathbf{g}(X)$ is a code polynomial in the (n,k) cyclic code. Now let $\mathbf{v}(X)$ be any code polynomial. Dividing $\mathbf{v}(X)$ by $\mathbf{g}(X)$ yields

$$\mathbf{v}(X) = \mathbf{a}(X)\mathbf{g}(X) + \mathbf{b}(X) \quad ,$$

where either $\mathbf{b}(X)$ is identical to zero or the degree of $\mathbf{b}(X)$ is less than the degree of $\mathbf{g}(X)$. Rearranging the above equation, we have

$$\mathbf{b}(X) \;=\; \mathbf{v}(X) + \mathbf{a}(X)\,\mathbf{g}(X) \quad .$$

Since $\mathbf{v}(X)$ and $\mathbf{a}(X)\mathbf{g}(X)$ are code polynomials and the code is linear, $\mathbf{b}(X)$ must also be a code polynomial. Suppose that $\mathbf{b}(X)$ is not identical to zero. Then $\mathbf{b}(X)$ is a non-zero code polynomial whose degree is less than the degree of $\mathbf{g}(X)$. This contradicts the assumption that $\mathbf{g}(X)$ is a code polynomial of minimum degree in the cyclic code. Thus, $\mathbf{b}(X)$ must be identical to zero. This proves that a code polynomial is a multiple of $\mathbf{g}(X)$.

Now we want to show that $\mathbf{g}(X)$ is unique. Suppose that there was another code polynomial $\mathbf{g}'(X)$ of degree r, say $\mathbf{g}'(X) = g_0{}' + g_1{}'X + \ldots + g_{r-1}{}'X^{r-1} + X^r$. Then $\mathbf{g}(X) + \mathbf{g}'(X) = (g_0 + g_0{}') + (g_1 + g_1{}')X + \ldots + (g_{r-1} + g_{r-1}{}')X^{r-1}$ is a code polynomial of degree less than r. If $\mathbf{g}(X) + \mathbf{g}'(X) \neq 0$, then the assumption that $\mathbf{g}(X)$ is a code polynomial of minimum degree is contradicted. Thus, $\mathbf{g}(X) + \mathbf{g}'(X) = 0$. This is to say that $\mathbf{g}'(X) = \mathbf{g}(X)$. Therefore, $\mathbf{g}(X)$ is unique.

The coefficient g_0 of $\mathbf{g}(X)$ must be equal to 1. If $g_0 = 0$, then $\mathbf{g}(X) = g_1X + g_2X^2 + \ldots + g_{r-1}X^{r-1} + X^r = X(g_1 + g_2X + \ldots + X^{r-1})$. After $n-1$ cyclic shifts of $\mathbf{g}(X)$, we would obtain a code polynomial

$$g_1 + g_2X + \ldots + g_{r-1}X^{r-2} + X^{r-1}$$

whose degree is less than r. This is a contradiction. Thus, g_0 cannot be equal to 0.

Now we want to show that r is equal to $n-k$. We have shown that a polynomial $\mathbf{v}(X)$ of degree $n-1$ or less is a code polynomial if and only if $\mathbf{v}(X)$ is a multiple of $\mathbf{g}(X)$. Thus, a code polynomial $\mathbf{v}(X)$ can be expressed as

$$\begin{aligned} \mathbf{v}(X) &= \mathbf{m}(X)\,\mathbf{g}(X) \\ &= (m_0 + m_1X + \ldots + m_{n-r-1}X^{n-r-1})\,\mathbf{g}(X) \quad . \end{aligned} \tag{4.7}$$

There are 2^{n-r} such code polynomials. Since there are 2^k code vectors in an (n,k) code, then 2^{n-r} must be equal to 2^k. That is, $r = n-k$. Thus, the code polynomial $\mathbf{g}(X)$ of minimum degree in an (n,k) cyclic code must be of the form

$$\mathbf{g}(X) = 1 + g_1 X + g_2 X^2 + \ldots + g_{n-k-1} X^{n-k-1} + X^{n-k} \quad .$$

The proof of the theorem is thus completed.

Q.E.D.

It follows from Theorem 4.1 that every code polynomial $\mathbf{v}(X)$ in an (n,k) cyclic code can be expressed in the following form:

$$\begin{aligned} \mathbf{v}(X) &= \mathbf{m}(X)\,\mathbf{g}(X) \\ &= (m_0 + m_1 X + m_2 X^2 + \ldots + m_{k-1} X^{k-1})\,\mathbf{g}(X) \quad . \end{aligned} \tag{4.8}$$

If the coefficients of $\mathbf{m}(X)$, $(m_0, m_1, \ldots, m_{k-1})$, are the k information digits to be encoded, then $\mathbf{v}(X)$ would be the corresponding code polynomial. Thus, the encoding of a message $\mathbf{m}(X)$ is equivalent to multiplying the message $\mathbf{m}(X)$ by $\mathbf{g}(X)$. Therefore, an (n,k) cyclic code is completely specified by the polynomial $\mathbf{g}(X)$ of Eq. (4.6). The polynomial $\mathbf{g}(X)$ is called the *generator polynomial* of the cyclic code. The degree $n-k$ of $\mathbf{g}(X)$ is equal to the number of parity check digits of the code.

Theorem 4.2: The generator polynomial $\mathbf{g}(X)$ of an (n,k) cyclic code is a factor of $X^n + 1$, i.e.,

$$X^n + 1 = \mathbf{g}(X)\,\mathbf{h}(X) \quad . \tag{4.9}$$

Proof: Consider the polynomial $X^k \mathbf{g}(X)$ of degree n. Dividing $X^k \mathbf{g}(X)$ by $X^n + 1$, we obtain

$$X^k \mathbf{g}(X) = (X^n + 1) + \mathbf{g}^{(k)}(X) \quad . \tag{4.10}$$

The remainder $\mathbf{g}^{(k)}(X)$ is a code polynomial obtained by shifting the generator polynomial $\mathbf{g}(X)$ cyclically k times. It follows from Theorem 4.1 that $\mathbf{g}^{(k)}(X)$ is a multiple of $\mathbf{g}(X)$, say $\mathbf{g}^{(k)}(X) = \mathbf{m}(X)\mathbf{g}(X)$. From Eq. (4.10), we have

$$X^n + 1 \;=\; [X^k + \mathbf{m}(X)]\; \mathbf{g}(X) \quad .$$

Thus, $\mathbf{g}(X)$ is a factor of $X^n + 1$. This completes the proof.

Q.E.D.

At this point, a natural question is whether, for any n and k, there exists an (n,k) cyclic code. This is answered by the following theorem.

Theorem 4.3: If $\mathbf{g}(X)$ is a polynomial of degree $n-k$ and is a factor of $X^n + 1$, then $\mathbf{g}(X)$ generates an (n,k) cyclic code.

Proof: Consider the k polynomials, $\mathbf{g}(X)$, $X\mathbf{g}(X)$, $X^2\mathbf{g}(X)$, . . ., $X^{k-1}\mathbf{g}(X)$ which all have degree $n - 1$ or less. Any linear combination of these k polynomials,

$$\begin{aligned}\mathbf{v}(X) &= m_0\mathbf{g}(X) + m_1 X\mathbf{g}(X) + \ldots + m_{k-1}X^{k-1}\mathbf{g}(X) \\ &= (m_0 + m_1 X + \ldots + m_{k-1}X^{k-1})\, \mathbf{g}(X)\end{aligned}$$

is also a polynomial of degree $n - 1$ or less and is a multiple of $\mathbf{g}(X)$. There are a total of 2^k such polynomials and they form a linear (n,k) code. Let $\mathbf{v}(X) = v_0 + v_1 X + v_2 X^2 + \ldots + v_{n-1}X^{n-1}$ be a code polynomial in this code. Consider

$$\begin{aligned}X\mathbf{v}(X) &= v_0 X + v_1 X^2 + \ldots + v_{n-2}X^{n-1} + v_{n-1}X^n \\ &= v_{n-1}(X^n + 1) + (v_{n-1} + v_0 X + v_1 X^2 + \ldots + v_{n-2}X^{n-1})\end{aligned}$$

$$= v_{n-1}(X^n + 1) + \mathbf{v}^{(1)}(X)$$

where $\mathbf{v}^{(1)}(X)$ is a cyclic shift of $\mathbf{v}(X)$. Since $X\mathbf{v}(X)$ and $(X^n + 1)$ are divisible by $\mathbf{g}(X)$, $\mathbf{v}^{(1)}(X)$ must be divisible by $\mathbf{g}(X)$. Thus, $\mathbf{v}^{(1)}(X)$ is a multiple of $\mathbf{g}(X)$ and can be expressed as a linear combination of $\mathbf{g}(X)$, $X\mathbf{g}(X), \ldots, X^{k-1}\mathbf{g}(X)$. This says that $\mathbf{v}^{(1)}(X)$ is also a code polynomial. It follows from Definition 4.1 that the linear code generated by $\mathbf{g}(X), X\mathbf{g}(X), \ldots, X^{k-1}\mathbf{g}(X)$ is an (n,k) cyclic code.

Q.E.D.

Example 4.1: The polynomial $X^7 + 1$ can be factored as follows:

$$X^7 + 1 = (1 + X + X^3)(1 + X + X^2 + X^4) .$$

The (7,4) cyclic code generated by $\mathbf{g}(X) = 1 + X + X^3$ has code polynomials or code vectors as shown in Table 4.1. The minimum distance of this code is 3. This is a single-error-correcting code. Notice that this code is not systematic.

Given the generator polynomial $\mathbf{g}(X)$ of an (n,k) cyclic code, the code can be put into *systematic form*. That is, *the first k digits of each code word are the unaltered information digits; the last $n-k$ digits are parity check digits*. Suppose that the message of k digits to be encoded is

$$\mathbf{m} = (m_0, m_1, m_2, \ldots, m_{k-1}) . \tag{4.11}$$

The corresponding message polynomial is

$$\mathbf{m}(X) = m_0 + m_1 X + m_2 X^2 + \ldots + m_{k-1} X^{k-1} . \tag{4.12}$$

Multiplying $\mathbf{m}(X)$ by X^{n-k}, we obtain

Messages	Code Polynomials	Code Vectors
(0 0 0 0)	$0 \cdot (1+X+X^3) = 0$	0 0 0 0 0 0 0
(1 0 0 0)	$1 \cdot (1+X+X^3) = 1+X+X^3$	1 1 0 1 0 0 0
(0 1 0 0)	$X(1+X+X^3) = X+X^2+X^4$	0 1 1 0 1 0 0
(1 1 0 0)	$(1+X)(1+X+X^3)$ $= 1+X^2+X^3+X^4$	1 0 1 1 1 0 0
(0 0 1 0)	$X^2(1+X+X^3) = X^2+X^3+X^5$	0 0 1 1 0 1 0
(1 0 1 0)	$(1+X^2)(1+X+X^3)$ $= 1+X+X^2+X^5$	1 1 1 0 0 1 0
(0 1 1 0)	$(X+X^2)(1+X+X^3)$ $= X+X^3+X^4+X^5$	0 1 0 1 1 1 0
(1 1 1 0)	$(1+X+X^2)(1+X+X^3)$ $= 1+X^4+X^5$	1 0 0 0 1 1 0
(0 0 0 1)	$X^3(1+X+X^3) = X^3+X^4+X^6$	0 0 0 1 1 0 1
(1 0 0 1)	$(1+X^3)(1+X+X^3)$ $= 1+X+X^4+X^6$	1 1 0 0 1 0 1
(0 1 0 1)	$(X+X^3)(1+X+X^3)$ $= X+X^2+X^3+X^6$	0 1 1 1 0 0 1
(1 1 0 1)	$(1+X+X^3)(1+X+X^3)$ $= 1+X^2+X^6$	1 0 1 0 0 0 1
(0 0 1 1)	$(X^2+X^3)(1+X+X^3)$ $= X^2+X^4+X^5+X^6$	0 0 1 0 1 1 1
(1 0 1 1)	$(1+X^2+X^3)(1+X+X^3)$ $= 1+X+X^2+X^3+X^4+X^5+X^6$	1 1 1 1 1 1 1
(0 1 1 1)	$(X+X^2+X^3)(1+X+X^3)$ $= X+X^5+X^6$	0 1 0 0 0 1 1
(1 1 1 1)	$(1+X+X^2+X^3)(1+X+X^3)$ $= 1+X^3+X^5+X^6$	1 0 0 1 0 1 1

Table 4.1. A (7,4) cyclic code generated by g(X) = $1+X+X^3$.

$$X^{n-k}\mathbf{m}(X) \;=\; m_0X^{n-k} + m_1X^{n-k+1} + \ldots + m_{k-1}X^{n-1} \; . \tag{4.13}$$

Dividing $X^{n-k}\mathbf{m}(X)$ by $\mathbf{g}(X)$, we have

$$X^{n-k}\mathbf{m}(X) \;=\; \mathbf{q}(X)\,\mathbf{g}(X) + \mathbf{r}(X) \tag{4.14}$$

where $\mathbf{q}(X)$ and $\mathbf{r}(X)$ are the quotient and the remainder respectively. Since the degree of the generator polynomial $\mathbf{g}(X)$ is n-k, the degree of $\mathbf{r}(X)$ must be $n - k - 1$ or less,

$$\mathbf{r}(X) \;=\; r_0 + r_1X + r_2X^2 + \ldots + r_{n-k-1}X^{n-k-1} \; . \tag{4.15}$$

Rearranging Eq. (4.14), we obtain

$$\mathbf{r}(X) + X^{n-k}\mathbf{m}(X) \;=\; \mathbf{q}(X)\,\mathbf{g}(X) \; . \tag{4.16}$$

This indicates that $\mathbf{r}(X) + X^{n-k}\mathbf{m}(X)$ is a multiple of $\mathbf{g}(X)$ and has degree $n - 1$ or less. Therefore, $\mathbf{r}(X) + X^{n-k}\mathbf{m}(X)$ is a code polynomial of the cyclic code generated by $\mathbf{g}(X)$. Writing out $\mathbf{r}(X) + X^{n-k}\mathbf{m}(X)$, we have

$$\begin{aligned} \mathbf{r}(X) + X^{n-k}\mathbf{m}(X) \;=\; & r_0 + r_1X + \ldots + r_{n-k-1}X^{n-k-1} \\ & + m_0X^{n-k} + m_1X^{n-k+1} + \ldots + m_{k-1}X^{n-1} \end{aligned} \tag{4.17}$$

which corresponds to the code word

$$(\underbrace{r_0, r_1, r_2, \ldots, r_{n-k-1}}_{\text{Parity check digits}}, \underbrace{m_0, m_1, \ldots, m_{k-1}}_{\text{Information digits}}) \; . \tag{4.18}$$

Therefore, the code word consists of the unaltered k-digits message block followed by $n - k$ parity check digits. In connection with cyclic codes, the following convention will be used. The first $n-k$ symbols, coefficients of $1, X, X^2, \ldots, X^{n-k-1}$, will be taken as parity check symbols, and the last k symbols, coefficients of $X^{n-k}, X^{n-k+1}, \ldots, X^{n-1}$, will be taken as information symbols. From now on, we shall only consider cyclic codes in systematic form.

Example 4.2: Consider the (7,4) cyclic code generated by $\mathbf{g}(X) = 1 + X + X^3$. Let $\mathbf{m} = (1\ 0\ 1\ 1)$ be the message to be encoded. Then the message polynomial is $\mathbf{m}(X) = 1 + X^2 + X^3$. Dividing $X^3\mathbf{m}(X) = X^3 + X^5 + X^6$ by $\mathbf{g}(X)$,

$$\begin{array}{r l}
 & X^3 + X^2 + X + 1 \quad \text{(Quotient)} \\
X^3 + X + 1 & \overline{)\; X^6 + X^5 + X^3} \\
 & \underline{X^6 + X^4 + X^3} \\
 & X^5 + X^4 \\
 & \underline{X^5 + X^3 + X^2} \\
 & X^4 + X^3 + X^2 \\
 & \underline{X^4 + X^2 + X} \\
 & X^3 + X \\
 & \underline{X^3 + X + 1} \\
 & 1 \quad \text{(Remainder)}
\end{array}$$

we obtain the remainder $\mathbf{r}(X) = 1$. Thus, the code polynomial is $\mathbf{v}(X) = \mathbf{r}(X) + X^3\mathbf{m}(X) = 1 + X^3 + X^5 + X^6$, and the corresponding code vector is $(1\ 0\ 0\ 1\ 0\ 1\ 1)$, where the rightmost 4 digits are the message digits. The 16 code vectors in systematic form are listed in Table 4.2.

The generator matrix of a cyclic code in systematic form can be formed as follows. Dividing X^{n-k+i} by the generator polynomial $\mathbf{g}(X)$ for $i = 0, 1, \ldots, k-1$, we obtain

$$X^{n-k+i} = \mathbf{q}_i(X)\mathbf{g}(X) + \mathbf{r}_i(X) \tag{4.19}$$

Messages	Code Vectors
(0 0 0 0)	(0 0 0 0 0 0 0)
(1 0 0 0)	(1 1 0 1 0 0 0)
(0 1 0 0)	(0 1 1 0 1 0 0)
(1 1 0 0)	(1 0 1 1 1 0 0)
(0 0 1 0)	(1 1 1 0 0 1 0)
(1 0 1 0)	(0 0 1 1 0 1 0)
(0 1 1 0)	(1 0 0 0 1 1 0)
(1 1 1 0)	(0 1 0 1 1 1 0)
(0 0 0 1)	(1 0 1 0 0 0 1)
(1 0 0 1)	(0 1 1 1 0 0 1)
(0 1 0 1)	(1 1 0 0 1 0 1)
(1 1 0 1)	(0 0 0 1 1 0 1)
(0 0 1 1)	(0 1 0 0 0 1 1)
(1 0 1 1)	(1 0 0 1 0 1 1)
(0 1 1 1)	(0 0 1 0 1 1 1)
(1 1 1 1)	(1 1 1 1 1 1 1)

Table 4.2. The (7,4) systematic code generated by $g(X) = 1 + X + X^3$.

where $\mathbf{r}_i(X) = r_{i0} + r_{i1}X + r_{i2}X^2 + \ldots + r_{i,n-k-1}X^{n-k-1}$. Thus, the polynomials $\mathbf{v}_i(X) = \mathbf{r}_i(X) + X^{n-k+i}$ for $i = 0, 1, \ldots, k-1$ are code polynomials. Arranging these k code polynomials as k rows of a matrix, we have

$$\mathbf{G} = \begin{bmatrix} \mathbf{v}_0 \\ \mathbf{v}_1 \\ \mathbf{v}_2 \\ \vdots \\ \mathbf{v}_{k-1} \end{bmatrix} = \begin{bmatrix} r_{00} & r_{01} & r_{02} & \cdots & r_{0,n-k-1} & 1\,0\,0 \ldots 0 \\ r_{10} & r_{11} & r_{12} & \cdots & r_{1,n-k-1} & 0\,1\,0 \ldots 0 \\ r_{20} & r_{21} & r_{22} & \cdots & r_{2,n-k-1} & 0\,0\,1 \ldots 0 \\ \vdots & & & & & \\ r_{k-1,0} & r_{k-1,1} & r_{k-1,2} & \cdots & r_{k,n-k-1} & 0\,0\,0 \ldots 1 \end{bmatrix} \quad (4.20)$$

which is the generator matrix of the cyclic code. *The first row of* $\mathbf{G}$ *is the generator polynomial of the code.* If $\mathbf{m} = (m_0, m_1, \ldots m_{k-1})$ are the k information digits to be encoded, then the corresponding code vector is

$$\mathbf{v} = \mathbf{mG} = (m_0, m_1, \ldots, m_{k-1}) \begin{bmatrix} \mathbf{v}_0 \\ \mathbf{v}_1 \\ \mathbf{v}_2 \\ \vdots \\ \mathbf{v}_{k-1} \end{bmatrix} \quad (4.21)$$

$$= m_0\mathbf{v}_0 + m_1\mathbf{v}_1 + \ldots + m_{k-1}\mathbf{v}_{k-1} \;.$$

In polynomial form,

$$\begin{aligned} \mathbf{v}(X) &= m_0\mathbf{v}_0(X) + m_1\mathbf{v}_1(X) + \ldots + m_{k-1}\mathbf{v}_{k-1}(X) \\ &= m_0\mathbf{r}_0(X) + m_1\mathbf{r}_1(X) + \ldots + m_{k-1}\mathbf{r}_{k-1}(X) \\ &\qquad + m_0X^{n-k} + m_1X^{n-k+1} + \ldots + m_{k-1}X^{n-1} \end{aligned}$$

$$= \mathbf{r}(X) + X^{n-k}\,\mathbf{m}(X) \tag{4.22}$$

where $\mathbf{m}(X) = m_0 + m_1 X + \ldots + m_{k-1} X^{k-1}$ and $\mathbf{r}(X) = m_0 \mathbf{r}_0(X) + m_1 \mathbf{r}_1(X) + \ldots + m_{k-1} \mathbf{r}_{k-1}(X)$. By Eq. (4.19), it is easy to see that $\mathbf{v}(X) = [m_0 \mathbf{q}_0(X) + m_1 \mathbf{q}_1(X) + \ldots + m_{k-1} \mathbf{q}_{k-1}(X)]\,\mathbf{g}(X)$ and $\mathbf{r}(X)$ is the remainder resulting from dividing $X^{n-k}\mathbf{m}(X)$ by $\mathbf{g}(X)$. Thus, $\mathbf{v}(X)$ is exactly the same form as in Eq. (4.17). From Eq. (4.20), we obtain the parity check matrix of the code as

$$\mathbf{H} = \begin{bmatrix} 1 & 0 & 0 & \ldots & 0 & r_{00} & r_{10} & r_{20} & \ldots & r_{k-1,0} \\ 0 & 1 & 0 & \ldots & 0 & r_{01} & r_{11} & r_{21} & \ldots & r_{k-1,1} \\ 0 & 0 & 1 & \ldots & 0 & r_{02} & r_{12} & r_{22} & \ldots & r_{k-1,2} \\ \vdots & & & & \vdots & \vdots & & & & \vdots \\ 0 & 0 & 0 & \ldots & 1 & r_{0,n-k-1} & r_{1,n-k-1} & r_{2,n-k-1} & \ldots & r_{k-1,n-k-1} \end{bmatrix} . \tag{4.23}$$

Cyclic codes are most easily mechanized by shift-register devices. The cyclic property and the property that each code polynomial is a multiple of the generator polynomial minimize the storage facilities for the encoding dictionary. Many subclasses of these codes can also be decoded in an efficient way.

4.2 ENCODING WITH AN $(n - k)$-STAGE SHIFT REGISTER

From Eq. (4.17), it is clear that the encoding of a message block $\mathbf{m}(X)$ of k digits is equivalent to calculating the parity check section $\mathbf{r}(X)$ which is the remainder of dividing $X^{n-k}\mathbf{m}(X)$ by the generator polynomial $\mathbf{g}(X)$. This can be accomplished by a dividing circuit which is a shift register with feedback connections according to the generator polynomial $\mathbf{g}(X) = 1 + g_1 X + g_2 X^2 + \ldots + g_{n-k-1} X^{n-k-1} + X^{n-k}$. An encoding circuit with an $(n-k)$-stage shift register[16,18] is shown in Fig. 4.1,

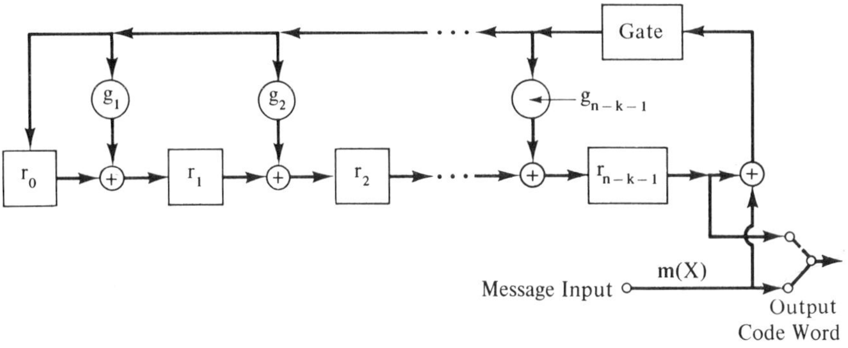

Fig. 4.1. An (n-k)-stage shift register encoding circuit.

where

(1) the symbol  denotes a single binary shift register stage (for instance, a flip-flop) which is shifted by an external synchronous clock so that its input at a particular time appears at its output one unit of time later;

(2) the symbol  denotes an Exclusive OR gate (or modulo-2 adder); and

(3) the symbol 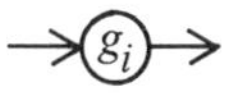 simply denotes a connection if $g_i = 1$; no connection if $g_i = 0$.

The encoding procedure is accomplished as follows:

Step 1. With the gate turned on, the k information digits $\mathbf{m}(X) = m_0 + m_1X + \ldots + m_{k-1}X^{k-1}$ are shifted into the register and simultaneously into the communication channel. As soon as the k information digits have entered the shift register, the n-k digits in the register are the parity check digits.

Step 2. Break the feedback connection by turning off the gate.

Step 3. Shift the contents of the shift register out and send them into the channel. These n-k parity check digits $\mathbf{r}(X) = r_0 + r_1X + \ldots + r_{n-k-1}X^{n-k-1}$ with the k information digits $X^{n-k}\mathbf{m}(X)$ make a complete code word $\mathbf{v}(X) = \mathbf{r}(X) + X^{n-k}\mathbf{m}(X)$.

The above encoding circuit consists of (1) $n-k$ shift register stages (say $n-k$ flip-flops), (2) approximately $(n-k)/2$ Exclusive OR gates, (3) one AND gate in the feedback connection, and (4) a counter to control the output switch and the gate in the feedback connection. Let m be the smallest integer such that $n < 2^m$. Then the counter requires m shift register stages (m flip-flops).

Example 4.3: Consider the (7,4) binary cyclic code generated by

$$g(X) = 1 + X + X^3 \ .$$

The encoding circuit is

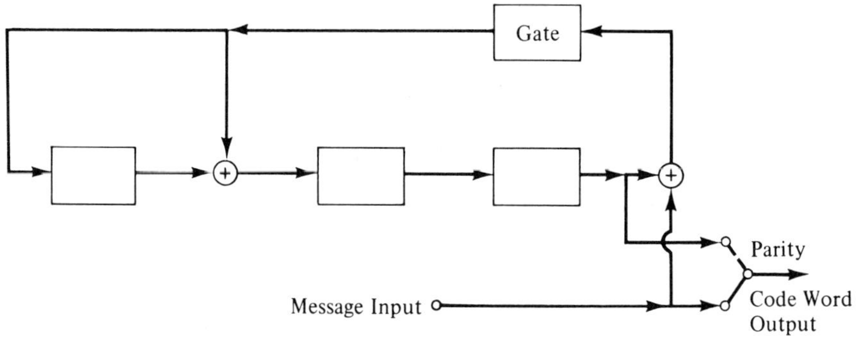

Fig. 4.2. An encoder for the (7,4) cyclic code.

Suppose that a 4-bit message

$$\mathbf{m} = (1\ 0\ 1\ 1) \longleftrightarrow \mathbf{m}(X) = 1 + X^2 + X^3$$

is to be encoded. As the information digits shift into the register sequentially, the contents in the register are as follows:

Input	Register Contents
	0 0 0 (Initial State)
1	1 1 0 (1st shift)
1	1 0 1 (2nd shift)
0	1 0 0 (3rd shift)
1	1 0 0 (4th shift) .

After 4 shifts, the contents of the register are (1 0 0). Thus, the complete code word is

$$(1\ 0\ 0\ 1\ 0\ 1\ 1)\ .$$

The code polynomial is

$$\mathbf{v}(X) = 1 + X^3 + X^5 + X^6\ .$$

4.3 ENCODING WITH A *k*-STAGE SHIFT REGISTER

It has been shown that an (n, k) cyclic code is completely specified by its generator polynomial $\mathbf{g}(X)$ which is a factor of $X^n + 1$. Let

$$X^n + 1 = \mathbf{g}(X)\,\mathbf{h}(X)\ .$$

Then the polynomial $\mathbf{h}(X)$ is of the form

$$\mathbf{h}(X) = h_0 + h_1X + h_2X^2 + \ldots + h_kX^k$$

where $h_0 = 1$ and $h_k = 1$. In the following, we shall show that the (n, k) cyclic code can also be specified completely by $\mathbf{h}(X)$.

Let $\mathbf{v}(X) = v_0 + v_1 X + v_2 X^2 + \ldots + v_{n-1} X^{n-1}$ be a code polynomial. Then $\mathbf{v}(X)$ is a multiple of $\mathbf{g}(X)$, say

$$\mathbf{v}(X) = \mathbf{q}(X)\,\mathbf{g}(X) \ .$$

In systematic form, $v_{n-k}, v_{n-k+1}, \ldots, v_{n-1}$ are the k information digits and $v_0, v_1, \ldots, v_{n-k-1}$ are the $n-k$ parity check digits. Multiplying $\mathbf{v}(X)$ by $\mathbf{h}(X)$, we have

$$\begin{aligned} \mathbf{v}(X)\,\mathbf{h}(X) &= \mathbf{q}(X)\,\mathbf{g}(X)\,\mathbf{h}(X) \\ &= \mathbf{q}(X)\,(X^n + 1) \\ &= X^n \mathbf{q}(X) + \mathbf{q}(X) \ . \end{aligned}$$

Since the degree of $\mathbf{q}(X)$ is $k-1$ or less, the powers $X^k, X^{k+1}, \ldots, X^{n-1}$ do not appear in $X^n\mathbf{q}(X) + \mathbf{q}(X)$. That is, in the expansion of $\mathbf{v}(X)\mathbf{h}(X)$, the coefficients of $X^k, X^{k+1}, \ldots, X^{n-1}$ must be zero, i.e.,

$$\sum_{i=0}^{k} h_i v_{n-i-j} = 0 \quad \text{for} \quad 1 \leqslant j \leqslant n-k \tag{4.24}$$

where $h_0 = 1$ and $h_k = 1$. From Eq. (4.24), we obtain

$$v_{n-k-j} = \sum_{i=0}^{k-1} h_i v_{n-i-j} \quad \text{for} \quad 1 \leqslant j \leqslant n-k \ , \tag{4.25}$$

which is known as a *difference equation*. Given the k information digits $v_{n-1}, v_{n-2}, \ldots, v_{n-k}$, this equation is a rule to determine the $n-k$ parity check digits $v_{n-k-1}, v_{n-k-2}, \ldots, v_0$ of the code polynomial $\mathbf{v}(X)$. Thus, the (n,k) cyclic code generated by $\mathbf{g}(X)$ is also completely specified by $\mathbf{h}(X) = (X^n + 1)/\mathbf{g}(X)$. The polynomial $\mathbf{h}(X)$ is called the *parity polynomial* of the cyclic code generated by $\mathbf{g}(X)$. An encoding circuit[9,21] based on Eq. (4.25) is shown in Fig. 4.3.

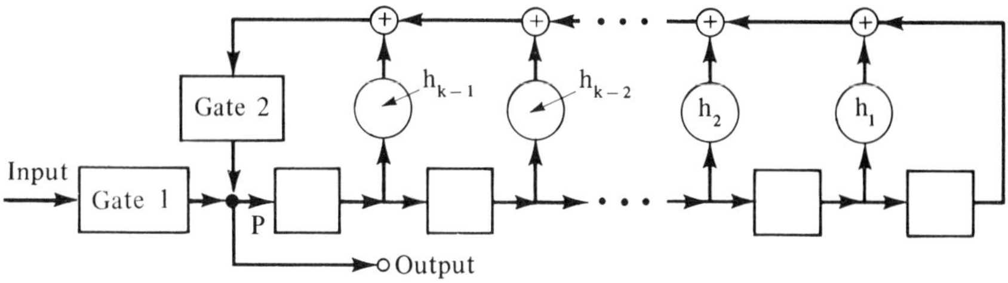

Fig. 4.3. A *k*-stage shift register encoding circuit.

The encoding procedure can be described in the following steps:

Step 1. Initially, Gate 1 is turned on and Gate 2 is turned off. The k information digits $\mathbf{m}(X) = m_0 + m_1X + \ldots + m_{k-1}X^{k-1}$ are shifted into the communication channel and the register simultaneously.

Step 2. As soon as the k information digits have entered the shift register, Gate 1 is turned off and Gate 2 is turned on. The first parity-check digit

$$\begin{aligned} v_{n-k-1} &= h_0v_{n-1} + h_1v_{n-2} + \ldots + h_{k-1}v_{n-k} \\ &= m_{k-1} + h_1m_{k-2} + \ldots + h_{k-1}m_0 \end{aligned}$$

is formed and appears at P.

Step 3. The register is shifted once. The first parity-check digit is shifted into the channel and is also shifted into the leftmost stage of the register. Now the second parity-check digit

$$\begin{aligned} v_{n-k-2} &= h_0v_{n-2} + h_1v_{n-3} + \ldots + h_{k-1}v_{n-k-1} \\ &= m_{k-2} + h_1m_{k-3} + \ldots + h_{k-2}m_0 + h_{k-1}v_{n-k-1} \end{aligned}$$

is formed and appears at P.

Step 4. Step 3 is repeated until $n - k$ parity-check digits have been shifted into the channel. Then Gate 1 is turned on and Gate 2 is turned off. The next message is now ready to be shifted into the register.

This encoding circuit consists of k shift register stages and at most $k-1$ Exclusive OR gates. A counter is also required. Comparing the encoding circuits discussed in the last and present sections, we can make the following conclusion: *for codes with more check digits than information digits, the k-stage encoder is more economical; otherwise, the (n - k)-stage encoder is preferable.*

Example 4.4: Consider the (7,4) code given in the last example with

$$\mathbf{g}(X) = 1 + X + X^3$$

and

$$\mathbf{h}(X) = (X^7 + 1)/(1 + X + X^3) = 1 + X + X^2 + X^4 \quad .$$

The encoding circuit based on $\mathbf{h}(X)$ is shown in Fig. 4.4.

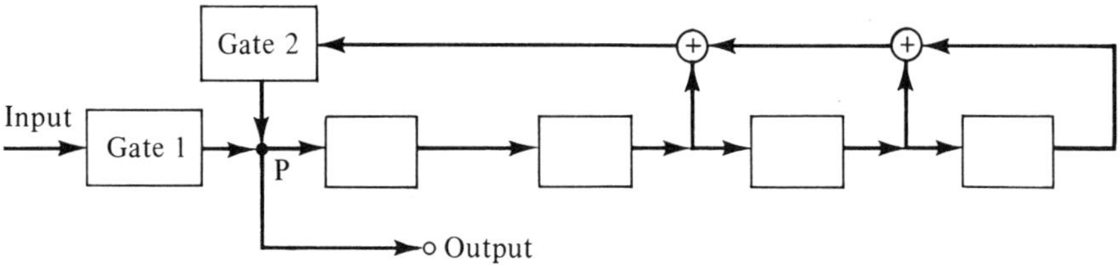

Fig. 4.4. An encoding circuit for the (7,4) cyclic code.

Each code polynomial is of the form

$$\mathbf{v}(X) = v_0 + v_1 X + v_2 X^2 + v_3 X^3 + v_4 X^4 + v_5 X^5 + v_6 X^6$$

where v_3, v_4, v_5, v_6 are information digits and v_0, v_1, v_2 are parity check digits. The difference equation which determines the parity check digits is

$$\begin{aligned} v_{3-j} &= 1 \cdot v_{7-j} + 1 \cdot v_{6-j} + 1 \cdot v_{5-j} + 0 \cdot v_{4-j} \\ &= v_{7-j} + v_{6-j} + v_{5-j} \quad \text{for} \quad 1 \leqslant j \leqslant 3 \ . \end{aligned}$$

Suppose the message to be encoded is (1 0 1 1). Then $v_6 = 1$, $v_5 = 1$, $v_4 = 0$, and $v_3 = 1$. The first parity check digit is

$$\begin{aligned} v_2 &= v_6 + v_5 + v_4 \\ &= 1 + 1 + 0 = 0 \ . \end{aligned}$$

The second parity check digit is

$$\begin{aligned} v_1 &= v_5 + v_4 + v_3 \\ &= 1 + 0 + 1 = 0 \ . \end{aligned}$$

The third parity check digit is

$$\begin{aligned} v_0 &= v_4 + v_3 + v_2 \\ &= 0 + 1 + 0 = 1 \ . \end{aligned}$$

Thus, the code vector which corresponds to message (1 0 1 1) is (1 0 0 1 0 1 1). This is the same code vector obtained in Example 4.2 and Example 4.3. The encoding operation is described in Table 4.3 on the following page.

The reader is referred to Reference 18 for further details concerning efficient encoding.

L	Gate status after L^{th} shift 1	2	Register contents after L^{th} shift	Symbol at P after L^{th} shift
7 (The last shift from the previous encoding)	on	off	x x x x (Remaining from the previous encoding)	1
1	on	off	1 x x x	1
2	on	off	1 1 x x	0
3	on	off	0 1 1 x	1
4	off	on	1 0 1 1	0
5	off	on	0 1 0 1	0
6	off	on	0 0 1 0	1
7	on	off	1 0 0 1	First information digit from the next message block

Table 4.3. The encoding operation of the circuit shown in Fig. 4.4.

4.4 SYNDROME CALCULATION AND ERROR DETECTION

When a code vector is transmitted over a noisy channel, it may be corrupted by noise. At the output of the channel, the received vector may or may not be the same as the transmitted code vector. The function of the decoder is to recover the transmitted code vector from knowledge of the received vector. Let the received vector be

$$\mathbf{r}(X) = r_0 + r_1 X + r_2 X^2 + \ldots + r_{n-1} X^{n-1}$$

where $r_0, r_1, \ldots, r_{n-k-1}$ are the received parity check digits and $r_{n-k}, \ldots, r_{n-1}$ are the received information digits. The decoder first tests whether or not the received vector is a code vector (or whether it is divisible by the generator polynomial $\mathbf{g}(X)$ of the code used at the encoder). This can be accomplished simply by calculating the syndrome of the received word. The syndrome $\mathbf{s}$ is obtained by taking the modulo-2 sum of the received parity check digits and the parity check digits calculated from the received information digits. That is, the syndrome $\mathbf{s}(X)$ is equal to the remainder resulting from dividing the received vector $\mathbf{r}(X)$ by the generator polynomial $\mathbf{g}(X)$, i.e.,

$$\mathbf{r}(X) = \mathbf{p}(X)\mathbf{g}(X) + \mathbf{s}(X) \ , \tag{4.26}$$

where $\mathbf{s}(X)$ is a polynomial of degree $n-k-1$ or less. Thus, the syndrome is an $(n-k)$-tuple. If the syndrome is zero, the received vector is divisible by the generator polynomial and is a code vector; the decoder will accept the received vector as the transmitted code vector. If the syndrome is a non-zero vector, the received vector is not a code vector and errors have been detected. Suppose that $\mathbf{v}(X)$ was the transmitted code vector. Then

$$\mathbf{r}(X) = \mathbf{v}(X) + \mathbf{e}(X) \ , \tag{4.27}$$

where $\mathbf{e}(X)$ is the error pattern caused by the channel disturbance. Since $\mathbf{v}(X)$ is a code polynomial, it must be a multiple of the generator polynomial $\mathbf{g}(X)$, say

$$\mathbf{v}(X) = \mathbf{m}(X)\mathbf{g}(X) \ . \tag{4.28}$$

Combining Eqs. (4.26), (4.27), and (4.28), we obtain

$$\mathbf{e}(X) = [\mathbf{p}(X) + \mathbf{m}(X)]\,\mathbf{g}(X) + \mathbf{s}(X) \ . \tag{4.29}$$

That is, the syndrome of $\mathbf{r}(X)$ is equal to the remainder resulting from dividing the error pattern by the generator polynomial $\mathbf{g}(X)$ of the code. Thus, *the syndrome of the received vector contains the information about the error pattern in the received vector, which will be used for error correction.*

The syndrome calculation is accomplished by a division circuit which is identical to the encoding circuit at the transmitter. If the circuit of Fig. 4.1

is used, then the syndrome calculator is as shown in Fig. 4.5a. The received vector is shifted into the register with all stages initially set to "0." After the entire received word has been entered into the shift register, the contents will be the syndrome. If the circuit of Fig. 4.3 is used, then the syndrome register is as shown in Fig. 4.5b. The received information digits are first shifted into the register (Gate 1 is turned on; Gates 2, 3, and 4 are turned off). After k shifts, Gate 1 is turned off; Gates 2, 3, and 4 are turned on. The syndrome is then obtained by taking the modulo-2 sum of the calculated parity check digits and the received parity check digits.

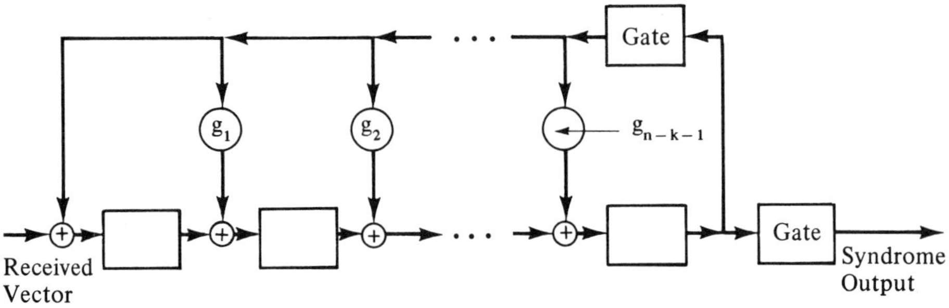

Fig. 4.5a. $(n-k)$-stage syndrome calculation circuit.

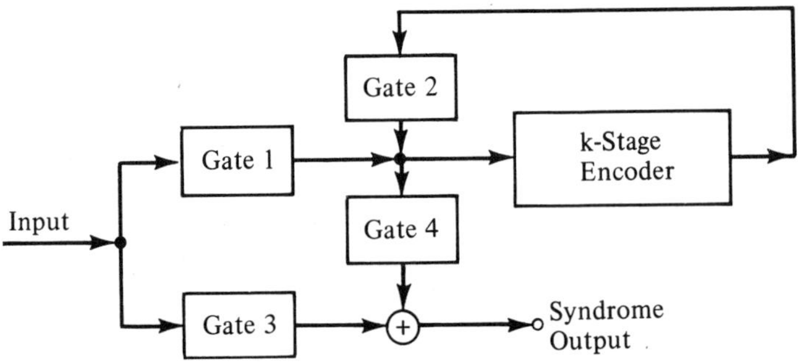

Fig. 4.5b. k-stage syndrome calculation circuit.

Cyclic codes are extremely well suited for error detection.[17,18] The detection circuit is just the syndrome calculator with a single additional flip-flop connected to the output of the calculator. If the syndrome is not zero, the flip-flop sets and an error has been detected; otherwise, the received word is a code vector.

4.5 A GENERAL DECODER FOR CYCLIC CODES (MEGGITT DECODER)

The decoding of a linear code consists of three basic steps. (1) Calculate the syndrome of the received vector. (2) Identify the correctable error pattern which corresponds to the syndrome calculated in Step 1. (The correspondence between the syndrome and a correctable error pattern is one-to-one.) This is the error pattern that presumably has occurred. (3) Correct the errors by taking the modulo-2 sum of the received vector and the error pattern found in Step 2.

A general decoder for an (n, k) cyclic code[11,12,18] is shown in Fig. 4.6. It consists of three major parts: (1) a syndrome register, (2) an error pattern detector, and (3) a buffer register. The error correction procedure can be described as follows:

Step 1. The syndrome is formed by shifting the entire received vector into the syndrome register. At the same time, the received vector is stored into the buffer.

Step 2. The syndrome is read into the detector and is tested for the corresponding error pattern. The detector is a combinational logic circuit which is designed in such a way that its output is "1" if and only if the syndrome in the syndrome register corresponds to a correctable error pattern with an error at the highest order position X^n. That is, if a "1" appears at the output of the detector, the received symbol in the rightmost stage of the buffer register is assumed to be erroneous and must be corrected; if a "0" appears at the output of the detector, the received symbol at the rightmost stage of the buffer register is assumed to be correct and no correction is necessary. Thus, the output of the detector is the estimated error value for the symbol to come out of the buffer.

Step 3. The first received symbol is read out of the buffer. At the same time, the syndrome register is shifted once. If the first received symbol is detected to be an erroneous symbol, it is then corrected by the output of the detector. The output of the detector is also fed

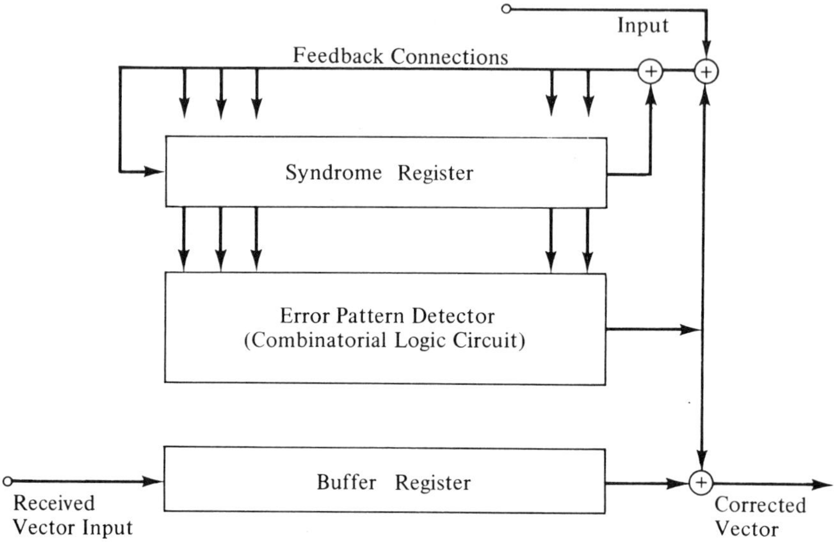

Fig. 4.6. A general cyclic code decoder.

back to the syndrome register to modify the syndrome (that is, to remove the error effect from the syndrome). This results in a new syndrome which corresponds to the altered received vector shifted one place to the right.

Step 4. The new syndrome formed in Step 3 is used to detect whether or not the second received symbol (now at the rightmost stage of the buffer register) is an erroneous symbol. The decoder repeats Steps 2 and 3. The second received symbol is corrected in exactly the same manner as the first received symbol was corrected.

Step 5. The decoder decodes the received vector symbol by symbol in the above manner until the entire received vector is read out of the buffer.

After the entire received vector is read out, the errors will have been corrected if they correspond to an error pattern built into the detector, and the syndrome register will contain all 0's. If the syndrome register does not contain all 0's at the end of the process, an uncorrectable error has been detected.

The above decoder applies in principle to any cyclic code. But whether or not this decoder is practical depends entirely on its combinational logic circuit. There are cases in which the logic circuits are simple. Several of these cases will be described in the next four chapters.

4.6 SHORTENED CYCLIC CODES

In system design, if a code of suitable natural length or suitable number of information digits cannot be found, it may be desirable to shorten a code to meet the requirements. A technique of shortening a cyclic code is described in the following. This technique leads to simple implementation of encoding and decoding for the shortened code.

Given an (n, k) cyclic code. Consider the set of code vectors whose η $(\eta < k)$ leading high-order information digits are zeros. There are $2^{k-\eta}$ such code vectors. If the η zero information digits are deleted from those code vectors, we obtain a set of $2^{k-\eta}$ vectors of $n-\eta$ digits. It is easy to see that this set of shortened code vectors form an $(n-\eta, k-\eta)$ linear code. This code is called a *shortened cyclic code*[18] and is not cyclic. A shortened cyclic code has at least the same error-correcting capability as the code from which it is derived. The encoding and syndrome calculation for a shortened cyclic code can be accomplished by the same circuits as employed by the original cyclic code. This is so because the deleted η leading zero information digits do not affect the parity-check calculations. The decoder for the original cyclic code can be used for decoding the shortened cyclic code simply by prefixing each received vector with η zeros. This prefixing can be eliminated, however, by modifying the feedback connections of the syndrome register.

PROBLEMS

4.1. Let $\mathbf{g}(X) = 1 + X + X^2 + X^4 + X^5 + X^8 + X^{10}$ be the generator polynomial of a (15,5) cyclic code.

(a) Find the parity polynomial $\mathbf{h}(X)$ of this code.

(b) Find the code polynomial for the message $\mathbf{m}(X) = 1 + X + X^4$ (in systematic form).

4.2. Find the generator matrix and the parity-check matrix for the code in Problem 4.1.

4.3. Construct a k-stage shift register encoder for the code in Problem 4.1.

4.4. Let n be the smallest integer such that the polynomial $\mathbf{g}(X)$ divides $X^n + 1$. Now consider the cyclic code of length n which is generated by $\mathbf{g}(X)$. Show that this code has minimum weight at least 3.

4.5. Show that $X + 1$ is a factor of $X^n + 1$.

4.6. Consider an (n,k) cyclic code whose generator polynomial is $\mathbf{g}(X)$. Suppose that n is odd and $X + 1$ is not a factor of $\mathbf{g}(X)$. Show that the vector of all 1's is a code vector.

4.7. A (15,7) cyclic code is generated by $\mathbf{g}(X) = 1 + X^4 + X^6 + X^7 + X^8$. Is $\mathbf{v}(X) = 1 + X + X^5 + X^{14}$ a code polynomial? If not, find the syndrome of $\mathbf{v}(X)$.

REFERENCES

1. Abramson, N. M., "A Class of Systematic Codes for Non-Independent Errors," *IRE Trans. on Information Theory*, **IT-5**, pp. 150-157, December, 1959.

2. Abramson, N. M., "Error Correcting Codes from Linear Sequential Networks," presented at the Fourth London Symposium on Information Theory, August, 1960.

3. Ash, R. B., *Information Theory*, Interscience Publishers, New York, 1965.

4. Berlekamp, E. R., *Algebraic Coding Theory,* McGraw-Hill, New York, 1968.

5. Elspas, B., "The Theory of Autonomous Linear Sequential Networks," *IRE Trans. on Computer Techniques*, **CT-6**, pp. 45-60, 1959.

6. Elspas, B., "A Note on P-nary Adjacent-Error-Correcting Codes," *IRE Trans. on Information Theory*, **IT-6**, pp. 13-15, March, 1960.

7. Fire, P., "A Class of Multiple-Error-Correcting Binary Codes for Non-Independent Errors," Sylvania Electronic Systems, Report RSL-E-2, March, 1959.

8. Gallager, R.G., *Information Theory and Reliable Communication*, John Wiley, New York, 1968.

9. Green, J. H., Jr., and R. L. San Soucie, "An Error-Correcting Encoder and Decoder of High Efficiency," *Proc. IRE*, **46**, pp. 1741-1744, 1958.

10. Lucky, R. W., J. Salz, and E. J. Weldon, Jr., *Principles of Data Communication*, McGraw-Hill, New York, 1968.

11. Meggitt, J. E., "Error Correcting Codes for Correcting Bursts of Errors," *IBM J. Research Develop.*, **4**, pp. 329-334, July, 1960.

12. Meggitt, J. E., "Error Correcting Codes and Their Implementation," *IRE Trans. on Information Theory*, **IT-7**, pp. 232-244, October, 1961.

13. Melas, C. M., "A New Group of Codes for Correction of Dependent-Errors in Data Transmission," *IBM J. Research Develop.*, **4**, pp. 58-65, January, 1960.

14. Melas, C. M., "A Cyclic Code for Double Error Correction," *IBM J. Research Develop.*, **4**, pp. 364-366, January, 1960.

15. Peterson, W. W., "Binary Coding for Error Control," *Proc. National Electronics Conference*, **16**, pp. 15-21, 1960.

16. Peterson, W. W., "Encoding and Error-Correction Procedures for the Bose-Chaudhuri Codes," *IRE Trans. on Information Theory*, **IT-6**, pp. 459-470, September, 1960.

17. Peterson, W. W., and D. T. Brown, "Cyclic Codes for Error Detection," *Proc. IRE,* **49**, pp. 228-235, January, 1961.

18. Peterson, W. W., *Error-Correcting Codes,* The M.I.T. Press, Cambridge, Massachusetts, and John Wiley, New York, 1961.

19. Peterson, W. W., and E. J. Weldon, Jr., *Error-Correcting Codes,* 2nd Edition, The M.I.T. Press, Cambridge, Massachusetts, 1970.

20. Prange, E., "Cyclic Error-Correcting Codes in Two Symbols," AFCRC-TN-57,103, Air Force Cambridge Research Center, Cambridge, Massachusetts, September, 1957.

21. Prange, E., "Some Cyclic Error-Correcting Codes with Simple Decoding Algorithms," AFCRC-TR-58-156, Air Force Cambridge Research Center, Cambridge, Massachusetts, April, 1958.

22. Prange, E., "The Use of Coset Equivalence in the Analysis and Decoding of Group Codes," AFCRC-TR-59-164, Air Force Cambridge Research Center, Cambridge, Massachusetts, June, 1959.

23. Prange, E., "The Use of Information Sets in Decoding Cyclic Codes," *IEEE Trans. on Information Theory,* **IT-8**, pp. 85-89, September, 1962.

24. Stern, T. E., and B. Friedland, "Application of Modular Sequential Circuits to Single-Error-Correcting P-nary Codes," *IRE Trans. on Information Theory,* **IT-5**, pp. 114-123, September, 1959.

CHAPTER 5

ERROR-TRAPPING DECODING FOR CYCLIC CODES

In principle, the general decoding method of Meggitt applies to any cyclic code, but refinements are necessary for practical implementation. In this chapter, a practical variation of Meggitt decoding, *error-trapping decoding*, is described. A decoder based on this decoding technique employs a very simple combinational logic circuit for error detection and correction. Error-trapping decoding is most effective for decoding single-error-correcting codes and some short double-error-correcting codes. When it is applied to long and high rate codes with large error-correcting capability, it becomes very ineffective and much error-correcting capability will be sacrificed. In an effort to extend its application to multiple-error-correcting codes, several modifications have been devised. One modification due to Kasami[12] is presented in Section 5.4. Some useful random-error-correcting codes which can be decoded effectively by error-trapping decoding (or Kasami's modification) are described in Sections 5.2, 5.3, and 5.5. The decoding of burst-error-correcting codes will be discussed in Chapter 8.

5.1 ERROR-TRAPPING DECODING

Suppose that a t-error-correcting (n, k) cyclic code is used for error control purposes. Let $\mathbf{v}(X)$ be the transmitted code vector and let $\mathbf{r}(X)$ be the received vector. Then the error pattern caused by the channel disturbance is $\mathbf{e}(X) = \mathbf{r}(X) + \mathbf{v}(X)$. As shown in Section 4.4, the syndrome $\mathbf{s}(X)$ of $\mathbf{r}(X)$ is equal to the remainder resulting from dividing the error pattern $\mathbf{e}(X)$ by the code generator polynomial $\mathbf{g}(X)$, i.e.,

$$\mathbf{e}(X) = \mathbf{q}(X)\mathbf{g}(X) + \mathbf{s}(X) \tag{5.1}$$

where $\mathbf{s}(X)$ is the remainder.

If the errors of $\mathbf{e}(X)$ are confined to the $n-k$ parity check positions $1, X, \ldots, X^{n-k-1}$ of $\mathbf{r}(X)$, then $\mathbf{e}(X)$ is a polynomial of degree $n-k-1$ or less.

It follows from Eq. (5.1) that $\mathbf{q}(X) = 0$ and $\mathbf{e}(X) = \mathbf{s}(X)$. That is, if the errors in $\mathbf{r}(X)$ are confined to the $n-k$ parity positions, then the syndrome of $\mathbf{r}(X)$ is identical to the error pattern $\mathbf{s}(X) = \mathbf{e}(X)$. Thus, correction can be accomplished simply by adding (modulo-2) the syndrome to the $n-k$ received parity check digits.

Suppose that the errors are not confined to the $n-k$ parity check positions of $\mathbf{r}(X)$ but are confined to $n-k$ consecutive positions (*including the end around case*), say $X^i, X^{i+1}, \ldots, X^{(n-k)+i-1}$. After $n-i$ cyclic shifts of $\mathbf{r}(X)$, the errors will be shifted to the $n-k$ parity check positions of the cyclically shifted received vector $\mathbf{r}^{(n-i)}(X)$. Then the syndrome of $\mathbf{r}^{(n-i)}(X)$ is identical to the errors confined to the positions $X^i, X^{i+1}, \ldots, X^{(n-k)+i-1}$ of $\mathbf{r}(X)$. As a result, the errors can be corrected. In the following we shall consider the error-trapping decoding[16,17,25]* which is based on the above facts.

An error-trapping decoder is shown in Fig. 5.1 on the following page. The operation of this decoder can be described in the following steps:

Step 1. Gate 1 is turned on; Gates 2 and 3 are turned off. The received vector is read into the syndrome register and simultaneously into the buffer register (since we are only interested in the recovery of the k transmitted information digits, the buffer register has only to store the k received information digits). As soon as the entire received vector has been shifted into the syndrome register, the contents of the register are the syndrome of the received vector.

Step 2. The weight of the syndrome is tested by an $(n-k)$-input threshold gate. The output of this gate is "1" when t or fewer of its inputs are "1"; otherwise, the output is zero.

Step 3. (a) If the weight of the syndrome is t or less, the errors are confined to the $(n-k)$ parity-check positions $X^0, X^1, \ldots, X^{n-k-1}$ of the received vector. Thus, the k received information digits in the buffer register are *error-free*. Gate 3 is then turned on and the information digits are sent to the data sink (Gate 2 is turned off). The decoding is completed. Return to Step 1. (b) If the weight of the syndrome calculated in the first step is greater than t, the syndrome register is then shifted once with Gate 1 turned on and Gates 2 and 3

* Error-trapping decoding was probably developed by Prange.

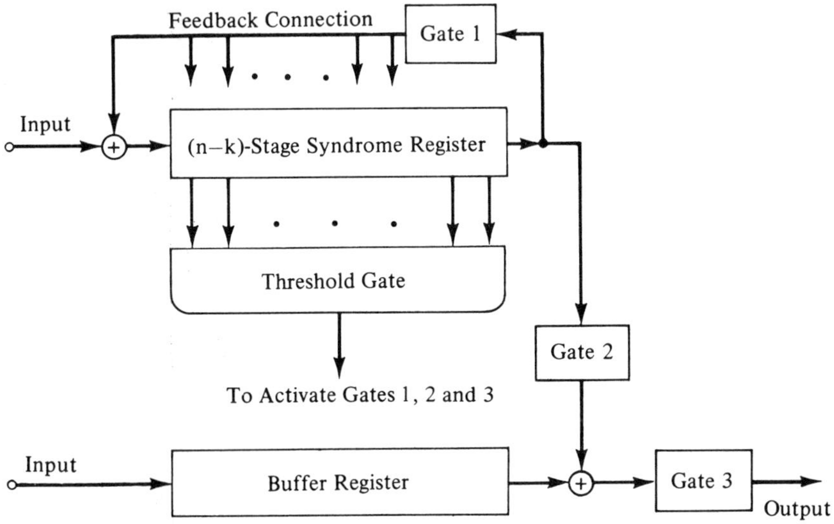

Fig. 5.1. An error-trapping decoder.

turned off. Go to Step 4.

Step 4. The weight of the new contents of the syndrome register is tested. (a) If the weight is t or less, the errors are confined to the positions X^{n-1}, X^0, X^1, . . ., X^{n-k-2} of the received vector. The leftmost digit in the syndrome register matches the error at the position X^{n-1} of the received vector; the other $n-k-1$ digits in the syndrome register match the errors at positions X^0, X^1, . . ., X^{n-k-2} of the received vector. The output of the threshold gate turns Gate 1 off and sets a clock to count from 2. The syndrome register is then shifted (in step with the clock) with Gate 1 turned off. As soon as the clock has counted to $n-k$, the contents of the syndrome register will be (0, 0, . . ., 0, 1). The rightmost digit matches the error at the position X^{n-1} of the received vector. The k received information digits are then read out of the buffer. The first received information digit is corrected by the "1" coming out from the syndrome register. The decoding is thus completed. Return to Step 1. (b) If the weight of the contents of the syndrome register (calculated in Step 3b) is greater than t, the syndrome register is shifted once again with Gate 1 turned on and Gates 2 and 3 turned off. Go to Step 5.

Step 5. Step 4b repeats until the weight of the contents of the syndrome register goes down to t or less. If the weight goes down to t or less after the ith shift, for $1 \leqslant i \leqslant n-k$, the clock starts to count from $i+1$. At the same time, the syndrome register is shifted with Gate 1 turned off. As soon as the clock has counted to $n-k$, the rightmost i digits in the syndrome register match the errors in the first i received information digits in the buffer register. The other information digits are error-free. Gates 2 and 3 are then turned on. The received information digits are read out of the buffer for correction. Return to Step 1.

Step 6. If the weight of the contents of the syndrome register never goes down to t or less by the time that the syndrome register has been shifted $n-k$ times (with Gate 1 turned on), Gate 3 is then turned on and the received information digits are read out of the buffer one at a time. At the same time the syndrome register is shifted with Gate 1 turned on. As soon as the weight of the contents of the syndrome register goes down to t or less, the contents match the errors in the next $n-k$ digits to come out of the buffer. Gate 2 is then turned on and the erroneous information digits are corrected by the digits coming out from the syndrome register with Gate 1 turned off. Gate 3 is turned off as soon as k information digits have been read out of the buffer.

If the weight of the contents of the syndrome register never goes down to t or less by the time the k received information digits have been read out of the buffer, then either an uncorrectable error pattern has occurred or a correctable error pattern with errors not confined to $n-k$ consecutive positions has occurred.

Error-trapping decoding is most effective for decoding single-error-correcting codes and burst-error-correcting codes. It is also effective for decoding some short double-error-correcting codes. When it is applied to long and high rate codes (small $n-k$) with large error-correcting capability, it becomes very ineffective and much of the error-correcting capability will be sacrificed. Several refinements of this simple decoding technique[12,14,22,25,26] have been proposed to extend its application to multiple-error-correcting codes. One of the refinements will be discussed in a later section.

5.2 HAMMING CODES

Let $\mathbf{p}(X)$ be a primitive polynomial of degree m. Then it can be shown that the smallest integer n such that $X^n + 1$ is divisible by $\mathbf{p}(X)$ is $2^m - 1$. A cyclic *Hamming code*[3,6,11,18,27] is a code whose generator polynomial is a primitive polynomial $\mathbf{p}(X)$ of degree m. This code has the following parameters:

Code length:	$n = 2^m - 1$
Number of parity check digits:	$n - k = m$
Number of information digits:	$k = 2^m - m - 1$
Error-correcting capability:	$t = 1$.

In the following, we shall show that for any positive integer m, a Hamming code is a single-error-correcting code.

Let $\mathbf{e}_i(X) = X^i$ be an error pattern with a single error at position X^i and let $\mathbf{e}_j(X)$ be an error pattern with a single error at position X^j, where $i \neq j$ and $0 \leqslant i, j < n$. The syndrome $\mathbf{s}_i(X)$ which corresponds to $\mathbf{e}_i(X)$ is equal to the remainder resulting from dividing $\mathbf{e}_i(X)$ by the code generator polynomial $\mathbf{p}(X)$,

$$\mathbf{e}_i(X) = \mathbf{q}_i(X)\,\mathbf{p}(X) + \mathbf{s}_i(X) \quad . \tag{5.2}$$

The syndrome $\mathbf{s}_j(X)$ which corresponds to $\mathbf{e}_j(X)$ is equal to the remainder resulting from dividing $\mathbf{e}_j(X)$ by $\mathbf{p}(X)$,

$$\mathbf{e}_j(X) = \mathbf{q}_j(X)\,\mathbf{p}(X) + \mathbf{s}_j(X) \quad . \tag{5.3}$$

Now we want to show that $\mathbf{s}_i(X) \neq \mathbf{s}_j(X)$. Suppose that $\mathbf{s}_i(X) = \mathbf{s}_j(X)$. Then, by combining Eqs. (5.2) and (5.3), we obtain

$$\mathbf{e}_j(X) + \mathbf{e}_i(X) \;=\; [\mathbf{q}_j(X) + \mathbf{q}_i(X)]\ \mathbf{p}(X) \ .$$

Assuming that $i < j$, we have

$$X^i(X^{j-i} + 1) \;=\; [\mathbf{q}_j(X) + \mathbf{q}_i(X)]\ \mathbf{p}(X) \ . \tag{5.4}$$

Equation (5.4) implies that $\mathbf{p}(X)$ divides $X^{j-i} + 1$, which is impossible since $j - i < 2^m - 1$ and $\mathbf{p}(X)$ is a primitive polynomial of degree m. Therefore, $\mathbf{s}_i(X) \neq \mathbf{s}_j(X)$ for $i \neq j$. That is, different error patterns of single error have different syndromes. There are $2^m - 1$ error patterns of single error. By Theorem 3.2, it is possible to form a standard array with all the $2^m - 1$ error patterns of single error as coset leaders. Thus, they are correctable error patterns. Since there are $2^{2^m - 1}$ $(2^m - 1)$-tuples and $2^{2^m - m - 1}$ code vectors, there are $2^{2^m - 1}/2^{2^m - m - 1} = 2^m$ cosets. Therefore, the standard array has the zero code vector and all the $2^m - 1$ error patterns of single error as all its coset leaders. This proves that a Hamming code corrects all error patterns of single error and no others. A t-error-correcting code is called a *perfect code* if it is possible to form a standard array with all error patterns of t or fewer errors and no others as coset leaders. Thus, Hamming codes are single-error-correcting perfect codes. The minimum distance of a Hamming code is exactly 3.

The encoding circuit consists of an m-stage shift register with feedback connections according to the generator polynomial $\mathbf{p}(X)$ as discussed in Section 4.2. Let

$$\mathbf{p}(X) \;=\; 1 + p_1 X + p_2 X^2 + \ldots + p_{m-1} X^{m-1} + X^m$$

where $p_i = 0$ or 1. The circuit is as shown in Fig. 5.2. This encoding circuit consists of: (1) m flip-flops; (2) approximately $m/2$ Exclusive OR gates (in many cases only 3 Exclusive OR gates are required); (3) one AND gate; and (4) a counter consisting of m flip-flops.

Decoding

Hamming codes can be decoded by the error-trapping method in a simple manner.[18] A decoder as shown in Fig. 5.3 consists of a syndrome

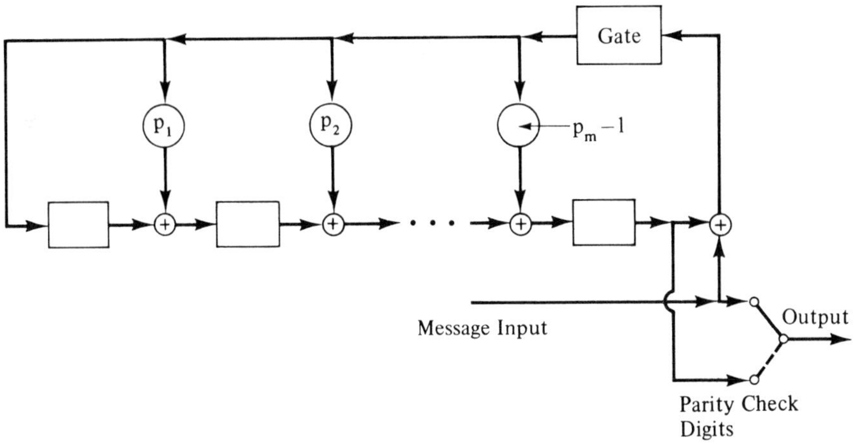

Fig. 5.2. An encoder for a $(2^m\text{-}1, 2^m\text{-}m\text{-}1)$ Hamming code.

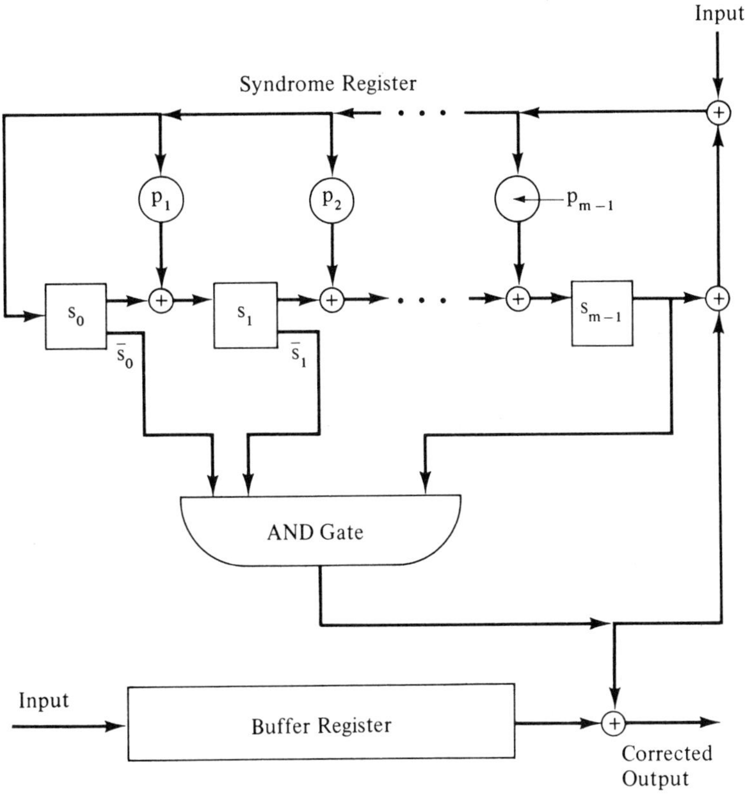

Fig. 5.3. A Hamming code decoder ($\bar{s}_1$ is the complement of s_1).

register, a buffer, and an m-input AND gate. The syndrome register is identical to the encoder. The detection of the occurrence of a single error is based on the following fact. Suppose that a single error has occurred at the position X^{n-1} in the received vector $\mathbf{r}(X)$. Since $\mathbf{r}(X)$ is read into the syndrome calculator from the rightmost stage, *which is equivalent to pre-shifting* $\mathbf{r}(X)$ *m times cyclically*, the error is then shifted to the position X^{m-1}. Therefore, the syndrome register contains the syndrome corresponding to $\mathbf{e}_{m-1}(X) = X^{m-1}$, which is just

$$\mathbf{s}_{m-1}(X) = X^{m-1} \quad ,$$

or $(0, 0, \ldots, 0, 1)$. That is, the syndrome register contains $(0, 0, \ldots, 0, 1)$ when a single error occurs at the position X^{n-1} in the received vector $\mathbf{r}(X)$.

The decoding procedure can be described in the following steps:

Step 1. The syndrome is obtained by shifting the entire received vector into the syndrome register. At the same time, the received vector is stored into the buffer. If the syndrome is zero, the decoder assumes that no error has occurred, and no correction is necessary. If the syndrome is not zero, the decoder assumes that a single error has occurred.

Step 2. The received word is read out of the buffer digit by digit. As each digit is read out of the buffer, the syndrome register is shifted cyclically once. As soon as the syndrome in the register is $(0, 0, 0, \ldots, 0, 1)$, the next digit to come out of the buffer is the erroneous digit, and the output of the m-input AND gate is "1."

Step 3. The erroneous digit is read out of the buffer and is corrected by the output of the m-input AND gate. The correction is accomplished by an Exclusive OR gate.

Step 4. The syndrome register is reset to zero after the entire received vector is read out of the buffer.

The above decoder is very simple; it consists of: (1) An m-stage shift register for syndrome calculation. This requires m flip-flops and approximately $m/2$ Exclusive OR gates. (2) A $(2^m - 1)$-stage buffer register for storing the received vector. This requires $2^m - 1$ flip-flops. (3) An m-input AND gate and an Exclusive OR gate for error detection and correction. (4) An Exclusive OR gate for syndrome resetting.

5.3 DOUBLE-ERROR-DETECTING AND SINGLE-ERROR-CORRECTING HAMMING CODES

A double-error-detecting and single-error-correcting Hamming code[1,18] is obtained by using $\mathbf{g}(X) = (1+X)\mathbf{p}(X)$ as the generator polynomial, where $\mathbf{p}(X)$ is a primitive polynomial of degree m. This code has the following parameters: $n = 2^m - 1$, $n - k = m + 1$, and $t = 1$.

Let $\mathbf{r}(X)$ be the received vector. The syndrome of $\mathbf{r}(X)$ may be calculated in such a way that the decoding of this code is slightly different from the decoding of a single-error-correcting Hamming code as discussed in the previous section. Dividing $\mathbf{r}(X)$ by $\mathbf{p}(X)$ and $(1+X)$ respectively, we obtain

$$\mathbf{r}(X) = \mathbf{q}_1(X)\mathbf{p}(X) + \mathbf{s}_p(X)$$

and

$$\mathbf{r}(X) = \mathbf{q}_2(X)(1+X) + s_a \tag{5.5}$$

where $\mathbf{s}_p(X)$ is of degree $m-1$ or less and s_a is either 0 or 1. If $\mathbf{s}_p(X) = 0$ and $s_a = 0$, then $\mathbf{r}(X)$ is divisible by $(1+X)\mathbf{p}(X)$ and is a code vector; otherwise, $\mathbf{r}(X)$ is not a code vector. Thus, the syndrome $\mathbf{s}(X)$ of $\mathbf{r}(X)$ consists of two parts, $\mathbf{s}_p(X)$ and s_a, or

$$\mathbf{s}(X) = X\,\mathbf{s}_p(X) + s_a \ . \tag{5.6}$$

If an error pattern of single error has occurred, then $\mathbf{s}_p(X) \neq 0$ and $s_a = 1$. The syndrome is

$$\mathbf{s}(X) = X\,\mathbf{s}_p(X) + 1 \ . \tag{5.7}$$

Following the argument in Section 5.2, it is possible to show that all error patterns of single error have different syndromes. Thus, they are correctable. Consider an error pattern of double errors, say $\mathbf{e}(X) = X^i + X^j$. This error pattern is divisible by $(1+X)$ but not by $\mathbf{p}(X)$. Thus, its syndrome is of the form

$$\mathbf{s}(X) = X\,\mathbf{s}_p(X) \,, \tag{5.8}$$

where $\mathbf{s}_p(X) \neq 0$. Comparing Eq. (5.7) and Eq. (5.8), it is obvious that an error pattern of double errors and an error pattern of single error cannot have the same syndrome; that is, they cannot be in the same coset. Now split $\mathbf{s}_p(X)$ into two parts, $\mathbf{s}_p^1(X)$ and $\mathbf{s}_p^2(X)$, such that

$$\mathbf{s}_p(X) = \mathbf{s}_p^1(X) + \mathbf{s}_p^2(X) \,. \tag{5.9}$$

Let X^k be the error pattern of single error whose syndrome is $X\mathbf{s}_p^1(X) + 1$ and let X^ℓ be the error pattern of single error whose syndrome is $X\mathbf{s}_p^2(X) + 1$. Then $X^k + X^\ell$ has syndrome $X\mathbf{s}_p(X)$, which is the same as the syndrome of $X^i + X^j$. Therefore, $X^i + X^j$ and $X^k + X^\ell$ are in the same coset of the standard array. If $X^i + X^j$ is used as the coset leader, then $X^k + X^\ell$ is an uncorrectable error pattern. Thus, all the error patterns of double errors are detectable, but not all of them are correctable. For any $t > 2$, it is possible to show that there exists at least one error pattern $\mathbf{e}(X)$ of t errors which is undetectable. That is, an incorrect decoding will result when $\mathbf{e}(X)$ occurs.

A decoder for a double-error-detecting and single-error-correcting Hamming code is shown in Fig. 5.4. The correction and detection is done as follows:

(1) For $s_a = 0$ and $\mathbf{s}_p(X) \equiv 0$, the decoder assumes that there is no error in the received vector. No corrective action takes place.

(2) For $s_a = 1$ and $\mathbf{s}_p(X) \not\equiv 0$, the decoder assumes that a single error has occurred and proceeds with the corrective action as described in the decoding of a single-error-correcting Hamming code.

(3) For $s_a = 0$ and $\mathbf{s}_p(X) \not\equiv 0$, the decoder assumes that an error pattern of double errors has occurred. The error alarm is turned on.

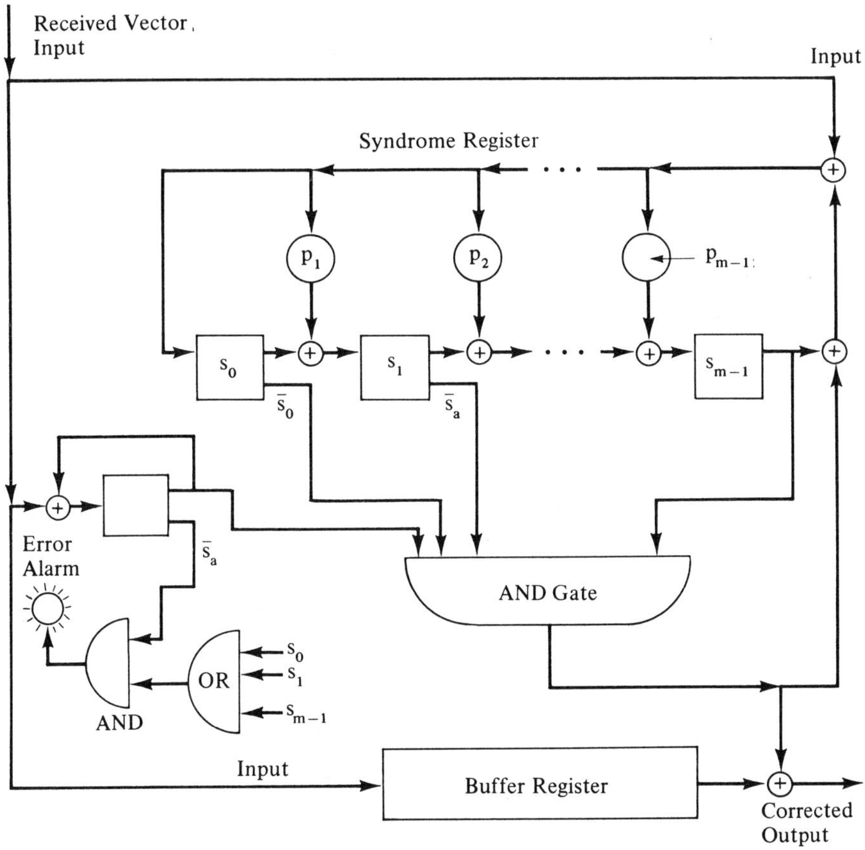

Fig. 5.4. A double-error-detecting and single-error-correcting Hamming code decoder.

(4) For $s_a = 1$ and $\mathbf{s}_p(X) \equiv 0$, the error alarm is also turned on. There must have been an odd number of errors greater than one.

Since every code polynomial $\mathbf{v}(X) = a_0 + a_1X + \ldots + a_{n-1}X^{n-1}$ has $(1+X)$ as a factor, then $\mathbf{v}(1) = a_0 + a_1 + \ldots + a_{n-1} = 0$. That is, each code vector must have even weight. Since this code corrects all error patterns of single error, its minimum weight (or minimum distance) is at least 4. We have shown that, for any error pattern $X^i + X^j$, there exists an error pattern $X^k + X^\ell$ which has the same syndrome as that of $X^i + X^j$. Therefore, $X^i + X^j + X^k + X^\ell$ is divisible by $\mathbf{g}(X) = (1+X)\,\mathbf{p}(X)$ and is a code polynomial of weight 4. Thus, we conclude that the minimum weight of this code is exactly 4.

5.4 A MODIFIED ERROR-TRAPPING DECODING

The error-trapping decoding discussed in Section 5.1 can be modified to correct error patterns such that, for each error pattern, most errors are confined to $n-k$ consecutive positions and fewer errors are outside the $(n-k)$-digit span. This modification needs additional equipment. The complexity of the additional equipment depends on how many errors outside an $(n-k)$-digit span are to be corrected. A modification proposed by Kasami[12] will be discussed here.

The error pattern $\mathbf{e}(X) = e_0 + e_1X + e_2X^2 + \ldots + e_{n-1}X^{n-1}$ which corrupted the transmitted code vector can be segmented into two parts:

$$\mathbf{e}_p(X) = e_0 + e_1X + \ldots + e_{n-k-1}X^{n-k-1}$$

$$\mathbf{e}_I(X) = e_{n-k}X^{n-k} + \ldots + e_{n-1}X^{n-1}$$

where $\mathbf{e}_I(X)$ contains the errors in the information section of the received vector and $\mathbf{e}_p(X)$ contains the errors in the parity section of the received vector. Dividing $\mathbf{e}_I(X)$ by the code generator polynomial $\mathbf{g}(X)$, we obtain

$$\mathbf{e}_I(X) = \mathbf{q}(X)\mathbf{g}(X) + \rho(X) , \tag{5.10}$$

where $\rho(X)$ is the remainder with degree $n-k-1$ or less. Adding $\mathbf{e}_p(X)$ to both sides of Eq. (5.10), we obtain

$$\mathbf{e}(X) = \mathbf{e}_p(X) + \mathbf{e}_I(X) = \mathbf{q}(X)\mathbf{g}(X) + \rho(X) + \mathbf{e}_p(X) . \tag{5.11}$$

Since $\mathbf{e}_p(X)$ has degree $n-k-1$ or less, $\rho(X) + \mathbf{e}_p(X)$ must be the remainder resulting from dividing the error pattern $\mathbf{e}(X)$ by the generator polynomial. Thus, $\rho(X) + \mathbf{e}_p(X)$ is equal to the syndrome of the received vector $\mathbf{r}(X)$,

$$\mathbf{s}(X) = \rho(X) + \mathbf{e}_p(X) . \tag{5.12}$$

Rearranging Eq. (5.12), we have

$$\mathbf{e}_p(X) = \mathbf{s}(X) + \boldsymbol{\rho}(X) \ . \qquad (5.13)$$

That is, if the error pattern $\mathbf{e}_I(X)$ in the information positions is known, the error pattern $\mathbf{e}_p(X)$ in the parity position can be found.

Kasami's modification of error-trapping decoding requires finding a set of polynomials $[\phi_j(X)]_{j=1}^N$ of degree $k-1$ or less such that, for any correctable error $\mathbf{e}(X)$, there is one polynomial $\phi_j(X)$ such that $X^{n-k}\phi_j(X)$ matches the information section of $\mathbf{e}(X)$ or the information section of a cyclic shift of $\mathbf{e}(X)$. Let $\rho_j(X)$ be the remainder resulting from dividing $X^{n-k}\phi_j(X)$ by the generator polynomial $\mathbf{g}(X)$ of the code.

The decoding procedure can be described in the following steps:

Step 1. Calculate the syndrome $\mathbf{s}(X)$ by entering the entire received word into the syndrome register.

Step 2. Calculate the weight of the sum $\mathbf{s}(X) + \rho_j(X)$ for each $j = 1, 2, \ldots, N$, i.e.,

$$\omega[\mathbf{s}(X) + \rho_j(X)]$$

for $j = 1, 2, \ldots, N$.

Step 3. If, for some ℓ,

$$\omega[\mathbf{s}(X) + \rho_\ell(X)] \leqslant t - \omega[\phi_\ell(X)] \ ,$$

then $X^{n-k}\phi_\ell(X)$ matches the error pattern in the information section of $\mathbf{e}(X)$ and $\mathbf{s}(X) + \rho_\ell(X)$ matches the error pattern in the parity section of $\mathbf{e}(X)$. Thus,

$$\mathbf{e}(X) = \mathbf{s}(X) + \rho_\ell(X) + X^{n-k}\phi_\ell(X) \ .$$

Correction is then accomplished by taking the modulo-2 sum $\mathbf{r}(X) + \mathbf{e}(X)$. This step requires N $(n-k)$-input threshold gates to test the weights of $\mathbf{s}(X) + \rho_j(X)$ for $j = 1, 2, \ldots, N$.

Step 4. If $\omega[\mathrm{s}(X) + \rho_j(X)] > t - \omega[\phi_j(X)]$ for all $j = 1, 2, \ldots, N$, both syndrome and buffer registers are shifted cyclically once. Then the new contents $\mathbf{s}_1(X)$ of the syndrome register is the syndrome corresponding to $\mathbf{e}^{(1)}(X)$ which is obtained by shifting the error pattern $\mathbf{e}(X)$ cyclically one place to the right.

Step 5. The weight of $\mathrm{s}_1(X) + \rho_j(X)$ is calculated for $j = 1, 2, \ldots, N$. If, for some ℓ,

$$\omega[\mathrm{s}_1(X) + \rho_\ell(X)] \leqslant t - w[\phi_\ell(X)] \quad ,$$

then $X^{n-k}\phi_\ell(X)$ matches the errors in the information section of $\mathrm{e}^{(1)}(X)$ and $\mathrm{s}_1(X) + \rho_\ell(X)$ matches the errors in the parity section of $\mathrm{e}^{(1)}(X)$. Thus,

$$\mathrm{e}^{(1)}(X) = \mathrm{s}_1(X) + \rho_\ell(X) + X^{n-k}\phi_\ell(X) \quad .$$

Correction is then accomplished by taking the modulo-2 sum $\mathbf{r}^{(1)}(X) + \mathrm{e}^{(1)}(X)$. If

$$\omega[\mathrm{s}_1(X) + \rho_j(X)] > t - \omega[\phi_j(X)]$$

for all $j = 1, 2, \ldots, N$, both syndrome and buffer registers are shifted cyclically once again.

Step 6. The syndrome and buffer registers are continuously shifted until $\mathrm{s}_i(X)$ (the syndrome after the ith shift) is found such that, for some ℓ,

$$\omega[\mathrm{s}_i(X) + \rho_\ell(X)] \leqslant t - \omega[\phi_\ell(X)] \quad .$$

Then,

$$\mathrm{e}^{(i)}(X) = \mathrm{s}_i(X) + \rho_\ell(X) + X^{n-k}\phi_\ell(X) \quad ,$$

where $e^{(i)}(X)$ is the ith cyclic-shift of $e(X)$. If the weight $\omega[s_i(X) + \rho_j(X)]$ never goes down to $t - \omega[\phi_j(X)]$ or less for all j by the time that the syndrome and buffer registers have been cyclically shifted $n-1$ times, then an uncorrectable error pattern is detected.

The complexity of a decoder which employs the above decoding method depends on N, the number of polynomials in $\{\phi_j(X)\}_{j=1}^{N}$. The combinational logical circuitry consists of N $(n-k)$-input threshold gates. To find the set of polynomials $\{\phi_j(X)\}_{j=1}^{N}$ for a specific code is not an easy problem. Several methods for finding this set can be found in References 7, 12, and 24.

This modified error-trapping method is applicable to many double- and triple-error-correcting codes. However, it is still only applicable to relatively short and low rate codes. When the code length n and error-correcting capability t become large, the number of threshold gates required in the error-detecting logical circuitry becomes very large and impractical.

Two earlier decoding techniques which are similar to Kasami's can be found in References 23 and 25.

5.5 THE GOLAY CODE

The Golay (23,12) code[10, 20, 21] is the only known multiple-error-correcting binary perfect code which is capable of correcting any combination of three or fewer random errors in a block of 23 digits. This code has been used in several real communication systems and, for this reason, it is emphasized here. The generator polynomial of this code is either

$$g_1(X) = 1 + X^2 + X^4 + X^5 + X^6 + X^{10} + X^{11}$$

or

$$g_2(X) = 1 + X + X^5 + X^6 + X^7 + X^9 + X^{11} .$$

Both $g_1(X)$ and $g_2(X)$ are factors of $X^{23} + 1$,

$$X^{23}+1 = (1+X)\,g_1(X)\,g_2(X) \quad .$$

The encoding can be accomplished by an 11-stage shift register with feedback connections according to either $g_1(X)$ or $g_2(X)$. There are several practical ways to decode this code. Two of the best are discussed in this section.

*Kasami Decoder**

The Golay code can be easily decoded by Kasami's modification of the error-trapping technique. The set of polynomials $\{\phi_j(X)\}_{j=1}^{N}$ is chosen as follows:

$$\phi_1(X) = 0 \quad ,$$
$$\phi_2(X) = X^5 \quad ,$$
$$\phi_3(X) = X^6 \quad .$$

Let $g_1(X) = 1 + X^2 + X^4 + X^5 + X^6 + X^{10} + X^{11}$ be the generator polynomial. Dividing $X^{11}\phi_j(X)$ by $g_1(X)$ for $j = 1, 2, 3$, we obtain the following remainders:

$$\rho_1(X) = 0 \ ,$$
$$\rho_2(X) = X + X^2 + X^5 + X^6 + X^8 + X^9 \quad ,$$
$$\rho_3(X) = X^2 + X^3 + X^6 + X^7 + X^9 + X^{10} \quad .$$

A decoder based on the Kasami modification of error-trapping decoding is shown in Fig. 5.5. For implementation purposes, the received vector $\mathbf{r}(X) = r_0 + r_1X + r_2X^2 + \ldots + r_{22}X^{22}$ is shifted into the syndrome register from the rightmost stage; this is equivalent to pre-shifting the received vector 11 times cyclically. After the entire received vector has entered the syndrome register, the syndrome in the register corresponds to $\mathbf{r}^{(11)}(X)$ which is the

* The material presented here is primarily based on the work of T. Kasami.[12]

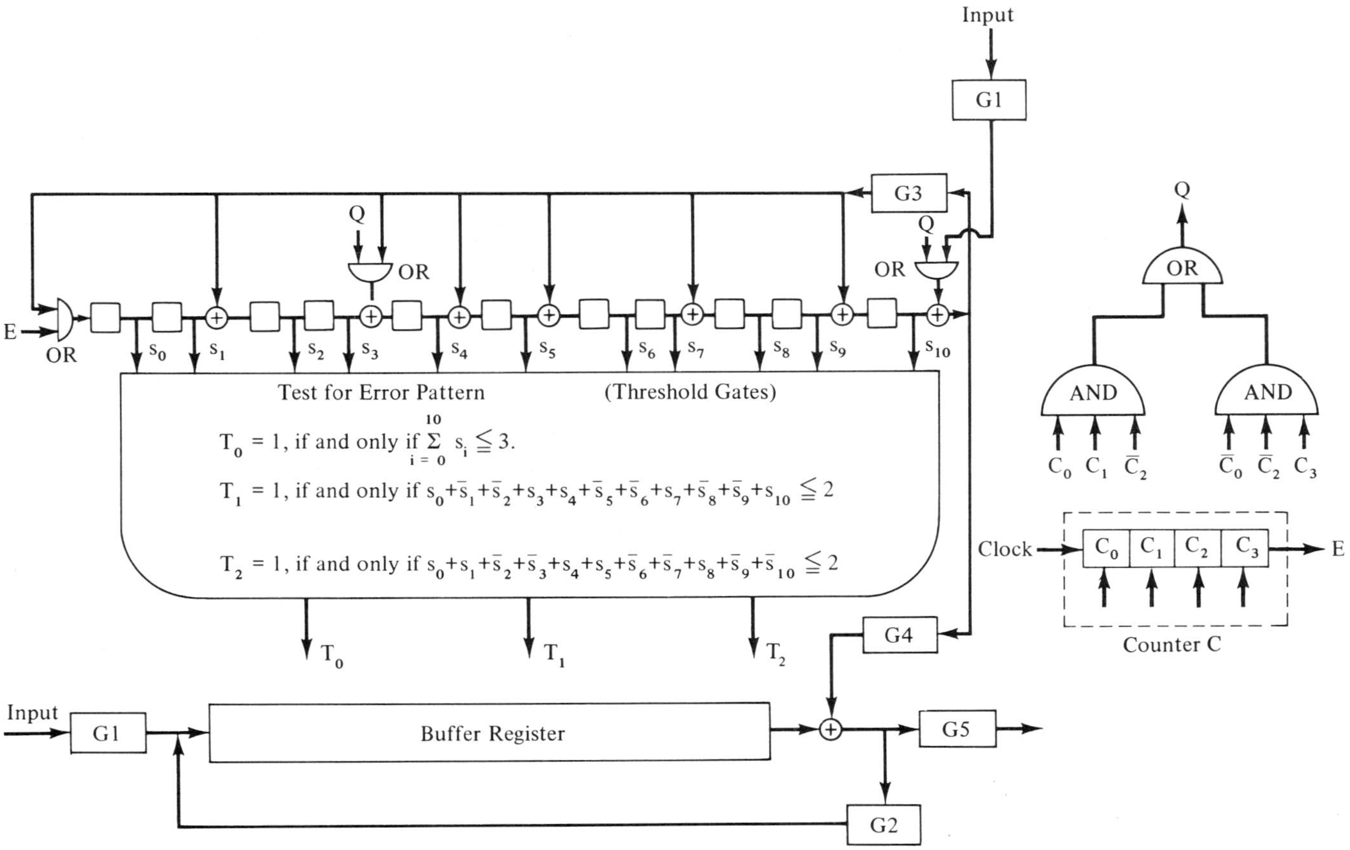

Fig. 5.5. An Error-Trapping Decoder for the Golay code. (From T. Kasami, "A Decoding Procedure for Multiple-Error-Correcting Cyclic Codes," *IEEE Trans. on Information Theory*, **IT-10**, Fig. 2, p. 136, April, 1964. Redrawn by permission.)

Test for Error Pattern

$T_0 = 1$, if and only if $\sum_{i=0}^{10} s_i \leqq 3$.

$T_1 = 1$, if and only if $s_0 + \bar{s}_1 + \bar{s}_2 + s_3 + s_4 + \bar{s}_5 + s_6 + s_7 + \bar{s}_8 + \bar{s}_9 + s_{10} \leqq 2$

$T_2 = 1$, if and only if $s_0 + s_1 + \bar{s}_2 + s_3 + s_4 + s_5 + s_6 + \bar{s}_7 + s_8 + \bar{s}_9 + s_{10} \leqq 2$

(Threshold Gates)

11th cyclic-shift of $\mathbf{r}(X)$. In this case, if the errors are confined to the first 11 high-order positions $X^{12}, X^{13}, \ldots, X^{22}$ of $\mathbf{r}(X)$, the syndrome matches the errors in those positions. The error correction procedure of this decoder can be described in the following steps:

Step 1. Gates 1, 3, and 5 are turned on; Gates 2 and 4 are turned off. The received vector $\mathbf{r}(X)$ is read into the syndrome register and simultaneously into the buffer register; the vector in the buffer resulting from the previous decoding is read out to the data sink. The syndrome $\mathbf{s}(X) = s_0 + s_1X + s_2X^2 + \ldots + s_{10}X^{10}$ is formed and is read into three threshold gates.

Step 2. Gates 1, 4, and 5 are turned off; Gates 2 and 3 are turned on. The syndrome is tested for correctable error patterns as follows:

a) If the weight

$$\omega[\mathbf{s}(X)] \leqslant 3 \ ,$$

all the errors are confined to the 11 high-order positions of $\mathbf{r}(X)$ and $\mathbf{s}(X)$ matches the errors. Thus, the erroneous symbols are the next 11 digits to come out of the buffer register. The output of the threshold gate T_0 turns Gate 4 on and Gate 3 off. Digits are read out one at a time from the syndrome register and from the buffer register. The digit coming out of the syndrome register is added (modulo-2) to the digit coming out of the buffer. This corrects the errors.

b) If $\omega[\mathbf{s}(X)] > 3$, the weight of $\mathbf{s}(X) + \rho_2(X)$ is tested. If

$$\omega[\mathbf{s}(X) + \rho_2(X)] \leqslant 2 \ ,$$

then $\mathbf{s}(X) + \rho_2(X) = s_0 + \bar{s}_1X + \bar{s}_2X^2 + s_3X^3 + s_4X^4 + \bar{s}_5X^5 + \bar{s}_6X^6 + s_7X^7 + \bar{s}_8X^8 + \bar{s}_9X^9 + s_{10}X^{10}$ is identical to the error pattern in the 11 high-order positions of the received word and a single error occurs at location X^5, where $\bar{s}_i = 1 + s_i$. Gate 4 is turned on, and Gate 3 is turned off. The counter C starts to count from 2. At the same time, the syndrome register is shifted without feedback. The output Q, which is "1" when and only when C counts 3 and 4, is fed into the syndrome register to form the error pattern $\mathbf{s}(X) + \rho_2(X)$. When the counter C counts 8, the output E is "1" and the leftmost stage of the syndrome register is set to "1." This "1" is used for correcting the error at location X^5 in the received vector $\mathbf{r}(X)$. The digits coming out of the buffer are then corrected by the digits coming out of the syndrome register.

c) If $\omega[\mathbf{s}(X)] > 3$ and $\omega[\mathbf{s}(X) + \rho_2(X)] > 2$, the weight of $\mathbf{s}(X) + \rho_3(X)$ is tested. If

$$\omega[\mathbf{s}(X) + \rho_3(X)] \leqslant 2,$$

then $\mathbf{s}(X) + \rho_3(X) = s_0 + s_1 X + \bar{s}_2 X^2 + \bar{s}_3 X^3 + s_4 X^4 + s_5 X^5 + \bar{s}_6 X^6 + \bar{s}_7 X^7 + s_8 X^8 + \bar{s}_9 X^9 + \bar{s}_{10} X^{10}$ is identical to the error pattern in the 11 high-order positions of the received word and a single error occurs at position X^6. The correction is the same as in b, except that counter C starts to count from 3. If $\omega[\mathbf{s}(X)] > 3$, $\omega[\mathbf{s}(X) + \rho_2(X)] > 2$ and $\omega[\mathbf{s}(X) + \rho_3(X)] > 2$, then the decoder moves to Step 3.

Step 3. Both the syndrome and buffer registers are cyclically shifted once with Gates 1, 4, and 5 turned off and Gates 2 and 3 turned on. The new contents of the syndrome register are $\mathbf{s}_1(X)$. Step 2 is then repeated.

Step 4. The decoding operation is completed as soon as the buffer register has been cyclically shifted 46 times. Gate 5 is then turned on and the vector in the buffer is shifted out to the data sink.

If there are three or fewer errors in the received vector, the vector in the buffer at the end of decoding will be the transmitted code vector. If there are more than three errors in the received vector, the vector in the buffer at the end of decoding will not be the transmitted code vector.

Systematic Search Decoder[28]

This decoding method is based on the fact that every pattern of three or fewer errors in a block of 23 digits can be cyclically shifted so that at most one of the errors lies outside a specified 11-digit section of the word. The decoding procedure can be described as follows:

Step 1. Calculate the syndrome from the received vector.

Step 2. Shift the syndrome and the received vector 23 times, checking whether the weight of the syndrome ever falls to 3 or less. If it does, the syndrome with weight 3 or less matches the error pattern and correction can be made.

Step 3. If it does not, the first information digit is inverted and Step 2 is repeated, checking for a syndrome of weight 2 or less. If one is found, the first (inverted) information digit was incorrect and the other two errors are specified by the syndrome. This completes the decoding.

Step 4. If no syndrome of weight 2 or less is found in Step 3, the first information digit was originally correct. In this case, this bit must be re-inverted.

Step 5. Repeat Step 3 by inverting the 2nd, 3rd, . . ., and 12th information digits. Since not all the errors are in the parity check section, an error must be corrected in this manner.

In every pattern of 3 or fewer errors, there is at least one error which, if corrected, will leave the remaining error or errors within eleven successive positions. When the digit corresponding to this error is inverted, the remaining errors are within the parity section and are corrected as in ordinary error-trapping. Note that if no more than three errors occurred, incorrect decoding cannot result with this method since the code has minimum distance 7. After the inversion there are at most 4 errors in the vector and only 2 additional corrections are permitted.

Compared to the Kasami decoder, the systematic search decoder has the advantage that only one weight sensing gate (threshold gate) is required. However, it has the disadvantage that the clock and timing circuitry is more complex than the Kasami decoder since 12 different digits must be inverted sequentially. Also, the Kasami decoder operates faster than the systematic search decoder.

This systematic search technique can be generalized for decoding other multiple-error-correcting cyclic codes.

PROBLEMS

5.1. Construct an encoding circuit for a (15,11) Hamming code generated by $\mathbf{g}(X) = 1 + X + X^4$.

5.2. Construct a decoding circuit for the code in Problem 5.1.

5.3. Use the decoder which you obtained in Problem 5.2 to decode the received vector $\mathbf{r}(X) = 1 + X + X^4 + X^{10}$.

5.4. Consider the $(2^m - 1, m)$ cyclic code generated by the parity-check polynomial $\mathbf{h}(X)$ of a $(2^m - 1, 2^m - m - 1)$ Hamming code. Let $\mathbf{v}(X)$ be a code vector and let $\mathbf{v}^{(i)}(X)$ be the code vector obtained by shifting $\mathbf{v}(X)$ cyclically i times.

(a) Show that, for $1 \leqslant i \leqslant 2^m - 2$, $\mathbf{v}(X) \neq \mathbf{v}^{(i)}(X)$.

(b) Show that the code contains an all-zero code vector and $2^m - 1$ code vectors of the same weight.

Hint: Use Eq. (4.5) and the fact that the smallest integer n such that $X^n + 1$ is divisible by a primitive polynomial $\mathbf{p}(X)$ of degree m is $2^m - 1$.

5.5. The circuit in Fig. 5.6 is a decoder for the (7,3) cyclic code generated by $\mathbf{g}(X) = 1 + X^2 + X^3 + X^4$. This decoder corrects single and double adjacent errors. Suppose that a certain code word was transmitted and $\mathbf{r}(X) = X^2 + X^3 + X^4 + X^6$ $[\mathbf{r} = (0\ 0\ 1\ 1\ 1\ 0\ 1)]$ is received.

(a) Find the contents in the syndrome register after the received vector has been read into the buffer.

(b) Find the contents in the syndrome register after each shift. Stop after a total of 8 shifts.

(c) Find the code vector at the output of the decoder. (The switch S is closed after the buffer register has shifted cyclically 7 times, and it is opened again after the contents of the buffer register have been shifted out.)

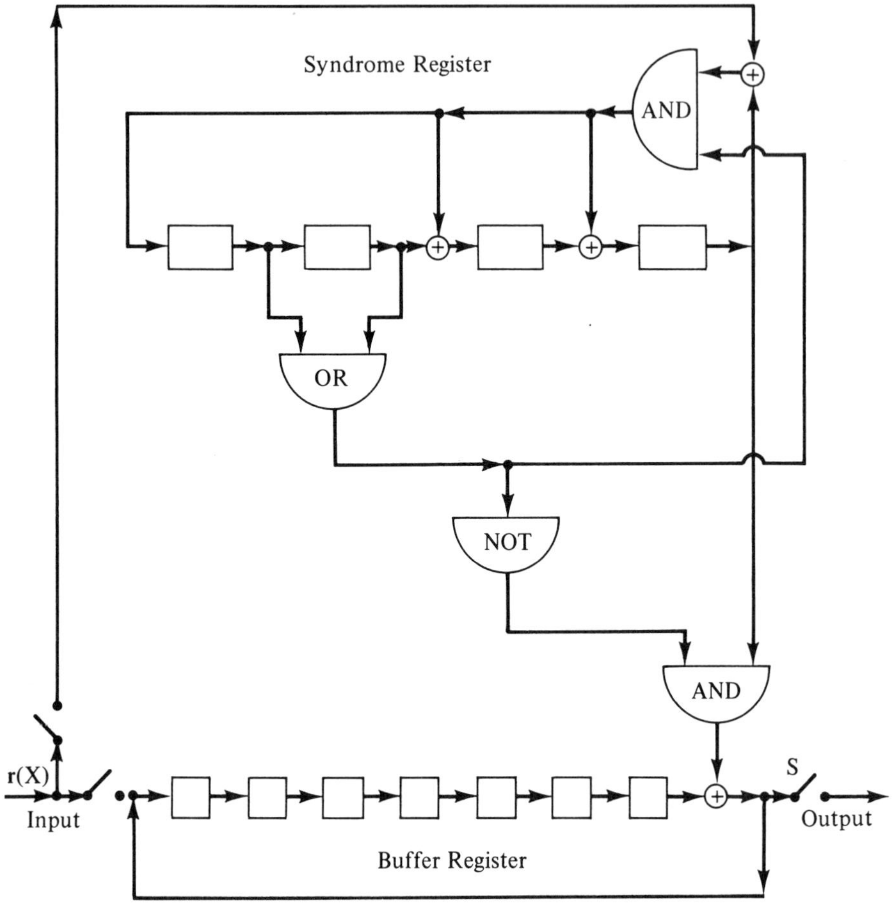

Fig. 5.6. A decoder for the single- and double-adjacent-error-correcting (7,3) cyclic code.

5.6. Since the (23,12) Golay code is a perfect code, its minimum distance is exactly 7.

(a) Show that there are code vectors of weight 16.

(b) Show that the number of code vectors of weight 7 is equal to the number of code vectors of weight 16.

5.7. Use the error-trapping decoder in Fig. 5.5 to decode the following received vectors:

(a) $\mathbf{r}(X) = X^{11} + X^{12} + X^{19}$.

(b) $\mathbf{r}(X) = X^{4} + X^{11} + X^{21}$.

(c) $\mathbf{r}(X) = X^{5} + X^{19}$.

At each step in the decoding process, write down the contents in the syndrome register.

REFERENCES

1. Abramson, N. M., "A Class of Systematic Codes for Non-Independent Errors," *IRE Trans. on Information Theory*, **IT-5**, pp. 150-157, December, 1959.
2. Abramson, N. M., and B. Elspas, "Double-Error-Correcting Encoders and Decoders for Non-Independent Binary Errors," presented at the UNESCO Information Processing Conference, Paris, France, 1959.
3. Abramson, N., "A Note on Single Error Correcting Binary Codes," *IRE Trans. on Information Theory*, **IT-6**, pp. 502-503, September, 1960.
4. Berlekamp, E. R., *Algebraic Coding Theory*, McGraw-Hill, New York, 1968.
5. Cocke, J., "Lossless Symbol Coding with Nonprimes," *IRE Trans. on Information Theory*, **IT-5**, pp. 33-34, March, 1959.
6. Elspas, B., "A Note on P-nary Adjacent-Error-Correcting Codes," *IRE Trans. on Information Theory*, **IT-6**, pp. 13-15, March, 1960.
7. Foata, D. C., "On a Program for Ray-Chaudhuri's Algorithm for a Minimum Cover of an Abstract Complex," *Comm. ACM*, **4**, pp. 504-506, November, 1961.
8. Golay, M. J. E., "Binary Coding," *IRE Trans. on Information Theory*, **IT-4**, pp. 23-28, September, 1954.

9. Golay, M. J. E., "Notes on Penny-Weighting Problem, Lossless Symbol Coding with Nonprimes, etc.," *IRE Trans. on Information Theory*, **IT-4**, pp. 103-109, 1958.

10. Golay, M. J. E., "Notes on Digital Coding," *Proc. IRE*, **37**, pp. 657, June, 1949.

11. Hamming, R. W., "Error Detecting and Error Correcting Codes," *Bell Systems Tech. J.*, **29**, pp. 147-160, April, 1950.

12. Kasami, T., "A Decoding Procedure for Multiple-Error-Correcting Cyclic Codes," *IEEE Trans. on Information Theory*, **IT-10**, pp. 134-139, April, 1964.

13. Lucky, R. W., J. Salz, and E. J. Weldon, Jr., *Principles of Data Communication*, McGraw-Hill, New York, 1968.

14. MacWilliams, F. J., "Permutation Decoding of Systematic Codes," *Bell Systems Tech. J.*, **43**, Part I, pp. 485-505, January, 1964.

15. Meggitt, J. E., "Error Correcting Codes and Their Implementation for Data Transmission Systems," *IEEE Trans. on Information Theory*, **IT-7**, pp. 234-244, October, 1961.

16. Mitchell, M. E., "Error-Trap Decoding of Cyclic Codes," G. E. Report No. 62MCD3, General Electric Military Communications Department, Oklahoma City, Oklahoma, December, 1962.

17. Mitchell, M. E., et al., "Coding and Decoding Operations Research," G. E. Advanced Electronics Final Report on Contract AF19(604)-6183, Air Force Cambridge Research Labs., Cambridge, Massachusetts, 1960.

18. Peterson, W. W., *Error-Correcting Codes*, The M.I.T. Press, Cambridge, Massachusetts, and John Wiley, New York, 1961.

19. Peterson, W. W., and E. J. Weldon, Jr., *Error-Correcting Codes*, 2nd Edition, The M.I.T. Press, Cambridge, Massachusetts, 1970.

20. Prange, E., "Cyclic Error-Correcting Codes in Two Symbols," AFCRC-TN-57-103, Air Force Cambridge Research Labs., Cambridge, Massachusetts, September, 1957.

21. Prange, E., "Some Cyclic Error-Correcting Codes with Simple Decoding Algorithms," AFCRC-TR-58-156, Air Force Cambridge Research Labs., Cambridge, Massachusetts, April, 1958.

22. Prange, E., "The Use of Coset Equivalence in the Analysis and Decoding of Group Codes," AFCRC-TR-59-164, Air Force Cambridge Research Labs., Cambridge, Massachusetts, June, 1959.

23. Prange, E., "The Use of Information Sets in Decoding Cyclic Codes," *IEEE Trans. on Information Theory*, **IT-8**, pp. 85-89, September, 1962.

24. Pyne, I. B., and E. J. McCluskey, "The Reduction of Redundancy in Solving Prime Implicant Tables," *IRE Trans. on Electronic Computers*, **EC-11**, pp. 473-482, August, 1962.

25. Rudolph, L., "Easily Implemented Error-Correction Encoding-Decoding," G. E. Report 62MCD2, General Electric Corporation, Oklahoma City, Oklahoma, December, 1962.

26. Rudolph, L., and M. E. Mitchell, "Implementation of Decoders for Cyclic Codes," *IEEE Trans. on Information Theory*, **IT-10**, pp. 259-260, July, 1964.

27. Stern, T. E., and B. Friedland, "Application of Modular Sequential Circuits to Single-Error-Correcting P-Nary Codes," *IRE Trans. on Information Theory*, **IT-5**, pp. 114-123, September, 1959.

28. Weldon, E. J., Jr., "A Comparison of an Interleaved Golay Code and a Three-Dimensional Product Code," Final Report, USNELC Contract N0095368M5345, August, 1968.

CHAPTER 6

BOSE-CHAUDHURI-HOCQUENGHEM CODES

Of the numerous classes of random-error-correcting codes proposed to date, the class discovered by Hocquenghem[17] in 1959 and independently by Bose and Chaudhuri[6,7] in 1960 is by far the most extensive and powerful one. The *BCH* codes are cyclic codes. They were first defined in binary symbols and then were generalized to codes in p^m symbols (where p is any prime and m is any positive integer) by Gorenstein and Zierler[15] in 1960. The first efficient decoding algorithm for binary *BCH* codes was devised by Peterson[28] in 1960. Since then, Peterson's algorithm has been generalized and refined by Gorenstein and Zierler,[15] Chien,[9] Berlekamp,[2,3,5] Forney[11] and Massey.[25,26]

In this chapter, we consider primarily a subclass of the binary *BCH* codes which is the most important subclass from the standpoint of both theory and implementation. Nonbinary *BCH* codes are discussed briefly. For a detailed description of the *BCH* codes and their decoding algorithms, the reader is particularly referred to References 5, 26, 29, and 32.

6.1 DESCRIPTION OF THE CODES

For any positive integers m and t $(t < 2^{m-1})$, there exists a Bose-Chaudhuri-Hocquenghem (*BCH*) code[6,7,17] with the following parameters:

Block length:	$n = 2^m - 1$
Number of parity-check digits:	$n - k \leqslant mt$
Minimum Distance:	$d \geqslant 2t + 1$.

Clearly, this code is capable of correcting any combination of t or fewer errors in a block of $n = 2^m$-1 digits. We shall call this code a t-error-correcting *BCH* code. The generator polynomial of this code is described as follows. Let α be a primitive element of the Galois field $GF(2^m)$. Consider the following sequence of consecutive powers of α:

$$\alpha, \alpha^2, \alpha^3, \ldots, \alpha^{2t} \quad . \tag{6.1}$$

Let $m_i(X)$ be the minimum polynomial of α^i. Then the generator polynomial of the t-error-correcting BCH code is the least common multiple of $m_1(X), m_2(X), \ldots, m_{2t}(X)$,[29] i.e.,

$$g(X) = \text{LCM}\,(m_1(X), m_2(X), \ldots, m_{2t}(X)) \quad . \tag{6.2}$$

Clearly, $\alpha, \alpha^2, \ldots, \alpha^{2t}$ are roots of $g(X)$, i.e., $g(\alpha^i) = 0$ for $i = 1, 2, \ldots, 2t$. If i is an even integer, it can be expressed as a product of the following form:

$$i = i' \, 2^{\ell} \quad ,$$

where i' is an odd integer and $\ell \geqslant 1$. It follows from the results in Section 2.1 that α^i and $\alpha^{i'}$ have the same minimum polynomial, i.e.,

$$m_i(X) = m_{i'}(X) \quad .$$

Therefore, every even power of α in the sequence of Eq. (6.1) has the same minimum polynomial as some previous odd power of α in the sequence. As a result, the generator polynomial of the t-error-correcting BCH given by Eq. (6.2) is reduced to

$$g(X) = \text{LCM}\,(m_1(X), m_3(X), \ldots, m_{2t-1}(X))^* \quad . \tag{6.3}$$

Since the degree of each minimum polynomial is m or less, the degree of $g(X)$ is at most mt. In other words, the number of parity-check digits, $n-k$, is at most equal to mt. There is no simple formula for calculating $n-k$, but if t is small, $n-k$ is exactly equal to mt.[4,5,24] The parameters for all binary BCH codes of length $2^m - 1$ with $m \leqslant 10$ are given in Table 6.1. For many

* The BCH code generated by $g(X)$ of Eq. (6.3) has been called a *narrow-sense* (or *primitive*) BCH code.

n	k	t
7	4	1
15	11	1
	7	2
	5	3
31	26	1
	21	2
	16	3
	11	5
	6	7
63	57	1
	51	2
	45	3
	39	4
	36	5
	30	6
	24	7
	18	10
	16	11
	10	13
	7	15
127	120	1
	113	2
	106	3
	99	4
	92	5
	85	6
	78	7
127	71	9
	64	10
	57	11
	50	13
	43	14
	36	15
	29	21
	22	23
	15	27
	8	31
255	247	1
	239	2
	231	3
	223	4
	215	5
	207	6
	199	7
	191	8
	187	9
	179	10
	171	11
	163	12
	155	13
	147	14
	139	15
	131	18
	123	19
	115	21
255	107	22
	99	23
	91	25
	87	26
	79	27
	71	29
	63	30
	55	31
	47	42
	45	43
	37	45
	29	47
	21	55
	13	59
	9	63
511	502	1
	493	2
	484	3
	475	4
	466	5
	457	6
	448	7
	439	8
	430	9
	421	10
	412	11
	403	12
	394	13
	385	14

Table 6.1.* ***BCH*** **codes generated by primitive elements of order less than** 2^{10}.

* Part of this table is taken from W. W. Peterson, *Error-Correcting Codes,* Table 9.1, p. 166, M.I.T. Press, 1961, by permission.

n	*k*	*t*
511	376	15
	367	16
	358	18
	349	19
	340	20
	331	21
	322	22
	313	23
	304	25
	295	26
	286	27
	277	28
	268	29
	259	30
	250	31
	241	36
	238	37
	229	38
	220	39
	211	41
	202	42
	193	43
	184	45
	175	46
	166	47
	157	51
	148	53
	139	54
	130	55
	121	58
	112	59
	103	61
511	94	62
	85	63
	76	85
	67	87
	58	91
	49	93
	40	95
	31	109
	28	111
	19	119
	10	121
1023	1013	1
	1003	2
	993	3
	983	4
	973	5
	963	6
	953	7
	943	8
	933	9
	923	10
	913	11
	903	12
	893	13
	883	14
	873	15
	863	16
	858	17
	848	18
	838	19
	828	20
1023	818	21
	808	22
	798	23
	788	24
	778	25
	768	26
	758	27
	748	28
	738	29
	728	30
	718	31
	708	34
	698	35
	688	36
	678	37
	668	38
	658	39
	648	41
	638	42
	628	43
	618	44
	608	45
	598	46
	588	47
	578	49
	573	50
	563	51
	553	52
	543	53
	533	54
	523	55
	513	57

Table 6.1. (cont'd.)

n	k	t	n	k	t	n	k	t
1023	503	58	1023	328	90	1023	153	125
	493	59		318	91		143	126
	483	60		308	93		133	127
	473	61		298	94		123	170
	463	62		288	95		121	171
	453	63		278	102		111	173
	443	73		268	103		101	175
	433	74		258	106		91	181
	423	75		248	107		86	183
	413	77		238	109		76	187
	403	78		228	110		66	189
	393	79		218	111		56	191
	383	82		208	115		46	219
	378	83		203	117		36	223
	368	85		193	118		26	239
	358	86		183	119		16	147
	348	87		173	122		11	255
	338	89		163	123			

Table 6.1. (cont'd.)

of these codes, the minimum distance has been shown to be exactly $2t + 1$.

The results described above can be best explained by examples. Let α be a primitive element of the Galois field $GF(2^4)$ given in Table 2.2 and let $\mathbf{m}_1(X)$, $\mathbf{m}_3(X)$, and $\mathbf{m}_5(X)$ be the minimum polynomials of α, α^3, and α^5 respectively. We shall use the technique described in Section 2.1 to find $\mathbf{m}_1(X)$, $\mathbf{m}_2(X)$, and $\mathbf{m}_5(X)$.† To find $\mathbf{m}_1(X)$, we first form the following sequence:

$$\alpha, \alpha^2, \alpha^{2^2} = \alpha^4, \alpha^{2^3} = \alpha^8, \alpha^{2^4} = \alpha^{16} = \alpha,$$

$$\alpha^{2^5} = \alpha^{32} = \alpha^2, \ldots .$$

In this sequence, there are only four distinct elements, $\alpha, \alpha^2, \alpha^4$, and α^8. Thus, $\mathbf{m}_1(X)$ has $\alpha, \alpha^2, \alpha^4$, and α^8 as all its roots, and

$$\mathbf{m}_1(X) = (X+\alpha)(X+\alpha^2)(X+\alpha^4)(X+\alpha^8) .$$

Multiplying with the aid of Table 2.2, we obtain

$$\mathbf{m}_1(X) = 1 + X + X^4 .$$

In the same manner, we can find that

$$\mathbf{m}_3(X) = 1 + X + X^2 + X^3 + X^4$$

$$\mathbf{m}_5(X) = 1 + X + X^2 .$$

According to Eq. (6.3), the double-error-correcting *BCH* code of length $n = 2^4 - 1 = 15$ is generated by

† Other methods of finding the minimum polynomial of a Galois field element can be found in References 5, 10, 13, and 29.

$$g(X) = \text{LCM}(m_1(X), m_3(X)) .$$

Since $m_1(X)$ and $m_2(X)$ are two distinct irreducible polynomials,

$$\begin{aligned} g(X) &= m_1(X)\, m_3(X) \\ &= (1+X+X^4)(1+X+X^2+X^3+X^4) \\ &= 1+X^4+X^6+X^7+X^8 . \end{aligned}$$

Thus, the code is a (15,7) cyclic code with minimum distance $d \geqslant 5$. Since the generator polynomial is a code polynomial of weight 5, the minimum distance of this code is exactly equal to 5. As another example, the triple-error-correcting *BCH* code of length $n = 15$ is generated by

$$\begin{aligned} g(X) &= \text{LCM}(m_1(X), m_3(X), m_5(X)) \\ &= m_1(X)\, m_3(X)\, m_5(X) \\ &= (1+X+X^4)(1+X+X^2+X^3+X^4)(1+X+X^2) \\ &= 1+X+X^2+X^4+X^5+X^8+X^{10} . \end{aligned}$$

This triple-error-correcting *BCH* code is a (15,5) cyclic code with minimum distance $d \geqslant 7$. Since the weight of the generator polynomial is 7, the minimum distance of this *BCH* code is exactly 7.

According to Eq. (6.3), the single-error-correcting *BCH* code of length $2^m - 1$ is generated by

$$g(X) = m_1(X) .$$

Since α is a primitive element of $GF(2^m)$, $m_1(X)$ is a primitive polynomial of degree m. Therefore, the Hamming code of length $n = 2^m - 1$ is the single-error-correcting *BCH* code of length $n = 2^m - 1$ for any positive integer $m \geqslant 3$.

Thus, the Hamming codes form a subclass of the (primitive) *BCH* codes. References 5, 12, 29, and 32 contain excellent expositions of *BCH* codes.

6.2 DECODING OF THE *BCH* CODES

Let

$$\mathbf{v}(X) = v_0 + v_1 X + v_2 X^2 + \ldots + v_{n-1} X^{n-1}$$

be the transmitted code vector and let

$$\mathbf{r}(X) = r_0 + r_1 X + r_2 X^2 + \ldots + r_{n-1} X^{n-1}$$

be the received vector. Then the error pattern added by the noisy channel is

$$\mathbf{e}(X) = \mathbf{r}(X) + \mathbf{v}(X) \quad . \tag{6.4}$$

As usual, the first step of decoding a code is to calculate the syndrome from the received vector $\mathbf{r}(X)$. For decoding a *BCH* code, the syndrome is defined as a vector $\mathbf{S}$ with $2t$ components as follows:[28, 29]

$$\begin{aligned} \mathbf{S}_i &= \mathbf{r}(\alpha^i) \\ &= r_0 + r_1\alpha^i + r_2(\alpha^i)^2 + \ldots + r_{n-1}(\alpha^i)^{n-1} \end{aligned} \tag{6.5}$$

for $i = 1, 2, \ldots, 2t$. Combining Eqs. (6.4) and (6.5), we obtain

$$\mathbf{S}_i = \mathbf{v}(\alpha^i) + \mathbf{e}(\alpha^i)$$

for $i = 1, 2, \ldots, 2t$. Since $\alpha^1, \alpha^2, \ldots, \alpha^{2t}$ are roots of the code polynomial $\mathbf{v}(X)$ ($\mathbf{v}(\alpha^i) = 0$ for $i = 1, 2, \ldots, 2t$), then

$$\mathbf{S}_i = \mathbf{e}(\alpha^i) \tag{6.6}$$

for $i = 1, 2, \ldots, 2t$. Assume that $\mathbf{e}(X)$ is an error pattern of ν errors, say

$$\mathbf{e}(X) = X^{j_1} + X^{j_2} + \ldots + X^{j_\nu} \ . \tag{6.7}$$

It follows from Eq. (6.6) that we have

$$\begin{aligned} \mathbf{S}_1 &= \alpha^{j_1} + \alpha^{j_2} + \ldots + \alpha^{j_\nu} \\ \mathbf{S}_2 &= (\alpha^{j_1})^2 + (\alpha^{j_2})^2 + \ldots + (\alpha^{j_\nu})^2 \\ \mathbf{S}_3 &= (\alpha^{j_1})^3 + (\alpha^{j_2})^3 + \ldots + (\alpha^{j_\nu})^3 \\ &\vdots \\ \mathbf{S}_{2t} &= (\alpha^{j_1})^{2t} + (\alpha^{j_2})^{2t} + \ldots + (\alpha^{j_\nu})^{2t} \ . \end{aligned} \tag{6.8}$$

Any error correction procedure is a method of solving this set of equations for $\alpha^{j_1}, \alpha^{j_2}, \ldots, \alpha^{j_\nu}$. Once $\alpha^{j_1}, \alpha^{j_2}, \ldots, \alpha^{j_\nu}$ have been found, then the powers $j_1, j_2, \ldots, j_\nu$ will tell us the error locations in $\mathbf{e}(X)$ as in Eq. (6.7). In general, these equations have many (but finite) possible solutions. Each solution yields a different error pattern. If the number of errors in the actual error pattern $\mathbf{e}(X)$ is t or less $(\nu \leqslant t)$, then the solution which yields an error pattern with the smallest number of errors is the right solution. The error pattern corresponding to this solution is the actual error pattern $\mathbf{e}(X)$ caused by the channel noise. For large t, solving the above equations for α^{j_ℓ} is difficult and ineffective. In the following, we shall describe an effective procedure to determine α^{j_ℓ} from the syndrome components $\mathbf{S}_i$'s. For convenience, we call

$$\beta_\ell = \alpha^{j_\ell} \quad \text{for} \quad 1 \leqslant \ell \leqslant \nu \tag{6.9}$$

the *error location numbers*.[28,29] Now Eq. (6.9) can be expressed in the following form:

$$\begin{aligned}
\mathbf{S}_1 &= \beta_1 + \beta_2 + \ldots + \beta_\nu \\
\mathbf{S}_2 &= \beta_1^2 + \beta_2^2 + \ldots + \beta_\nu^2 \\
&\vdots \\
\mathbf{S}_{2t} &= \beta_1^{2t} + \beta_2^{2t} + \ldots + \beta_\nu^{2t} \; .
\end{aligned} \tag{6.10}$$

These $2t$ syndrome components are symmetric functions in $\beta_1, \beta_2, \ldots, \beta_\nu$, which are known as *power-sum symmetric functions*.

Define the *error location polynomial*[28, 29] as follows:

$$\begin{aligned}
\sigma(X) &= (1+\beta_1 X)(1+\beta_2 X)\ldots(1+\beta_\nu X) \\
&= \sigma_0 + \sigma_1 X + \sigma_2 X^2 + \ldots + \sigma_\nu X^\nu
\end{aligned} \tag{6.11}$$

where

$$\begin{aligned}
\sigma_0 &= 1 \\
\sigma_1 &= \beta_1 + \beta_2 + \ldots + \beta_\nu \\
\sigma_2 &= \beta_1\beta_2 + \beta_1\beta_3 + \ldots + \beta_{\nu-1}\beta_\nu \\
&\vdots \\
\sigma_\nu &= \beta_1\beta_2 \ldots \beta_\nu \; .
\end{aligned} \tag{6.12}$$

The roots of $\sigma(X)$ are $\beta_1^{-1}, \beta_2^{-1}, \ldots, \beta_\nu^{-1}$, which are the inverses of error location numbers. It is clear from Eqs. (6.10) and (6.12) that the coefficients of $\sigma(X)$ are related to the syndrome components $\mathbf{S}_i$ for $i = 1, 2, \ldots 2t$. Therefore, if it is possible to find $\sigma(X)$ from $\mathbf{S}_i$'s, then the error location numbers can be found and the error pattern $\mathbf{e}(X)$ can be determined. The coefficients $\sigma_1, \sigma_2, \ldots, \sigma_\nu$ are known as *elementary symmetric functions* of $\beta_1, \beta_2, \ldots, \beta_\nu$. At this point, it would be appropriate to outline the error-correcting procedure. The procedure consists of three major steps:[28, 29]

(1) Calculate the syndrome $\mathbf{S} = (\mathbf{S}_1, \mathbf{S}_2, \ldots, \mathbf{S}_{2t})$ from the received vector $\mathbf{r}(X)$.

(2) Find the error location polynomial $\sigma(X)$ from $\mathbf{S}_1, \mathbf{S}_2, \ldots, \mathbf{S}_{2t}$.

(3) Determine the error location numbers β_j by finding the roots of $\sigma(X)$.

Step 1 has been explained at the beginning of this section. In the following, we shall describe Steps 2 and 3. Step 2 is the most difficult part of decoding a *BCH* code.

An Iterative Algorithm for Finding the Error Location Polynomial $\sigma(X)$

This algorithm is credited to Berlekamp.[3,5] In the following, we shall simply describe the algorithm without giving any proof. The reader who is interested in the details of this algorithm is referred to References 5, 12, 26, and 32.

To find $\sigma(X)$, we begin with the table

μ	$\sigma^{(\mu)}(X)$	d_μ	ℓ_μ	$\mu - \ell_\mu$
-1	1	1	0	-1
0	1	$\mathbf{S}_1$	0	0
1				
2				
$\vdots$				
$2t$				

Table 6.2

and proceed to fill out the table. Assuming that we have filled out all rows up to and including the μth row, we fill out the $(\mu+1)^{\text{th}}$ row as follows:

(1) If $d_\mu = 0$, then $\sigma^{(\mu+1)}(X) = \sigma^{(\mu)}(X)$ and $\ell_{\mu+1} = \ell_\mu$.

(2) If $d_\mu \neq 0$, find another row preceding the μth row, say the ρth row, such that the number $\rho - \ell_\rho$ in the last column of the table has the largest value and $d_\rho \neq 0$. Then

$$\sigma^{(\mu+1)}(X) = \sigma^{(\mu)}(X) - d_\mu d_\rho^{-1} X^{\mu-\rho} \sigma^{(\rho)}(X) \quad , \tag{6.13}$$

and

$$\ell_{\mu+1} = \max\,[\ell_\mu, \ell_\rho + \mu - \rho] \quad . \tag{6.14}$$

In either case,

$$d_{\mu+1} = \mathbf{S}_{\mu+2} + \sigma_1^{(\mu+1)} \mathbf{S}_{\mu+1} + \ldots + \sigma_{\ell_{\mu+1}}^{(\mu+1)} \mathbf{S}_{\mu+2-\ell_{\mu+1}} \quad , \tag{6.15}$$

where the $\sigma_i^{(\mu+1)}$ are the coefficients of $\sigma^{(\mu+1)}(X)$,

$$\sigma^{(\mu+1)}(X) = 1 + \sigma_1^{(\mu+1)} X + \sigma_2^{(\mu+1)} X^2 + \ldots + \sigma_{\ell_{\mu+1}}^{(\mu+1)} X^{\ell_{\mu+1}} \quad . \tag{6.16}$$

The polynomial $\sigma^{(2t)}(X)$ in the last row should be the required $\sigma(X)$. If it has degree greater than t, there were more than t errors, and generally it is not possible to locate them.

In the following, an example of computation is given for the triple-error-correcting code of length $2^4-1 = 15$ considered in Section 6.1. Assume that the code vector of all zeros

$$\mathbf{v} = (0\,0\,0\,\ldots\,0)$$

is transmitted and the vector

$$\mathbf{r} = (0\,0\,0\,1\,0\,1\,0\,0\,0\,0\,0\,0\,1\,0\,0)$$

is received. Then $\mathbf{r}(X) = X^3 + X^5 + X^{12}$. By Eq. (6.5), we obtain

$$S_1 = r(\alpha) = \alpha^3 + \alpha^5 + \alpha^{12} = 1$$

$$S_2 = r(\alpha^2) = \alpha^6 + \alpha^{10} + \alpha^{24} = \alpha^6 + \alpha^{10} + \alpha^9 = 1$$

$$S_3 = r(\alpha^3) = \alpha^9 + \alpha^{15} + \alpha^{36} = \alpha^9 + 1 + \alpha^6 = \alpha^{10}$$

$$S_4 = r(\alpha^4) = \alpha^{12} + \alpha^{20} + \alpha^{48} = \alpha^{12} + \alpha^5 + \alpha^3 = 1$$

$$S_5 = r(\alpha^5) = \alpha^{15} + \alpha^{25} + \alpha^{60} = 1 + \alpha^{10} + 1 = \alpha^{10}$$

$$S_6 = r(\alpha^6) = \alpha^{18} + \alpha^{30} + \alpha^{72} = \alpha^3 + 1 + \alpha^{12} = \alpha^5 .$$

By the iterative procedure described above, we obtain the following table:

μ	$\sigma^{(\mu)}(X)$	d_μ	ℓ_μ	$\mu - \ell_\mu$
-1	1	1	0	-1
0	1	1	0	0
1	$1+X$	0	1	0 (Take $\rho = -1$)
2	$1+X$	α^5	1	1
3	$1+X+\alpha^5X^2$	0	2	1 (Take $\rho = 0$)
4	$1+X+\alpha^5X^2$	α^{10}	2	2
5	$1+X+\alpha^5X^3$	0	3	2 (Take $\rho = 2$)
6	$1+X+\alpha^5X^3$	--	3	3

Table 6.3

Thus, the error location polynomial is

$$\sigma(X) = \sigma^{(6)}(X) = 1 + X + \alpha^5 X^3 .$$

The algorithm for finding $\sigma(X)$ described above not only applies to binary *BCH* codes but also applies to nonbinary *BCH* codes.

A Simplified Algorithm for Finding $\sigma(X)$

For binary *BCH* codes, it is not necessary to fill out the empty $2t$ rows of Table 6.2 for finding $\sigma(X)$. A simplified algorithm[5,26,32] can be obtained that requires filling out a table with only t empty rows. This table is as follows:

μ	$\sigma^{(\mu)}(X)$	d_μ	ℓ_μ	$2\mu - \ell_\mu$
$-1/2$	1	1	0	-1
0	1	S_1	0	0
1				
2				
.				
.				
.				
t				

Table 6.4

Assuming that we have filled out all rows up to and including the μth row, we fill out the $(\mu+1)^{th}$ row as follows:

(1) If $d_\mu = 0$, then $\sigma^{(\mu+1)}(X) = \sigma^{(\mu)}(X)$.

(2) If $d_\mu \neq 0$, find another two preceding the μth, say the ρth, such that the number $2\rho - \ell_\rho$ in the last column is as large as possible and $d_\rho \neq 0$. Then

$$\sigma^{(\mu+1)}(X) = \sigma^{(\mu)}(X) + d_\mu d_\rho^{-1} X^{2(\mu-\rho)} \sigma^{(\rho)}(X) .$$

In either case, $\ell_{\mu+1}$ is exactly the degree of $\sigma^{(\mu+1)}(X)$, and

$$d_{\mu+1} = S_{2\mu+3} + \sigma^{(\mu+1)} S_{2\mu+2} + \sigma_2^{(\mu+1)} S_{2\mu+1} + \ldots + \sigma_{\ell_{\mu+1}}^{(\mu+1)} S_{2\mu+3-\ell_{\mu+1}} . \tag{6.17}$$

The polynomial $\sigma^{(t)}(X)$ in the last line should be the required $\sigma(X)$. If it has degree greater than t, there were more than t errors, and generally it is not possible to locate them. The simplified table for the previous example is as follows:

μ	$\sigma^{(\mu)}(X)$	d_μ	ℓ_μ	$2\mu - \ell_\mu$
$-\frac{1}{2}$	1	1	0	-1
0	1	$S_1 = 1$	0	0
1	$1+S_1X = 1+X$	$S_3+S_2S_1 = \alpha^5$	1	1 (Take $\rho = -\frac{1}{2}$)
2	$1+X+\alpha^5X^2$	α^{10}	2	2 (Take $\rho = 0$)
3	$1+X+\alpha^5X^3$	--	3	3 (Take $\rho = 1$)

It is clear that $\sigma(X) = \sigma^{(3)}(X) = 1 + X + \alpha^5 X^5$, which is identical to the solution found in the previous example. Thus, the computation required in this simplified algorithm is one-half of the computation required in the general algorithm. We must remember that the simplified algorithm applies only to binary *BCH* codes.

Calculation of Error Locations and Error Correction

The last step in decoding a *BCH* code is to find the error location numbers which are the reciprocals of the roots of $\sigma(X)$. The roots of $\sigma(X)$ can be found simply by substituting $1, \alpha, \alpha^2, \ldots, \alpha^{n-1}$ $(n = 2^m - 1)$ into $\sigma(X)$. Since $\alpha^n = 1$, $\alpha^{-\ell} = \alpha^{n-\ell}$. Therefore, if α^ℓ is a root of $\sigma(X)$, $\alpha^{n-\ell}$ is an error location number and the received digit $r_{n-\ell}$ is an erroneous digit. Consider the previous example. The error location polynomial has been found to be

$$\sigma(X) = 1 + X + \alpha^5 X^3 .$$

By substituting $1, \alpha, \alpha^2, \ldots, \alpha^{14}$ into $\sigma(X)$, we find that α^3, α^{10}, and α^{12} are roots of $\sigma(X)$. Therefore, the error location numbers are α^{12}, α^5, and α^3.

The error pattern is

$$\mathbf{e}(X) = X^3 + X^5 + X^{12} ,$$

which is exactly the assumed error pattern. The decoding of the code is completed by adding (modulo-2) $\mathbf{e}(X)$ to the received vector $\mathbf{r}(X)$.

A procedure credited to Chien[9] and used for testing error locations is described in the following. The received vector $\mathbf{r}(X) = r_0 + r_1X + r_2X^2 + \ldots + r_{n-1}X^{n-1}$ is decoded on a bit-by-bit basis. The high-order bits are decoded first. To decode r_{n-1}, the decoder tests whether α^{n-1} is an error location number; this is equivalent to testing whether α is a root of $\sigma(X)$. If α is a root, we have

$$\sigma_0 + \sigma_1\alpha + \sigma_2\alpha^2 + \ldots + \sigma_\nu\alpha^\nu = 0 .$$

Since $\sigma_0 = 1$,

$$\sigma_1\alpha + \sigma_2\alpha^2 + \ldots + \sigma_\nu\alpha^\nu = 1 .$$

Therefore, to decode r_{n-1}, the decoder forms $\sigma_1\alpha, \sigma_2\alpha^2, \ldots, \sigma_\nu\alpha^\nu$. If the sum $\sigma_1\alpha + \sigma_2\alpha^2 + \ldots + \sigma_\nu\alpha^\nu$ is 1, then α^{n-1} is an error location number and r_{n-1} is an erroneous digit; otherwise, r_{n-1} is a correct digit. To decode $r_{n-\ell}$, the decoder forms $\sigma_1\alpha^\ell, \sigma_2\alpha^{2\ell}, \ldots, \sigma_\nu\alpha^{\nu\ell}$ and tests the sum

$$\sigma_1\alpha^\ell + \sigma_2\alpha^{2\ell} + \ldots + \sigma_\nu\alpha^{\nu\ell} .$$

If this sum is equal to 1, then α^ℓ is a root of $\sigma(X)$ and $r_{n-\ell}$ is an erroneous digit; otherwise, $r_{n-\ell}$ is a correct digit.

The testing procedure for error locations described above can be implemented in a straightforward manner by a circuit such as that shown in Fig. 6.1.[9] The t σ-registers are initially stored with $\sigma_1, \sigma_2, \ldots, \sigma_t$ calculated in Step 2 of the decoding ($\sigma_{\nu+1} = \sigma_{\nu+2} = \ldots = \sigma_t = 0$ for $\nu < t$).

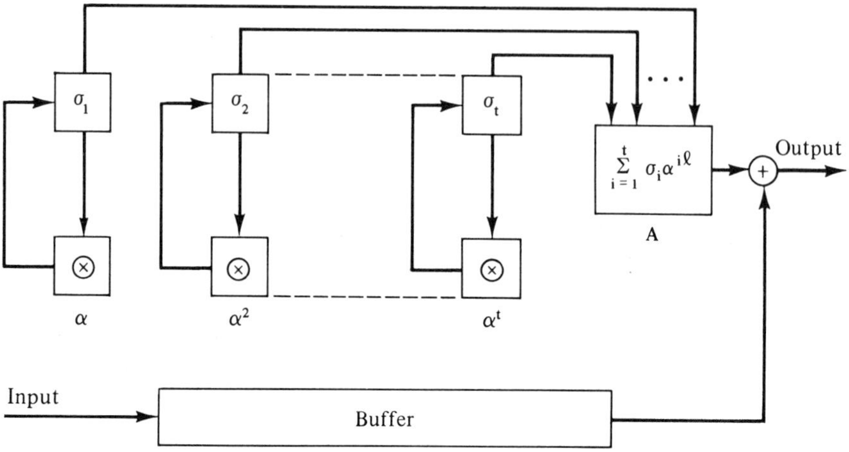

Fig. 6.1. Cyclic error location unit.

Immediately before $r_{n\text{-}1}$ is read out of the buffer, the t multipliers X are pulsed once. The multiplications are performed and $\sigma_1\alpha$, $\sigma_2\alpha^2, \ldots, \sigma_\nu\alpha^\nu$ are stored in the σ-registers. The output of the logic circuit A is 1 if and only if the sum $\sigma_1\alpha + \sigma_2\alpha^2 + \ldots + \sigma_\nu\alpha^\nu = 1$; otherwise, the output of A is 0. The digit $r_{n\text{-}1}$ is read out of the buffer and corrected by the output of A. Having decoded $r_{n\text{-}1}$, the t multipliers are pulsed again. Now $\sigma_1\alpha^2$, $\sigma_2\alpha^4$, $\sigma_\nu\alpha^{2\nu}$ are stored in the σ-registers. The sum

$$\sigma_1\alpha^2 + \sigma_2\alpha^4 + \ldots + \sigma_\nu\alpha^{2\nu}$$

is tested for 1. The digit $r_{n\text{-}2}$ is read out of the buffer and corrected in the same manner as $r_{n\text{-}1}$ was corrected. This process continues until the whole received vector is read out of the buffer.

From the above discussion, we see that the decoding of *BCH* codes requires computations which use Galois field arithmetic. Galois field arithmetic can be implemented more easily than ordinary arithmetic because there are no carries. Addition of field symbols is done as described in Chapter 2. This is the same as the "Exclusive-OR" instruction which is built into most modern computers and requires m "Exclusive-OR" gates. Multiplication can be done in several ways:

(1) For m up to about 7, it can be implemented in a $2m$-input m-output combinational logic circuit.

(2) A multiply unit similar to, but simpler than, multiplying circuits for ordinary arithmetic can be built. It requires the same number of steps as ordinary multiplication but may be faster because there are no carries.

(3) The equivalent procedure can be programmed – it would require roughly $5m$ instruction executions.

(4) It can be done by a simple table look-up process that requires two tables with 2^{m+1} symbols in each table.

Subtraction is the same as addition. Division is done by using the fact that, for any non-zero byte β, $\beta^{-1} = \beta^{2^m-2}$; this can be computed by multiplying.

6.3 IMPLEMENTATION OF ERROR CORRECTION

Each step in the decoding of a *BCH* code as described in Section 6.2 can be implemented either by digital hardware or by software (programmed on a general-purpose computer). Each implementation has certain advantages. In the following, we consider both kinds of implementations.

Step 1. To compute the syndrome components $\mathbf{S}_1, \mathbf{S}_2, \ldots, \mathbf{S}_{2t}$, the field elements $\alpha, \alpha^2, \ldots, \alpha^{2t}$ are substituted into the received polynomial $\mathbf{r}(X) = r_{n-1}X^{n-1} + r_{n-2}X^{n-2} + \ldots + r_1X + r_0$. For software implementation, substituting into a polynomial is best accomplished in the following form:

$$AX^3 + BX^2 + CX + D \quad = \quad ((AX+B)X + C)X + D \quad .$$

For a polynomial of degree $n-1$, $n-1$ additions and $n-1$ multiplications are required. For binary codes, it can be shown that $\mathbf{S}_{2i} = \mathbf{S}_i^{\,2}$. With this equality, the $2t$ $\mathbf{S}_i$ can be computed with $(n-1)t$ additions and nt multiplications.

These $\mathbf{S}_i$ can also be computed by feedback shift registers. In view of the equality $\mathbf{S}_{2i} = \mathbf{S}_i{}^2$, it is sufficient to calculate $\mathbf{S}_1, \mathbf{S}_3, \mathbf{S}_5, \ldots \mathbf{S}_{2t\text{-}1}$. Each requires an m-stage shift register with multiple feedback connections. The advantage of this method is speed.

Step 2. For this step the software computation requires somewhat less than t additions and t multiplications to compute each $\sigma^{(\mu)}(X)$ and each d_μ, and since there are t of each, the total is roughly $2t^2$ additions and $2t^2$ multiplications. A pure hardware implementation requires the same total, and speed would depend upon how much is done in parallel. A very fast hardware implementation of this step would probably be very expensive, whereas a simple hardware implementation would probably be organized much like a general-purpose computer, except with a wired rather than a stored program.

Step 3. In the worse case, this step requires substituting n numbers in a degree-t polynomial. In software this requires $n(t-1)$ multiplications and nt additions. This can also be done in hardware, as shown in Fig. 6.1, where each multiplier is an m-stage feedback shift register. The circuit A for detecting the condition $\sum_{i=1}^{t} \sigma_i \alpha^{i\ell} = 1$ consists of a simple adder, an m-input OR gate, and an inverter. The adder consists of m t-input modulo-2 adders. The t σ-registers are part of the hardware in Step 2.

Steps 1 and 3 involve roughly the same amount of computation. Since n is generally much larger than t, $4nt$ is much larger than $4t^2$, and Steps 1 and 3 involve most of the computation. Thus, the hardware implementation of these steps can be quite important. With hardware implementation, Step 1 can be done as data is read in and Step 3 as it is being read out, and in this case the computation time required in Steps 1 and 3 is essentially negligible. Table 6.5 gives some rough comparisons assuming that the computer instruction times are 2 μsec for addition and 2 μsec for multiplication and that in addition to the multiplications and additions, an equal number of other 2 μsec instructions are needed. These computations indicate that a small computer with a 1 μsec memory programmed for a code up to $n = 1023$ and $t = 10$ can correct several thousand bits per second. Also, the speed can be increased by almost two orders of magnitude if the syndrome computation and the final error correction step are done with shift registers.

Code	(127,92) 5-error-correcting	(1023,923) 10-error-correcting
Step 1	13,060 μsec	132,990 μsec
Step 2	1,000 μsec	5,200 μsec
Step 3	12,171 μsec	122,760 μsec
Total	26,231 μsec	260,950 μsec
Bits per second, complete software implementation (n/Total time))	4,800	3,900
Bits per second, Steps 1 and 3 hardware and Step 2 software (n/(Step 2 time))	127,000	190,000

Table 6.5. Rough estimates of time for *BCH* correction by computer.

6.4 NONBINARY *BCH* CODES AND REED-SOLOMON CODES

In addition to the binary codes, there are nonbinary codes. In fact, if p is a prime number and q is any power of p, there are codes with code symbols from a q-symbol alphabet. These codes are called *q-ary codes*. For any choice of positive integers s and t there exists a q-ary *BCH* code[15] of length $n = q^s - 1$ which corrects any combination of t or fewer errors and requires no more than $2st$ parity-check digits. For details of q-ary *BCH* codes, the reader is referred to References 5, 15, 29, 32, and 35.

The special subclass of q-ary *BCH* codes for which $s = 1$ is the well known class of *Reed-Solomon codes.*[33] A t-error-correcting Reed-Solomon code has the following parameters:

Block length:	$n = q - 1$
Number of parity digits:	$n - k = 2t$
Minimum distance:	$d = 2t + 1$

In the following, we shall consider Reed-Solomon codes with code symbols from the Galois field $GF(2^m)$, i.e., $q = 2^m$. The generator polynomial of a t-error-correcting Reed-Solomon code of length 2^m-1 is

$$\mathbf{g}(X) = (X+\alpha)(X+\alpha^2)\ldots(X+\alpha^{2t}) , \qquad (6.18)$$

where α is a primitive element of $GF(2^m)$. Let

$$\mathbf{v}(X) = v_0 + v_1 X + v_2 X^2 + \ldots + v_{n-1} X^{n-1}$$

be the transmitted code vector and let

$$\mathbf{r}(X) = r_0 + r_1 X + r_2 X^2 + \ldots + r_{n-1} X^{n-1}$$

be the received vector. Then the error pattern added by the channel is

$$\mathbf{e}(X) = e_0 + e_1 X + e_2 X^2 + \ldots + e_{n-1} X^{n-1}$$

$$= \mathbf{r}(X) - \mathbf{v}(X) ,$$

where $e_i = r_i - v_i$ is a symbol from $GF(2^m)$. Suppose that the error pattern $\mathbf{e}(X)$ contains $\nu \leqslant t$ errors (non-zero components) at positions X^{j_1}, X^{j_2}, X^{j_ν}, where $0 \leqslant j_1 < j_2 < \ldots < j_\nu \leqslant n-1$. Then

$$\mathbf{e}(X) = e_{j_1} X^{j_1} + e_{j_2} X^{j_2} + \ldots + e_{j_\nu} X^{j_\nu} .$$

Thus, in order to specify $\mathbf{e}(X)$, we need to know the error locations j_ℓ and the error values e_{j_ℓ}. As with binary codes, we define

$$\beta_\ell = \alpha^{j_\ell} \text{ for } \ell = 1, 2, \ldots, \nu$$

as error location numbers. In decoding a Reed-Solomon code (or any q-ary *BCH* code), the same three steps used for decoding a binary *BCH* code are required; in addition, a fourth step involving calculation of the error values is required. The error value at the location corresponding to β_ℓ is given by the following equation:

$$e_{j_\ell} = \frac{\mathbf{Z}(\beta_\ell^{-1})}{\prod_{\substack{i=1 \\ i \neq \ell}}^{\nu} (1 + \beta_i \beta_\ell^{-1})} , \qquad (6.19)$$

where

$$\mathbf{Z}(X) = 1 + (\mathbf{S}_1 + \sigma_1)X + (\mathbf{S}_2 + \sigma_1 \mathbf{S}_1 + \sigma_2)X^2 + \ldots$$

$$+ (\mathbf{S}_\nu + \sigma_1 \mathbf{S}_{\nu-1} + \sigma_2 \mathbf{S}_{\nu-2} + \ldots + \sigma_\nu) X^\nu \ . \qquad (6.20)$$

The decoding computation for a Reed-Solomon code is best explained by an example. Consider a triple-error-correcting Reed-Solomon code with symbols from $GF(2^4)$. The generator polynomial of this code is

$$\mathbf{g}(X) = (X + \alpha)(X + \alpha^2)(X + \alpha^3)(X + \alpha^4)(X + \alpha^5)(X + \alpha^6)$$

$$= \alpha^4 + \alpha^{10} X + \alpha^3 X^2 + \alpha^9 X^3 + \alpha^9 X^4 + \alpha^3 X^5 + X^6 \ .$$

Let the all-zero vector be the transmitted code vector and let $\mathbf{r} = (0\ 0\ 0\ \alpha^7\ 0\ 0\ \alpha^3\ 0\ 0\ 0\ 0\ 0\ \alpha^4\ 0\ 0)$ be the received vector. Thus, $\mathbf{r}(X) = \alpha^7 X^3 + \alpha^3 X^6 + \alpha^4 X^{12}$.

Step 1. The syndrome components are computed as follows (use Table 2.2):

$$
\begin{aligned}
\mathbf{S}_1 &= \mathbf{r}(\alpha) &&= \alpha^{10} + \alpha^9 + \alpha &&= \alpha^{12} \\
\mathbf{S}_2 &= \mathbf{r}(\alpha^2) &&= \alpha^{13} + 1 + \alpha^{13} &&= 1 \\
\mathbf{S}_3 &= \mathbf{r}(\alpha^3) &&= \alpha + \alpha^6 + \alpha^{10} &&= \alpha^{14} \\
\mathbf{S}_4 &= \mathbf{r}(\alpha^4) &&= \alpha^4 + \alpha^{12} + \alpha^7 &&= \alpha^{10} \\
\mathbf{S}_5 &= \mathbf{r}(\alpha^5) &&= \alpha^7 + \alpha^3 + \alpha^4 &&= 0 \\
\mathbf{S}_6 &= \mathbf{r}(\alpha^6) &&= \alpha^{10} + \alpha^9 + \alpha &&= \alpha^{12} \ .
\end{aligned}
$$

Step 2. To find the error location polynomial $\sigma(X)$, we fill out Table 6.2 as follows:

μ	$\sigma^{(\mu)}(X)$	d_μ	ℓ_μ	$\mu - \ell_\mu$
-1	1	1	0	-1
0	1	α^{12}	0	1
1	$1+\alpha^{12}X$	α^7	1	0 (Take $\rho = -1$)
2	$1+\alpha^3X$	1	1	1 (Take $\rho = 0$)
3	$1+\alpha^3X+\alpha^3X^2$	α^7	2	1 (Take $\rho = 0$)
4	$1+\alpha^4X+\alpha^{12}X^2$	α^{10}	2	2 (Take $\rho = 2$)
5	$1+\alpha^7X+\alpha^4X^2+\alpha^6X^3$	0	3	2 (Take $\rho = 3$)
6	$1+\alpha^7X+\alpha^4X^2+\alpha^6X^3$	--	--	--

Thus, $\sigma(X) = 1 + \alpha^7X + \alpha^4X^2 + \alpha^6X^3$.

Step 3. By substituting $1, \alpha, \alpha^2, \ldots, \alpha^{14}$ into $\sigma(X)$, we find that α^3, α^9, and α^{12} are roots of $\sigma(X)$. The reciprocals of these roots are α^{12}, α^6, and α^3, which are the error location numbers of the error pattern $\mathbf{e}(X)$. Thus, errors occur at positions X^3, X^6, and X^{12}.

Step 4. By Eq. (6.19), we obtain

$$e_3 = \frac{1+\alpha^2\alpha^{-3}+\alpha^{-6}+\alpha^6\alpha^{-9}}{(1+\alpha^6\alpha^{-3})\,(1+\alpha^{12}\alpha^{-3})}$$

$$= \frac{1+\alpha^{14}+\alpha^9+\alpha^{12}}{\alpha^{14}\alpha^7} = \frac{\alpha^{13}}{\alpha^6}$$

$$= \alpha^7$$

$$e_6 = \frac{1+\alpha^2\alpha^{-6}+\alpha^{-12}+\alpha^6\alpha^{-18}}{(1+\alpha^3\alpha^{-6})\,(1+\alpha^{12}\alpha^{-6})}$$

$$= \frac{1+\alpha^{11}+\alpha^3+\alpha^3}{\alpha^9} = \frac{\alpha^{12}}{\alpha^9} = \alpha^3$$

$$e_{12} = \frac{1+\alpha^2\alpha^{-12}+\alpha^{-24}+\alpha^6\alpha^{-36}}{(1+\alpha^3\alpha^{-12})\,(1+\alpha^6\alpha^{-12})}$$

$$= \frac{1+\alpha^5+\alpha^6+1}{\alpha^5} = \frac{\alpha^9}{\alpha^5} = \alpha^4 \;.$$

Thus, the error pattern is

$$\mathbf{e}(X) = \alpha^7X^3 + \alpha^3X^6 + \alpha^4X^{12} \;,$$

which is exactly the difference between the received vector and the transmitted vector. The decoding is completed by taking $\mathbf{r}(X) - \mathbf{e}(X)$.

PROBLEMS

6.1. The polynomial $\mathbf{p}(X) = 1 + X^2 + X^5$ is a primitive polynomial of degree 5. Assuming that $\mathbf{p}(\alpha) = 0$, construct the table of Galois field of 2^5 elements, $GF(2^5)$, similar to Table 2.2.

6.2. Let α be a primitive element in $GF(2^5)$. Find the minimum polynomials of α and α^3.

6.3. Find the generator polynomial of a double-error-correcting $(t = 2)$ *BCH* code of length 31.

6.4. Suppose that the code which you obtained in Problem 6.3 is used. Use the decoding method described in Section 6.2 to decode the received vector $\mathbf{r}(X) = X + X^7$.

6.5. Find the generator polynomial of a triple-error-correcting *BCH* code of length 31. Suppose this code is used for error control purposes. Decode the received vector $\mathbf{r}(X) = 1 + X + X^{11}$.

6.6. Find the generator polynomial of a double-error-correcting Reed-Solomon code with symbols from $GF(2^5)$. Suppose that a certain code word in this code was transmitted and $\mathbf{r}(X) = \alpha X^3 + \alpha^{11} X^7$ was received, where α is a primitive element in $GF(2^5)$. Decode $\mathbf{r}(X)$ by the decoding method described in Section 6.4.

REFERENCES

1. Bartee, T. C., and D. I. Schneider, "An Electronic Decoder for Bose-Chaudhuri-Hocquenghem Error Correcting Codes," *IEEE Trans. on Information Theory*, **IT-8**, pp. 17-24, September, 1962.

2. Berlekamp, E. R., "On Decoding Binary Bose-Chaudhuri-Hocquenghem Codes," *IEEE Trans. on Information Theory*, **IT-11**, pp. 577-580, October, 1965.

3. Berlekamp, E. R., "Nonbinary *BCH* Decoding," presented at the IEEE International Symposium on Information Theory, San Remo, Italy, 1967.

4. Berlekamp, E. R., "The Enumeration of Information Symbols in *BCH* Codes, *Bell Systems Tech. J.*, **46**, pp. 1861-1880, October, 1967.

5. Berlekamp, E. R., *Algebraic Coding Theory*, McGraw-Hill, New York, 1968.

6. Bose, R. C., and D. K. Ray-Chaudhuri, "On a Class of Error Correcting Binary Group Codes," *Information and Control*, **3**, pp. 68-79, March, 1960.

7. Bose, R. C., and D. K. Ray-Chaudhuri, "Further Results on Error Correcting Binary Group Codes," *Information and Control*, **3**, pp. 279-290, September, 1960.

8. Chen, C. L., and S. Lin, "Further Results on Polynomial Codes," *Information and Control*, **15**, pp. 38-60, July, 1969.

9. Chien, R. T., "Cyclic Decoding Procedure for the Bose-Chaudhuri Hocquenghem Codes," *IEEE Trans. on Information Theory*, **IT-10**, pp. 357-363, October, 1964.

10. Daykin, D. E., "Generation of Irreducible Polynomials over a Finite Field," *Am. Math. Monthly*, **72**, pp. 646-648, June-July, 1965.

11. Forney, G. D., "On Decoding *BCH* Codes," *IEEE Trans. on Information Theory*, **IT-11**, pp. 549-557, October, 1965.

12. Gallager, R. G., *Information Theory and Reliable Communication*, John Wiley, New York, 1968.

13. Golomb, S. W., *Shift Register Sequences*, Holden-Day, Inc., San Francisco, California, 1967.

14. Gorenstein, D. C., W. W. Peterson, and N. Zierler, "Two-Error-Correcting *BCH* Codes are Quasi-Perfect," *Information and Control*, **3**, pp. 291-294, September, 1960.

15. Gorenstein, D., and N. Zierler, "A Class of Cyclic Linear Error-Correcting Codes in p^m Symbols," *J. Soc. Indust. Appl. Math.*, **9**, pp. 107-214, June, 1961.

16. Gross, A. J., "Augmented *BCH* Codes Which Correct Single Bursts of Errors," *IEEE Trans. on Information Theory*, **IT-9**, p. 121, April, 1963.

17. Hocquenghem, A., "Codes Correcteurs D'erreurs," *Chiffres*, **2**, pp. 147-156, 1959.

18. Kasami, T., "Weight Distributions of Bose-Chaudhuri-Hocquenghem Codes," Proceedings of the Symposium on Combinatorial Mathematics and Its Applications, Chapel Hill, North Carolina, April, 1967.

19. Kasami, T., S. Lin, and W. W. Peterson, "Linear Codes Which are Invariant under the Affine Group and Some Results on Minimum Weights in *BCH* Codes," *J. Inst. Elect. Commun. Eng. Japan*, **50**, pp. 1617-1622, September, 1967.

20. Kasami, T., and N. Tokura, "Some Remarks on *BCH* Bounds and Minimum Weights of Binary Primitive *BCH* Codes," *IEEE Trans. on Information Theory*, **IT-15**, pp. 408-413, May, 1969.

21. Knee, D., and H. D. Goldman, "Quasi-Self-Reciprocal Polynomials and Potentially Large Minimum Distance *BCH* Codes," *IEEE Trans. on Information Theory*, **IT-15**, pp. 118-121, January, 1969.

22. Lin, S., and E. J. Weldon, Jr., "Long *BCH* Codes are Bad," *Information and Control*, **11**, pp. 445-451, October, 1967.

23. Lin, S., and W. W. Peterson, "Review on Error-Correcting Codes," Final Report, Part 4, Systems Research Corporation, Honolulu, Hawaii, May, 1969. (Also Research and Development Report, Naval Electronics Lab. Center, San Diego, California.)

24. Mann, H. B., "On the Number of Information Symbols in Bose-Chaudhuri Codes," *Information and Control*, **5**, pp. 153-162, June, 1962.

25. Massey, J. L., "Step-by-Step Decoding of the Bose-Chaudhuri-Hocquenghem Codes," *IEEE Trans. on Information Theory*, **IT-11**, pp. 580-585, October, 1965.

26. Massey, J. L., "Shift-Register Synthesis and *BCH* Decoding," *IEEE Trans. on Information Theory*, **IT-15**, pp. 122-127, January, 1969.

27. Mattson, H. F., and G. Solomon, "A New Treatment of Bose-Chaudhuri Codes," *J. Soc. Indust. Appl. Math.*, **9**, pp. 654-669, December, 1961.

28. Peterson, W. W., "Encoding and Error-Correction Procedures for the Bose-Chaudhuri Codes," *IRE Trans. on Information Theory*, **IT-6**, pp. 459-470, September, 1960.

29. Peterson, W. W., *Error-Correcting Codes*, The M.I.T. Press, Cambridge, Massachusetts, and John Wiley, New York, 1961.

30. Peterson, W. W., "Some New Results on Finite Fields and their Application to the Theory of *BCH* Codes," Proceedings of the Symposium on Combinatorial Mathematics and Its Applications, Chapel Hill, North Carolina, April, 1967.

31. Peterson, W. W., "On the Weight Structure and Symmetry of *BCH* Codes," *J. Inst. Elect. Commun. Eng. Japan*, **50**, pp. 1183-1190, July, 1967.

32. Peterson, W. W., and E. J. Weldon, Jr., *Error-Correcting Codes*, 2nd Edition, The M.I.T. Press, Cambridge, Massachusetts, 1970.

33. Reed, I. S., and G. Solomon, "Polynomial Codes over Certain Finite Fields," *J. Soc. Indust. Appl. Math.*, **8**, pp. 300-304, June, 1960.

34. Tzeng, K. K. M., "On Iterative Decoding of *BCH* Codes and Decoding Beyond the *BCH* Bound," CSL Report R-404, University of Illinois, Urbana, Illinois, 1969.

35. Zierler, N., "A Complete Theory for Generalized *BCH* Codes," Proceedings of the 1968 Symposium on Error Correcting Codes, edited by H. B. Mann, John Wiley, New York, 1969.

CHAPTER 7

MAJORITY-LOGIC DECODING FOR CYCLIC CODES

The majority-logic decoding presented in this chapter is another effective decoding scheme for certain classes of block codes (especially for certain classes of cyclic codes). The first majority-logic decoding algorithm was devised in 1954 by Reed[28] for a class of multiple-error-correcting codes discovered by Muller.[23] Reed's algorithm was later extended and generalized by many coding investigators. The first unified formulation of majority-logic decoding algorithms was due to Massey.[20] The material presented in Sections 7.1 and 7.3 are primarily based on Massey's work.

Most majority-logic decodable block codes found so far are cyclic codes. Important cyclic codes of this category are presented in Sections 7.2 and 7.4. The reader who is interested in other majority-logic decodable block codes is referred to References 8 and 36.

7.1 ONE-STEP MAJORITY-LOGIC DECODING

As described in Section 4.1, the parity-check matrix $\mathbf{H}$ of an (n,k) cyclic code can be arranged in the following form:

$$\mathbf{H} = \begin{bmatrix} \mathbf{h}_0 \\ \mathbf{h}_1 \\ \mathbf{h}_2 \\ \vdots \\ \mathbf{h}_{n-k-1} \end{bmatrix} = \begin{bmatrix} 1\,0\,0\,0 \ldots 0 & c_{00} & c_{01} & c_{02} & \cdots & c_{0,k-1} \\ 0\,1\,0\,0 \ldots 0 & c_{10} & c_{11} & c_{12} & \cdots & c_{1,k-1} \\ 0\,0\,1\,0 \ldots 0 & c_{20} & c_{21} & c_{22} & \cdots & c_{2,k-1} \\ \vdots & \vdots & & & & \vdots \\ 0\,0\,0\,0 \ldots 1 & c_{n-k-1,0} & c_{n-k-1,1} & c_{n-k-1,2} & \cdots & c_{n-k-1,k-1} \end{bmatrix}. \tag{7.1}$$

Let $\mathbf{e} = (e_0, e_1, e_2, \ldots, e_{n-1})$ be an error pattern. According to the convention used for cyclic codes, the digits $e_0, e_1, \ldots, e_{n-k-1}$ are parity error digits and

$e_{n-k}, e_{n-k+1}, \ldots, e_{n-1}$ are message error digits. The syndrome corresponding to $\mathbf{e}$ is

$$\mathbf{s} = (s_0, s_1, s_2, \ldots, s_{n-k-1}) = \mathbf{e}\mathbf{H}^T \quad ,$$

where $\mathbf{H}^T$ is the transpose of $\mathbf{H}$. Multiplying out $\mathbf{e}\mathbf{H}^T$ yields the following syndrome bits:

$$\begin{aligned}
s_0 &= e_0 + c_{00}\, e_{n-k} + \ldots + c_{0,k-1}\, e_{n-1} \\
s_1 &= e_1 + c_{10}\, e_{n-k} + \ldots + c_{1,k-1}\, e_{n-1} \\
s_2 &= e_2 + c_{20}\, e_{n-k} + \ldots + c_{2,k-1}\, e_{n-1} \\
&\vdots \\
s_{n-k-1} &= e_{n-k-1} + c_{n-k-1,0}\, e_{n-k} + \ldots + c_{n-k-1,k-1}\, e_{n-1} \quad .
\end{aligned} \tag{7.2}$$

(Equation (7.2) can also be obtained from Eq. (4.25).) Since c_{ij} is either 0 or 1, each syndrome bit is a (modulo-2) sum of certain error digits. Now we consider a (modulo-2) sum of syndrome bits of the following form:

$$\mathrm{A} = a_0 s_0 + a_1 s_1 + \ldots + a_{n-k-1} s_{n-k-1} \quad ,$$

where a_i is either 0 or 1. It follows from Eq. (7.2) that A is also a sum of error bits as follows:

$$\mathrm{A} = b_0 e_0 + b_1 e_1 + \ldots + b_{n-1} e_{n-1} \quad , \tag{7.3}$$

where b_i is either 0 or 1. This sum A of error digits is generally called a *parity-check sum*, or simply a *check sum*. The error digit e_ℓ is said to be checked by A if the coefficient b_ℓ of e_ℓ in A is 1.

Definition 7.1:[20] *A set of parity-check sums* $A_1, A_2, \ldots, A_J$ *is said to be orthogonal on the error digit* e_ℓ *if* e_ℓ *is checked by each check sum* $\mathbf{A}_j$ *in the set and no other error digit is checked by more than one check sum.*

It follows from the above definition that each check sum orthogonal on e_ℓ is of the form

$$\mathbf{A}_j = \sum_{i \neq \ell} e_i + e_\ell \quad . \tag{7.4}$$

If all error digits e_i in the sum $\mathbf{A}_j$ are zero for $i \neq \ell$, then the error digit e_ℓ is equal to $\mathbf{A}_j$, i.e.,

$$e_\ell = \mathbf{A}_j \quad . \tag{7.5}$$

The parity-check sums orthogonal on e_ℓ and Eq. (7.5) can be used to estimate e_ℓ (or decode the received digit r_ℓ).

Suppose that it is possible to form J parity-check sums $A_1, A_2, \ldots, A_J$ orthogonal on the highest order error digit e_{n-1} and assume that there are $[J/2]$ or fewer errors in the error vector $\mathbf{e} = (e_0, e_1, \ldots, e_{n-1})$ (that is, $[J/2]$ or fewer error digits of $\mathbf{e}$ are 1). If $e_{n-1} = 0$, then the non-zero error digits can distribute among at most $[J/2]$ check sums. Hence, at least $J - [J/2]$, or at least one-half of the check sums orthogonal on e_{n-1}, are equal to $e_{n-1} = 0$. If, on the other hand, $e_{n-1} = 1$, then the other non-zero error digits can distribute among at most $[J/2] - 1$ check sums orthogonal on e_{n-1}. Hence, at least $J - [J/2] + 1$, or more than one-half of the check sums, are equal to $e_{n-1} = 1$. Thus, the value of the error digit e_{n-1} is given as the value assumed by a clear *majority* of the parity-check sums orthogonal on e_{n-1}; if no value is assumed by a clear majority (i.e., there is a tie), the error digit e_{n-1} is zero. Based on the above facts, an algorithm for decoding e_{n-1} can be formulated as follows: *The error digit* e_{n-1} *is decoded as* "1" *if a clear majority of the check sums is* "1"*; otherwise,* e_{n-1} *is decoded as* "0." Correct decoding of e_{n-1} is guaranteed if $[J/2]$ or fewer errors occur in the error vector $\mathbf{e}$ added by the noisy channel. If it is possible to form J parity-check sums orthogonal on e_{n-1}, then it is possible to form J parity-check sums orthogonal on any error digit because of the cyclic symmetry of the code. From Eq. (7.4), it can be seen that the parity-check sums orthogonal on $e_{\ell-1}$ can be obtained from the check sums orthogonal on e_ℓ by simply shifting the error vector **e** to the right one place cyclically. Thus, we have

$$\mathbf{A}'_j = \sum_{i-1 \neq \ell-1} e_{i-1} + e_{\ell-1} \quad .$$

(Note that $e_{-t} = e_{n-t}$.) Thus, the decodings of $e_{n-2}, e_{n-3}, \ldots, e_{n-k}$ are identical to the decoding of e_{n-1}. The decoding algorithm described above is called *one-step majority-logic decoding*. If J is the maximum number of parity-check sums orthogonal on any error digit that can be formed, then, by one-step majority-logic decoding, any error pattern of $[J/2]$ or fewer errors can be corrected. Let d be the minimum distance of a code. Clearly, the one-step majority-logic decoding is effective for this code only if $[J/2]$ is equal to or close to the error-correcting capability $[(d-1)/2]$ of the code (in other words, J should be equal to or close to $d-1$).

Definition 7.2:[20] *A cyclic code with minimum distance d is said to be completely orthogonalizable in one step if and only if it is possible to form $J = d - 1$ parity-check sums orthogonal on every error digit.*

At this point, an example would be helpful in clarifying the notions developed above. Consider a (15,7) cyclic code whose generator polynomial is

$$\mathrm{g}(X) = 1 + X^4 + X^6 + X^7 + X^8 \quad .$$

It follows from Eqs. (4.19) and (4.23) that the parity-check matrix of these codes are found as follows:

$$\mathbf{H} = \begin{bmatrix} 1&0&0&0&0&0&0&0&1&1&0&1&0&0&0 \\ 0&1&0&0&0&0&0&0&0&1&1&0&1&0&0 \\ 0&0&1&0&0&0&0&0&0&0&1&1&0&1&0 \\ 0&0&0&1&0&0&0&0&0&0&0&1&1&0&1 \\ 0&0&0&0&1&0&0&0&1&1&0&1&1&1&0 \\ 0&0&0&0&0&1&0&0&0&1&1&0&1&1&1 \\ 0&0&0&0&0&0&1&0&1&1&1&0&0&1&1 \\ 0&0&0&0&0&0&0&1&1&0&1&0&0&0&1 \end{bmatrix} .$$

Let $\mathbf{e} = (e_0, e_1, e_2, e_3, e_4, e_5, e_6, e_7, e_8, e_9, e_{10}, e_{11}, e_{12}, e_{13}, e_{14})$ be an error vector. The syndrome corresponding to $\mathbf{e}$ is

$$\begin{aligned} \mathbf{s} &= (s_0, s_1, s_2, s_3, s_4, s_5, s_6, s_7) \\ &= \mathbf{e}\mathbf{H}^T . \end{aligned}$$

Multiplying out $\mathbf{e}\mathbf{H}^T$ gives the following eight syndrome bits:

$$\begin{aligned} s_0 &= e_0 + e_8 + e_9 + e_{11} \\ s_1 &= e_1 + e_9 + e_{10} + e_{12} \\ s_2 &= e_2 + e_{10} + e_{11} + e_{13} \\ s_3 &= e_3 + e_{11} + e_{12} + e_{14} . \\ s_4 &= e_4 + e_8 + e_9 + e_{11} + e_{12} + e_{13} \\ s_5 &= e_5 + e_9 + e_{10} + e_{12} + e_{13} + e_{14} \\ s_6 &= e_6 + e_8 + e_9 + e_{10} + e_{13} + e_{14} \\ s_7 &= e_7 + e_8 + e_{10} + e_{14} . \end{aligned}$$

From these eight syndrome bits, four (no more) parity-check sums orthogonal on e_{14} can be formed as follows:

$$\begin{aligned}
A_1 &= s_3 &&= e_3 + e_{11} + e_{12} + e_{14} \\
A_2 &= s_1 + s_5 &&= e_1 + e_5 + e_{13} + e_{14} \\
A_3 &= s_0 + s_2 + s_6 &&= e_0 + e_2 + e_6 + e_{14} \\
A_4 &= s_7 &&= e_7 + e_8 + e_{10} + e_{14} \quad .
\end{aligned}$$

It can be checked easily that e_{14} is checked by all four sums and no other error digit is checked by more than one sum. If $e_{14} = 1$ and if there is one or no error occurring among the other 14 digit positions, then at least three (majority) of the four sums, A_1, A_2, A_3, and A_4, are equal to $e_{14} = 1$. If $e_{14} = 0$ and if there are two or fewer errors occurring among the other 14 digit positions, then at least two of the sums are equal to $e_{14} = 0$. Thus, if there are two or fewer errors in **e**, the one-step majority-logic decoding always results in correct decoding of e_{14}. Since the code is cyclic, 4 parity-check sums orthogonal on any other message error can be formed. The four parity-check sums orthogonal on e_{13} are

$$\begin{aligned}
A'_1 &= s_2 &&= e_2 + e_{10} + e_{12} + e_{13} \\
A'_2 &= s_0 + s_4 &&= e_0 + e_4 + e_{12} + e_{13} \\
A'_3 &= s_1 + s_5 &&= e_1 + e_5 + e_{13} + e_{14} \\
A'_4 &= s_6 + s_7 &&= e_6 + e_7 + e_9 + e_{13} \quad .
\end{aligned}$$

It can be checked that 4 is the maximum number of parity-check sums orthogonal on any message digit that can be formed. Thus, by one-step majority-logic decoding, this code is capable of correcting any error pattern with two or fewer errors. It can be shown that there exists at least one error pattern with three errors which cannot be corrected by the one-step majority-logic decoding. Consider an error pattern of three errors which are e_0, e_3, and e_8

(i.e., $e_0 = e_3 = e_8 = 1$). From the four parity-check sums orthogonal on e_{14}, we obtain $A_1 = 1$, $A_2 = 0$, $A_3 = 1$, and $A_4 = 1$. Since majority of the four sums are 1, according to the decoding algorithm, e_{14} is decoded as "1." This is an incorrect decoding. In fact, this code is a *BCH* code with minimum distance exactly 5. Thus, this code is completely orthogonalizable. Majority-logic decoding for this code was first studied by Massey.[20]

The one-step majority-logic decoding algorithm can be implemented easily with a single *J*-input majority-logic gate. The *J* parity-check sums orthogonal on an error digit are the *J*-inputs to this gate. The output of this gate is "1" if and only if more than one-half of its inputs are "1"; otherwise, the output is zero. The output is the estimated value of an error digit. A general one-step majority-logic decoder (Type I)[20] is shown in Fig. 7.1. The error correction procedure can be described as follows:

Step 1. The syndrome is calculated as usual.

Step 2. The set of *J* parity-check sums orthogonal on e_{n-1} is formed from the $n-k$ syndrome bits by *J* multiple-input modulo-2 adders. These *J* check sums are fed into a *J*-input majority gate. If the output of the majority gate is "1," the decoder assumes that the first received digit is erroneous. If the output of the majority gate is "0," the decoder assumes that the first received digit is correct.

Step 3. The first received digit is read out of the buffer register and corrected by the output of the majority gate, which is the estimated error bit e_{n-1}. The correction is done by an Exclusive OR gate.

Step 4. The syndrome and buffer registers are shifted once. If $e_{n-1} = 1$, the effect of e_{n-1} on the syndrome should be removed. This is achieved by adding $\rho(X) = \rho_0 + \rho_1 X + \rho_2 X^2 + \ldots + \rho_{n-k-1} X^{n-k-1}$ to the syndrome, where $\rho(X)$ is the remainder resulting from dividing X^{n-1} by the generator polynomial. (This is called syndrome resetting.) The new contents in the syndrome register form the syndrome of the altered received vector shifted one place to the right.

Step 5. The new syndrome formed in Step 4 is used to decode the second received digit. The decoder repeats Steps 2, 3, and 4. The second received digit is corrected in exactly the same manner as the first received digit was corrected.

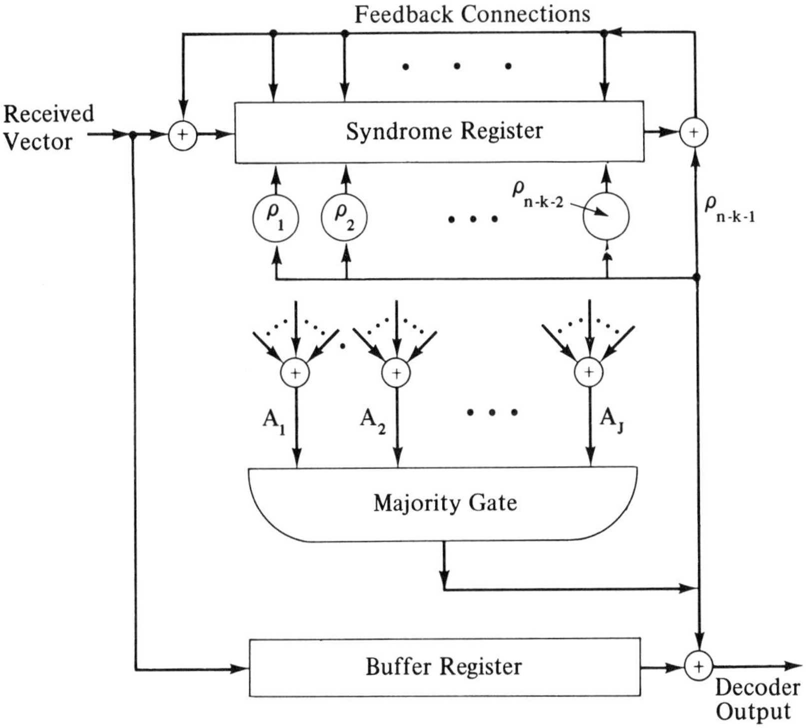

Fig. 7.1. A general Type I one-step majority-logic decoder. (The symbol (ρ_i) denotes a connection if $\rho_i = 1$; no connection if $\rho_i = 0$.)

Step 6. The decoder decodes the received vector digit by digit in the above manner until a total of n received digits have been decoded. Correct decoding is guaranteed provided that $[J/2]$ or fewer errors occurred in the received vector.

After the n received digits are read out of the buffer, the syndrome register should contain all 0's if the decoder output is a code vector. If the syndrome register does not contain all 0's at the end of the decoding, an uncorrectable error has been detected.

It is possible to form orthogonal parity-check sums in a different way. Consider an (n,k) cyclic code with parity-check matrix $\mathbf{H}$. Let $\mathbf{w} = (w_0, w_1, \ldots, w_{n-1})$ be a vector in the null space of the code; i.e., $\mathbf{w}$ is a vector in the row space of $\mathbf{H}$. Let $\mathbf{v} = (v_0, v_1, \ldots, v_{n-1})$, $\mathbf{e} = (e_0, e_1, \ldots, e_{n-1})$, and $\mathbf{r} = (r_0, r_1, \ldots, r_{n-1})$ be the transmitted code vector, the error vector, and the received vector respectively. Then the inner product of $\mathbf{r}$ and $\mathbf{w}$ is

$$\mathbf{r}\mathbf{w} = (\mathbf{v}+\mathbf{e})\mathbf{w} = \mathbf{v}\mathbf{w} + \mathbf{e}\mathbf{w} \ .$$

Since $\mathbf{v}\mathbf{w} = 0$, then

$$\mathbf{r}\mathbf{w} = \mathbf{e}\mathbf{w}$$

or

$$w_0 r_0 + w_1 r_1 + \ldots + w_{n-1} r_{n-1} = w_0 e_0 + w_1 e_1 + \ldots + w_{n-1} e_{n-1} \ . \quad (7.6)$$

Obviously, $\mathbf{r}\mathbf{w} = w_0 r_0 + w_1 r_1 + \ldots + w_{n-1} r_{n-1}$ is a parity-check sum. Now finding J parity-check sums orthogonal on e_{n-1} is equivalent to finding J vectors, $\mathbf{w}^{(j)} = (w_0^{(j)}, w_1^{(j)}, \ldots, w_{n-1}^{(j)})$ for $1 \leqslant j \leqslant J$, in the null space of the code such that the $(n-1)^{\text{th}}$ component $w_{n-1}^{(j)} = 1$ for $j = 1, 2, \ldots, J$ and no other component is 1 in more than one vector. Therefore, by Eq. (7.6), the J parity-check sums orthogonal on e_{n-1} are

$$\begin{aligned} A_1 &= \mathbf{r}\mathbf{w}^{(1)} = w_0^{(1)} r_0 + w_1^{(1)} r_1 + \ldots + w_{n-1}^{(1)} r_{n-1} \\ A_2 &= \mathbf{r}\mathbf{w}^{(2)} = w_0^{(2)} r_0 + w_1^{(2)} r_1 + \ldots + w_{n-1}^{(2)} r_{n-1} \\ &\vdots \\ A_J &= \mathbf{r}\mathbf{w}^{(J)} = w_0^{(J)} r_0 + w_1^{(J)} r_1 + \ldots + w_{n-1}^{(J)} r_{n-1} \ . \end{aligned} \quad (7.7)$$

That is, the J orthogonal parity-check sums can be formed by taking sums of J sets of appropriate received digits. The vector $\mathbf{w}^{(j)}$ tells what received digits should be summed up to form check sum A_j. The polynomial associated with $\mathbf{w}^{(j)}$ is

$$\mathbf{w}^{(j)}(X) = w_0^{(j)} + w_1^{(j)}X + w_2^{(j)}X^2 + \ldots + w_{n-1}^{(j)}X^{n-1} ,$$

which is called an *orthogonal polynomial* (or a polynomial orthogonal on e_{n-1}). Consider the following linear combination of syndrome bits:

$$\begin{aligned} \mathrm{A} &= a_0 s_0 + a_1 s_1 + \ldots + a_{n-k-1} s_{n-k-1} \\ &= b_0 e_0 + b_1 e_1 + \ldots + b_{n-1} e_{n-1} \ . \end{aligned}$$

If A is a parity-check sum orthogonal on e_{n-1}, then $\mathbf{b}(X) = b_0 + b_1 X + \ldots + b_{n-1} X^{n-1}$ must be a polynomial orthogonal on e_{n-1}.

A second type of one-step majority-logic decoding based on Eq. (7.7) is shown in Fig. 7.2. The error correction procedure can be described as follows:

Step 1. With Gate 1 on and Gate 2 off, the received vector is read into the buffer register.

Step 2. The J parity-check sums orthogonal on e_{n-1} are formed by summing appropriate received digits. This is done by J multi-input modulo-2 adders.

Step 3. The J orthogonal check sums are fed into a majority-logic gate. The first received digit r_{n-1} is read out of the buffer and corrected by the output of the majority gate; the correction is accomplished by an Exclusive OR gate.

Step 4. After Step 3, the buffer register has been shifted one place to the right. Now the second received digit is in the first stage of the buffer register and will be corrected in exactly the same manner as the first received digit was. The decoder repeats Steps 2 and 3.

Step 5. The received vector is decoded digit by digit in the above manner until a total of n digits have been decoded. Correct decoding is guaranteed, provided that $[J/2]$ or fewer errors occurred in the received vector.

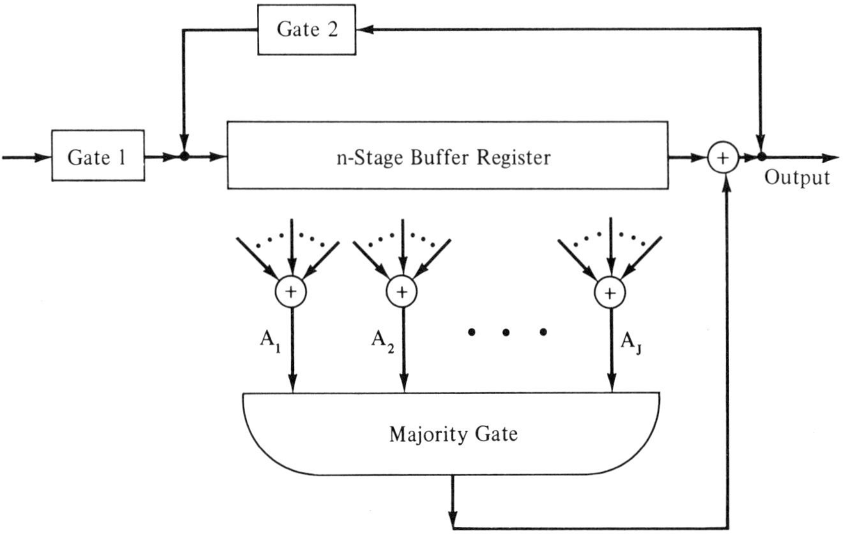

Fig. 7.2. A general Type II one-step majority-logic decoder.

After completion of the decoding, the buffer register should contain a code vector, and the inputs to the majority gate are zero. If any inputs are 1, an uncorrectable error pattern has been detected.

It is possible to construct the Type 1 one-step majority-logic decoder from the set of orthogonal polynomials. Consider the following parity-check sum

$$\begin{aligned} A &= a_0 s_0 + a_1 s_1 + \ldots + a_{n-k-1} s_{n-k-1} \\ &= b_0 e_0 + b_1 e_1 + \ldots + b_{n-1} e_{n-1} \quad . \end{aligned}$$

From Eq. (7.2), it is clear that

$$a_i = b_i$$

for $i = 0, 1, \ldots, n-k-1$. Thus, if $\mathbf{b}(X) = b_0 + b_1 X + \ldots + b_{n-1} X^{n-1}$ is a polynomial orthogonal on e_{n-1}, then the following linear combination of syndrome bits

$$A = b_0 s_0 + b_1 s_1 + \ldots + b_{n-k-1} s_{n-k-1}$$

must be a parity-check sum orthogonal on e_{n-1}. Thus, knowing the set of orthogonal polynomials on e_{n-1}, one is able to form the set of linear combinations of syndrome bits which are orthogonal on e_{n-1}. Based on this set of linear combinations of syndrome bits, one can construct the Type I one-step majority-logic decoder for the code.

Both the Type I and Type II decoders employ a total of n stages of shift register. Which type is more simply implemented depends on the structure of the given code. One-step majority-logic decoding is most efficient for codes which are completely orthogonalizable, or for codes with large J compared to $d - 1$ (d is the minimum distance of the code). When J is small compared to $d - 1$, however, one-step majority-logic decoding becomes very inefficient, and much of the error-correcting capability of the code is sacrificed.

7.2 ONE-STEP MAJORITY-LOGIC DECODABLE CODES

As pointed out in the previous section, one-step majority-logic decoding is most effective for cyclic codes which are completely orthogonalizable. Unfortunately, there exist very few good cyclic codes in this category. The double-error-correcting (15,7) code considered in Example 7.1 is the only known BCH code which is completely orthogonalizable in one step. In the following, two small classes of one-step completely orthogonalizable cyclic codes are presented.

Maximum-Length Codes

For any integer $m \geqslant 2$, there exists a maximum-length code with the following parameters:

Block Length:	$n = 2^m - 1$
Number of Information Digits:	$k = m$
Minimum Distance:	$d = 2^{m-1}$.

The generator polynomial of this code is

$$\mathbf{g}(X) = (X^n + 1)/\mathbf{p}(X) \ , \tag{7.8}$$

where the parity polynomial $\mathbf{p}(X)$ is any primitive polynomial of degree m. This code consists of the all-zero code vector and $2^m - 1$ code vectors of weight 2^{m-1}. Thus, the minimum distance of this code is exactly 2^{m-1}. Maximum-length codes were first shown to be majority-logic decodable by Yale[39] and Zierler[40] independently.

Let $\mathbf{p}'(X) = X^m \mathbf{p}(X^{-1})$. The polynomial $\mathbf{p}'(X)$ is also a primitive polynomial of degree m and is called the *reciprocal polynomial* of $\mathbf{p}(X)$. It can be shown that the $(2^m - 1, 2^m - m - 1)$ Hamming code generated by $\mathbf{p}'(X)$ is the null space of the maximum-length code generated by $\mathbf{g}(X)$ of Eq. (7.8).[24] Thus, the null space of a maximum-length code contains vectors of weight exactly 3. Consider the following set of distinct code polynomials

$$\mathbf{Q} = \{\mathbf{w}(X) = X^i + X^j + X^{n-1} \mid 0 \leqslant i < j < n-1\} \tag{7.9}$$

in the Hamming code generated by $\mathbf{p}'(X)$. No two polynomials in $\mathbf{Q}$ can have any common terms except the term X^{n-1}. Otherwise, the sum of these two polynomials would be a code polynomial of only two terms in the Hamming code generated by $\mathbf{p}'(X)$. This is impossible since the minimum weight of a Hamming code is 3. Therefore, the set $\mathbf{Q}$ contains polynomials orthogonal on the error digit e_{n-1} for the maximum-length code generated by $\mathbf{g}(X)$ of Eq. (7.8). To find $\mathbf{w}(X)$, we start with a polynomial $X^{n-1} + X^j$, for $0 \leqslant j < n-1$, and then determine X^i such that $X^{14} + X^j + X^i$ is divisible by $\mathbf{p}'(X)$. This can be done as follows. Divide $X^{n-1} + X^j$ by $\mathbf{p}'(X)$ step-by-step with long division until a single term X^i appears at the end of a certain step. Then $\mathbf{w}(X) = X^{n-1} + X^j + X^i$ is a polynomial orthogonal on e_{n-1}. Clearly, if we start with $X^{n-1} + X^i$, we would obtain the same polynomial $\mathbf{w}(X)$. Thus, we can find $(n-1)/2 = 2^{m-1} - 1$ polynomials orthogonal on e_{n-1}. That is, $J = 2^{m-1} - 1$ parity-check sums orthogonal on e_{n-1} can be formed. Thus, a maximum-length code is completely orthogonalizable.

Example 7.1: Consider the maximum-length code with $m = 4$ and parity polynomial $\mathbf{p}(X) = 1 + X + X^4$. This code has block length $n = 15$ and minimum distance $d = 8$. The generator polynomial of this code is

$$\begin{aligned} \mathbf{g}(X) &= (X^{15} + 1)/\mathbf{p}(X) \\ &= 1 + X + X^2 + X^3 + X^5 + X^7 + X^8 + X^{11} \quad . \end{aligned}$$

The null space of this code is generated by

$$\mathbf{p}'(X) \;=\; X^4\mathbf{p}(X^{-1}) \;=\; X^4 + X^3 + 1.$$

Divide $X^{14} + X^{13}$ by $\mathbf{p}'(X) = X^4 + X^3 + 1$ with long division as shown in the following:

$$\begin{array}{r|l} & X^{10} \\ \hline X^4 + X^3 + 1 & X^{14} + X^{13} \\ & X^{14} + X^{13} + X^{10} \\ \cline{2-2} & \qquad\qquad\quad X^{10} \text{ (stop)} \quad . \end{array}$$

A single term X^{10} appears at the end of the 1st step of the long division. Then $\mathbf{w}^{(1)}(X) = X^{14} + X^{13} + X^{10}$ is a polynomial orthogonal on e_{14}. Now divide $X^{14} + X^{12}$ by $\mathbf{p}'(X)$ as follows:

$$\begin{array}{r|l} & X^{10} + X^9 + X^6 \\ \hline X^4 + X^3 + 1 & X^{14} \qquad\quad + X^{12} \\ & X^{14} + X^{13} \qquad\qquad + X^{10} \\ \cline{2-2} & \qquad X^{13} + X^{12} + X^{10} \\ & \qquad X^{13} + X^{12} \qquad\quad + X^9 \\ \cline{2-2} & \qquad\qquad\qquad X^{10} + X^9 \\ & \qquad\qquad\qquad X^{10} + X^9 + X^6 \\ \cline{2-2} & \qquad\qquad\qquad\qquad\quad X^6 \text{ (stop)} \quad . \end{array}$$

Then $\mathbf{w}^{(2)}(X) = X^{14} + X^{12} + X^6$ is another polynomial orthogonal on e_{14}. The rest of the polynomials orthogonal on e_{14} can be found in the same manner; they are

$$\begin{aligned}
\mathbf{w}^{(3)}(X) &= X^{14} + X^{11} + 1 \\
\mathbf{w}^{(4)}(X) &= X^{14} + X^9 + X^4 \\
\mathbf{w}^{(5)}(X) &= X^{14} + X^8 + X \\
\mathbf{w}^{(6)}(X) &= X^{14} + X^7 + X^5 \\
\mathbf{w}^{(7)}(X) &= X^{14} + X^3 + X^2
\end{aligned}$$

From the set of polynomials orthogonal on e_{14}, we obtain the following set of parity-check sums orthogonal on e_{14}:

$$\begin{aligned}
A_1 &= e_{10} + e_{13} + e_{14} \\
A_2 &= e_6 + e_{12} + e_{14} \\
A_3 &= e_0 + e_{11} + e_{14} \\
A_4 &= e_4 + e_9 + e_{14} \\
A_5 &= e_1 + e_8 + e_{14} \\
A_6 &= e_5 + e_7 + e_{14} \\
A_7 &= e_2 + e_3 + e_{14} \quad .
\end{aligned}$$

In terms of syndrome bits, we have $A_1 = s_{10}$, $A_2 = s_6$, $A_3 = s_0$, $A_4 = s_4 + s_9$, $A_5 = s_1 + s_8$, $A_6 = s_5 + s_7$, and $A_7 = s_2 + s_3$. The Type I and Type II one-step majority-logic decoders for this code are shown in Fig. 7.3 and Fig. 7.4 respectively.

Difference-Set Codes

The formulation of difference-set codes is based on the construction of *perfect difference-set*. Let $\mathbf{P} = \{\ell_0, \ell_1, \ell_2, \ldots, \ell_q\}$ be a set of $q + 1$

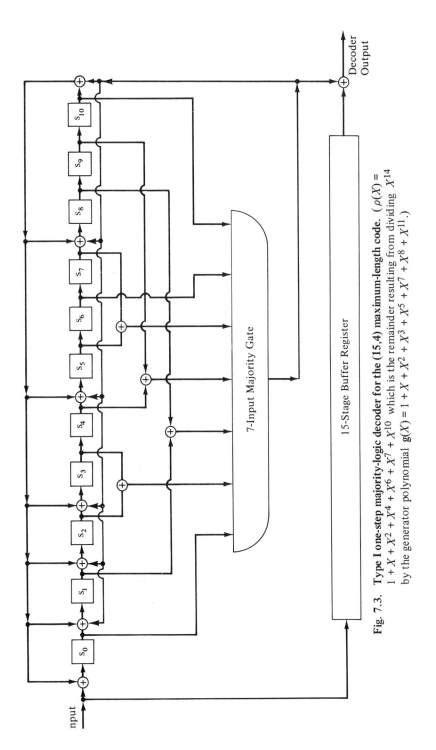

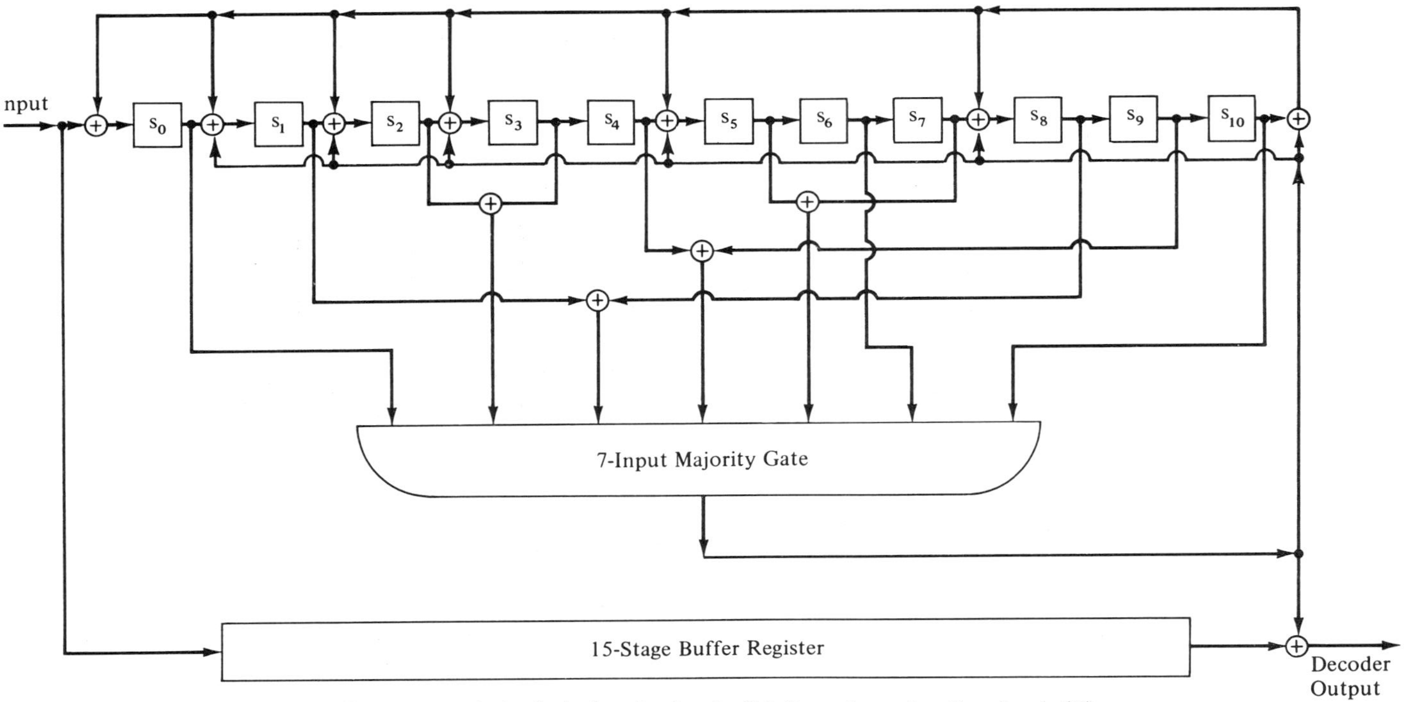

Fig. 7.3. Type I one-step majority-logic decoder for the (15,4) maximum-length code. ($\rho(X) = 1 + X + X^2 + X^4 + X^6 + X^7 + X^{10}$ which is the remainder resulting from dividing X^{14} by the generator polynomial $\mathbf{g}(X) = 1 + X + X^2 + X^3 + X^5 + X^7 + X^8 + X^{11}$.)

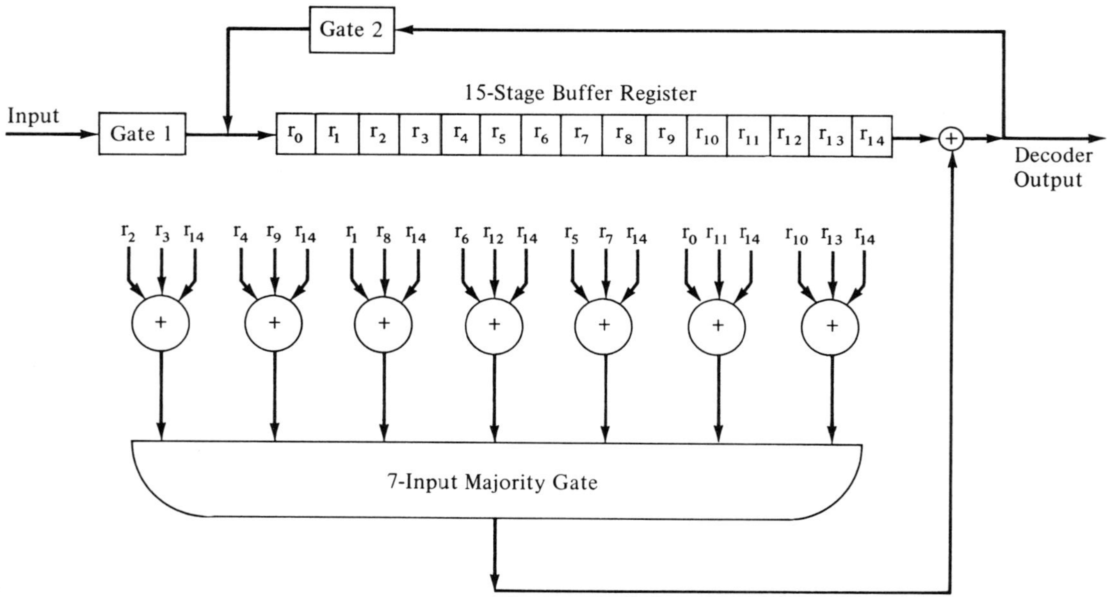

Fig. 7.4. Type II one-step majority-logic decoder for the (15,4) maximum-length code.

non-negative integers such that

$$0 \leqslant \ell_0 < \ell_1 < \ell_2 < \ldots < \ell_q \leqslant q(q+1) \quad .$$

From this set of integers, it is possible to form $q(q+1)$ *ordered differences* as follows:

$$\mathbf{D} \;=\; \{\ell_j - \ell_i \mid j \neq i\} \quad .$$

Obviously, half of the differences in **D** are positive and the other half are negative. The set **P** is said to be a *perfect simple difference-set of order* q if and only if it has the following properties:

1) All the positive differences in **D** are distinct.
2) All the negative differences in **D** are distinct.
3) If $\ell_j - \ell_i$ is a negative difference in **D**, then $q(q+1)+1-(\ell_i - \ell_j)$ is not equal to any positive difference in **D**.

Clearly, it follows from the definition that $\mathbf{P}' = \{0, \ell_1 - \ell_0, \ell_2 - \ell_0, \ldots, \ell_q - \ell_0\}$ is also a perfect difference-set.

Example 7.2: Consider the set $\mathbf{P} = \{0, 2, 7, 8, 11\}$ with $q = 4$. The $4 \times 5 = 20$ ordered differences are

$$\mathbf{D} \;=\; \{\,2, 7, 8, 11, 5, 6, 9, 1, 4, 3, -2, -7$$
$$-8, -11, -5, -6, -9, -1, -4, -3\} \quad .$$

It can be checked easily that **P** satisfies all three properties of a perfect difference-set.

Singer[32] has constructed perfect difference-sets for order $q = p^s$, where p is a prime and s is any positive integer. (Also see Reference 7.) In the following, we shall only be concerned with $q = 2^s$.

Let $\mathbf{P} = \{\ell_0 = 0, \ell_1, \ell_2, \ldots, \ell_{2^s}\}$ be a perfect simple difference set of order 2^s. Define the following polynomial,

$$z(X) = 1 + X^{\ell_1} + X^{\ell_2} + \ldots + X^{\ell_{2^s}} \tag{7.10}$$

Let $n = 2^s(2^s+1)+1$ and $\mathbf{h}(X)$ be the greatest common divisor of $\mathbf{z}(X)$ and $X^n + 1$, i.e.,

$$\begin{aligned} \mathbf{h}(X) &= \text{GCD}\{\mathbf{z}(X), X^n+1\} \\ &= 1 + h_1 X + h_2 X^2 + \ldots + h_{k-1} X^{k-1} + X^k \end{aligned} \tag{7.11}$$

Then a difference-set code of length n is defined as the cyclic code generated by

$$\begin{aligned} \mathbf{g}(X) &= (X^n+1)/\mathbf{h}(X) \\ &= 1 + g_1 X + g_2 X^2 + \ldots + X^{n-k} \quad . \end{aligned} \tag{7.12}$$

This code has the following parameters:

Code Length: $n = 2^{2s} + 2^s + 1$

Number of Parity-Check Digits: $n\text{-}k = 3^s + 1$

Minimum Distance: $d = 2^s + 2$.

Difference-set codes were discovered by Rudolph[29] and Weldon[34] independently. The formula for the number of information digits, k, was derived by Graham and MacWilliams.[12]

Example 7.3: In Example 7.2, we have shown that the set $\mathbf{P} = \{0, 2, 7, 8, 11\}$ is a perfect simple difference-set of order $q = 2^2$. Let $\mathbf{z}(X) = 1 + X^2 + X^7 + X^8 + X^{11}$. Then

$$\begin{aligned} \mathbf{h}(X) &= \text{GCD}\{1 + X^2 + X^7 + X^8 + X^{11}, 1 + X^{21}\} \\ &= 1 + X^2 + X^7 + X^8 + X^{11} \quad . \end{aligned}$$

The generator polynomial of the difference-set code of length $n = 21$ is

$$\mathbf{g}(X) = (X^{21}+1)/\mathbf{h}(X)$$
$$= 1 + X^2 + X^4 + X^6 + X^7 + X^{10} \quad .$$

Thus, the code is a (21,11) cyclic code.

Let $\mathbf{h}'(X) = X^k\mathbf{h}(X^{-1})$ be the reciprocal polynomial of $\mathbf{h}(X)$. Then the $(n,n\text{-}k)$ cyclic code generated by $\mathbf{h}'(X)$ is the null space of the difference-set code generated by $\mathbf{g}(X)$ of Eq. (7.12). Let

$$\mathbf{z}'(X) = X^{\ell_{2s}}\mathbf{z}(X^{-1})$$
$$= 1 + \ldots + X^{\ell_{2s}-\ell_2} + X^{\ell_{2s}-\ell_1} + X^{\ell_{2s}} \quad . \tag{7.13}$$

Since $\mathbf{z}(X)$ is divisible by $\mathbf{h}(X)$, $\mathbf{z}'(X)$ is divisible by $\mathbf{h}'(X)$. Thus, $\mathbf{z}'(X)$ is in the null space of the difference-set code generated by $\mathbf{g}(X)$ of Eq. (7.12). Let

$$\mathbf{w}(X) = X^{n-1-\ell_{2s}}\mathbf{z}'(X)$$
$$= X^{n-1-\ell_{2s}} + \ldots + X^{n-1-\ell_2} + X^{n-1-\ell_1} + X^{n-1} \quad .$$

Obviously, $\mathbf{w}(X)$ is divisible by $\mathbf{h}(X)$ and is also in the null space of the difference-set code generated by $\mathbf{g}(X)$ of Eq. (7.12). Now let

$$\mathbf{w}^{(i)}(X) = X^{\ell_i-\ell_{i-1}-1} + X^{\ell_i-\ell_{i-2}-1} + \ldots + X^{\ell_i-\ell_1-1} + X^{\ell_i-1}$$
$$+ X^{n-1-\ell_{2s}+\ell_i} + X^{n-1-\ell_{2s-1}+\ell_i} + \ldots + X^{n-1} \tag{7.14}$$

be the vector obtained by shifting $\mathbf{w}(X)$ cyclically to the right ℓ_i times.

Since $\{\ell_0 = 1, \ell_1, \ell_2, \ldots, \ell_{2^s}\}$ is a perfect difference set, no two polynomials $\mathbf{w}^{(i)}(X)$ and $\mathbf{w}^{(j)}(X)$, for $i \neq j$, can have any common term except X^{n-1}. Thus, $\mathbf{w}(X), \mathbf{w}^{(1)}(X), \ldots, \mathbf{w}^{(2^s)}(X)$ form a set of $J = 2^s + 1$ polynomials orthogonal on the error digit e_{n-1}.

Example 7.4: Consider the code given in Example 7.3, which is specified by the perfect difference-set $\mathbf{P} = \{0, 2, 7, 8, 11\}$ of order 2^2. Thus, we have

$$\mathbf{z}'(X) = X^{11}\mathbf{z}(X^{-1}) = 1 + X^3 + X^4 + X^9 + X^{11} ,$$

and

$$\mathbf{w}(X) = X^9 \mathbf{z}'(X) = X^9 + X^{12} + X^{13} + X^{18} + X^{20} .$$

By shifting $\mathbf{w}(X)$ cyclically to the right 2 times, 7 times, 8 times, and 11 times, we obtain

$$\begin{aligned}
\mathbf{w}^{(1)}(X) &= X + X^{11} + X^{14} + X^{15} + X^{20} \\
\mathbf{w}^{(2)}(X) &= X^4 + X^6 + X^{16} + X^{19} + X^{20} \\
\mathbf{w}^{(3)}(X) &= 1 + X^5 + X^7 + X^{17} + X^{20} \\
\mathbf{w}^{(4)}(X) &= X^2 + X^3 + X^8 + X^{10} + X^{20} .
\end{aligned}$$

Clearly, $\mathbf{w}(X), \mathbf{w}^{(1)}(X), \mathbf{w}^{(2)}(X), \mathbf{w}^{(3)}(X)$, and $\mathbf{w}^{(4)}(X)$ are 5 polynomials orthogonal on e_{20}. From these 5 orthogonal polynomials, we can form the following parity-check sums orthogonal on e_{20},

$$\begin{aligned}
A_1 &= s_9 = e_9 + e_{12} + e_{13} + e_{18} + e_{20} \\
A_2 &= s_1 = e_1 + e_{11} + e_{14} + e_{15} + e_{20} \\
A_3 &= s_4 + s_6 = e_4 + e_6 + e_{16} + e_{19} + e_{20}
\end{aligned}$$

$$A_4 = s_0 + s_5 + s_7 = e_0 + e_5 + e_7 + e_{17} + e_{20}$$

$$A_5 = s_2 + s_3 + s_8 = e_2 + e_3 + e_8 + e_{10} + e_{20} \; .$$

The two types of one-step majority-logic decoders for the (21,11) difference-set code are shown in Figs. 7.5 and 7.6 respectively.

Difference-set codes are nearly as powerful as the best known cyclic codes in the range of practical interest. Unfortunately, there are relatively few codes with useful parameters in this class. A list of the first few codes with their generator polynomials and their corresponding perfect simple difference-set is given in Table 7.1.

7.3 *L*-STEP MAJORITY-LOGIC DECODING

The one-step majority-logic decoding for a cyclic code is based on the assumption that a set of J parity-check sums orthogonal on an error digit can be constructed. This decoding method is effective for codes which are completely orthogonalizable, or for codes with large J compared to the minimum distance d. Unfortunately, there are only several small classes of cyclic codes known to be in this category. However, the concept of a set of parity-check sums orthogonal on a single error digit can be generalized in such a way that more cyclic codes can be decoded by employing several levels of majority gates. Let $\mathbf{E} = \{e_{i_1}, e_{i_2}, \ldots, e_{i_M}\}$ be a set of M error digits. The number of error digits in $\mathbf{E}$ is called the *size* of the set $\mathbf{E}$.

Definition 7.3:[20] *A set of J parity-check sums* $A_1, A_2, \ldots, A_J$ *is said to be orthogonal on the set* $\mathbf{E}$ *if and only if:* (1) *every error digit* e_{i_ℓ} *in* $\mathbf{E}$ *is checked by every check sum* $\mathbf{A}_j$ *for* $j = 1, 2, \ldots, J$, and (2) *no other error digit is checked by more than one check sum.*

For example, the following four parity-check sums are orthogonal on the set $\mathbf{E} = \{e_0, e_1\}$,

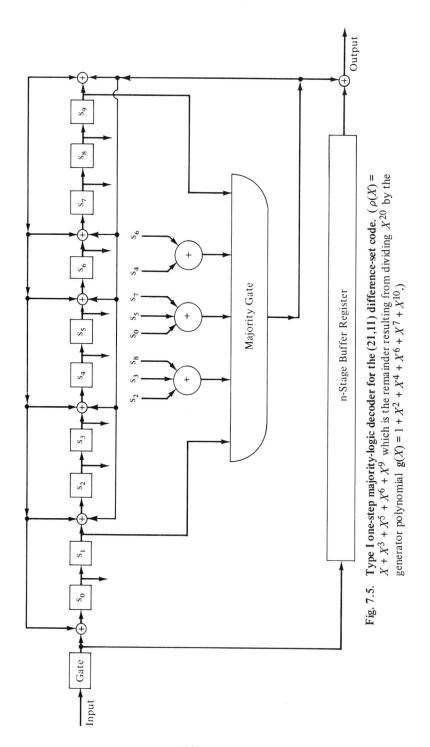

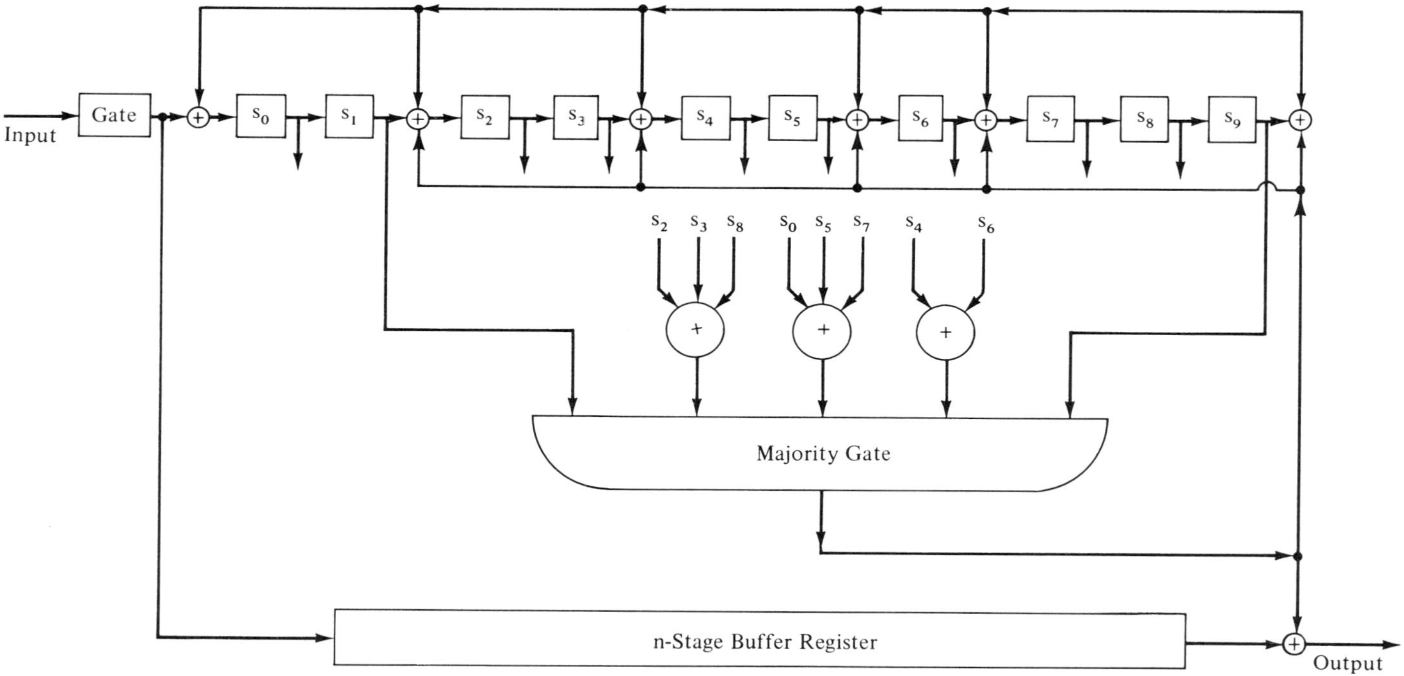

Fig. 7.5. Type I one-step majority-logic decoder for the (21,11) difference-set code. ($\rho(X) = X + X^3 + X^5 + X^6 + X^9$ which is the remainder resulting from dividing X^{20} by the generator polynomial $\mathbf{g}(X) = 1 + X^2 + X^4 + X^6 + X^7 + X^{10}$.)

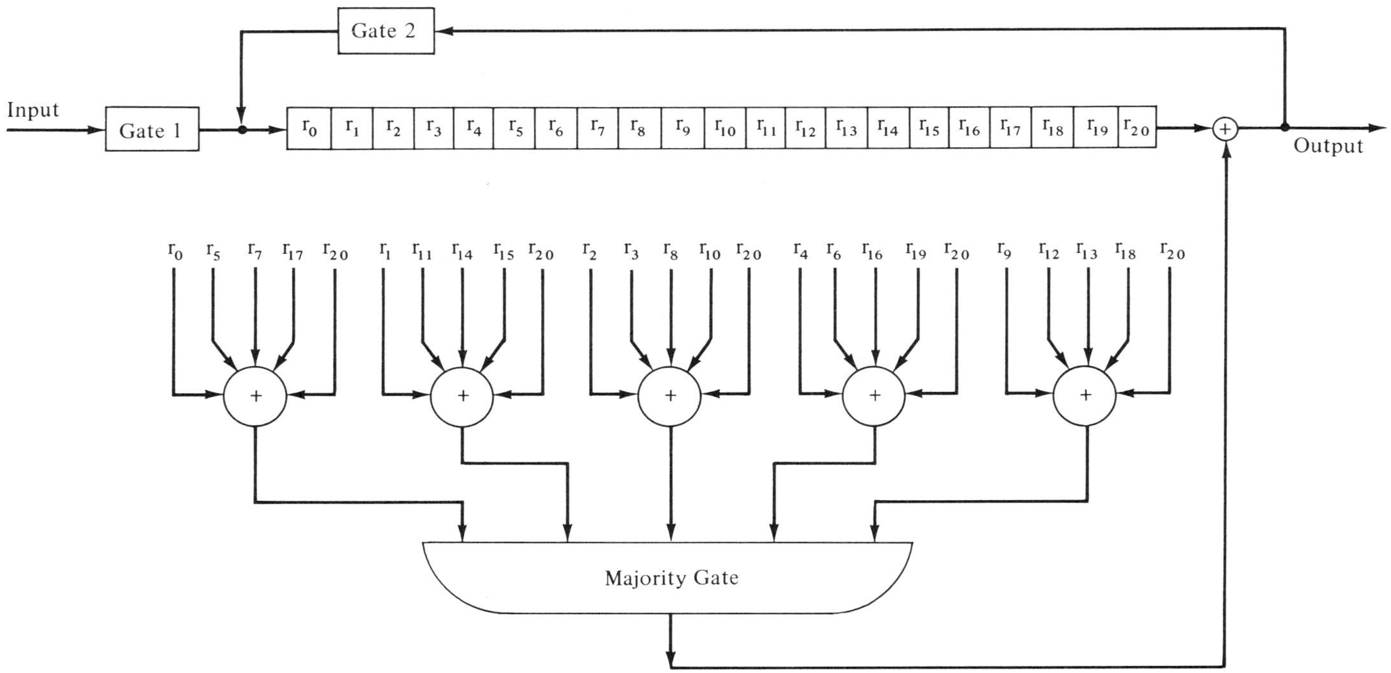

Fig. 7.6. Type II one-step majority-logic decoder for the (21,11) difference-set code.

s	n	k	d	t	Generator Polynomial, **g**(X)	Associated Difference-Set
1	7	3	4	1	0,2,3,4	0,2,3
2	21	11	6	2	0,2,4,6,7,10	0,2,7,8,11
3	45	45	10	4	0,2,4,6,8,12,16,22,25,28	0,2,10,24,25,29,36,42,45
4	273	191	18	8	0,4,10,18,22,24,34,36,40,48,52, 56,66,67,71,76,77,82	0,18,24,46,50,67,103,112,115, 126,128,159,166,167,186,196,201
5	1057	813	34	16	0,1,3,4,5,11,14,17,18,22,23,26 27,28,32,33,35,37,39,41,43, 45,47,48,51,52,55,59,62,68, 70,71,72,74,75,76,79,81,83, 88,95,96,98,101,103,105,106, 108,111,114,115,116,120,121, 122,123,124,126,129,131,132, 135,137,138,141,142,146,147, 149,150,151,153,154,155,158, 160,161,164,165,166,167,169, 174,175,176,177,178,179,180, 181,182,183,184,186,188,189, 191,193,194,195,198,199,200, 201,202,203,208,209,210,211, 212,214,216,222,224,226,228, 232,234,236,242,244	0,1,3,7,15,31,54,63,109,127, 138,219,255,277,298,338,348,439, 452,511,528,555,597,677,697,702, 754,792,897,905,924,990,1023

Table 7.1.* List of binary difference-set cyclic codes.

Note: Each generator polynomial is represented by the exponents of its non-zero terms. For example, {0,2,3,4} represents $\mathbf{g}(X) = 1 + X^2 + X^3 + X^4$.

* This table is taken from E.J. Weldon, Jr., "Difference-Set Cyclic Codes," Bell Systems Tech. Journal, Table 1, p. 1048, September, 1966. (Copyright, 1966, The American Telephone and Telegraph Co., reprinted by permission.)

$$
\begin{aligned}
A_1 &= e_0 + e_1 + e_2 \\
A_2 &= e_0 + e_1 \qquad\quad + e_3 + e_4 \\
A_3 &= e_0 + e_1 \qquad\qquad\qquad + e_5 \\
A_4 &= e_0 + e_1 \qquad\qquad\qquad\qquad + e_6 + e_7 \ .
\end{aligned}
$$

Following the same argument employed in Section 7.1, the sum of error digits in $\mathbf{E}$, $e_{i_1} + e_{i_2} + \ldots + e_{i_M}$, can be determined correctly from the check sums $A_1, A_2, \ldots, A_J$ orthogonal on $\mathbf{E}$ provided that $[J/2]$ or fewer errors occurred in the error vector added by the noisy channel. This sum can be considered as an additional check sum and used for decoding.

Consider an (n,k) cyclic code which is used for error control purposes. Let $\mathbf{e} = (e_0, e_1, \ldots, e_{n-1})$ denote the error vector which is added to the transmitted code vector by the channel. Let $\mathbf{E}_1^1, \mathbf{E}_2^1, \ldots, \mathbf{E}_i^1, \ldots$ be selected sets of error digits of $\mathbf{e}$. Let $S(\mathbf{E}_i^1)$ be the modulo-2 sum of error digits in $\mathbf{E}_i^1$. Suppose that, for each set $\mathbf{E}_i^1$, it is possible to form at least J parity-check sums orthogonal on it. Then the sum $S(\mathbf{E}_i^1)$ can be estimated from these J orthogonal check sums. The estimation can be done by a J-input majority gate with the J orthogonal check sums as inputs. The estimated value of $S(\mathbf{E}_i^1)$ is the output of the majority gate which is "1" if and only if more than one-half of the inputs are "1"; otherwise, it is "0." This estimation is correct provided that $[J/2]$ or fewer errors occurred in the error vector $\mathbf{e}$. The estimated sums $S(\mathbf{E}_i^1)$'s are then used to estimate the sums of error digits in the second selected sets $\mathbf{E}_1^2, \mathbf{E}_2^2, \ldots$ with size smaller than that of the first selected sets. The process of estimating sums from sums of larger size is called *orthogonalization*.[20] The orthogonalization process continues until a set of J or more parity-check sums orthogonal on only a single error digit e_ℓ is obtained. Then the value of e_ℓ can be estimated from these orthogonal check sums by a majority gate. Because of the cyclic symmetry of the code, every error digit can be estimated in this manner. A code is said to be *L-step orthogonalizable* (or *L-step majority-logic decodable*) if L steps of orthogonalization are required to make a decoding decision on an error digit e_ℓ. The code is said to be *completely L-step orthogonalizable* if J is equal to $d-1$, where d is the minimum distance of the code. Since majority gates are used to estimate certain selected sums of error digits at each step of orthogonalization, a total of L levels of majority gates are required for decoding. The number of majority gates required at each levels depends on the structure of the code. The above decoding scheme is best illustrated by an example.

Consider the (7,4) Hamming code generated by $\mathbf{g}(X) = 1 + X + X^3$. The generator matrix $\mathbf{G}$ and parity-check matrix $\mathbf{H}$ are found as follows:

$$\mathbf{G} = \begin{bmatrix} 1 & 1 & 0 & 1 & 0 & 0 & 0 \\ 0 & 1 & 1 & 0 & 1 & 0 & 0 \\ 1 & 1 & 1 & 0 & 0 & 1 & 0 \\ 1 & 0 & 1 & 0 & 0 & 0 & 1 \end{bmatrix}$$

$$\mathbf{H} = \begin{bmatrix} 1 & 0 & 0 & 1 & 0 & 1 & 1 \\ 0 & 1 & 0 & 1 & 1 & 1 & 0 \\ 0 & 0 & 1 & 0 & 1 & 1 & 1 \end{bmatrix} .$$

The syndrome $\mathbf{s} = (s_0, s_1, s_2)$ of the received vector is equal to $\mathbf{e}\mathbf{H}^T$. Thus,

$$\begin{aligned} s_0 &= e_0 + e_3 + e_5 + e_6 \\ s_1 &= e_1 + e_3 + e_4 + e_5 \\ s_2 &= e_2 + e_4 + e_5 + e_6 . \end{aligned}$$

Let $\mathrm{E}_1 = \{e_5, e_6\}$ and $\mathrm{E}_2 = \{e_4, e_6\}$ be two selected sets. It is easy to see that the check sums s_0 and s_2 are orthogonal on set E_1, and the check sums $s_0 + s_1$ and s_2 are orthogonal on set E_2. Thus, J is equal to 2. Let $\mathrm{B}_1 = e_5 + e_6$ be the estimated sum of e_5 and e_6 and let $\mathrm{B}_2 = e_4 + e_6$ be the estimated sum of e_4 and e_6. These two estimated check sums are orthogonal on e_6. Thus, e_6 can be estimated from B_1 and B_2. If a single error has occurred in the error vector, then the estimations of B_1 and B_2 are correct and the estimation of e_6 is also correct. Therefore, this code can correct any single error by 2-step majority-logic decoding. Since the minimum distance d of this code is 3 and J is equal to 2, this code is 2-step completely orthogonalizable. A Type I majority-logic decoder for this code is shown in Fig. 7.7 and a Type II majority-logic decoder is shown in Fig. 7.8.

A general Type I decoder for an L-step orthogonalizable code is shown in Fig. 7.9. The decoding procedure can be described as follows:

Step 1. As usual, the syndrome is calculated by shifting the received vector into the syndrome calculator. At the same time, the received vector is stored into a buffer.

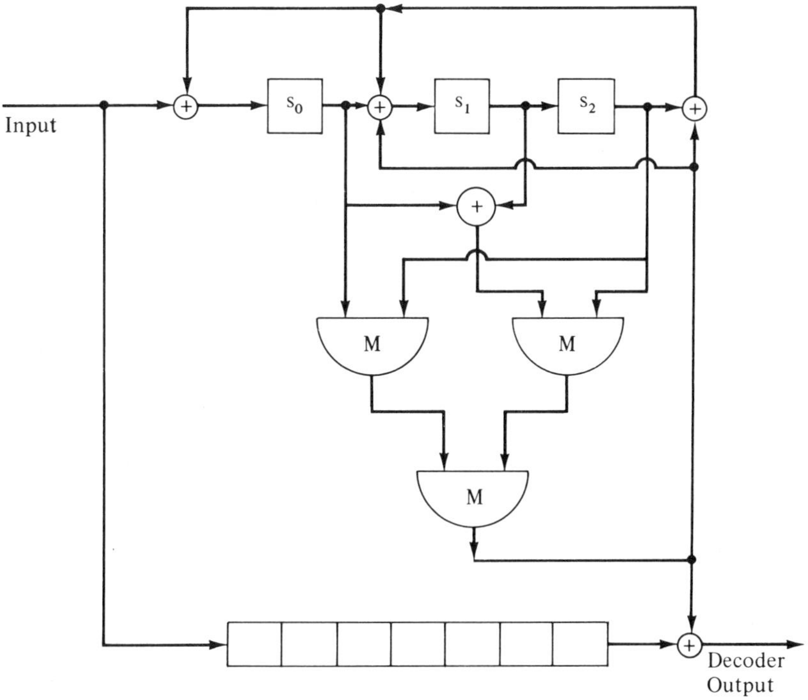

Fig. 7.7. Type I 2-step majority-logic decoder for the (7,4) Hamming code. ($p(X) = 1 + X^2$.)

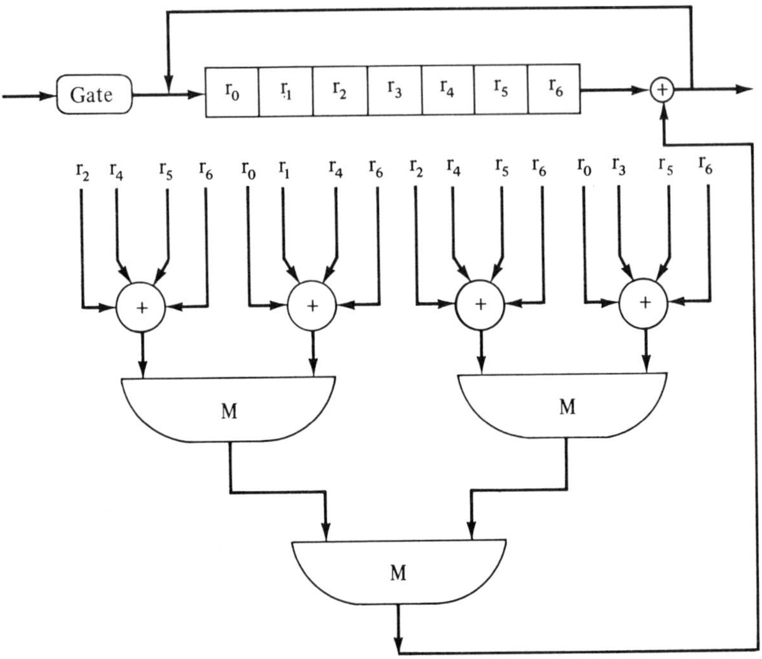

Fig. 7.8. Type II 2-step majority-logic decoder for the (7,4) Hamming code.

Step 2. A set of check sums [approximately $(J)^L$ of them] is formed orthogonal on certain selected sets of error digits. This set of check sums is fed into the first level majority gates; there are $(J)^{L-1}$ of them, each with J inputs. The outputs of the first level of majority-logic gates are then fed into the second level of majority-logic gates; there are $(J)^{L-2}$ of them, each with $2t$ inputs. The outputs of the second level of majority-logic gates are then fed into the third level majority-logic gates; there are $(J)^{L-3}$ of them, each with J inputs. This continues until the last level of majority-logic gates; there is only one gate at the last level. The J inputs to this gate are parity-check sums orthogonal on the first error digit e_{n-1}. If the output of this gate is "1," the decoder assumes that the first received information digit is incorrect. Otherwise, the decoder assumes that the first received information digit is correct.

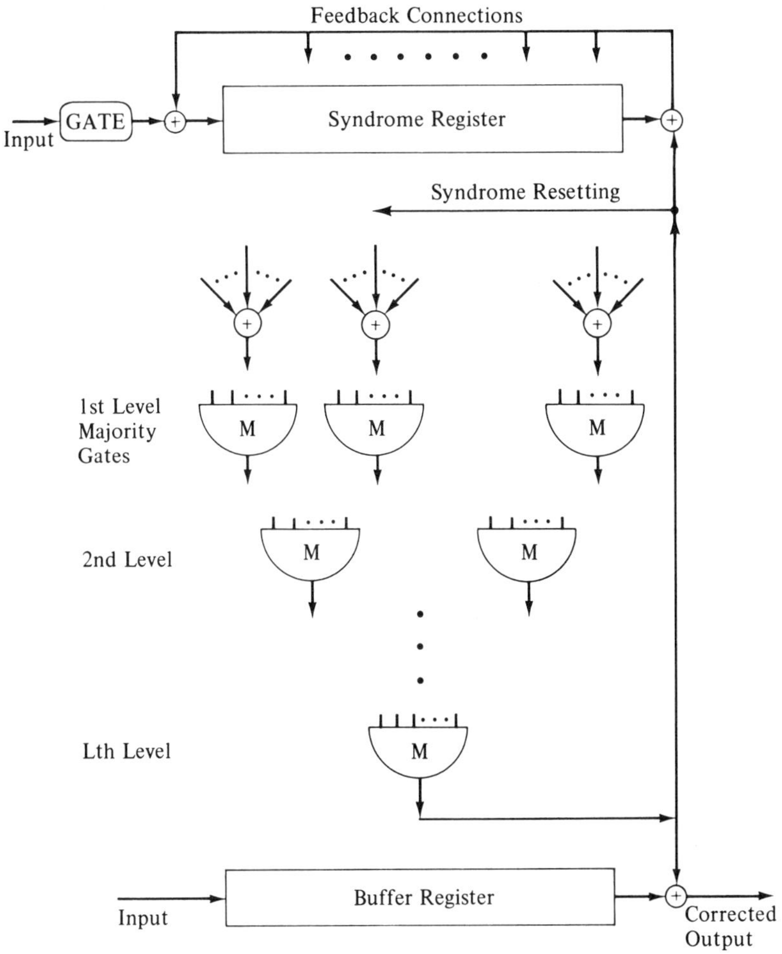

Fig. 7.9. A general Type I majority-logic decoder for an *L*-step orthogonalizable code.

Step 3. The first received digit is read out of the buffer and is corrected by the output of the last majority gate. This correction is accomplished by an Exclusive OR gate.

Step 4. Both the syndrome and buffer registers are shifted cyclically once. The new syndrome in the register is then used for decoding the second received digit in exactly the same manner as decoding the first received digit. The decoder repeats Steps 2 and 3.

Step 5. The received vector is decoded digit by digit in the manner described in Steps 2, 3, and 4 until the received vector is read out of the buffer. Correct decoding is guaranteed, provided that $[J/2]$ or fewer errors occurred in the received vector.

A general Type II L-step majority-logic decoder is shown in Fig. 7.10. The error correction procedure can be explained as follows:

Step 1. With Gate 1 opened and Gate 2 closed, the received vector is read into the buffer register.

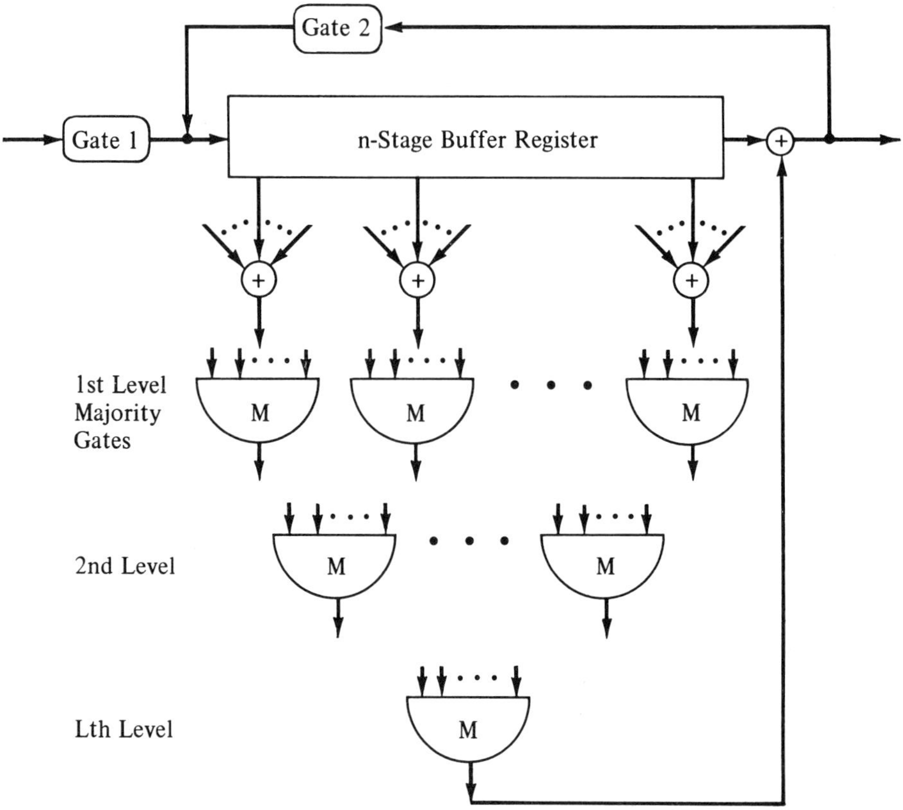

Fig. 7.10. A general Type II majority-logic decoder for an *L*-step orthogonalizable code.

Step 2. Parity-check sums orthogonal on certain selected sets of error digits are formed by summing appropriate sets of received digits. The rest of the orthogonalization process is the same as described in Step 2 of Type I L-step decoding.

Step 3. The first received digit r_{n-1} is read out of the buffer and is corrected by the output of the last level majority gate. The correction is done by an Exclusive OR gate.

Step 4. After Step 3, the buffer register has been shifted one place to the right. Now the second received digit is in the first stage of the buffer register and will be corrected in exactly the same manner as the first received digit was. The decoder repeats Steps 2 and 3.

Step 5. The received vector is decoded digit by digit in the above manner until a total of n digits has been decoded.

An L-step majority-logic decoder requires L levels of majority-logic gates. In general, at the ith level, $(J)^{L-i}$ gates are required. Thus, a total of

$$\sum_{i=1}^{L} (J)^{L-i}$$

gates are needed. Therefore, the complexity of an L-step majority-logic decoder is an exponential function of L. If L is large, the decoder is likely to be impractical. Fortunately, there are many cyclic codes with useful parameters which can be decoded with a reasonably small L.

7.4 L-STEP MAJORITY-LOGIC DECODABLE CODES

It has been shown[20] that the $(2^m, 2^m\text{-}m\text{-}1)$ Hamming code is completely orthogonalizable in $m\text{-}1$ steps. Thus, the Hamming codes can be decoded by the majority-logic decoding described in the previous section. However, the error-trapping decoding for Hamming codes described in Section 5.2 can be much more simply implemented than the majority-logic decoding. The *BCH* codes which are known to be completely orthogonalizable are: (1) the subclass $(2^{m-2}\text{-}1)$-error-correcting $(2^m\text{-}1, m\text{+}1)$ codes for

$m \geqslant 3$ (2-step orthogonalizable); (2) the double-error-correcting (15,7) code (1-step orthogonalizable); and (3) the triple-error-correcting (31,16) code (3-step orthogonalizable). Besides the above codes, several classes of cyclic codes have been recently found to be L-step majority-logic decodable. The construction and the rules for orthogonalization of these codes are based on the properties of finite geometries. To discuss finite geometries is beyond the scope of this introductory book. In the following, only the parameters and generator polynomials of these codes are given.

Let h be a non-negative integer less than 2^{ms}, where m and s are two positive integers. The integer h can be expressed in radix-2^s form as follows:

$$h = \delta_0 + \delta_1 2^s + \delta_2 2^{2s} + \ldots + \delta_{m-1} 2^{(m-1)s} , \tag{7.15}$$

where $0 \leqslant \delta_i < 2^s$ for $i = 0, 1, 2, \ldots, m-1$. For example, let $m = 3$ and $s = 2$; then $h = 45$ can be expressed as

$$h = 1 + 3 \cdot 2^2 + 2 \cdot 2^{2 \cdot 2} ,$$

where $\delta_0 = 1$, $\delta_1 = 3$, and $\delta_2 = 2$. Define the 2^s-*weight* of h as the sum (ordinary sum) of the coefficients in its radix-2^s expansion,

$$W_{2^s}(h) = \sum_{i=0}^{m-1} \delta_i . \tag{7.16}$$

For example, the 2^2-weight of $h = 45$ is 6. Consider the difference

$$h - W_{2^s}(h) = \delta_1(2^s-1) + \delta_2(2^s-1) + \ldots + \delta_{m-1}(2^s-1) .$$

It is obvious that h is divisible by $2^s - 1$ if and only if $W_{2^s}(h)$ is divisible by $2^s - 1$. Let $h^{(\ell)}$ be the remainder resulting from dividing $2^\ell h$ by $2^{ms} - 1$, i.e.,

$$2^{\ell}h = q(2^{ms}-1) + h^{(\ell)} \quad . \tag{7.17}$$

Finite Projective Geometry Codes (*PG Codes*)

Since the construction and rules for orthogonalization of this class of codes are based on the properties of *finite projective geometry*, the codes are therefore called *finite projective geometry codes.* For any two positive integers m and s, there exists an L-step orthogonalizable code ($L < m$) with the following parameters:

$$n = \frac{2^{ms}-1}{2^s-1}$$

$$n-k = \left[\begin{array}{l}\text{The number of non-negative integers } h \\ \text{less than } 2^{ms}-1 \text{ which are divisible by} \\ 2^s-1 \text{ and such that } \max\limits_{0\leq \ell<s} W_{2^s}[h^{(\ell)}] = \\ j(2^s-1) \text{ with } 0 \leqslant j < m-L.\end{array}\right] \tag{7.18}$$

$$J = \frac{2^{(m-L)}-1}{2^s-1} \quad .$$

This code is capable of correcting any combination of $[J/2]$ or fewer errors by L-step majority-logic decoding. The minimum distance of this code is at least $J+1$. Let α be a primitive element of the Galois field GF(2^{ms}) and let h be a non-negative integer less than 2^{ms}. The generator polynomial $g(X)$ of this code has α^h as a root if and only if: (1) h is divisible by 2^s-1; and (2) $\max\limits_{0\leq \ell<s} W_{2^s}[h^{(\ell)}] = j(2^s-1)$ with $0 \leqslant j < m-L$, where $h^{(\ell)}$ is the remainder resulting from dividing $2^{\ell}h$ by 2^{ms}-1. In terms of linear factors, $g(X)$ is equal to

$$g(X) = (X+\alpha^{h_1})(X+\alpha^{h_2})\ldots(X+\alpha^{h_{n-k}}) \quad .$$

Using the table of $GF(2^{ms})$, $\mathbf{g}(X)$ can be expressed as a polynomial with binary coefficients,

$$\mathbf{g}(X) = g_0 + g_1 X + g_2 X^2 + \ldots + g_{n-k} X^{n-k} ,$$

where $g_0 = g_{n-k} = 1$. Except for certain special cases, there is no simple formula for enumerating the number $n-k$ of parity-check digits specified by Eq. (7.18).

For $L = 1$, we obtain a class of one-step majority-logic decodable codes which contains the Difference-Set cyclic codes ($m = 3$) as a subclass. For $L = 1$ and $s = 1$, it yields the class of maximum length sequence codes as discussed in Section 7.2.

Euclidean Geometry Codes (EG Codes)

This is another large class of multi-step majority-logic decodable codes. The construction and rules of orthogonalization are based on *Euclidean geometry*. An L-step majority-logic decodable code of this class has the following parameters:

$$n = 2^{ms} - 1$$

$$n - k = \left[\begin{array}{l} \text{The number of non-negative integers} \\ \text{less than } 2^{ms}\text{-1 such that } 0 < \\ \max\limits_{0 \leq \ell < s} W_{2^s}[h^{(\ell)}] \leqslant (m-L)(2^s-1). \end{array} \right] \qquad (7.19)$$

$$J = \frac{2^{(m-L+1)s} - 1}{2^s - 1} - 1 ,$$

where m, s, and L are positive integers with $L < m$. Let α be a primitive element of the Galois field $GF(2^{ms})$ and let h be a non-negative integer less than 2^{ms}. The generator polynomial $\mathbf{g}(X)$ of this code has α^h as a root if and only if $0 < \max_{0 \leq \ell < s} W_{2^s}[h^{(\ell)}] \leqslant (m - L)(2^s - 1)$. Again, except for certain special cases, there is no simple formula for enumerating the number of parity-check digits specified by Eq. (7.19).

For $s = 1$, we obtain a subclass of Euclidean geometry codes which are of practical interest. This subclass of codes is known as the *Reed-Muller codes*. An L-step majority-logic decodable Reed-Muller code has the following parameters:

$$n = 2^m - 1$$

$$k = \sum_{i=0}^{L-1} \binom{m}{i}$$

$$J = 2^{m-L+1} - 2 \quad .$$

The minimum distance of this code was shown to be exactly $J + 1$. Therefore, this code is completely orthogonalizable. Non-cyclic Reed-Muller codes were first discovered by Muller in 1954.[23] In the same year, Reed[28] devised a majority-logic decoding algorithm for these codes.

For moderate length n, the error-correcting capability of a geometry code is slightly inferior to that of a comparable *BCH* code. However, the majority-logic decoding algorithm for geometry codes is more simply implemented than the known decoding algorithms for *BCH* codes. Thus, for moderate n, geometry codes provide rather effective error control. For large n, geometry codes become much inferior to the comparable *BCH* codes, and the number of majority-logic gates required for the majority-logic decoder becomes prohibitively large. In this case, *BCH* codes are definitely superior to geometry codes in error-correcting capability and decoder complexity. Some geometry codes with useful parameters are given in Tables 7.2, 7.3, and 7.4.

Geometry codes were first studied by Rudolph.[29] Rudolph's work was later extended and generalized by many other coding investigators. For algebraic structures and rules for orthogonalization of geometry codes, the reader is referred to References 6, 9, 14, 15, 16, 25, 33, 35, 37, and 38.

Code (n, k)	J	Number of Orthogonalization Steps L	Number of Majority Gates Required M
(21,11)	4	1	1
(73,45)	8	1	1
(85,24)	20	1	1
(85,68)	4	2	5
(273,191)	16	1	1
(341,45)	84	1	1
(341,195)	20	2	21
(341,315)	4	3	21
(585,184)	72	1	1
(585,520)	8	2	9
(1057,813)	32	1	1
(1365,78)	340	1	1
(1365,483)	84	2	85
(1365,1063)	20	3	421
(1365,1328)	4	4	85

Table 7.2. A list of some finite projective geometry codes.

Code (n, k)	J	Number of Orthogonalization Steps L	Number of Majority Gates Required M
(63,13)	20	1	1
(63,37)	8	1	1
(255,175)	16	1	1
(255,231)	4	3	21
(255,127)	20	2	21
(255,19)	84	1	1

Table 7.3. A list of Euclidean geometry codes, $s \geqslant 2$.

Code (n, k)	J	Number of Orthogonalization Steps L	Number of Majority Gates Required M
(15,5)	6	1	1
(15,11)	2	1	1
(31,6)	14	2	2
(31,16)	6	3	6
(31,26)		Hamming code	
(63,7)	30	2	2
(63,22)	14	2	7
(63,42)	6	2	7
(63,57)	2	Hamming code	
(127,8)	62	2	2
(127,29)	30	3	8
(127,64)	14	4	23
(127,99)	6	5	43
(255,9)	126	2	2
(255,37)	62	2	9
(255,93)	30	3	30
(255,163)	14	2	15
(255,219)	6	3	43
(255,247)	2	Hamming code	
(511,10)	254	2	2
(511,46)	126	3	10
(511,130)	62	2	38
(511,256)	30	3	94
(511,382)	14	4	164
(511,466)	6	3	43
(511,502)	2	4	15
(1023,11)	510	2	2
(1023,56)	254	2	11
(1023,176)	126	3	47
(1023,386)	62	3	131
(1023,638)	30	2	31
(1023,848)	14	3	383
(1023,968)	6	4	259
(1023,1013)	2	4	15

Table 7.4. A list of Reed-Muller codes.

PROBLEMS

7.1. In Section 7.1, we have shown that the double-error-correcting (15,7) *BCH* code is completely orthogonalizable in one-step. Construct both Type I and Type II one-step majority-logic decoders for this code.

7.2. Consider an (11,6) linear code whose parity-check matrix is

$$\mathbf{H} = \begin{bmatrix} 1&0&0&0&0&1&1&1&1&1&1 \\ 0&1&0&0&0&1&1&0&1&0&0 \\ 0&0&1&0&0&1&0&1&0&1&0 \\ 0&0&0&1&0&0&1&1&0&0&1 \\ 0&0&0&0&1&0&0&0&1&1&1 \end{bmatrix}$$

(This code is not cyclic.)

(a) Show that the minimum distance of this code is exactly 4.

(b) Let $\mathbf{e} = (e_0, e_1, e_2, e_3, e_4, e_5, e_6, e_7, e_8, e_9, e_{10})$ be an error vector. Find the syndrome bits in terms of error digits.

(c) Construct all possible parity-check sums orthogonal on each message error digit e_i for $i = 5, 6, 7, 8, 9, 10$.

(d) Is this code completely orthogonalizable in one-step?

7.3. Show that the all one vector is not a code vector in a maximum-length code.

7.4. Let $\mathbf{v}(X) = v_0 + v_1X + v_2X^2 + \ldots + v_{2^m-2}X^{2^m-2}$ be a non-zero code vector in the $(2^m-1, m)$ maximum-length code whose parity polynomial is $\mathbf{p}(X)$. Show that the other 2^m-2 non-zero code vectors are cyclic shifts of $\mathbf{v}(X)$. (Hint: Let $\mathbf{v}^{(i)}(X)$ and $\mathbf{v}^{(j)}(X)$ be the ith cyclic shift and the jth cyclic shift of $\mathbf{v}(X)$ with $0 \leqslant i < j < 2^m-2$. Show that $\mathbf{v}^{(i)}(X) \neq \mathbf{v}^{(j)}(X)$.)

7.5. Arrange the 2^m-1 non-zero code vectors of a maximum-length code as rows of a $(2^m-1) \times (2^m-1)$ array.

(a) Show that each column of this array has 2^{m-1} ones and $2^{m-1}-1$ zeros.

(b) Show that the weight of each non-zero code vector is exactly 2^{m-1}.

7.6. Consider the (31,5) maximum-length code whose parity-check polynomial is $\mathbf{p}(X) = 1 + X^2 + X^5$. Find all the polynomials orthogonal on the error digit e_{30}.

7.7. Use Eqs. (7.10) and (7.11) to find the parity-check polynomial of the (7,3) difference-set code whose associate perfect simple difference-set is $\mathbf{P} = \{0, 2, 3\}$. Find the polynomials orthogonal on the error digit e_6.

7.8. Consider the triple-error-correcting (15,5) BCH code whose generator polynomial is

$$\mathbf{g}(X) = 1 + X + X^2 + X^4 + X^5 + X^8 + X^{10} .$$

Let $\mathbf{e} = (e_0, e_1, e_2, e_3, e_4, e_5, e_6, e_7, e_8, e_9, e_{10}, e_{11}, e_{12}, e_{13}, e_{14})$ be an error vector.

(a) Find the parity-check matrix of this code.

(b) Find the syndrome bits in terms of error digits.

(c) Find the parity-check sums orthogonal on $E_1 = \{e_{10}, e_{11}\}$, $E_2 = \{e_{11}, e_{12}\}$, $E_3 = \{e_{12}, e_{13}\}$, $E_4 = \{e_{10}, e_{12}\}$, $E_5 = \{e_{10}, e_{13}\}$, and $E_6 = \{e_{11}, e_{13}\}$.

(d) Show that this code is completely orthogonalizable in two steps. Construct the Type I two-step majority-logic decoder for this code.

7.9. Let $m = 2$, $s = 2$, and $L = 1$. Find the generator polynomial $\mathbf{g}(X)$ of the one-step majority-logic decodable EG code of length 15 and $J = 4$. (Use the Galois field GF(2^4) of Table 2.2.) Show that this EG code is actually the double-error-correcting (15,7) BCH code.

7.10. Let $\mathbf{P} = \{\ell_0, \ell_1, \ell_2, \ldots, \ell_{2^s}\}$ be a perfect simple difference-set of order 2^s such that

$$0 \leqslant \ell_0 < \ell_1 < \ell_2 < \ldots < \ell_{2^s} \leqslant 2^s(2^s+1) \quad .$$

Construct a vector of $n = 2^{2s} + 2^s + 1$ components,

$$\mathbf{v} = (v_0, v_1, v_2, \ldots, v_{n-1}) \quad ,$$

whose non-zero components are $v_{\ell_0}, v_{\ell_1}, \ldots, v_{\ell_{2^s}}$, i.e.,

$$v_{\ell_0} = v_{\ell_1} = \ldots = v_{\ell_{2^s}} = 1 \quad .$$

Consider the following $n \times 2n$ matrix:

$$\mathbf{G} = [\mathbf{Q} \quad \mathbf{I}_n]$$

where (1) $\mathbf{I}_n$ is an $n \times n$ identity matrix, and (2) $\mathbf{P}$ is an $n \times n$ matrix whose n rows are $\mathbf{v}$ and $n-1$ cyclic shifts of $\mathbf{v}$. The code generated by $\mathbf{G}$ is a $(2n,n)$ linear code (not cyclic) whose parity-check matrix is

$$\mathbf{H} = [\mathbf{I}_n \quad \mathbf{Q}^T] \quad .$$

(a) Show that $J = 2^s + 1$ parity-check sums orthogonal on any message error digit can be formed.

(b) Show that the minimum distance of this code is $d = J+1 = 2^2+2$.

(This code is referred to as a half-rate *quasi-cyclic code*.[37])

REFERENCES

1. Berlekamp, E. R., *Algebraic Coding Theory*, McGraw-Hill, New York, 1968.
2. Carmichael, R. D., *Introduction to the Theory of Groups of Finite Order*, Dover Press, 1937.
3. Chow, D. K., "A Geometric Approach to Coding Theory with Application to Information Retrieval," CSL Report R-368, University of Illinois, Urbana, Illinois, 1967.
4. Chow, D. K., "On Threshold Decoding of Cyclic Codes," *Information and Control*, **13**, pp. 471-483, November, 1968.
5. Delsarte, P., "A Geometric Approach to a Class of Cyclic Codes," *J. of Combinatorial Theory*, **6**, pp. 340-358, 1969.
6. Delsarte, P., J. M. Goethals, and J. MacWilliams, "On GRM and Related Codes," *Information and Control*, in press.
7. Evans, T. A., and H. B. Mann, "On Simple Difference Sets," *Sankhya*, **11**, pp. 464-481, 1955.
8. Gallager, R. G., *Low-Density Parity Check Codes*, The M.I.T. Press, Cambridge, Massachusetts, 1963.
9. Goethals, J.M., and P. Delsarte, "On a Class of Majority-Logic Decodable Codes," *IEEE Trans. on Information Theory*, **IT-14**, March, 1968.
10. Gore, W. C., "Generalized Threshold Decoding and the Reed-Solomon Codes," *IEEE Trans. on Information Theory*, **IT-15**, pp. 78-81, January, 1969.
11. Gore, W. C., "The Equivalence of L-step Orthogonalization and a Reed Decoding Procedure," *IEEE Trans. on Information Theory*, **IT-15**, pp. 184-186, January, 1969.
12. Graham, F. L., and J. MacWilliams, "On the Number of Parity Checks in Difference-Set Cyclic Codes," *Bell Systems Tech. J.*, **45**, pp. 1046-1070, September, 1966.

13. Green, J. H., and R. L. San Soucie, "An Error-Correction Encoder and Decoder of High Efficiency," *Proc. IRE*, **46**, pp. 1741-1744, 1958.

14. Kasami, T., S. Lin, and W. W. Peterson, "New Generations of the Reed-Muller Codes—Part I: Primitive Codes," *IEEE Trans. on Information Theory*, **IT-14**, March, 1968.

15. Kasami, T., S. Lin, and W. W. Peterson, "Polynomial Codes," *IEEE Trans. on Information Theory*, **IT-14**, pp. 807-814, November, 1968.

16. Lin, S., "On a Class of Cyclic Codes," Chapter 7, *Error-Correcting Codes*, H. Mann, Ed., John Wiley, New York, 1968.

17. Lin, S., and E. J. Weldon, Jr., "Further Results on Cyclic Product Codes," *IEEE Trans. on Information Theory*, to appear in 1970.

18. Lucky, R. W., J. Salz, and E. J. Weldon, Jr., *Principles of Data Communication*, McGraw-Hill, New York, 1968.

19. Mann, H. B., *Analysis and Design of Experiments*, Dover Press, 1949.

20. Massey, J. L., *Threshold Decoding*, The M.I.T. Press, Cambridge, Massachusetts, 1963.

21. Massey, J. L., *Advances in Threshold Decoding Advances in Communication Systems*, 2, A. V. Balakrishnan, Ed., Academic Press, 1968.

22. Mitchell, M. E., et al., "Coding and Decoding Operations Research," Final Report on Contract AF 19 (604)-6183, AFCRL8, 1961.

23. Muller, D. E., "Applications of Boolean Algebra to Switching Circuit Design and to Error Detection," *IRE Trans.*, **EC-3**, pp. 6-12, September, 1954.

24. Peterson, W. W., *Error-Correcting Codes*, The M.I.T. Press, Cambridge, Massachusetts, and John Wiley, New York, 1961.

25. Peterson, W. W., and E. J. Weldon, Jr., *Error-Correcting Codes*, 2nd Edition, The M.I.T. Press, Cambridge, Massachusetts, 1970.

26. Prange, E., "Some Cyclic Error Correcting Codes with Simple Decoding Algorithms," AFCRC-TN-38-156, Air Force Cambridge Research Labs., Cambridge, Massachusetts, April, 1958.

27. Prange, E., "The Use of Coset Equivalence in the Analysis and Design of Group Codes," AFCRC-TR-59-164, Air Force Cambridge Research Labs., Cambridge, Massachusetts, June 1959.

28. Reed, I. S., "A Class of Multiple-Error-Correcting Codes and the Decoding Scheme," *IRE Trans.*, **IT-4**, pp. 38-49, September, 1954.

29. Rudolph, L. D., "Geometric Configuration and Majority Logic Decodable Codes," MEE Thesis, University of Oklahoma, Norman, Oklahoma, 1964.

30. Rudolph, L. D., "A Class of Majority Logic Decodable Codes," *IEEE Trans. on Information Theory*, **IT-13**, pp. 305-307, April, 1967.

31. Rudolph, L. D., "Threshold Decoding of Cyclic Codes," *IEEE Trans. on Information Theory*, **IT-15**, pp. 414-418, May, 1969.

32. Singer, J., "A Theorem in Finite Projective Geometry and Some Applications to Number Theory," *AMS Trans.*, **43**, pp. 377-385, 1938.

33. Smith, K. J. C., "Majority Decodable Codes Derived from Finite Geometries," Institute of Statistics Mimeo Series No. 561, University of North Carolina, Chapel Hill, North Carolina, 1967.

34. Weldon, E. J., Jr., "Difference-Set Cyclic Codes," *Bell Systems Tech. J.*, **45**, pp. 1045-1055, September, 1966.

35. Weldon, E. J., Jr., "Euclidean Geometry Cyclic Codes," Proceedings of the Symposium of Combinatorial Mathematics at the University of North Carolina, Chapel Hill, North Carolina, April, 1967.

36. Weldon, E. J., Jr., "Quasi-Cyclic Codes," *IEEE Trans. on Information Theory*, **IT-12**, pp. 183-195, April, 1967.

37. Weldon, E. J., Jr., "New Generations of the Reed-Muller Codes–Part II: Non-primitive Codes," *IEEE Trans. on Information Theory*, **IT-14**, pp. 199-205, March, 1968.

38. Weldon, E. J., Jr., "Some Results on Majority-Logic Decoding," Chapter 8, *Error Correcting Codes*, H. Mann, Ed., John Wiley, 1968.

39. Yale, R. B., *Error Correcting Codes and Linear Recurring Sequences*, Lincoln Laboratory Report 34-77, Lincoln Labs., M.I.T. 1958.

40. Zierler, N., *On A Variation of the First Order Reed-Muller Codes*, Lincoln Laboratory Report 34-80, Lincoln Labs., M.I.T., 1958.

CHAPTER 8

SINGLE-BURST-ERROR-CORRECTING CODES

8.1 INTRODUCTION

In the previous chapters, we have been primarily concerned with coding techniques for channels on which transmission errors occur independently in digit positions, i.e., each transmitted digit is affected independently by noise. However, there are certain communication channels which are affected by disturbances that cause transmission errors to cluster into *bursts*. For example, on telephone lines, a stroke of lightning or a man-made electrical disturbance frequently affects several adjacent transmitted digits. On magnetic storage systems, magnetic tape defects usually affect more than one digit. In general, codes for correcting random errors are not efficient for correcting burst errors. Therefore, it is desirable to design codes specifically for correcting burst errors. Codes of this kind are called *burst-error-correcting codes*.

A burst of length ℓ is defined as a vector whose non-zero components are confined to ℓ consecutive digit positions, the first and last of which are non-zero. For example, the vector $\mathbf{v} = (0\ 0\ 0\ 1\ 0\ 0\ 1\ 0\ 1\ 0\ 0\ 0)$ is a burst of length 6. A linear code which is capable of correcting all burst errors of length ℓ or less (not all burst errors of length $\ell + 1$) is called an *ℓ-burst-error-correcting code*, or the code is said to have *burst-error-correcting capability* ℓ.

It is clear that, for given n and ℓ, we desire to construct an (n,k) code with as small a redundancy $n-k$ as possible. In the following, we shall establish certain restrictions on $n-k$ for given ℓ, or restrictions on ℓ for given $n-k$.

Theorem 8.1: A necessary condition for an (n,k) linear code to be able to correct all burst errors of length ℓ or less is that no burst of length 2ℓ or less can be a code vector.

Proof: Suppose that there exists a burst $\mathbf{v}$ of length 2ℓ or less as a code vector. This code vector $\mathbf{v}$ can be expressed as a vector sum of two bursts **u** and **w** of length ℓ or less (except the degenerate case in which **v** is a burst of length one). By Theorem 3.2, **u** and **w** must be in the same coset of a standard array for this code. If one of these two vectors is used as a coset leader (correctable error pattern), the other will be an uncorrectable error burst. As a result, this code would not be able to correct all burst errors of length ℓ or less. Therefore, in order to correct all burst errors of length ℓ or less, no burst of length 2ℓ or less can be a code vector.

Q.E.D.

Theorem 8.2: The number of parity check digits of an (n,k) linear code which has no burst of length b or less as a code vector is at least b, i.e.,

$$n - k \geqslant b \quad .$$

Proof: Consider the vectors whose non-zero components are confined to the first b digit positions. There are a total of 2^b of them. No two such vectors can be in the same coset of a standard array for this code; otherwise, their vector sum, which is a burst of length b or less, would be a code vector. Therefore, these 2^b vectors must be in 2^b distinct cosets. There are a total of 2^{n-k} cosets for an (n,k) code. Thus, $n-k$ must be at least equal to b; i.e., $n-k \geqslant b$.

Q.E.D.

It follows from Theorems 8.1 and 8.2 that we obtain a restriction on the number of parity check digits of an ℓ-burst-error-correcting code.

Theorem 8.3: The number of parity check digits of an ℓ-burst-error-correcting code must be at least 2ℓ, i.e.,

$$n - k \geqslant 2\ell \quad . \tag{8.1}$$

For given n and k, Theorem 8.3 implies that the burst-error-correcting capability of an (n,k) code is at most $[(n-k)/2]$, i.e.,

$$\ell \leqslant \frac{n-k}{2} \tag{8.2}$$

This is an upper bound on the burst-error-correcting capability of an (n,k) code and is called the Reiger bound.[38] Codes which meet the Reiger bound are said to be *optimal*. The ratio

$$z = \frac{2\ell}{n-k} \tag{8.3}$$

is used as a measure of the *burst-correcting efficiency* of the code. An optimal code has burst-correcting efficiency equal to 1.

It is possible to show[35] that if an (n,k) code is designed to correct all burst errors of length ℓ or less and simultaneously detect all burst errors of length $d \geqslant \ell$ or less, the number of parity check digits of the code must be at least $\ell + d$, i.e.,

$$n-k \geqslant \ell + d \quad .$$

In this chapter, we shall be primarily concerned with cyclic codes which are well suited for correcting a single burst of errors in a coded block of n digits. Cyclic codes for single-burst-error correction were first studied by Abramson.[1,2] In an effort to generalize Abramson's results, Fire[15] discovered a large class of burst-error-correcting cyclic codes with small redundancy $n-k$. Cyclic codes with minimum or near-minimum redundancy for correcting short bursts have been found by a number of researchers.[3,14,16,19,20,22,23,24,29,38] For cyclic codes, an error pattern with errors confined to the first i high-order positions and the $(b-i)$ low-order positions are considered as a burst of length b (this is an *end around burst*).

8.2 DECODING OF SINGLE-BURST-ERROR-CORRECTING CYCLIC CODES

An ℓ-burst-error-correcting cyclic code can be most easily decoded by the error-trapping technique with a slight variation. The decoding is based on the following facts. Let $\mathbf{r}(X)$ be the received vector, let $\mathbf{e}(X)$ be the error vector which contaminated the transmitted code vector, and let

$$\mathbf{s}(X) = s_0 + s_1 X + \ldots + s_{n-k-1} X^{n-k-1}$$

be the syndrome of $\mathbf{r}(X)$. If the errors of $\mathbf{e}(X)$ are confined to the ℓ high-order parity-check positions $X^{n-k-\ell}, \ldots, X^{n-k-2}, X^{n-k-1}$ of $\mathbf{r}(X)$, then according to Eq. (5.1), the ℓ high-order bits

$$s_{n-k-\ell}, \ldots, s_{n-k-2}, s_{n-k-1}$$

of $\mathbf{s}(X)$ match the errors of $\mathbf{e}(X)$ and the $n-k-\ell$ low-order bits

$$s_0, s_1, \ldots, s_{n-k-\ell-1}$$

of $\mathbf{s}(X)$ are zeros. Suppose that the errors of $\mathbf{e}(X)$ are not confined to the positions $X^{n-k-\ell}, \ldots, X^{n-k-2}, X^{n-k-1}$ of $\mathbf{r}(X)$ but are confined to certain ℓ consecutive positions of $\mathbf{r}(X)$ (including the end around case). Then, after a certain number of cyclic shifts of $\mathbf{r}(X)$, say i cyclic shifts, the errors will be shifted to the positions $X^{n-k-\ell}, \ldots, X^{n-k-2}, X^{n-k-1}$ of $\mathbf{r}^{(i)}(X)$, the ith shift of $\mathbf{r}(X)$. Let $\mathbf{s}_i(X)$ be the syndrome of $\mathbf{r}^{(i)}(X)$. Then the first ℓ high-order bits of $\mathbf{s}_i(X)$ match the errors and the $n-k-\ell$ low-order bits of $\mathbf{s}_i(X)$ are zeros.

An error-trapping decoder based on the above facts is shown in Fig. 8.1. The OR gate detects whether the $n-k-\ell$ low-order bits of $\mathbf{s}_i(X)$ are zeros. The decoding procedure can be described in the following steps:

Step 1. Gate 1 is turned on; Gates 2 and 3 are turned off. The syndrome $\mathbf{s}(X)$ is formed by shifting the entire received vector $\mathbf{r}(X)$ into the syndrome register. At the same time, the k received information digits of $\mathbf{r}(X)$ are stored into the buffer register.

Step 2. Gate 1 is turned on; Gates 2 and 3 are turned off. The syndrome register starts to shift. As soon as its $n-k-\ell$ leftmost stages contain only zeros, its ℓ rightmost stages contain the burst pattern.

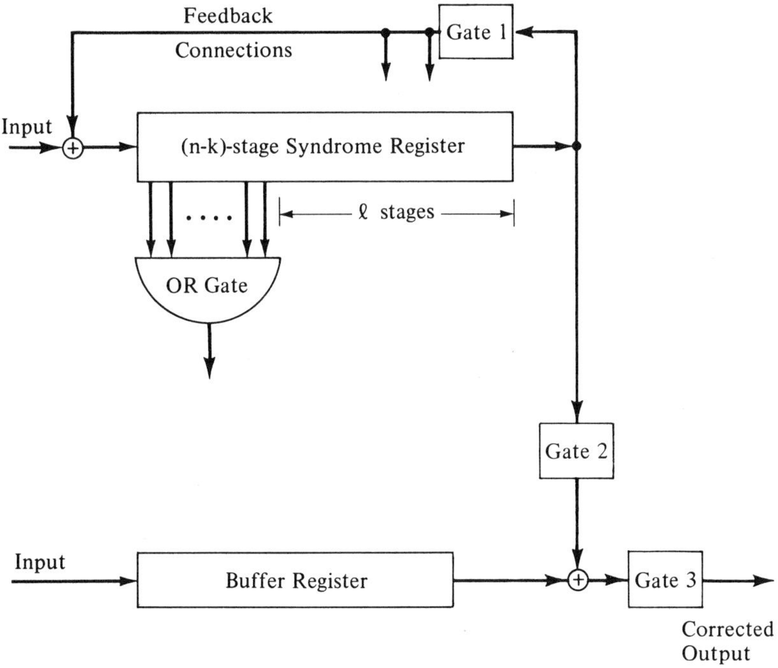

Fig. 8.1. An error-trapping decoder for a burst-error-correcting cyclic code.

Then the correction can be made. Three phases must be considered.

Step 3. If the $n-k-\ell$ leftmost stages of the syndrome register contain zeros after the ith shift for $0 \leqslant i \leqslant n-k-\ell$, then the errors of the burst $\mathbf{e}(X)$ are confined to the parity-check section of $\mathbf{r}(X)$. Thus, the k received information digits in the buffer are error-free. Gate 3 is then turned on and the k error-free information digits in the buffer are shifted out to the data sink. If the $n-k-\ell$ leftmost stages of the syndrome register never contain zeros during the first $n-k-\ell$ shifts of the syndrome register, then the burst is not confined to the $n-k$ parity-check positions of $\mathbf{r}(X)$.

Step 4. If the $n-k-\ell$ leftmost stages of the syndrome register contain zeros after the $(n-k-\ell+i)^{\text{th}}$ shift of the syndrome register for $1 \leqslant i \leqslant \ell$, then the burst is confined to the positions $X^{n-i}, \ldots, X^{n-1}$,

$X^0, \ldots, X^{\ell-i-1}$ of $\mathbf{r}(X)$. The i bits contained in the ℓth, $(\ell-1)^{\text{th}}, \ldots,$ $(\ell-i+1)^{\text{th}}$ stages of the syndrome register (from the right end) match the error bits at the positions $X^{n-i}, \ldots, X^{n-2}, X^{n-1}$ of $\mathbf{r}(X)$. At this instant, a clock starts to count from $(n-k-\ell+i+1)$. The syndrome register is shifted (in step with the clock) with Gate 1 turned off. As soon as the clock has counted up to $n-k$, the i rightmost bits in the syndrome register match the errors in the first i received information digits in the buffer register. Gates 2 and 3 are then turned on. The received information digits are read out of the buffer for correction.

Step 5. If the $n-k-\ell$ leftmost stages never contain all zeros by the time that the syndrome register has been shifted $n-k$ times, then Gate 3 is turned on and the received information digits are read out of the buffer one at a time. At the same time, the syndrome register is shifted with Gate 1 turned on. As soon as the $n-k-\ell$ leftmost stages of the syndrome register contain zeros, the contents of the ℓ rightmost stages of the syndrome register match the errors in the next ℓ received information digits to come out of the buffer. Gate 2 is then turned on and the erroneous information digits are corrected by the digits coming out from the syndrome register with Gate 1 turned off.

If the leftmost $n-k-\ell$ stages of the syndrome register never contain zeros by the time the k information digits have been read out of the buffer, then a burst of length longer than ℓ or an uncorrectable burst has been detected.

The decoder described above corrects only burst errors of length ℓ or less. The number of these burst error patterns is $n2^{\ell-1}$ which, for large n, is only a small fraction of 2^{n-k} correctable error patterns (coset leaders). It is possible to modify the above decoder in such a way that it corrects all the correctable burst errors of length $n-k$ or less. That is, besides correcting all the bursts of length ℓ or less, the decoder also corrects those bursts of length $\ell+1$ to $n-k$ which are used as coset leaders. This modified decoder operates as follows. The entire received vector is first shifted into the syndrome register. Before performing the error correction, the syndrome register is cyclically shifted n times (with feedback connections operative). During this cycling, the length b of the shortest burst which appears in the b rightmost stages of the syndrome register is recorded by a counter. This burst is assumed to be the error burst added by the channel. Having completed the above pre-correction shifts, the decoder begins its correction process. The syndrome register starts to shift again. As soon as the shortest burst reappears in the b rightmost stages of the syndrome register, the decoder starts to make corrections as described earlier. The above decoding is an optimum decoding for burst-error-correcting codes which was proposed by Gallager.[17]

8.3 SINGLE-BURST-ERROR-CORRECTING CODES

Fire Codes

This is the first class of cyclic codes constructed systematically for correcting or detecting a single burst of errors in a coded block of n digits. Let $\mathbf{p}(X)$ be an irreducible polynomial of degree m and let e be the smallest positive integer such that $X^e + 1$ is divisible by $\mathbf{p}(X)$. An ℓ-burst-error-correcting Fire code is generated by the polynomial

$$\mathbf{g}(X) = \mathbf{p}(X)(1 + X^{2\ell-1}) , \tag{8.4}$$

where $\ell \leqslant m$ and $2\ell - 1$ is not divisible by e. The length n of this code is equal to the least common multiple of e and $2\ell - 1$, i.e.,

$$n = \mathrm{LCM}(e, 2\ell - 1) . \tag{8.5}$$

The number of parity-check digits of this code is $m + 2\ell - 1$. For a proof of the above result, the reader is referred to References 15 and 35.

The burst-correcting efficiency of a Fire code is

$$z = \frac{2\ell}{m + 2\ell - 1} .$$

If ℓ is chosen to be equal to m, then

$$z = \frac{2m}{3m - 1} .$$

For large m, z is approximately 2/3. Thus, Fire codes are not very efficient with respect to the Reiger bound.

A Fire code which is capable of correcting any burst of length ℓ or less and of simultaneously detecting any burst of length $d \geqslant \ell$ is generated by

$$g(X) = p(X)(1 + X^c) , \tag{8.6}$$

where $c \geqslant \ell + d - 1$.[15,35] The length of this code is equal to the least common multiple of e and c.

Other Codes

Some very efficient cyclic codes and shortened cyclic codes for correcting short single bursts have been found by a number of coding investigators.[3,14,23,24,29,39] A list of these codes with their generator polynomials is given in Table 8.1. These codes and the codes derived from them by interlacing as described in the following section are the most efficient single-burst-error-correcting codes known.

8.4 INTERLACED CODES

Given an (n,k) cyclic code, it is possible to construct a $(\lambda n, \lambda k)$ cyclic code, i.e., a code λ times as long with λ times as many information digits, by *interlacing*. This is done simply by arranging λ code vectors in the original code into λ rows of a rectangular array and then transmitting them column by column. The resulting code is called an *interlaced code*. The parameter λ is referred to as the *interlacing degree*.

Obviously, a pattern of errors can be corrected for the whole array if and only if the pattern of errors in each row is a correctable pattern for the original code. No matter where it starts, a burst of length λ will affect no more than one digit in each row. Thus, if the original code corrects single errors, the interlaced code corrects single bursts of length λ or less. Similarly, if the original code corrects all combinations of t or fewer errors, the interlaced code will correct any combination of t bursts of length λ or less. If the original code corrects any single burst of length ℓ or less, the interlaced

$n-k-2\ell$	Code (n,k)	Burst-Correcting Ability ℓ	Generator Polynomial
0	(7,3)	2	35
	(15,9)	3	171
	(19,11)	4	1151
	(27,17)	5	2671
	(34,22)	6	15173
	(38,24)	7	114361
	(50,34)	8	224531
	(56,38)	9	1505773
	(59,39)	10	4003351
1	(15,10)	2	65
	(27,20)	3	311
	(38,29)	4	1151
	(48,37)	5	4501
	(67,54)	6	36365
	(103,88)	7	114361
	(96,79)	8	501001
2	(31,25)	2	161
	(63,55)	3	711
	(85,75)	4	2651
	(131,119)	5	15163
	(169,155)	6	55725
3	(63,56)	2	355
	(121,112)	3	1411
	(164,153)	4	6255
	(290,277)	5	24711
4	(511,499)	4	10451
5	(1023,1010)	4	22365

Table 8.1. Some burst-correcting cyclic and shortened cyclic codes.

Note: Generator polynomials are given in an octal representation. Each digit in the table represents three binary digits according to the following code:

$0 \longleftrightarrow 0\,0\,0$ $\quad 2 \longleftrightarrow 0\,1\,0$ $\quad 4 \longleftrightarrow 1\,0\,0$ $\quad 6 \longleftrightarrow 1\,1\,0$

$1 \longleftrightarrow 0\,0\,1$ $\quad 3 \longleftrightarrow 0\,1\,1$ $\quad 5 \longleftrightarrow 1\,0\,1$ $\quad 7 \longleftrightarrow 1\,1\,1$

The binary digits are then the coefficients of the polynomial, with the high-order coefficients at the left. For example, the binary representation of 171 is 0 0 1 1 1 1 0 0 1, and the corresponding polynomial is $\mathbf{g}(X) = X^6 + X^5 + X^4 + X^3 + 1$.

code will correct any single burst of length $\lambda\ell$ or less. If an (n,k) code has maximum possible burst-error-correcting capability, i.e., $n-k-2\ell = 0$, then the interlaced $(\lambda n, \lambda k)$ code also has maximum possible burst-error-correcting capability. By interlacing short codes with maximum possible burst-error-correcting capability, it is possible to construct codes of practically any length with maximum burst-error-correcting ability. Therefore, the interlacing technique reduces the problem of searching long efficient burst-error-correcting codes to searching good short codes.

The obvious way to implement an interlaced code is to set up the array and operate on rows in encoding and decoding. This is generally *not* the simplest implementation. The simplest implementation results from the observation that *if the original code is cyclic, then the interlaced code is also cyclic*. If the generator polynomial of the original code is $\mathbf{g}(X)$, then the generator polynomial for the interlaced code is $\mathbf{g}(X^{\lambda})$.[22] Thus, encoding and error correction can be accomplished by using shift registers. It turns out that the decoder for the interlaced code can be derived from the decoder of the original code simply by replacing each register-stage of the original decoder by λ stages without changing the other connections. This essentially allows the decoder circuitry to look at successive rows of the code array on successive decoder cycles. Therefore, if the decoder of the original code is simple (this is usually true for short codes), so is the decoder for the interlaced code.

The interlacing technique described above is effective not only for deriving long powerful single-burst-error-correcting codes from short optimal single-burst-error-correcting codes, but also for deriving long powerful burst-and-random-error-correcting codes from short codes as described in the following chapter.

8.5 PHASED-BURST-ERROR-CORRECTING CODES

Consider an (n,k) code whose length n is a multiple of an integer m, say $n = \sigma m$. Denote a code polynomial by

$$\mathbf{v}(X) = v_0 + v_1 X + v_2 X^2 + \ldots + v_{\sigma m-1} X^{\sigma m-1} .$$

Define the m consecutive code digits of the form

$$v_{im}, v_{im+1}, \ldots, v_{(i+1)m-1}$$

as a *sub-block*, where $0 \leqslant i \leqslant \sigma - 1$. Thus, a code vector of this code consists of σ sub-blocks. A burst of length λm or less is called a *phased-burst* if and only if it is confined to λ consecutive sub-blocks, where λ is a positive integer less than σ. A linear code of length $n = \sigma m$ which is capable of correcting all phased error bursts confined to λ or fewer sub-blocks is called a λm-phased-burst-error-correcting code. Since a burst of length $(\lambda - 1)m + 1$, no matter where it starts, can affect at most λ sub-blocks, it is clear that a λm-phased-burst-error-correcting code is capable of correcting any single burst of length $(\lambda - 1)m + 1$ or less. Thus, a λm-phased-burst-error-correcting code can be used as a $[(\lambda - 1)m + 1]$-single-burst-error-correcting code.

Burton Codes

Burton[5] has discovered a class of phased-burst-error-correcting cyclic codes which is similar to the class of Fire codes. Let $\mathbf{p}(X)$ be an irreducible polynomial of degree m, let e be the smallest positive integer such that $X^e + 1$ is divisible by $\mathbf{p}(X)$ and let n be the least common multiple of m and e, say

$$\begin{aligned} n &= \mathrm{LCM}(m,e) \\ &= \sigma m \ . \end{aligned}$$

Then, for any positive integer m, there exists an m-phased-burst-error-correcting Burton code of length $n = \sigma m$ which is generated by

$$\mathbf{g}(X) = \mathbf{p}(X)\,(1 + X^m) \ . \tag{8.7}$$

The number of parity-check digits of this code is $2m$. Thus, this is a $(\sigma m, (\sigma - 2)m)$ cyclic code. Each code vector consists of σ sub-blocks. In order to show that the Burton code of Eq. (8.7) is capable of correcting all phased-bursts confined to a single sub-block of m digits, it is necessary and sufficient to show that no two such bursts are in the same coset of a standard array for this code. For a proof of this result, the reader is referred to References 5 and 36.

The encoding of a Burton code can be accomplished with a $2m$-stage shifted register with feedback connections according to $\mathbf{g}(X)$. The decoding of this code can be accomplished with the decoder as described in Section 8.2 except that the contents of the m leftmost stages of the syndrome register are tested for zeros at every m^{th} shift.

It is possible to interlace an m-phased-burst-error-correcting Burton code in such a way that the interlaced $(\lambda n, \lambda k)$ code is capable of correcting any phased-burst which is confined to λ consecutive sub-blocks. Arrange λ code vectors in the m-phased-burst-error-correcting code into λ rows of a rectangular array as before. Now consider a sub-block of each row as a single element. Then the array consists of σ columns. Each column consists of λ sub-blocks. The array is transmitted column by column, one sub-block from each row at a time. Therefore, a code vector in the interlaced code consists of $\lambda\sigma$ sub-blocks. No matter where it starts, any phased-error-burst confined to λ or fewer sub-blocks will affect no more than one sub-block in each row. Thus, this phased-burst will be corrected if the received array is decoded on a row-by-row basis. If this interlaced code is used as a $[(\lambda-1)m+1]$-burst-error-correcting code, its burst-error-correcting efficiency is

$$z = \frac{2[(\lambda-1)m+1]}{\lambda(n-k)}$$

$$= \frac{2[(\lambda-1)m+1]}{2\lambda m} = 1 - \frac{1}{\lambda}\left(\frac{m-1}{m}\right) .$$

As λ approaches infinity, the burst-error-correcting efficiency of the code approaches one, i.e., $\lim_{\lambda\to\infty} z = 1$. Thus, by interlacing the Burton codes, it is possible to obtain a class of asymptotically optimal burst-error-correcting codes. For large λ, an interlaced Burton code is more efficient than a Fire code of the same burst-error-correcting capability.

The obvious way to implement an interlaced Burton code is to set up the code array and operate on rows in encoding and decoding. Thus, the encoder of the interlaced code consists of the encoder of the original code and a buffer for the storage of the row vectors of the code array; the decoder of the interlaced code consists of the decoder of the original code and a buffer for the storage of the received code array.

PROBLEMS

8.1. Show that a single-error-correcting and double-error-detecting Hamming code is capable of correcting any single burst of length 2 or less ($\ell = 2$).

8.2. Suppose that the single-error-correcting and double-error-detecting Hamming code of length 15 is used for correcting bursts of length 2 or less. Devise an error-trapping decoder for this code.

8.3. Let $\mathbf{p}(X)$ be a primitive polynomial of degree 5. Find the generator polynomial of a Fire code which is capable of correcting any single burst of length 5 or less ($\ell = 5$). What is the length of this code? Construct an error-trapping decoder for this code.

8.4. Use a code in Table 8.1 to derive a new code with burst-error-correcting capability $\ell = 51$, length $n = 255$, and burst-error-correcting efficiency $z = 1$. Construct a decoder for this new code.

8.5. Let $m = 5$. Construct a Burton code which is capable of correcting any phased-burst confined to a single sub-block of 5 digits. Suppose that this code is interlaced to a degree $\lambda = 6$. What are the length, the number of parity-check digits, and the burst-error-correcting capability of this interlaced code?

8.6. Interlace the (164,153) code in Table 8.1 to a degree $\lambda = 6$. Compare this interlaced code with the interlaced Burton code of the previous problem. Which code is more efficient?

REFERENCES

1. Abramson, N. M., "A Class of Systematic Codes for Non-Independent Errors," *IRE Trans. on Information Theory*, **IT-5**, pp. 150-157, December, 1959.

2. Abramson, N. M., and B. Elspas, "Double-Error-Correcting Coders and Decoders for Non-Independent Binary Errors," presented at the UNESCO Information Processing Conference in Paris, France, 1959.

3. Abramson, N. M., "Error Correcting Codes from Linear Sequential Networks," *Proc.* 4th *London Symposium on Information Theory*, C. Cherry, Ed., Butterworths, Washington, D. C., 1961.

4. Brown, D. T., and W. W. Peterson, "Cyclic Codes for Error Detection," *Proc. IRE*, **49**, pp. 228-235, January, 1961.

5. Burton, H. O., "A Class of Asymptotically Optimal Burst Correcting Block Codes," presented at the ICCC, Boulder, Colorado, June, 1969.

6. Calabi, L., and H. G. Haefeli, "A Class of Binary Systematic Codes Correcting Errors at Random and in Bursts," *IRE Trans. on Information Theory*, **IT-5**, Special Supplement, pp. 79-94, May, 1959.

7. Campopiano, C. N., "Bounds on Burst Error Correcting Codes," *IRE Trans. on Information Theory*, **IT-8**, pp. 257-259, April, 1962.

8. Chien, R. T., "Burst-Correcting Codes with High-Speed Decoding," *IEEE Trans. on Information Theory*, **IT-15**, pp. 109-113, January, 1969.

9. Cheilik, P., "A Note on Utilization of Cyclic Codes," *IEEE Trans. on Information Theory*, **IT-12**, p. 402, July, 1966.

10. Corr, F. P., "Multiple Burst Detection," *Proc. IRE*, **49**, p. 1337, 1961.

11. Corr, F. P., "A Shortened Cyclic Code for Multiple Errors," *IEEE Trans. on Information Theory*, **IT-12**, p. 404, July, 1966.

12. Elliott, E.O., "Estimates of Error Rates for Codes on Burst-Noise Channels," *Bell Systems Tech. J.*, **42**, pp. 1977-1998, September, 1963.

13. Elspas, B., "A Note on P-nary Adjacent-Error-Correcting Codes," *IRE Trans. on Information Theory*, **IT-6**, pp. 13-15, March, 1960.

14. Elspas, B., and R.A. Short, "A Note on Optimum Burst-Error-Correcting Codes," *IRE Trans. on Information Theory*, **IT-8**, pp. 39-42, January, 1962.

15. Fire, P., "A Class of Multiple-Error-Correcting Binary Codes for Non-Independent Errors," Sylvania Report RSL-E-2, Sylvania Electronic Defense Laboratory, Reconnaissance Systems Division, Mountain View, California, March, 1959.

16. Foulk, C. R., "Some Properties of Maximally-Efficient Cyclic Burst-Correcting Codes and Results of a Computer Search for Such Codes," File No. 375, Digital Computer Lab., University of Illinois, Urbana, Illinois, June 12, 1961.

17. Gallager, R. G., *Information Theory and Reliable Communication*, John Wiley, New York, 1968.

18. Gorog, E., "Some New Classes of Cyclic Codes Used for Burst Error Correction," *IBM J. Research Develop.*, **7**, pp. 102-111, 1963.

19. Gross, A. J., "Binary Group Codes which Correct in Bursts of Three or Less for Odd Redundancy," *IRE Trans. on Information Theory*, **IT-8**, pp. 356-359, October, 1962.

20. Gross, A. J., "A Note on Some Binary Group Codes which Correct Errors in Bursts of Four or Less," *IRE Trans. on Information Theory*, **IT-8**, p. 384, October, 1962.

21. Gross, A. J., "Augmented Bose-Chaudhuri Codes Which Correct Single Bursts of Errors," *IEEE Trans. on Information Theory*, **IT-9**, p. 121, April, 1963.

22. Kasami, T., "Cyclic Codes for Burst-Error-Correction," *J. Inst. Elec. Commun. Eng. Japan*, **45**, p. 9-16, January, 1962.

23. Kasami, T., "Optimum Shortened Cyclic Codes for Burst-Error-Correction," *IEEE Trans. on Information Theory*, **IT-9**, pp. 105-109, April, 1963.

24. Kasami, T., and S. Matoba, "Some Efficient Shortened Cyclic Codes for Burst-Error-Correction," *IEEE Trans. on Information Theory*, **IT-10**, pp. 252-253, July, 1964.

25. Lucky, R. W., J. Salz, and E. J. Weldon, Jr., *Principles of Data Transmission*, McGraw-Hill, New York, 1968.

26. Meggitt, J.E., "Error Correcting Codes for Correcting Bursts of Errors," *IBM J. Research Develop.*, **4**, pp. 329-334, July, 1960.

27. Meggitt, J.E., "Error Correcting Codes for Correcting Bursts of Errors," *Trans. AIEE*, **80**, pp. 708-711, January, 1961.

28. Meggitt, J. E., "Error-Correcting Codes and Their Implementation for Data Transmission Systems," *IRE Trans. on Information Theory*, **IT-7**, pp. 234-244, October, 1961.

29. Melas, C. M., "A New Group of Codes for Correction of Dependent Errors in Data Transmission," *IBM J. Research Develop.*, **4**, pp. 58-64, January, 1960.

30. Melas, C. M., "A Cyclic Code for Double Error Correction," *IBM J. Research Develop.*, **4**, pp. 364-366, January, 1960.

31. Melas, C. M., and E. Gorog, "A Note on Extending Certain Codes to Correct Error Bursts in Longer Messages," *IBM J. Research Develop.*, **7**, pp. 151-152, 1963.

32. Metzner, J. J., "Burst-Error Correcting for Randomly-Chosen Binary Group Codes," *IEEE Trans. on Information Theory*, **IT-9**, pp. 281-285, October, 1963.

33. Mitchell, M. E., "Simple Decoders and Correlators for Cyclic Error-Correcting Codes," *IEEE Trans. on Communications Systems*, **CS-10**, pp. 284-291, 1962.

34. Peterson, W. W., "Binary Coding for Error Control," *Proc. NEC*, **16**, pp. 15-21, 1960.

35. Peterson, W. W., *Error-Correcting Codes*, The M.I.T. Press, Cambridge, Massachusetts, and John Wiley, New York, 1961.

36. Peterson, W. W., and E. J. Weldon, Jr., *Error-Correcting Codes*, 2nd Edition, The M.I.T. Press, Cambridge, Massachusetts, 1970.

37. Posner, W., "Simultaneous Error-Correction and Burst-Error Detection Binary Linear Cyclic Codes," *J. Soc. Indust. Appl. Math.*, **13**, pp. 1087-1095, December, 1965.

38. Reiger, S. H., "Codes for the Correction of 'Clustered' Errors," *IRE Trans. on Information Theory*, **IT-6**, pp. 16-21, March, 1960.

39. Stone, J. J., "Multiple Burst Error Correction," *Information and Control*, **4**, pp. 324-331, December, 1961.

40. Tong, S. Y., "Burst Trapping Techniques for a Compound Channel," Bell Telephone Labs. Technical Memo., 1968.

41. Tavares, S. E., and S. G. S. Shiva, "Detecting and Correcting Multiple Bursts for Binary Cyclic Codes," to appear in the *IEEE Trans. on Information Theory*, **IT-16**, 1970.

42. Wolf, J. K., "On Codes Derivable from the Tensor Product of Check Matrices," *IEEE Trans. on Information Theory*, **IT-11**, pp. 281-284, April, 1965.

43. Zetterberg, L. H., "Cyclic Codes from Irreducible Polynomials for Correction of Multiple Errors," *IEEE Trans. on Information Theory*, **IT-8**, pp. 13-21, January, 1962.

CHAPTER 9

BURST-AND-RANDOM-ERROR-CORRECTING CODES

On many communication channels, errors occur neither independently at random nor in well-defined single bursts. Consequently, random-error-correcting codes or single-burst-error-correcting codes will be either inefficient or inadequate in attempts to combat these mixed disturbances. On such channels it is desirable to design codes which are capable of correcting random errors and/or single or multiple bursts.

Several methods of constructing codes for the correction of random errors as well as burst errors have been proposed. The most effective method is the interlacing technique as described in Section 8.4. By interlacing a t-random-error-correcting (n,k) code to degree λ, we obtain a $(\lambda n,\lambda k)$ code which is capable of correcting any combination of t bursts of length λ or less. Three other methods of deriving new codes from known codes for simultaneously correcting random errors and burst errors are presented in this chapter.

Other works on constructing burst-and-random-error-correcting codes can be found in References 2, 14, 19, 22, 23, 24, and 25. Reference 14 contains an extensive list of efficient burst-and-random-error-correcting codes.

9.1 PRODUCT CODES

Suppose $\mathbf{C}_1$ is an (n_1,k_1) code and $\mathbf{C}_2$ is an (n_2,k_2) code. A code with $n_1 n_2$ symbols can be formed by making a rectangular array of n_1 columns and n_2 rows in which every row is a code vector in $\mathbf{C}_1$ and every column is a code vector in $\mathbf{C}_2$, as shown in Fig. 9.1. The symbols in the upper left section of the array are all information digits. Thus, there are $k_1 k_2$ information digits and this is an $(n_1 n_2, k_1 k_2)$ code. This resulting code is called a *product code*.[10]

The digits in the upper right corner are calculated from the parity-check rules for code $\mathbf{C}_1$, and the ones in the lower left from the rules for code $\mathbf{C}_2$. The next question is, should we calculate the check digits in the lower right section by using the rules for code $\mathbf{C}_2$ on columns or the rules

$$
\begin{array}{cccc|ccc}
X_{11} & X_{12} & \cdots & X_{1k_1} & X_{1(k_1+1)} & \cdots & X_{1n_1} \\
X_{21} & X_{22} & \cdots & X_{2k_1} & X_{2(k_1+1)} & \cdots & X_{2n_1} \\
\vdots & & & & & & \\
X_{k_2 1} & X_{k_2 2} & \cdots & X_{k_2 k_1} & X_{k_2(k_1+1)} & \cdots & X_{k_2 n_1} \\
\hline
X_{(k_2+1)1} & X_{(k_2+1)2} & \cdots & X_{(k_2+1)k_1} & X_{(k_2+1)(k_1+1)} & \cdots & X_{(k_2+1)n_1} \\
\vdots & & & & & & \\
X_{n_2 1} & X_{n_2 2} & \cdots & X_{n_2 k_1} & X_{n_2(k_1+1)} & \cdots & X_{n_2 n_1}
\end{array}
$$

Fig. 9.1. A code array

for code C_1 on rows? It turns out that the answer is the same either way, and it is possible to have all row code vectors in C_1 and all column code vectors in C_2 simultaneously.

If the code C_1 has minimum weight d_1 and the code C_2 has minimum weight d_2, then the minimum weight of the product code is exactly $d_1 d_2$. A minimum weight code vector in the product code is formed by: (1) choosing a minimum weight code vector in C_1 and a minimum weight code vector in C_2; and (2) forming an array in which all columns corresponding to zeros in the code vector from C_1 are zeros and all columns corresponding to ones in the code vector from C_1 are the minimum weight code vector chosen from C_2.

It is not easy to characterize the correctable error patterns; this depends upon how the correction is actually done. One method involves using the correction first on rows and then on columns. In this case, a pattern will be correctable if and only if the uncorrectable patterns on rows after row correction leave correctable patterns on the columns. It generally improves the correction by decoding rows, columns, then columns and rows again.

The product code can correct any combination of $[(d_1 d_2 - 1)/2]$ errors, but the above method will not achieve this. For example, consider the product code of two Hamming single-error-correcting codes. The minimum distance of each is 3, so the minimum distance of the product is 9. A pattern of 4 errors at the corners of a rectangle gives 2 errors in each of the two rows and the two columns and is therefore not correctable by simple correction on rows and columns. Nevertheless, simple correction on rows and columns, although non-optimum, can be very effective.

Let ℓ_1 and ℓ_2 be the burst-error-correcting capabilities of code $\mathbf{C}_1$ and code $\mathbf{C}_2$ respectively. The burst-error-correcting capability of the product code of $\mathbf{C}_1$ and $\mathbf{C}_2$ can be analyzed as follows. Suppose that a code array is transmitted row by row and that, at the output of the channel, the received digits are rearranged back into an array row by row. No matter where it starts, any existing error burst of length $n_1 \ell_2$ or less will affect no more than $\ell_2 + 1$ consecutive rows; when the received digits are rearranged back into an array, each column is at most affected by a burst of length ℓ_2. Now if the array is decoded on a column-by-column basis, the burst will be corrected. Therefore, the burst-error-correcting capability of the product code is at least $n_1 \ell_2$. Suppose that a code array is transmitted on a column-by-column basis and decoded on a row-by-row basis. By a similar argument, it is possible to show that any error burst of length $n_2 \ell_1$ or less can be corrected. Thus, the burst-error-correcting capability of the product code is at least $n_2 \ell_1$. Consequently, we may conclude that the burst-error-correcting capability ℓ of the product code is at least $\max \{n_1 \ell_2, n_2 \ell_1\}$, i.e.,

$$\ell \geqslant \max \{ n_1 \ell_2, n_2 \ell_1 \} \quad . \tag{9.1}$$

So far we have considered a product code for either random-error correction or burst-error correction. However, a product code can be used for simultaneous random-error correction and burst-error correction. Let d_1 and d_2 be the minimum distances of codes $\mathbf{C}_1$ and $\mathbf{C}_2$ respectively. Then it is possible to show that the product code of $\mathbf{C}_1$ and $\mathbf{C}_2$ is capable of correcting any combination of $t = [(d_1 d_2 - 1)/2]$ random errors and of simultaneously correcting any error burst of length $\ell = \max(n_1 t_2, n_2 t_1)$ or less, where $t_1 = [(d_1 - 1)/2]$ and $t_2 = [(d_2 - 1)/2]$. Proof of this assertation can be found in References 4 and 18.

The obvious way to implement a product code is to set up the code array and operate on rows and then columns (or columns and then rows) in encoding and decoding, but there is an alternative that can be extremely attractive. In many cases the product code of cyclic codes is cyclic, and cyclic code implementation is much simpler.

If n_1 and n_2 are relatively prime and if $\mathbf{C}_1$ and $\mathbf{C}_2$ are cyclic codes, then the product code is cyclic if the digits are transmitted in the correct order. Start with the upper left corner and move down and to the right on a 45° diagonal, i.e., transmit $X_{11}, X_{22}, X_{33}, \ldots$ When you reach the end of a column, move to the top of the next column. When you reach the end of a row, move to the first digit of the next row.

Since n_1 and n_2 are relatively prime, there exists a pair of integers a and b such that

$$an_1 + bn_2 = 1 \ .$$

Let $\mathbf{g}_1(X)$ and $\mathbf{h}_1(X)$ be the generator and parity polynomials of the (n_1,k_1) cyclic code $\mathbf{C}_1$ and let $\mathbf{g}_2(X)$ and $\mathbf{h}_2(X)$ be the generator and parity polynomials of the (n_2,k_2) cyclic code $\mathbf{C}_2$. Then it is possible to show[4,15] that the generator polynomial $\mathbf{g}(X)$ of the cyclic product code of $\mathbf{C}_1$ and $\mathbf{C}_2$ is the greatest common divisor of $X^{n_1 n_2} - 1$ and $\mathbf{g}_1(X^{bn_2})\mathbf{g}_2(X^{an_1})$, i.e.,

$$\mathbf{g}(X) = \text{GCD}\,[X^{n_1 n_2} - 1, \mathbf{g}_1(X^{bn_2})\mathbf{g}_2(X^{an_1})] \tag{9.2}$$

and the parity polynomial $\mathbf{h}(X)$ of the cyclic product code is the greatest common divisor of $\mathbf{h}_1(X^{bn_2})$ and $\mathbf{h}_2(X^{an_1})$, i.e.,

$$\mathbf{h}(X) = \text{GCD}\,[\mathbf{h}_1(X^{bn_2}), \mathbf{h}_2(X^{an_1})] \ . \tag{9.3}$$

Suppose that the cyclic code $\mathbf{C}_1$ has random-error-correcting capability t_1 and burst-error-correcting capability ℓ_1 and the cyclic code $\mathbf{C}_2$ has random-error-correcting capability t_2 and burst-error-correcting capability

ℓ_2. Then the burst-error-correcting capability ℓ of the cyclic product code of $\mathbf{C}_1$ and $\mathbf{C}_2$ is at least equal to max $(n_1t_2+\ell_1, n_2t_1+\ell_2)$,[4] i.e.,

$$\ell \geqslant \max\,(n_1t_2+\ell_1, n_2t_1+\ell_2) \quad . \tag{9.4}$$

This can be shown as follows. Suppose that an error burst of length $n_2t_1+\ell_2$ or less occurred during the transmission of a code array. When the received digits are rearranged back into an array, all except ℓ_2 adjacent rows will contain t_1 or fewer errors. Each of these ℓ_2 adjacent rows will contain t_1+1 or fewer errors. If the rows are decoded first, then these ℓ_2 adjacent rows may contain errors after the row decoding. Therefore, after row decoding, each column of the array contains an error burst of length at most ℓ_2. Since the column code $\mathbf{C}_2$ is capable of correcting any error burst of length ℓ_2 or less, all the remaining errors in the array will be corrected by column decoding. By a similar argument, any error burst of length $n_1t_2+\ell_1$ or less will be corrected if the column decoding is performed before the row decoding. Therefore, we obtain the result as stated by Eq. (9.4).

The complexity of the decoder for cyclic product codes is comparable to the complexity of the decoders for both the (n_1, k_1) code and the (n_2,k_2) code. At the receiving end of the channel, the received vector may again be rearranged as a rectangular array. Thus, the decoder can decode each of the row (or column) code vectors separately and then decode each of the column (or row) code vectors. Alternatively, in the transmitted code vector, the set of n_1 digits formed by selecting every n_2^{th} digit are the n_1 digits of a code vector of $\mathbf{C}_1$ permuted in a fixed way. They can be permuted back to their original form and corrected in a Meggitt-type decoder. The digits in the permuted form are a code vector in a related code and can be decoded directly in this form in a Meggitt-type decoder. Similarly, correction for the column code $\mathbf{C}_2$ can be done by selecting every n_1^{th} digit from the large code vector. Thus, the total equipment required is roughly that required to decode the two individual codes.

There is room for a good deal of engineering ingenuity in devising decoding procedures for cyclic product codes.[1,4,15,18]

9.2 BINARY CODES DERIVED FROM REED-SOLOMON CODES

In Chapter 2, it was pointed out that any element β in the Galois field $GF(2^m)$ can be expressed uniquely as a sum of $1, \alpha, \alpha^2, \ldots, \alpha^{m-1}$ in the following form:

$$\beta = a_0 + a_1\alpha + a_2\alpha^2 + \ldots + a_{m-1}\alpha^{m-1}$$

where α is a primitive element in $GF(2^m)$ and $a_\ell = 0$ or 1. Thus, the correspondence between β and $(a_0, a_1, \ldots, a_{m-1})$ is one-to-one. We shall call the m-tuple $(a_0, a_1, \ldots, a_{m-1})$ an *m-bit byte* representation of β.

Consider a t-error-correcting Reed-Solomon code with code symbols from $GF(2^m)$. If each symbol is represented by its corresponding m-bit byte, then we obtain a binary code with the following parameters:

$$n = m(2^m - 1) \text{ binary digits}$$

$$n - k = 2mt \text{ binary check digits} \quad .$$

This code is capable of correcting any error pattern that affects t or fewer m-bit bytes. It is immaterial whether a byte has one error or whether all the m bits are in error; it is counted as one byte error. This can be seen as follows. At the channel output, the binary received vector is divided into $2^m - 1$ bytes; each byte is transformed back into a symbol in $GF(2^m)$. Thus, if an error pattern affects t or fewer bytes, it affects t or fewer symbols in a Reed-Solomon code. Obviously, the error pattern can be corrected by the decoding method described in Sections 6.2 and 6.4. We shall call this binary code a *t-byte-correcting code*. Actually, this code is a multiple-phased-burst-error-correcting code.

Binary codes derived from Reed-Solomon codes are more effective against clustered errors than random errors since clustered errors usually involve several errors per byte and thus relatively few byte errors. Thus, for example, since a burst of length $3m + 1$ cannot affect more than 4 bytes, a four-byte correcting code can correct any single burst of length $3m + 1$ or less. It can also simultaneously correct any combination of two bursts of length $m+1$ or less because each such burst can affect no more than 2 bytes. At the same time, it can correct any combination of 4 or fewer random errors. In general, a t-byte-correcting binary Reed-Solomon code is capable of correcting any combination of

$$\lambda = \frac{t}{1 + \frac{\ell + m - 2}{m}}$$

or fewer bursts of length ℓ (or correcting any single burst of length $(t-1)m+1$ or less). Simultaneously, it corrects any combination of t or fewer random errors.

9.3 CONCATENATED CODES

A concatenated code[12] is formed from two codes, an (n_1,k_1) binary code $\mathbf{C}_1$ and an (n_2,k_2) non-binary code $\mathbf{C}_2$ for which the symbols are bytes consisting of k_1 binary symbols. Usually, a Reed-Solomon code is used as $\mathbf{C}_2$. The resulting code has n_1n_2 binary symbols of which k_1k_2 are information digits, just as in the case of product codes.

Encoding consists of two steps. First, the k_1k_2 information digits are divided into k_2 bytes of k_1 information digits each. These k_2 bytes are encoded according to the rules for $\mathbf{C}_2$ to form an n_2 byte code vector. Second, each k_1-digit byte is encoded into a code vector in $\mathbf{C}_1$, resulting in a string of n_2 code vectors of $\mathbf{C}_1$, a total of n_2n_1 digits. These digits are then transmitted, one $\mathbf{C}_1$ code vector at a time in succession.

Decoding is also done in two steps. First, decoding is done for each $\mathbf{C}_1$ code vector as it arrives, and the check digits are removed, leaving a sequence of n_2 k_1-digit bytes. These bytes are then decoded according to the method for $\mathbf{C}_2$ to leave the final corrected message.

Decoding implementation is the straightforward combination of the implementation for codes $\mathbf{C}_1$ and $\mathbf{C}_2$, and the amount of hardware required is roughly that required for both codes.

Concatenated codes are effective against a mixture of random errors and bursts, and the pattern of bytes not correctable by the $\mathbf{C}_1$ code must form a correctable pattern for C_2 if the concatenated code is to correct the pattern. Scattered random errors are corrected by C_1. Bursts will affect relatively few bytes, but probably so badly that C_1 cannot correct them. These few bytes can then be corrected by C_2.

PROBLEMS

9.1. Let C_1 be the (3,1) cyclic code generated by $g_1(X) = 1 + X + X^2$ and let C_2 be the (7,3) maximum-length code generated by $g_2(X) = 1 + X + X^2 + X^4$. Find the generator and parity-check polynomials of the cyclic product code of C_1 and C_2. What is the minimum distance of the product code?

9.2. In the previous problem, both codes C_1 and C_2 are completely orthogonalizable in one step. Show that the product of these two codes is also completely orthogonalizable in one step.

9.3. Consider the cyclic product code whose component codes are the (3,2) cyclic code generated by $g_1(X) = 1 + X$ and the (7,4) Hamming code generated by $g_2(X) = 1 + X + X^3$. The component code C_1 is completely orthogonalizable in one step and the component code C_2 is completely orthogonalizable in two steps. Show that the product code is completely orthogonalizable in two steps. (In general, if one component code is completely orthogonalizable in one step and the other component code is completely orthogonalizable in L steps, then the product code is completely orthogonalizable in L steps.[15])

REFERENCES

1. Abramson, N. M., "Cascade Decoding of Cyclic Product Codes," *IEEE Trans. on Communication Technology*, **COM-16**, pp. 398-402, 1968.

2. Bahl, L., and R. T. Chien, "A Class of Multiple-Burst-Error-Correcting Codes," presented at the IEEE International Symposium on Information Theory, Ellenville, New York, 1969.

3. Berlekamp, E. R., *Algebraic Coding Theory*, McGraw-Hill, New York, 1968.

4. Burton, H. O., and E. J. Weldon, Jr., "Cyclic Product Codes," *IEEE Trans. on Information Theory*, **IT-11**, pp. 433-440, July, 1965.

5. Calabi, L., "Additions and Multiplications of Codes," Technical Memo No. 11, Contract AF19 (604)-3471, Park Math. Labs., Carlisle, Massachusetts, June, 1959.

6. Calabi, L., and H. G. Haefeli, "A Class of Binary Systematic Code Correcting Errors Occurring at Random and in Bursts," *IRE Trans. on Information Theory*, **IT-5**, pp. 79-94, May, 1959.

7. Calabi, L., "A Study of the Sum and the Product of Two Codes," Scientific Report No. 3, Contract AF19 (604)-7493, Park Math. Labs., Carlisle, Massachusetts, August, 1961.

8. Chang, S. H., and L. J. Weng, "Dual Product Codes," presented at the IEEE International Symposium on Information Theory, Los Angeles, California, 1966.

9. Corr, F. P., "Multiple Burst Detection," *Proc. IRE*, **49**, p. 1337, 1961.

10. Elias, P., "Error-Free Coding," *IRE Trans. on Information Theory*, **PGIT-4**, pp. 29-37, September, 1954.

11. Elspas, B., "A Note on Multidimensional Coding," presented at the IEEE International Symposium on Information Theory, San Remo, Italy, 1967.

12. Forney, G. D., Jr., *Concatenated Codes*, The M.I.T. Press, Cambridge, Massachusetts, 1966.

13. Gallager, R. G., *Information Theory and Reliable Communication*, John Wiley, New York, 1968.

14. Hsu, H. T., T. Kasami, and R. T. Chien, "Error-Correcting Codes for a Compound Channel," *IEEE Trans. on Information Theory*, **IT-14**, pp. 135-139, January, 1968.

15. Lin, S., and E. J. Weldon, Jr., "Further Results on Cyclic Product Codes," to appear in the *IEEE Trans. on Information Theory*, 1970.

16. Lucky, R. W., J. Salz, and E. J. Weldon, Jr., *Principles of Data Communication*, McGraw-Hill, 1968.

17. Peterson, W. W., *Error-Correcting Codes*, The M.I.T. Press, Cambridge, Massachusetts, and John Wiley, New York, 1961.

18. Peterson, W. W., and E. J. Weldon, Jr., *Error-Correcting Codes*, 2nd Edition, The M.I.T. Press, Cambridge, Massachusetts, 1970.

19. Posner, W., "Simultaneous Error-Correction and Burst-Error Detection Binary Linear Cyclic Codes," *J. Soc. Indust. Appl. Math.*, **13**, pp. 1087-1095, December, 1965.

20. Reed, J. S., and G. Solomon, "Polynomial Codes over Certain Finite Fields," *J. Soc. Indust. Appl. Math.*, **8**, pp. 300-304, 1960.

21. Slepian, D., "Some Further Theory of Group Codes," *Bell Systems Tech. J.*, **39**, pp. 1219-1252, 1960.

22. Stone, J. J., "Multiple Burst Error Correction," *Information and Control*, **4**, pp. 324-331, March, 1961.

23. Tong, S. Y., "Burst Trapping Techniques for a Compound Channel," *Bell Telephone Labs. Tech. Memo.*, 1968.

24. Tavares, S. E., and S. G. S. Shiva, "Detecting and Correcting Multiple Bursts for Binary Cyclic Codes," to appear in the *IEEE Trans. on Information Theory*, **IT-16**, 1970.

25. Wolf, J. K., "On Codes Derivable from the Tensor Product of Check Matrices," *IEEE Trans. on Information Theory*, **IT-11**, pp. 281-284, April, 1965.

CHAPTER 10

CONVOLUTIONAL CODES

Convolutional codes (or recurrent codes) were first introduced by Elias in 1955.[5] These codes differ from the block codes discussed in previous chapters. In a block code, the block of n code digits generated by the encoder in any particular time unit depends only on the block of k input message digits within that time unit. However, in a convolutional code, the block of n code digits generated by the encoder in a particular time unit depends not only on the block of k message digits within that time unit, but also on the blocks of message digits within a previous span of $N - 1$ time units ($N > 1$). For convolutional codes, k and n are, in general, small integers.

Similar to block codes, convolutional codes can be devised for correcting random errors, burst errors, or both types of errors. Encoding of convolutional codes can be accomplished with shift registers. Several practical decoding schemes for these codes have been developed.[7,12,16,23,25,34,36] Recent studies have shown that convolutional codes are equal or superior to block codes in performance in many practical error control situations.

In this chapter, basic structures of convolutional codes are presented. The use of complicated notations seems unavoidable. It is hoped that the reader will not be deterred from going through this chapter. For further details on convolutional codes, the reader is referred to References 3, 23, and 38.

10.1 GENERAL DESCRIPTION OF CONVOLUTIONAL CODES

The operation of a general convolutional decoder as shown in Fig. 10.1 can be described as follows. The input to the encoder is a sequence $\mathbf{m}$ of message digits and the output is the corresponding sequence $\mathbf{c}$ of code digits. At any time unit, a block of k message digits (called a message block) is fed into the encoder, and a block of n code digits (called a code block) is generated at the output of the decoder, where $k < n$. The n-digit code block depends not only on the k-digit message block of the same time unit,

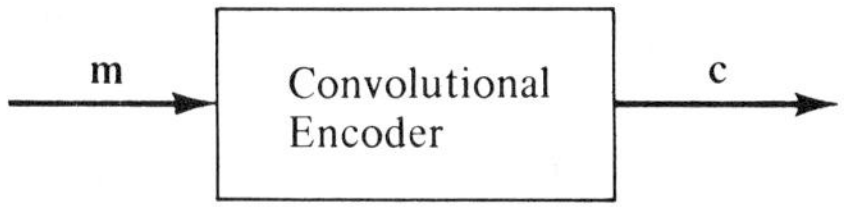

Fig. 10.1. A general convolutional encoder.

but also on the previous $(N-1)$ message blocks. The code generated by the above encoder is called an (n,k) *convolutional code* of constraint length N blocks (or nN digits). The rate of this code is $R = k/n$. For convolutional codes, the parameters k and n are, in general, small integers.

Consider a set of $k(n-k)$ vectors of N binary digits,

$$\mathbf{g}(i,j) = (g_0(i,j), g_1(i,j), g_2(i,j), \ldots, g_{N-1}(i,j)) \tag{10.1}$$

for $i = 1, 2, \ldots, k$ and $j = 1, 2, \ldots, n-k$. From these $k(n-k)$ vectors, we form the following matrix of k rows,

$$\mathbf{Q}_0 = \begin{bmatrix} \mathbf{g}_\infty(1) \\ \mathbf{g}_\infty(2) \\ \vdots \\ \mathbf{g}_\infty(k) \end{bmatrix} = [\mathbf{I}_k\ \mathbf{P}_0\ \mathbf{O}\ \mathbf{P}_1\ \mathbf{O}\ \mathbf{P}_2 \ldots \mathbf{O}\ \mathbf{P}_{N-1} \xrightarrow{\text{zeros}} \infty] \tag{10.2}$$

where (1) $\mathbf{I}_k$ is a k-by-k identity matrix,

(2) $\mathbf{O}$ is a k-by-k zero matrix, and

(3) $\mathbf{P}_\ell$ is a k-by-$(n-k)$ matrix of the following form:

$$\mathbf{P}_\ell = \begin{bmatrix} g_\ell(1,1) & g_\ell(1,2) & g_\ell(1,3) & \ldots & g_\ell(1,n-k) \\ g_\ell(2,1) & g_\ell(2,2) & g_\ell(2,3) & \ldots & g_\ell(2,n-k) \\ \vdots & & & & \\ g_\ell(k,1) & g_\ell(k,2) & g_\ell(k,3) & \ldots & g_\ell(k,n-k) \end{bmatrix} \tag{10.3}$$

for $0 \leqslant \ell \leqslant N-1$.

Thus, each row $\mathbf{g}_\infty(i)$ is a semi-infinite vector with non-zero components confined to the first nN digit positions. For any positive integer λ, we define a shift operator D^λ as follows: When D^λ is applied on the sequence $\mathbf{g}_\infty(i)$, it shifts every component of $\mathbf{g}_\infty(i)$ to the right by λn digit positions and prefixes $\mathbf{g}_\infty(i)$ with λn zeros. Thus,

$$D^\lambda \mathbf{g}_\infty(i) = (\overset{\longleftarrow \lambda n \longrightarrow}{0\,0 \ldots 0} \overset{\mathbf{g}_\infty(i)}{\overline{\qquad\qquad}}) \; . \tag{10.4}$$

An (n,k) convolutional code is a linear code which is generated by the following matrix:

$$\mathbf{G}_\infty = \begin{bmatrix} \mathbf{I}_k\mathbf{P}_0 & \mathbf{O}\,\mathbf{P}_1 & \mathbf{O}\,\mathbf{P}_2 & \ldots & \mathbf{O}\,\mathbf{P}_{N-1} & \xrightarrow{\text{zeros}} & & \\ & \mathbf{I}_k\mathbf{P}_0 & \mathbf{O}\,\mathbf{P}_1 & \ldots & \mathbf{O}\,\mathbf{P}_{N-2} & \mathbf{O}\,\mathbf{P}_{N-1} & \xrightarrow{\text{zeros}} & \\ & & \mathbf{I}_k\mathbf{P}_0 & \ldots & \mathbf{O}\,\mathbf{P}_{N-3} & \mathbf{O}\,\mathbf{P}_{N-2} & \mathbf{O}\,\mathbf{P}_{N-1} & \xrightarrow{\text{zeros}} \\ & & & & \vdots & & & \\ & \text{(zeros)} & & & \mathbf{I}_k\mathbf{P}_0 & \mathbf{O}\,\mathbf{P}_1 & \mathbf{O}\,\mathbf{P}_2 & \ldots \\ & & & & & \downarrow & & \\ & & & & & \infty & & \end{bmatrix} \tag{10.5}$$

with

$$\{\mathbf{g}_\infty(1), \mathbf{g}_\infty(2), \ldots, \mathbf{g}_\infty(k), D\mathbf{g}_\infty(1), D\mathbf{g}_\infty(2), \ldots, D\mathbf{g}_\infty(k),$$
$$D^2\mathbf{g}_\infty(1), D^2\mathbf{g}_\infty(2), \ldots, D^2\mathbf{g}_\infty(k), \ldots\}$$

as rows.

Let $\mathbf{m}$ be a semi-infinite message sequence to be encoded. This message sequence is segmented into ordered message blocks as follows:

$$\mathbf{m} = (m_0(1)\, m_0(2) \ldots m_0(k)\, m_1(1)\, m_1(2) \ldots$$
$$m_1(k)\, m_2(1)\, m_2(2) \ldots m_2(k) \ldots) \;, \qquad (10.6)$$

where the ℓth message block $\underline{\mathbf{m}}_\ell$ consists of k message digits,

$$\underline{\mathbf{m}}_\ell = m_\ell(1)\, m_\ell(2) \ldots m_\ell(k) \;.$$

The code sequence which corresponds to $\mathbf{m}$ is

$$\begin{aligned}
\mathbf{c} &= \mathbf{m}\,\mathbf{G}_\infty \\
&= m_0(1)\,\mathbf{g}_\infty(1) + m_0(2)\,\mathbf{g}_\infty(2) + \ldots + m_0(k)\,\mathbf{g}_\infty(k) + \\
&\quad m_1(1)\,\mathrm{D}\mathbf{g}_\infty(1) + m_1(2)\,\mathrm{D}\mathbf{g}_\infty(2) + \ldots + m_1(k)\,\mathrm{D}\mathbf{g}_\infty(k) + \\
&\quad \vdots \\
&\quad m_\ell(1)\,\mathrm{D}^\ell\mathbf{g}_\infty(1) + m_\ell(2)\,\mathrm{D}^\ell\mathbf{g}_\infty(2) + \ldots + m_\ell(k)\,\mathrm{D}^\ell\mathbf{g}_\infty(k) + \\
&\quad \vdots \\
&= \sum_{\ell=0}^{\infty} m_\ell(1)\,\mathrm{D}^\ell\mathbf{g}_\infty(1) + \sum_{\ell=0}^{\infty} m_\ell(2)\,\mathrm{D}^\ell\mathbf{g}_\infty(2) + \ldots + \\
&\quad \sum_{\ell=0}^{\infty} m_\ell(k)\,\mathrm{D}^\ell\mathbf{g}_\infty(k) \;. \qquad (10.7)
\end{aligned}$$

This code sequence $\mathbf{c}$ consists of ordered code blocks as follows:

$$\mathbf{c} = (c_0(1)\, c_0(2) \ldots c_0(n)\, c_1(1)\, c_1(2) \ldots$$
$$c_1(n)\, c_2(1)\, c_2(2) \ldots c_2(n) \ldots) \;, \qquad (10.8)$$

where the ℓth code block $\underline{\mathbf{c}}_\ell$ consists of n code digits

$$\underline{c}_\ell = c_\ell(1)\, c_\ell(2) \ldots c_\ell(n) \quad .$$

From Eqs. (10.3) and (10.5), the n digits of the ℓth code block are found as follows:

$$c_\ell(i) = m_\ell(i) \quad \text{for} \quad i = 1, 2, \ldots, k \tag{10.9}$$

and

$$c_\ell(k+j) = \sum_{i=1}^{k} m_\ell(i)\, g_0(i,j) + \sum_{i=1}^{k} m_{\ell-1}(i)\, g_1(i,j) + \ldots + \sum_{i=1}^{k} m_{\ell-N+1}(i)\, g_{N-1}(i,j) \tag{10.10}$$

for $j = 1, 2, \ldots, n-k$. (Note that $m_t(i)$ is assumed to be zero for $t < 0$.) From Eq. (10.9), we can see that the first k digits of the ℓth code block are identical to the k message digits fed into the encoder at the ℓth time unit. The last $n-k$ digits of the ℓth code block are parity-check digits. Equation (10.10) shows that these $n-k$ parity-check digits are determined not only by the present message block, but also by the previous $N-1$ message blocks. In other words, the parity-check digits of the ℓth code block check not only the message block at the ℓth time unit, but also the previous $N-1$ message blocks. Thus, in convolutional encoding, each k-digit message block affects a code vector over a span of N blocks.

We have shown that an (n,k) convolutional code is completely specified by the set of $k(n-k)$ vectors of Eq. (10.1). These $k(n-k)$ vectors are called *sub-generators* of the (n,k) convolutional code. Let $\mathbf{g}(i)$ be the vector which consists of the first nN components of $\mathbf{g}_\infty(i)$ defined by Eq. (10.2). The k vectors $\mathbf{g}(1)$, $\mathbf{g}(2)$, . . ., $\mathbf{g}(k)$ are called *generators* (or *generator sequences*) of the code. These k generators are obtained by interlacing the $k(n-k)$ sub-generators according to Eqs. (10.2) and (10.3). If the k generators of an (n,k) code are given, then the $k(n-k)$ sub-generators of the code can be found by decomposing the generators. The matrix $\mathbf{G}_\infty$ defined by Eq. (10.5) is called the *generator matrix* of the code. The parameter N is referred to as the *constraint length*. Since, at any time unit, the first k digits of a code block are unaltered message digits, the code is in systematic form. A non-systematic (n,k) code is obtained if the first k rows (non-zero components confined to the first nN positions) of $\mathbf{G}_\infty$ are not in the form of Eq.(10.2). To specify a non-systematic (n,k) code, a set of kn sub-generators of N digits long is required. In this book, we shall be primarily concerned with systematic convolutional codes.

Example 10.1: Consider a (2,1) convolutional code of constraint length $N = 4$, which is generated by the following sub-generator:

$$\mathbf{g}(1,1) = (1\ 1\ 0\ 1) \ .$$

The generator is $\mathbf{g}(1) = (1\ 1\ 0\ 1\ 0\ 0\ 0\ 1)$. The generator matrix of this code is

$$\mathbf{G}_\infty = \begin{bmatrix} 11 & 01 & 00 & 01 & & & & \\ & 11 & 01 & 00 & 01 & & & \\ & & 11 & 01 & 00 & 01 & & \\ & & & 11 & 01 & 00 & 01 & \\ & & & & 11 & 01 & 00 & 01 \\ & & & & & \downarrow & & \\ & & & & & \infty & & \end{bmatrix} .$$

Let $\mathbf{m} = (\underline{1}\ \underline{0}\ \underline{0}\ \underline{1}\ \underline{1} \ldots)$ be the message sequence to be encoded. The corresponding code sequence is

$$\mathbf{c} = \mathbf{m}\mathbf{G}_\infty = (\underline{1\,1}\ \ \underline{0\,1}\ \ \underline{0\,0}\ \ \underline{1\,0}\ \ \underline{1\,0}\ \ldots) \ .$$

Example 10.2: Consider a (3,2) code of constraint length $N = 3$ which is generated by the following sub-generators:

$$g(1,1) = 1\,0\,1 \;,$$

$$g(2,1) = 1\,1\,0 \;.$$

The two generators are

$$g(1) = 1\,0\,1\,0\,0\,0\,0\,0\,1 \;,$$

$$g(2) = 0\,1\,1\,0\,0\,1\,0\,0\,0 \;.$$

The generator matrix of this code is

$$G_\infty = \begin{bmatrix}
1&0&1&0&0&0&0&0&1&&&&&& \\
0&1&1&0&0&1&0&0&0&&&&&& \\
&&&1&0&1&0&0&0&0&0&1&&& \\
&&&0&1&1&0&0&1&0&0&0&&& \\
&&&&&&1&0&1&0&0&0&0&0&1 \\
&&&&&&0&1&1&0&0&1&0&0&0 \\
&&&&&&&&&&\downarrow&&&& \\
&&&&&&&&&&\infty&&&&
\end{bmatrix} .$$

Let $m = (\underline{1\;1}\;\;\underline{0\;0}\;\;\underline{1\;0}\;\ldots)$ be the message sequence to be encoded. Then the corresponding code sequence is

$$c = m\,G_\infty = (\underline{1\,1\,0}\;\;\underline{0\,0\,1}\;\;\underline{1\,0\,0}\;\;\ldots) \;.$$

Since an (n,k) convolutional code is a linear code, it is also specified by its parity-check matrix. The parity-check matrix of this code is

$$
\mathbf{H}_\infty = \left[\begin{array}{llllllllll}
\mathbf{P}_0^T & \mathbf{I}_k & & & & & & & & \\
\mathbf{P}_1^T & \mathbf{O} & \mathbf{P}_0^T & \mathbf{I}_k & & & & & & \\
\mathbf{P}_2^T & \mathbf{O} & \mathbf{P}_1^T & \mathbf{O} & \mathbf{P}_0^T & \mathbf{I}_k & & & & \\
\vdots & & & & & & & & & \\
\mathbf{P}_{N-1}^T & \mathbf{O} & \mathbf{P}_{N-2}^T & \mathbf{O} & \mathbf{P}_{N-3}^T & \mathbf{O} & \ldots & \mathbf{P}_0^T & \mathbf{I}_k & \\
\text{zeros} & & \mathbf{P}_{N-1}^T & \mathbf{O} & \mathbf{P}_{N-2}^T & \mathbf{O} & \ldots & \mathbf{P}_1^T\ \mathbf{O} & \mathbf{P}_0^T\ \mathbf{I} & \\
\downarrow & & \text{zeros} & & \mathbf{P}_{N-1}^T & \mathbf{O} & \ldots & \mathbf{P}_2^T\ \mathbf{O} & \mathbf{P}_1^T\ \mathbf{O} & \\
\infty & & \downarrow\ \infty & & \text{zeros}\ \downarrow\ \infty & & & & &
\end{array}\right] \quad (10.11)
$$

where $\mathbf{P}_\ell^T$ is the transpose of $\mathbf{P}_\ell$. We can easily see that $\mathbf{G}_\infty \mathbf{H}_\infty^T = 0$. Thus, $\mathbf{c}$ is a code sequence if and only if $\mathbf{c}\mathbf{H}^T = 0$.

10.2 ENCODING OF CONVOLUTIONAL CODES

Encoding of an (n,k) convolutional code can be implemented easily by using shift registers with connections according to the set of $k(n-k)$ subgenerators which specifies the code. The expressions of Eqs. (10.9) and (10.10) suggest an encoding circuit which employs $n-k$ $(N-1)$-stage shift registers as shown in Fig. 10.2. This circuit was devised by Wozencraft and Reiffen.[36] Equation (10.10) can be rewritten in the following form:

$$
c_\ell(k+j) = \sum_{t=0}^{N-1} m_{\ell-t}(1)\, g_t(1,j) + \sum_{t=0}^{N-1} m_{\ell-t}(2)\, g_t(2,j) + \ldots + \sum_{t=0}^{N-1} m_{\ell-t}(k)\, g_t(k,j) \quad . \qquad (10.12)
$$

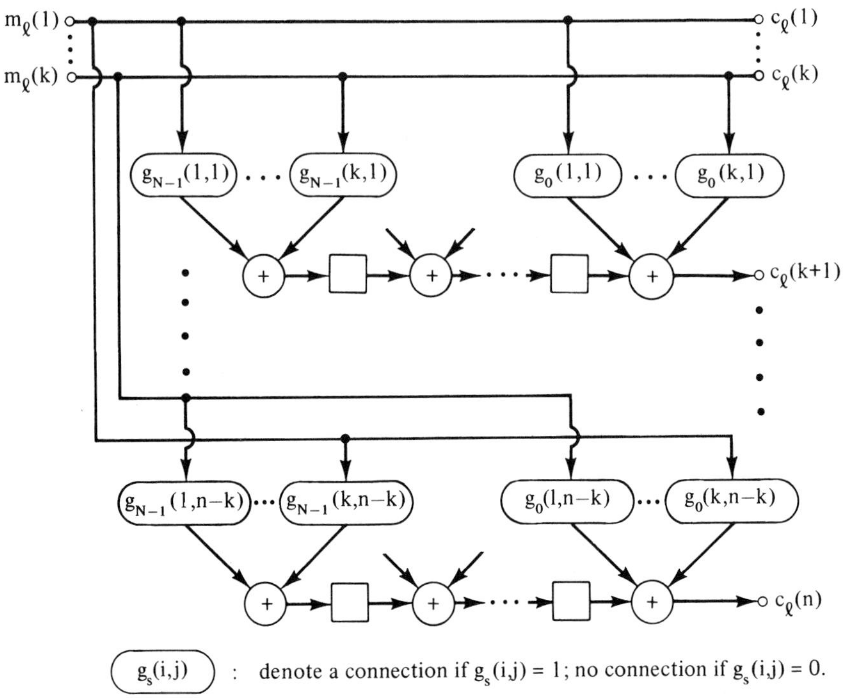

Fig. 10.2. An $(n-k)(N-1)$-stage encoder (Type I encoder). (From J. L. Massey, *Threshold Decoding*, Fig. 6, p. 23, M.I.T. Press, 1963. Redrawn by permission.)

Based on the expressions of Eqs. (10.9) and (10.12), we obtain a second type of encoding circuit which employs k $(N-1)$-stage shift registers as shown in Fig. 10.3. This circuit was developed by Massey.[23] Since both types of encoding circuits accept message digits in parallel form, a serial-to-parallel commutator is required at the input of either circuit to transform the message sequence $\mathbf{m}$ into k synchronous sub-sequences as follows:

$$
\begin{aligned}
\mathbf{m}^{(1)} &= m_0(1)\, m_1(1)\, m_2(1) \ldots m_\ell(1) \ldots \\
\mathbf{m}^{(2)} &= m_0(2)\, m_1(2)\, m_2(2) \ldots m_\ell(2) \ldots \\
&\;\;\vdots \\
\mathbf{m}^{(k)} &= m_0(k)\, m_1(k)\, m_2(k) \ldots m_\ell(k) \ldots
\end{aligned}
\tag{10.13}
$$

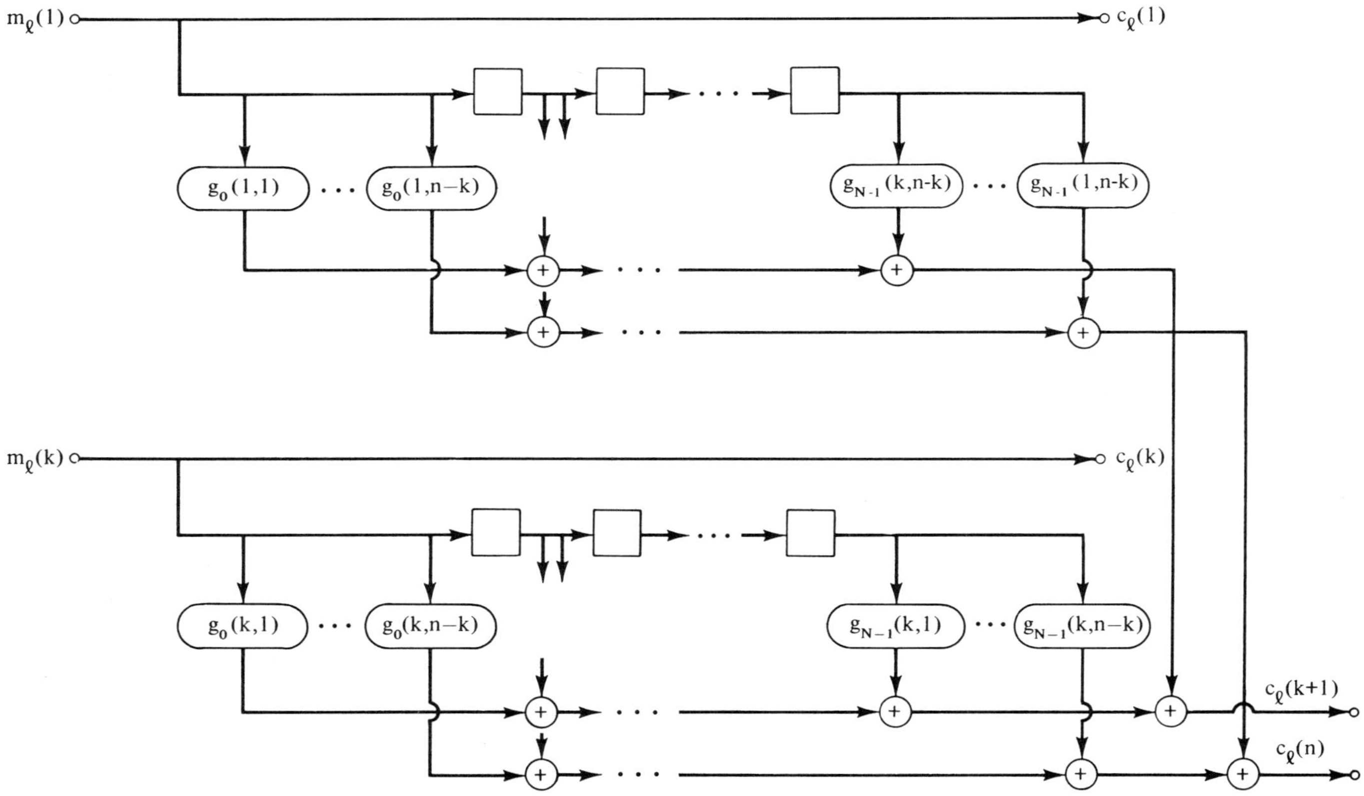

Fig. 10.3. A $k(N\text{-}1)$-stage encoder (Type II encoder). (From J. L. Massey, *Threshold Decoding*, Fig. 5, p. 22, M.I.T. Press, 1963. Redrawn by permission.)

During the ℓth time unit, the ℓth message block $(m_\ell(1), m_\ell(2), \ldots, m_\ell(k))$ is fed into the encoding circuit, the registers of the circuit are shifted once, and the ℓth code block $(c_\ell(1), c_\ell(2), \ldots, c_\ell(n))$ is generated at the n output terminals of the circuit. If the code digits are to be transmitted serially, a parallel-to-serial commutator is required at the output of the encoder to serialize the code digits.

For high-rate codes $(k > n-k)$, the first type of encoding circuit is more economical than the second type. Otherwise, the second type is more economical than the first type. The two types of encoding circuits for the (2,1) code given in Example 10.1 are shown in Fig. 10.4 and Fig. 10.5 respectively.

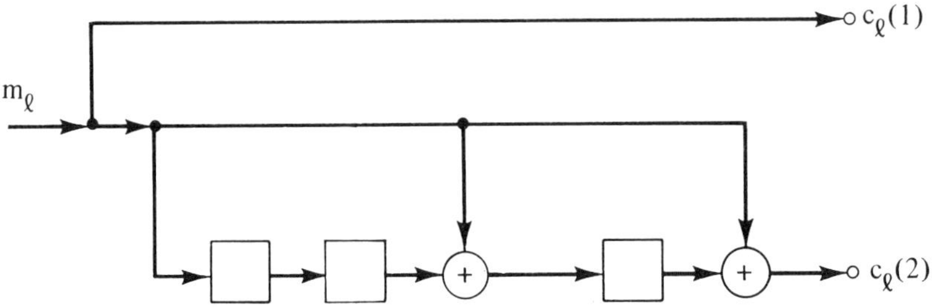

Fig. 10.4. Type I encoder for the (2,1) convolutional code of Example 10.1.

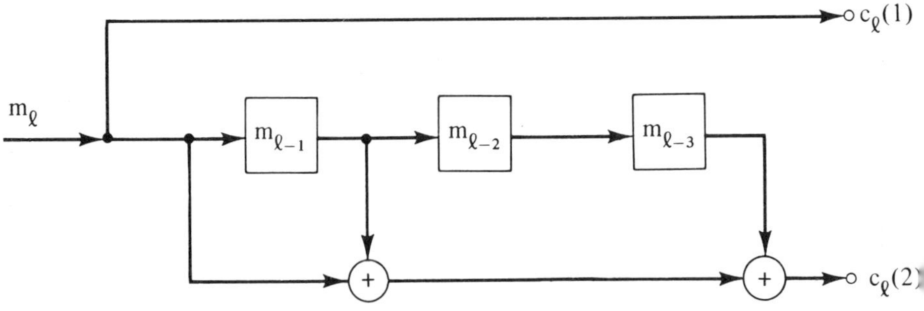

Fig. 10.5. Type II encoder for the (2,1) convolutional code of Example 10.1.

10.3 SYNDROME CALCULATION

Let $\mathbf{c}$ be the transmitted code sequence and let $\mathbf{e}$ be the noise sequence added by the noisy channel. Then the received sequence at the output of the channel is

$$\mathbf{r} = \mathbf{c} + \mathbf{e} \ .$$

The received sequence $\mathbf{r}$ can be expressed as follows:

$$\mathbf{r} = (r_0(1)\, r_0(2) \ldots r_0(n)\, r_1(1)\, r_1(2) \ldots r_1(n)\, r_2(1)\, r_2(2) \ldots r_2(n) \ldots r_\ell(1)\, r_\ell(2) \ldots r_\ell(n) \ldots) \ ,$$

where

$$r_\ell(i) = c_\ell(i) + e_\ell(i)$$

for $i = 1, 2, \ldots, n$. The syndrome of this received sequence is defined as

$$\mathbf{s} = \mathbf{r}\, \mathbf{H}_\infty^T \ . \tag{10.14}$$

Thus, $\mathbf{s}$ is also a semi-infinite sequence which consists of ordered blocks

$$\mathbf{s} = (s_0(1)\, s_0(2) \ldots s_0(n-k)\, s_1(1)\, s_1(2) \ldots s_1(n-k) \ldots s_\ell(1)\, s_\ell(2) \ldots s_\ell(n-k) \ldots) \ , \tag{10.15}$$

where the ℓth block consists of $n-k$ syndrome digits

$$s_\ell(1)\, s_\ell(2) \ldots s_\ell(n-k) \ .$$

From Eq. (10.14), the $n-k$ syndrome digits of the ℓth block are obtained as follows:

$$s_\ell(j) = r_\ell(k+j) + \sum_{i=1}^{k} r_\ell(i)\, g_0(i,j) + \sum_{i=1}^{k} r_{\ell-1}(i)\, g_1(i,j)$$

$$+ \ldots + \sum_{i=1}^{k} r_{\ell-N+1}(i)\, g_{N-1}(i,j) \qquad (10.16)$$

for $j = 1, 2, \ldots, n-k$. Since $\mathbf{r} = \mathbf{c} + \mathbf{e}$ and $\mathbf{c}\mathbf{H}_\infty^T = \mathbf{0}$, we obtain

$$\begin{aligned} \mathbf{s} &= \mathbf{r}\,\mathbf{H}_\infty^T \\ &= (\mathbf{c}+\mathbf{e})\,\mathbf{H}_\infty^T \\ &= \mathbf{c}\mathbf{H}_\infty^T + \mathbf{e}\mathbf{H}_\infty^T \\ &= \mathbf{e}\,\mathbf{H}_\infty^T \ . \end{aligned} \qquad (10.17)$$

It follows from Eq. (10.17) that the syndrome digits can be expressed in terms of error digits,

$$s_\ell(j) = e_\ell(k+j) + \sum_{i=1}^{k} e_\ell(i)\, g_0(i,j) + \sum_{i=1}^{k} e_{\ell-1}(i)\, g_1(i,j)$$

$$+ \ldots + \sum_{i=1}^{k} e_{\ell-N+1}(i)\, g_{N-1}(i,j) \qquad (10.18)$$

for $j = 1, 2, \ldots, n-k$ ($e_t = 0$ for $t < 0$). Thus, the syndrome of the received sequence contains information about the error sequence and can be used for decoding.

The syndrome can be calculated at the decoder by encoding the received message digits and adding the resulting parity-check digits to the received parity-check digits as shown in Fig. 10.6. Hence, both of the encoders described above can be modified to calculate the syndrome of the received sequence.

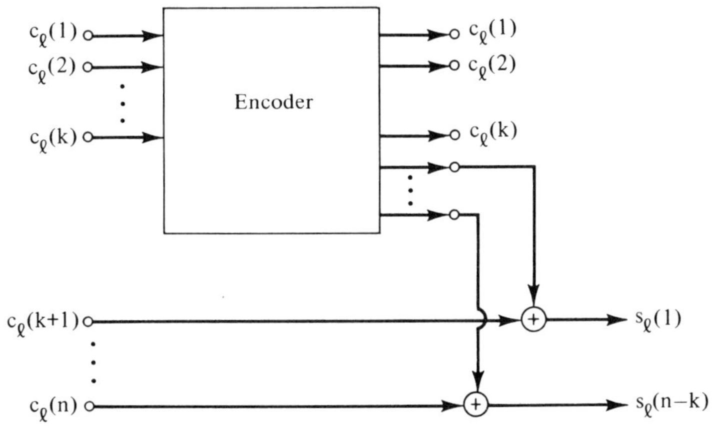

Fig. 10.6. A syndrome calculator for convolutional codes.

10.4 DECODING OF CONVOLUTIONAL CODES AND ERROR PROPAGATION

Since the encoding of a convolutional code is performed block by block (k message digits to n code digits at a time), the received sequence is therefore decoded a block of n digits at a time. As we have shown in Section 10.3, the syndrome of the received sequence contains information about the error sequence which is introduced by the noisy channel. Thus, it can be used for estimating errors. In order to illustrate the decoding of a block of n received digits, we expand Eq. (10.18) as follows:

$$s_0(j) = e_0(k+j) + \sum_{i=1}^{k} e_0(i)\, g_0(i,j)$$

$$s_1(j) = e_1(k+j) + \sum_{i=1}^{k} e_1(i)\, g_0(i,j) + \sum_{i=1}^{k} e_0(i)\, g_1(i,j)$$

$$\vdots$$

$$s_{N-1}(j) = e_{N-1}(k+j) + \sum_{i=1}^{k} e_{N-1}(i)\, g_0(i,j) + \ldots + \sum_{i=1}^{k} e_0(i)\, g_{N-1}(i,j)$$

$$s_N(j) = e_N(k+j) + \sum_{i=1}^{k} e_N(i)\, g_0(i,j) + \ldots + \sum_{i=1}^{k} e_1(i)\, g_{N-1}(i,j)$$

$$s_{N+1}(j) = e_{N+1}(k+j) + \sum_{i=1}^{k} e_{N+1}(i)\, g_0(i,j) + \ldots + \sum_{i=1}^{k} e_2(i)\, g_{N-1}(i,j)$$

$$\vdots \qquad (10.19)$$

with $j = 1, 2, \ldots, n-k$. By examining this set of equations, we notice that the error digits $e_0(1), e_0(2), \ldots, e_0(n)$ in the 0th block of the error sequence are only checked by the first $N(n-k)$ equations. Therefore, in decoding the 0th block of the received sequence, only the first $N(n-k)$ syndrome digits from the 0th block to the $(N-1)^{th}$ block are to be used. After the errors in the 0th block have been found, their effect on the syndrome sequence is removed. The removal of this error effect from the syndrome is called *syndrome resetting*. Having decoded the 0th block of the received sequence, the decoder begins to decode the 1st block of the received sequence. Since the error digits in the 1st block are only checked by the $N(n-k)$ syndrome digits from the 1st block to the Nth block of the received sequence, the 1st block of the received sequence is therefore decoded by examining the modified syndrome from the 1st block to the Nth block. If the decoding of the 0th received block is correct, the syndrome resetting will result in a modified syndrome sequence as follows:

$$s_0'(j) = 0$$

$$s_1'(j) = e_1(k+j) + \sum_{i=1}^{k} e_1(i)\, g_0(i,j)$$

$$s_2'(j) = e_2(k+j) + \sum_{i=1}^{k} e_2(i)\, g_0(i,j) + \sum_{i=1}^{k} e_1(i)\, g_1(i,j)$$

$$\vdots$$

$$s_{N-1}'(j) = e_{N-1}(k+j) + \sum_{i=1}^{k} e_{N-1}(i)\, g_0(i,j) + \ldots + \sum_{i=1}^{k} e_1(i)\, g_{N-2}(i,j)$$

$$s_N(j) = e_N(k+j) + \sum_{i=1}^{k} e_N(i)\, g_0(i,j) + \ldots + \sum_{i=1}^{k} e_1(i)\, g_{N-1}(i,j)$$

$$s_{N+1}(j) = e_{N+1}(k+j) + \sum_{i=1}^{k} e_{N+1}(i)\, g_0(i,j) + \ldots + \sum_{i=1}^{k} e_2(i)\, g_{N-1}(i,j)$$

$$\vdots \tag{10.20}$$

where only the syndrome bits from the 0th block to the $(N-1)^{th}$ block are altered. We notice that the modified syndrome bits from the 1st block to the Nth block which are used for decoding the 1st received block are exactly in the same form as the syndrome bits which were used for decoding the 0th received block. Therefore, the decoding of the 1st received block is identical to the decoding of the 0th received block. After the 1st block of the received sequence has been decoded, the syndrome must be reset again. The decoding proceeds in this manner sequentially. To decode the ℓth block of the received sequence, the syndrome (with previous error effects removed) from the ℓth block to the $(\ell-N+1)^{th}$ block will be used.

A general decoder for an (n,k) convolutional code[25] is shown in Fig. 10.7. Its operation can be described as follows:

Step 1. For decoding the 0th block of the received sequence, the first $N(n-k)$ syndrome digits from the 0th block to the $(N-1)^{th}$ block of the syndrome sequence **s** are calculated by shifting the first N blocks of the received sequence into the syndrome generator (all the register stages initially contain zeros).

Step 2. These $N(n-k)$ syndrome digits are read into the logic circuit and are tested for errors in the 0th block of the received sequence. Usually, we are only concerned with the errors at the k message positions. Thus, the output of the logic circuit are the estimated errors at the k message positions of the 0th block of the received sequence.

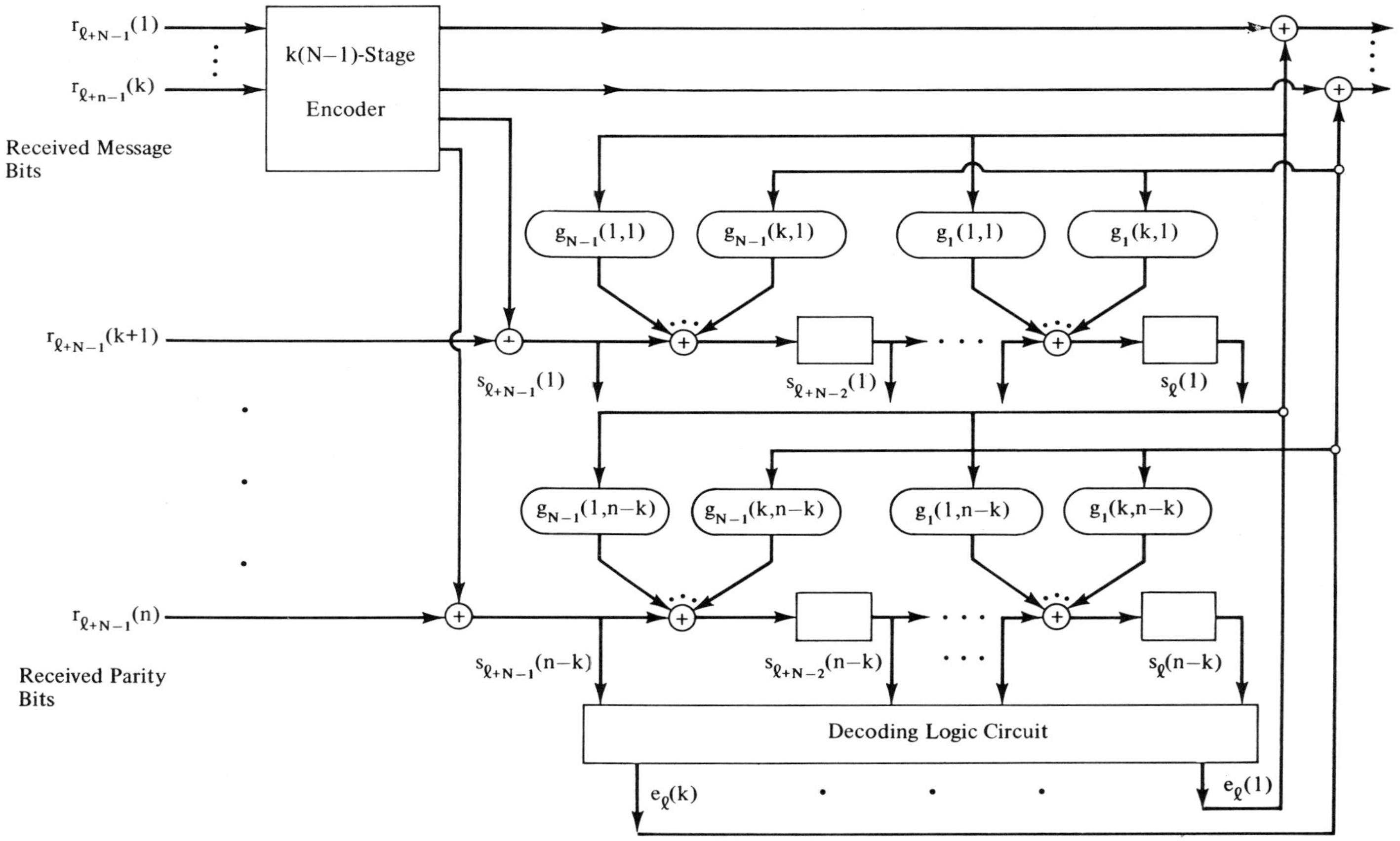

Fig. 10.7. A general decoder for convolutional codes.

Step 3. The k received message digits $r_0(1), r_0(2), \ldots, r_0(k)$ are read out of the encoder and are corrected by the output of the logic circuit. The corrections are done by k Exclusive OR gates. At the same time, the errors are fed back into the syndrome register to remove their effect on the syndrome sequence (syndrome resetting).

Step 4. As soon as the k received message digits are shifted out of the encoder, the $n-k$ syndrome registers are shifted to the right once. The Nth block of the received sequence is shifted into the syndrome generator, and its corresponding $n-k$ syndrome digits are calculated and stored in the leftmost stages of the $n-k$ syndrome registers.

Step 5. Now the syndrome registers contain the modified syndrome of $N(n-k)$ digits from the 1st block to the Nth block. The decoder starts to decode the 1st block of the received sequence in exactly the same manner as it decoded the 0th block of the received sequence. The decoder repeats Steps 2, 3, and 4.

Step 6. The decoder proceeds in the above manner sequentially and decodes n received digits at a time.

With the possible exception of the logic circuit which performs the decoding algorithm, the entire decoder is simple. Whether or not the decoder is practical depends entirely on the complexity of the logic circuit. The syndrome resetting after each decoding decision results in feedback connections within the decoder. Thus, the decoder is called a *feedback decoder* and the decoding operation with syndrome resetting is called *feedback decoding*.

A major disadvantage of feedback decoding is the tendency of a decoding mistake to trigger a succession of further decoding mistakes even in the absence of additional channel errors. This phenomenon is called *error propagation*.[23] The error propagation effect results from incorrect resetting of the syndrome after a decoding mistake. Several methods have been proposed to limit the extent of error propagation. One method is based on the following fact. Suppose that the decoder is decoding the ℓth block of the received sequence. From Eq. (10.18), we notice that the channel errors which occur earlier than the $(\ell-N+1)^{th}$ time unit have no effect on the syndrome bits after the $(\ell-1)^{th}$ time unit. Thus, if a decoding mistake were made earlier than the $(\ell-N+1)^{th}$ time unit and no decoding mistake were made from the $(\ell-N+1)^{th}$ time unit to the $(\ell-1)^{th}$ time unit, then the syndrome resettings would result in a correct syndrome for decoding the ℓth received block. That is, if a decoding mistake is followed by N-1 successive correct decodings, the decoder will return to normal operating mode, and the error propagation will be terminated. This fact suggests the following approach to control error propagation.[36] First, a known sequence of $k(N-1)$ digits (usually an all-zero sequence) is injected into the message sequence at prescribed intervals before encoding—say after every kL regular message digits. This injection results in a separation of the semi-infinite message sequence into sections. The known sequence of $k(N-1)$ digits will be called the *resynchronization sequence* because of the manner in which we will utilize it. The modified message sequence is then encoded and transmitted. Whenever the $(N-1)$ received blocks which correspond to the resynchronization sequence are fed into the decoder, the decoder automatically decodes them into the resynchronization sequence. This operation guarantees $N-1$ correct decodings. Thus, any existing error propagation will be terminated after the $N-1$ resynchronizing decoding operations. Therefore, error propagation is confined to $L+N-1$ time units. The above method of controlling error propagation is called *periodic resynchronization* and will reduce the effective information transmission rate to

$$R' = \frac{L}{L+N-1} R$$

where $R = k/n$. If L is large enough, the reduction will not be substantial.

If a feedback channel is available, error propagation can be controlled by *error counting*.[23,36] Basically, this method involves counting the number of errors corrected by the decoder over a certain span of consecutive received digits. Whenever this number exceeds the error correcting capability of the code over that span, the decoder assumes that either a decoding mistake has been made or the channel has temporarily become too noisy for reliable decoding operation. Then a signal is sent back to the transmitter over the feedback channel to request retransmission of data from some early time at which the high density of errors began.

A third method of combatting error propagation is to design codes and decoders with *automatic recovery properties*[23,24,31,32,33] which enable the decoder to return to correct decoding operation after a short span of erroneous decoding. Codes with automatic recovery properties will be discussed in Chapter 11. Since error propagation is caused by incorrect syndrome resetting after a decoding mistake, it therefore can be totally prevented if the code is decoded without syndrome resetting after each decoding decision. Decoding without syndrome resetting is called *definite decoding*.[13, 32] A decoder which employs definite decoding does not have feedback connections. The price that we must pay for preventing error propagation by using definite decoding is a reduction in the performance of the code (or the error-correcting capability of the code), and we can debate whether or not this is worthwhile. From theoretical and experimental studies, we have found that error propagation is not a serious problem for certain classes of codes and certain decoding algorithms and that the corresponding performance of a feedback decoder is always superior to that of a definite decoder.

Similar to block codes, convolutional codes can be designed to correct random errors, to correct burst errors, or to correct both. A random-error-correcting convolutional code is said to be a *t-error-correcting code* if it is capable of correcting any error sequence $\mathbf{e}$, provided that no set of nN consecutive digits of $\mathbf{e}$ contains more than t errors.[38] A burst-error-correcting convolutional code is said to be an *ℓ-burst-error-correcting code* if it is capable of correcting any error sequence $\mathbf{e}$, provided that the errors of any nN consecutive digit positions of $\mathbf{e}$ are confined to a burst of length ℓ.[38] Convolutional codes have one inherent advantage over block codes. Because data are handled in much smaller blocks, it is simpler to acquire or reacquire block synchronization with convolutional codes.

10.5 TREE STRUCTURE AND DISTANCE PROPERTIES OF CONVOLUTIONAL CODES

A convolutional code has a very interesting structure that allows the semi-infinite code sequences to be arranged diagrammatically in the form of an infinite tree with nodes spaced n digits apart and 2^k branches stemming from each node.[36] Each branch of the tree is an n-digit code block which corresponds to a certain k-digit message block. Thus, a code sequence is represented as a path in the infinite tree.

For simplicity, we shall first consider an $(n,1)$ convolutional code. As we have shown in Section 10.1, an $(n,1)$ convolutional code is specified by a set of $n-1$ sub-generators,

$$\mathbf{g}(1,j) = (g_0(1,j), g_1(1,j), g_2(1,j), \ldots, g_{N-1}(1,j))$$

for $j = 1, 2, \ldots, n-1$. The generator of this code is

$$\begin{aligned}\mathbf{g}(1) = (&1\, g_0(1,1)\; g_0(1,2) \ldots g_0(1,n-1)\; 0\; g_1(1,1)\; g_1(1,2) \\ &\ldots g_1(1,n-1)\; 0\; g_2(1,1)\; g_2(1,2) \ldots g_2(1,n-1) \\ &\ldots 0\; g_{N-1}(1,1)\; g_{N-1}(1,2) \ldots g_{N-1}(1,n-1)) \ .\end{aligned} \tag{10.21}$$

For convenience, we will use the following notation:

$$\underline{g}_0 = 1\, g_0(1,1)\, g_0(1,2) \ldots g_0(1,n-1) \ ,$$

and

$$\underline{g}_\ell = 0\, g_\ell(1,1)\, g_\ell(1,2) \ldots g_\ell(1,n-1) \ .$$

for $\ell = 1, 2, \ldots, N-1$. Then the generator $\mathbf{g}(1)$ is represented as follows:

$$\mathbf{g}(1) = \underline{g}_0\; \underline{g}_1\; \underline{g}_2 \cdots \underline{g}_{N-1} \ ,$$

where $\underline{g}_\ell$ is called the ℓth branch (or block) of $\mathbf{g}(1)$. The generator matrix of the code is

$$\mathbf{G}_\infty = \begin{bmatrix} \mathbf{g}_\infty(1) \\ \mathbf{D}\mathbf{g}_\infty(1) \\ \mathbf{D}^2\mathbf{g}_\infty(1) \\ \mathbf{D}^3\mathbf{g}_\infty(1) \\ \vdots \end{bmatrix} = \begin{bmatrix} \underline{g}_0 & \underline{g}_1 & \underline{g}_2 & \underline{g}_3 & \cdots & \underline{g}_{N-1} & \underline{0} & \underline{0} & \underline{0} & \cdots \\ \underline{0} & \underline{g}_0 & \underline{g}_1 & \underline{g}_2 & \cdots & \underline{g}_{N-2} & \underline{g}_{N-1} & \underline{0} & \underline{0} & \cdots \\ \underline{0} & \underline{0} & \underline{g}_0 & \underline{g}_1 & \cdots & \underline{g}_{N-3} & \underline{g}_{N-2} & \underline{g}_{N-1} & \underline{0} & \cdots \\ \underline{0} & \underline{0} & \underline{0} & \underline{g}_0 & \cdots & \underline{g}_{N-4} & \underline{g}_{N-3} & \underline{g}_{N-2} & \underline{g}_{N-1} & \\ & & & & \downarrow & & & & & \\ & & & & \infty & & & & & \end{bmatrix} \tag{10.22}$$

where $\underline{0}$ denotes a block of n zeros. Let $\mathbf{m} = (m_0\ m_1\ m_2\ m_3 \ldots)$ be the message sequence to be encoded and let $\mathbf{c} = (\mathbf{c}_0\ \mathbf{c}_1\ \mathbf{c}_2\ \mathbf{c}_3 \ldots)$ be the corresponding code sequence, where $\mathbf{c}_\ell$ is the ℓth block of code digits, i.e.,

$$\underline{c}_\ell = c_\ell(1)\ c_\ell(2) \ldots c_\ell(n) \quad .$$

Then,

$$\begin{aligned} \mathbf{c} &= (\underline{c}_0\ \underline{c}_1\ \underline{c}_2\ \underline{c}_3 \ldots) \\ &= \mathbf{m}\,\mathbf{G}_\infty \\ &= m_0\mathbf{g}_\infty(1) + m_1\mathbf{D}\mathbf{g}_\infty(1) + m_2\mathbf{D}^2\mathbf{g}_\infty(1) + \ldots \quad . \end{aligned} \tag{10.23}$$

By examining Eq. (10.22) or Eq. (10.23), we notice that $\underline{c}_0 = \underline{0}$ if $m_0 = 0$, and $\underline{c}_0 = \underline{g}_0$ if $m_0 = 1$. That is, the code can be partitioned into two subsets of equal size. One subset, $\mathbf{S}_0$, contains all the code sequences which correspond to $m_0 = 0$; therefore, all the code sequences in this subset have the same prefix $\underline{0}$. The other subset, $\mathbf{S}_1$, contains all the code sequences which correspond to $m_0 = 1$; therefore, all the code sequences in this subset have the same prefix $\underline{g}_0$. The partitioning is diagrammed as in Fig. 10.8. We can also partition $\mathbf{S}_0$ into two equal subsets, $\mathbf{S}_{00}$ and $\mathbf{S}_{01}$. The subset $\mathbf{S}_{00}$ contains all the code sequences which correspond to $m_0 = m_1 = 0$; thus, all the

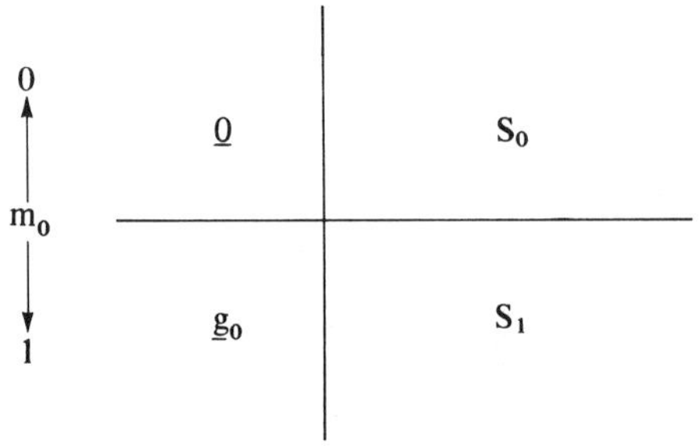

Fig. 10.8.

code sequences in $\mathbf{S}_{00}$ have the same prefix $\underline{0}\ \underline{0}$. The subset $\mathbf{S}_{01}$ contains all the code sequences which correspond to $m_0 = 0$ and $m_1 = 1$; thus, the code sequences in $\mathbf{S}_{01}$ have the same prefix $\underline{0}\ \underline{g}_0$. Likewise, $\mathbf{S}_1$ can be partitioned into two equal subsets, $\mathbf{S}_{10}$ and $\mathbf{S}_{11}$. The subset $\mathbf{S}_{10}$ contains all the code sequences which correspond to $m_0 = 1$ and $m_1 = 0$; thus, all the code sequences in $\mathbf{S}_{10}$ have the same prefix $\underline{g}_0\, \underline{g}_1$. The subset $\mathbf{S}_{11}$ contains all the code sequences which correspond to $m_0 = m_1 = 1$; all the code sequences in $\mathbf{S}_{11}$ have the same prefix $\underline{g}_0\ \underline{g}_0 + \underline{g}_1$. The second partitioning is shown in Fig. 10.9. The partitioning process can be carried on indefinitely. Thus, all the code sequences of the code can be arranged diagrammatically into an infinite tree with nodes spaced n digits apart and two branches stemming from each node. Each branch is an n-digit code block which corresponds

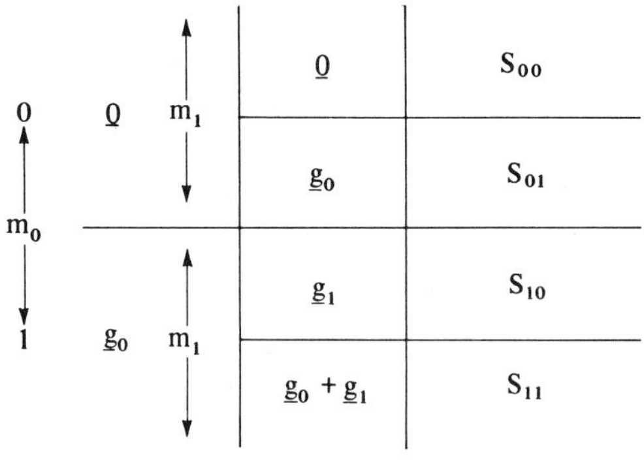

Fig. 10.9.

to a particular message digit and a code sequence is a path in this tree. A topological representation of this infinite tree is shown in Figs. 10.10a and 10.10b. At this point, an example will serve to explain all the notions developed above.

Example 11.3: Consider the (3,1) code of constraint length $N = 4$ generated by the following sub-generators:

$$\begin{aligned} g(1,1) &= 1\ 0\ 1\ 1 \\ g(1,2) &= 1\ 1\ 0\ 1\ . \end{aligned}$$

The generator of this code is

$$g(1) = (\underline{1\,1\,1}\ \ \underline{0\,0\,1}\ \ \underline{0\,1\,0}\ \ \underline{0\,1\,1})\ .$$

The generator matrix of this code is

$$G_\infty = \begin{bmatrix} 111001010011 & & & \\ & 111001010011 & & \\ & & 111001010011 & \\ & & & 111001010011 \\ & & & \downarrow \\ & & & \infty \end{bmatrix} .$$

The tree associated with this code is shown in Fig. 10.11.

The encoding operation can be viewed as a process in which the encoder traces a particular path through the tree according to the instructions given by the input message digits. Each message digit gives instructions as follows. At a given node, the encoder selects the upper branch as the output code block if the input message digit is 0; otherwise, it selects the lower branch as the output code block. Thus, the sequence of selections at

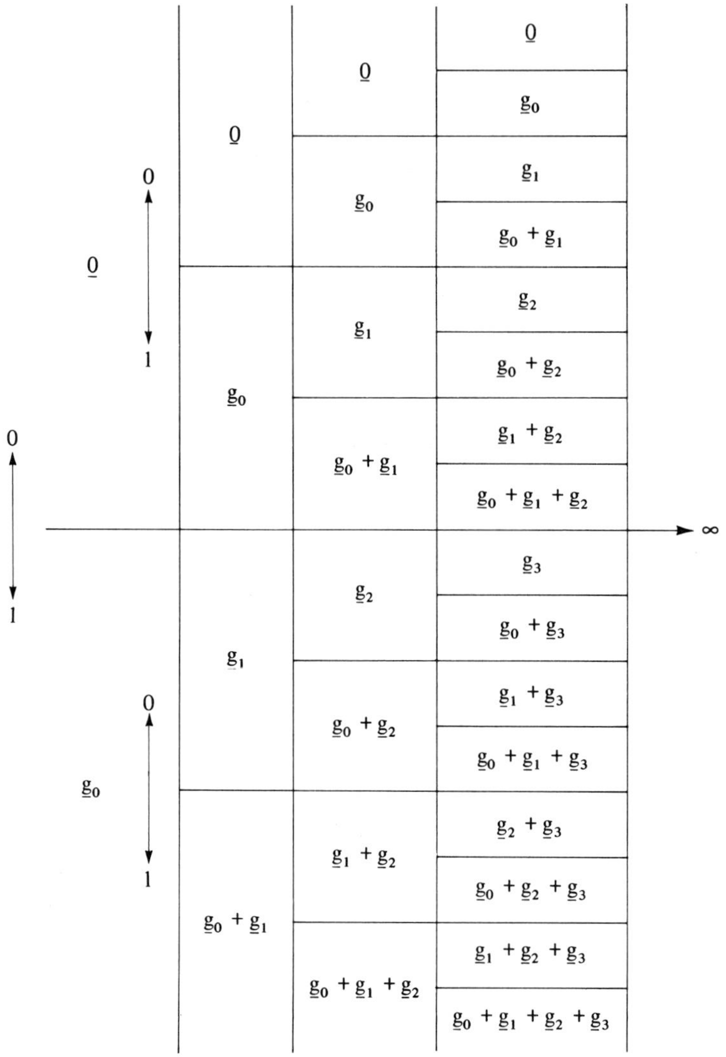

Fig. 10.10a. Table showing the development of an infinite tree for an $(n,1)$ convolutional code.

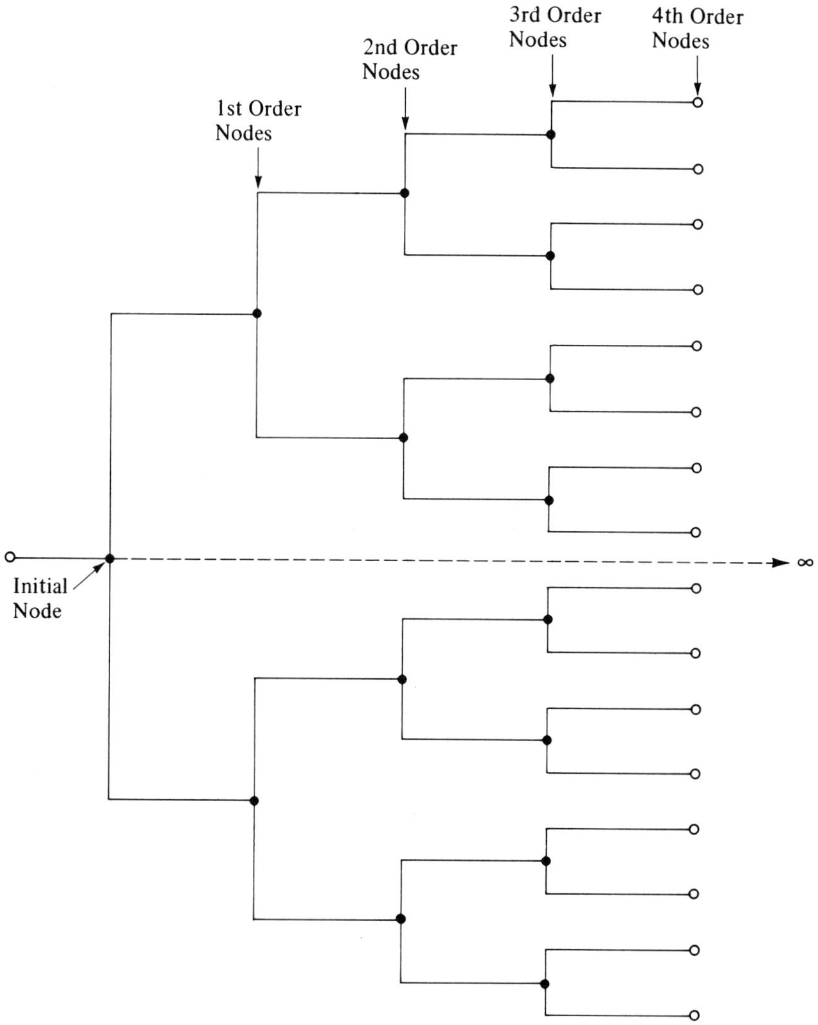

Fig. 10.10b. An infinite tree for an (n,1) convolutional code.

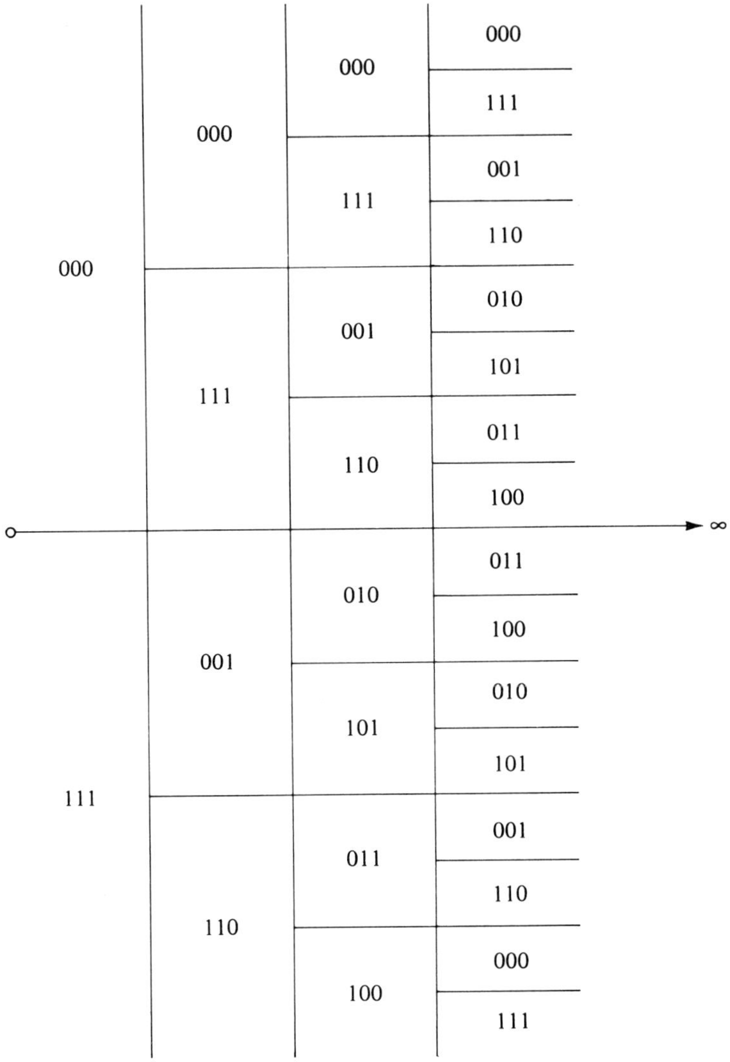

Fig. 10.11. The infinite tree structure of the (3,1) convolutional code of Example 11.3.

consecutive nodes uniquely determines the output code sequence. Consider the infinite tree shown in Fig. 10.11. The path corresponding to $\mathbf{m} = (1\ 0\ 0\ 1 \ldots)$ is $\mathbf{c} = (\underline{1\ 1\ 1}\ \ \underline{0\ 0\ 1}\ \ \underline{0\ 1\ 0}\ \ \underline{1\ 0\ 0} \ldots)$.

The notion of an infinite tree associated with an $(n,1)$ convolutional code can be readily extended to an (n,k) convolutional code. Since there are 2^k possible k-bit messages at the 0th time unit, all the code sequences can be partitioned into 2^k subsets $\mathbf{S}_0, \mathbf{S}_1, \ldots, \mathbf{S}_{2^k-1}$. The code sequences in $\mathbf{S}_i$ have the same 0th block which contains a particular 0th message block. The set $\mathbf{S}_i$ can also be partitioned into 2^k subsets, each containing all the code sequences in $\mathbf{S}_i$ which have the same 0th and 1st blocks. By continuing this partitioning process, we would obtain an infinite tree with nodes spaced n digits apart and 2^k branches from each node as shown in Fig. 10.12. Each branch is a code block which contains a certain k-bit message block. At the ℓth time unit, the encoder is at one of the ℓth order nodes; if the input message block is $m_\ell(1) \ldots m_\ell(k)$, the encoder will select the branch which contains this message block as an output code block. The tree representation of a convolutional code is very useful in explaining a probabilistic decoding scheme which is known as *sequential decoding*.[36]

In the following, we shall study the distance property of a convolutional code by considering the finite tree $\mathcal{L}$ of N branches long which is truncated from the infinite code tree. This finite tree $\mathcal{L}$ consists of 2^{kN} paths of N branches long stemming from the initial node of the infinite tree. The paths in $\mathcal{L}$ shall be called *initial code vectors*, and all of these vectors form an (nN, kN) linear code which is generated by the kN-by-nN submatrix at the upper left corner of the generator matrix $\mathbf{G}_\infty$ of Eq. (10.5), i.e.,

$$\mathbf{G} = \begin{bmatrix} \mathbf{I}_k\mathbf{P}_0 & \mathbf{O}\,\mathbf{P}_1 & \mathbf{O}\,\mathbf{P}_2 & \cdots & \mathbf{O}\,\mathbf{P}_{N-1} \\ & \mathbf{I}_k\mathbf{P}_0 & \mathbf{O}\,\mathbf{P}_1 & \cdots & \mathbf{O}\,\mathbf{P}_{N-2} \\ & & \mathbf{I}_k\mathbf{P}_0 & \cdots & \mathbf{O}\,\mathbf{P}_{N-3} \\ & & & & \vdots \\ & & & & \mathbf{I}_k\mathbf{P}_0 \end{bmatrix} . \tag{10.24}$$

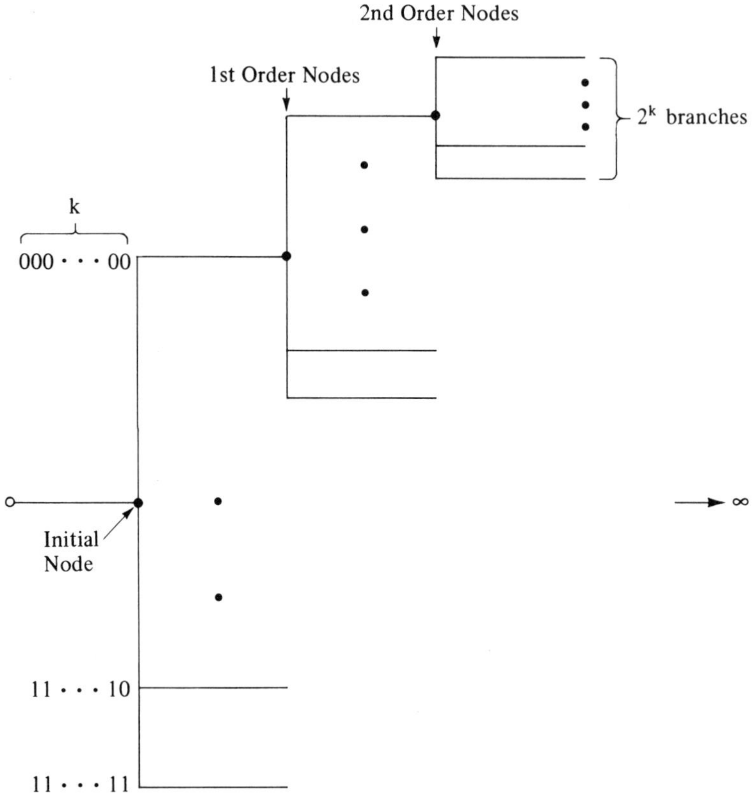

Fig. 10.12. An infinite tree for an (n,k) convolutional code.

The parity-check matrix of $\mathcal{L}$ is

$$H = \begin{bmatrix} P_0^T & I_{n-k} & & & & & & \\ P_1^T & O & P_0^T & I_{n-k} & & & & \\ P_2^T & O & P_1^T & O & P_0^T & I_{n-k} & & \\ \vdots & & & & & & & \\ P_{N-1}^T & O & P_{N-2}^T & O & P_{N-3}^T & O & \ldots & P_0^T \, I_{n-k} \end{bmatrix} \tag{10.25}$$

which is the $(n-k)N$-by-nN submatrix at the upper left corner of $\mathbf{H}_\infty$ of Eq. (10.11). It can be easily shown that $\mathbf{G}\mathbf{H}^T = 0$. Therefore, a vector $\mathbf{v}$ of nN digits is an initial code vector in $\mathcal{L}$ if and only if

$$\mathbf{v} \cdot \mathbf{H}^T = \mathbf{0} \ .$$

The finite code tree $\mathcal{L}$ obviously can be partitioned into 2^k subsets $[\mathbf{S}_0]$, $[\mathbf{S}_1]$, . . ., $[\mathbf{S}_{2^k-1}]$. Each subset $[\mathbf{S}_i]$ contains $2^{k(N-1)}$ initial code vectors which have the same 0th block. Two initial code vectors from two different subsets disagree in the 0th block. Let $d(\mathbf{u},\mathbf{v})$ be the Hamming distance between two initial code vectors $\mathbf{u}$ and $\mathbf{v}$ which disagree in the 0th block.

Definition 11.1: *The minimum distance d_{min} of an (n,k) convolutional code is equal to the smallest Hamming distance $d(\mathbf{u},\mathbf{v})$ between two initial code vectors $\mathbf{u}$ and $\mathbf{v}$ which disagree in the 0th block. Mathematically, this is expressed as follows:*

$$d_{min} = \min_{\substack{i,j \\ i \neq j}} \{d(\mathbf{u},\mathbf{v}): \ \mathbf{u} \in [\mathbf{S}_i] \ \text{and} \ \mathbf{v} \in [\mathbf{S}_j]\} \ . \tag{10.26}$$

Let $\mathbf{z} = \mathbf{u} + \mathbf{v}$. Then $\mathbf{z}$ is also an initial code vector. Since $\mathbf{u}$ and $\mathbf{v}$ disagree in the 0th block, the 0th block of $\mathbf{z}$ cannot be all zeros $\underline{0}$. Let $\omega(\mathbf{z})$ be the weight of $\mathbf{z}$. Then $d(\mathbf{u},\mathbf{v}) = \omega(\mathbf{z})$. It follows from the above definition that the minimum distance of a convolutional code is equal to the minimum weight of an initial code vector whose 0th block is non-zero. For a convolutional code correcting random errors, the minimum distance is an important parameter which gives the error-correcting capability of the code.

Consider an (n,k) convolutional code. An error sequence $\mathbf{e}$ is said to be *correctable* by the code if, by examining the $N(n-k)$-bit syndrome from the ℓth time unit to the $(\ell+N-1)^{th}$ unit, the decoder gives correct estimations of the errors in the ℓth block of $\mathbf{e}$ for $\ell = 0, 1, 2, \ldots$ Since the decoding of any received block is identical to the decoding of the 0th received block, we shall only consider the decoding of the 0th received block. Let $\mathbf{e}_1$ and $\mathbf{e}_2$

be two correctable error sequences which disagree in the 0th block. An obvious requirement for decoding the 0th received block correctly is that $\mathbf{e}_1$ and $\mathbf{e}_2$ cannot yield the same $N(n-k)$-bit syndrome from the 0th time unit to the $(N-1)^{th}$ time unit; otherwise, by examining the syndrome, the decoder would not be able to tell whether the 0th block of $\mathbf{e}_1$ has occurred or the 0th block of $\mathbf{e}_2$ has occurred. Suppose that the correctable error sequences which disagree in the 0th block yield different syndromes from the 0th time unit to the $(N-1)^{th}$ time unit. Then it is possible to show that the decoding of the 0th error block is unique and correct if the error sequence added by the noisy channel is correctable. To see this,[38] we first group all error sequences (only the first N blocks) into subsets E_i's. Each subset E_i contains all the error sequences which have the same 0th block, say $\underline{e}_0^{(i)} = (e_0(1)\, e_0(2) \ldots e_0(n))^{(i)}$. Thus, the correspondence between E_i and $\underline{e}_0^{(i)}$ is one-to-one. For each E_i, we compute the corresponding set A_i of syndromes. It then follows the given condition that the correspondence between A_i and $\underline{e}_0^{(i)}$ is one-to-one. Thus, by examining the $N(n-k)$-bit syndrome, the decoder can exactly tell the error pattern in the 0th received block, and the decoding will be correct. Therefore, we may conclude that the necessary and sufficient condition for a set of error sequences which disagree in the 0th block to be correctable is that they yield different syndromes from the 0th time unit to the $(N-1)^{th}$ time unit. Based on this fact, convolutional codes can be designed to correct random errors, burst errors, or both types.

Let $d_{\min}$ be the minimum distance of an (n,k) convolutional code. The random-error-correcting capability of this code can be determined from the following theorem.

Theorem 13.1: Let $\mathbf{e}_1$ and $\mathbf{e}_2$ be two error sequences of N blocks long that disagree in the 0th block. If both $\mathbf{e}_1$ and $\mathbf{e}_2$ contain $[(d_{\min}-1)/2]$ or fewer errors, then $\mathbf{e}_1$ and $\mathbf{e}_2$ cannot yield the same syndrome, i.e.,

$$\mathbf{e}_1 \mathbf{H}^T \neq \mathbf{e}_2 \mathbf{H}^T \ .$$

Proof: Since $\mathbf{e}_1$ and $\mathbf{e}_2$ disagree in the 0th block, then the 0th block of $\mathbf{e}_1 + \mathbf{e}_2$ must be non-zero. Suppose that $\mathbf{e}_1\mathbf{H}^T = \mathbf{e}_2\mathbf{H}^T$. Then we obtain

$$(\mathbf{e}_1 + \mathbf{e}_2)\,\mathbf{H}^T = \mathbf{0} \ .$$

Therefore, $\mathbf{e}_1 + \mathbf{e}_2$ must be an initial code vector with a non-zero 0th block. This is impossible since the weight of $\mathbf{e}_1 + \mathbf{e}_2$ is less than d_{min}, which is equal to the minimum weight of an initial code vector with a non-zero 0th block. Therefore, we conclude that $\mathbf{e}_1 \mathbf{H}^T \neq \mathbf{e}_2 \mathbf{H}^T$.

Q.E.D.

This theorem implies that any error sequence with $[(d_{min}-1)/2]$ or fewer errors in any span of nN consecutive positions is correctable. It is possible to show that there exists an error sequence with $[(d_{min}-1)/2]+1$ errors in the 1st span of nN consecutive positions which is not correctable. Let $\mathbf{u}$ be an initial code vector with a non-zero 0th block whose weight $\omega(\mathbf{u})$ is equal to d_{min}. We construct two error sequences $\mathbf{e}_1$ and $\mathbf{e}_2$ from $\mathbf{u}$ with the following properties:

(1) $\mathbf{e}_1 + \mathbf{e}_2 = \mathbf{u}$.

(2) The set of errors in $\mathbf{e}_1$ and the set of errors in $\mathbf{e}_2$ are disjoint. (Obviously, $\mathbf{e}_1$ and $\mathbf{e}_2$ disagree in the 0th block.)

(3) The weight $\omega(\mathbf{e}_1)$ of $\mathbf{e}_1$ is equal to $[(d_{min}-1)/2]+1$ and the weight $\omega(\mathbf{e}_2)$ of $\mathbf{e}_2$ is equal to $d_{min} - [(d_{min}-1)/2] - 1$.

From the first property, we obtain $\mathbf{u}\mathbf{H}^T = (\mathbf{e}_1 + \mathbf{e}_2)\,\mathbf{H}^T = 0$, which implies that $\mathbf{e}_1 \mathbf{H}^T = \mathbf{e}_2 \mathbf{H}^T$. Since $\mathbf{e}_1$ and $\mathbf{e}_2$ yield the same syndrome, at least one of them is not correctable. There are two cases to be considered. First, if d_{min} is odd, then we have

$$\frac{d_{min}-1}{2} = w(\mathbf{e}_2) < w(\mathbf{e}_1) = \frac{d_{min}-1}{2} + 1 \ .$$

In other words, $\mathbf{e}_2$ is guaranteed to be correctable. Therefore, $\mathbf{e}_1$ with $[(d_{min}-1)/2]+1$ will not be correctable. Second, if d_{min} is even, then we obtain

$$w(\mathbf{e}_1) = w(\mathbf{e}_2) = \frac{d_{min}-1}{2} + 1 \ .$$

In this case, at least one of them is not correctable. We can thus conclude that a convolutional code with minimum distance d_{min} is capable of correcting any error sequence with $[(d_{min}-1)/2]$ or fewer errors in any span of nN consecutive positions.

It is now clear that for random error correction, an (n,k) convolutional code should be constructed with as large a minimum distance as possible within a given constraint length N. For given values of n, k, and N, upper and lower bounds on the minimum distance attainable have been derived.[3,19,20,23,30,35,36,38] Unfortunately, no systematic method has been found for constructing codes with attainable minimum distance within a given constraint length. Some algorithms which can be used to search for good codes have been proposed. All of these algorithms rely on computer methods.[3,4,6,8,20]

PROBLEMS

10.1. Consider a (2,1) convolutional code which is specified by the following sub-generator:

$$g(1,1) = (1\ 1\ 0\ 1\ 0\ 1) .$$

(a) Find the generator sequence of this code.

(b) Construct the generator matrix for this code.

(c) Construct the parity-check matrix for this code.

10.2. Construct both Type I and Type II encoders for the convolutional code given in Problem 10.1.

10.3. (a) Find the sub-generators for the (3,1) convolutional code whose generator sequence is

$$g(1) = (111\ 001\ 010\ 010\ 001\ 011) .$$

(b) Construct the generator matrix for this code.

(c) Construct the Type II encoder for this code.

10.4. Consider the (2,1) convolutional code given in Problem 10.1. Let $\mathbf{e} = (e_0(1)\ e_0(2)\ e_1(1)\ e_1(2)\ e_2(1)\ e_2(2)\ e_3(1)\ e_3(2)\ e_4(1)\ e_4(2)\ e_5(1)\ e_5(2)\ \ldots)$ be an error sequence. Express the first 6 syndrome bits in terms of the error digits $e_\ell(i)$ for $\ell = 0, 1, 2, 3, 4$, and 5.

10.5. Construct the code tree (6 branches long) for the (3,1) code given in Problem 10.3. What is the minimum distance of this code?

10.6. Construct a (4,1) convolutional code with minimum distance $d = 9$ and constraint length $N = 4$.

10.7. Consider a non-systematic (3,1) convolutional code whose generator sequence is

$$\mathbf{g}(1) = (111\ 101\ 001\ 110)\ .$$

(a) Construct an encoder for this code.

(b) Construct the code tree of 4 branches for this code.

(c) What is the minimum distance of this code?

REFERENCES

1. Berlekamp, E. R., "A Class of Convolutional Codes," *Information and Control*, **6**, pp. 1-13, March, 1963.

2. Berlekamp, E. R., "Note on Recurrent Codes," *IEEE Trans. on Information Theory*, **IT-10**, pp. 257-259, July, 1964.

3. Bussgang, J. J., "Some Properties of Binary Convolutional Code Generators," *IEEE Trans. on Information Theory*, **IT-11**, pp. 90-100, January, 1965.

4. Costello, D. J., "A Construction Technique for Random Error Correcting Convolutional Codes," *IEEE Trans. on Information Theory*, **IT-15**, pp. 631-636, September, 1969.

5. Elias, P., "Coding for Noisy Channels," *IRE Convention Record*, Part 4, pp. 37-47, 1955.

6. Epstein, M. A., "Construction of Convolutional Codes by Sub-optimalization," Technical Report No. 341, M.I.T. Research Lab. of Electronics, Cambridge, Massachusetts, 1959.

7. Fano, R. M., "A Heuristic Discussion of Probabilistic Decoding," *IEEE Trans. on Information Theory*, **IT-9**, pp. 64-74, April, 1963.

8. Forney, G. D., "Final Report on a Study of a Simple Sequential Decoder," U. S. Army Satellite Communication Agency Report DAABO7-68-0093, Appendix A, Codex Corporation, Watertown, Massachusetts, 1968.

9. Forney, G. D., "Algebraic Structure of Convolutional Codes," presented at the IEEE International Symposium on Information Theory, Ellenville, New York, 1969.

10. Freiman, C. V., and J. P. Robinson, "A Comparison of Block and Recurrent Codes for the Correction of Independent Errors," *IEEE Trans. on Information Theory*, **IT-11**, pp. 445-449, July, 1965.

11. Gallager, R. G., *Information Theory and Reliable Communication*, John Wiley, New York, 1968.

12. Hagelbarger, D. W., "Recurrent Codes: Easily Mechanized, Burst-Correcting, Binary Codes," *Bell Systems Tech. J.*, **38**, pp. 969-984, 1959.

13. Hagelbarger, D. W., "Recurrent Codes for the Binary Symmetric Channel," lecture notes from the University of Michigan Summer Conference on Coding Theory, 1962.

14. Heller, J. A., "Short Constraint Length Convolutional Codes," presented at the IEEE International Conference on Communications, Boulder, Colorado, 1969.

15. Hsu, H. T., "A New Class of Recurrent Codes," *IEEE Trans. on Information Theory*, **IT-15**, pp. 592-597, September, 1969.

16. Iwadare, Y., "On Type-B1 Burst-Error-Correcting Convolutional Codes," *IEEE Trans. on Information Theory*, **IT-14**, pp. 577-583, July, 1968.

17. Kilmer, W. L., "Some Results on Best Recurrent-Type Binary-Error-Correcting Codes," *IRE Convention Record*, Part 4, pp. 135-147, 1960.

18. Kilmer, W. L., "Linear-Recurrent Binary Error-Correcting Codes for Memoryless Channels," *IRE Trans. on Information Theory*, **IT-7**, pp. 7-12, January, 1961.

19. Kolor, R. W., "A Gilbert Bound for Convolutional Codes," M.S. Thesis, Massachusetts Institute of Technology, Cambridge, Massachusetts, 1967.

20. Lin, S., and H. Lyne, "Some Results on Binary Convolutional Code Generators," *IEEE Trans. on Information Theory*, **IT-13**, pp. 134-139, January, 1967.

21. Lucky, R. W., J. Salz, and E. J. Weldon, Jr., *Principles of Data Communication*, McGraw-Hill, New York, 1968.

22. Macy, J. R., "Theory of Serial Codes," Ph.D. Thesis, Stevens Institute of Technology, Hoboken, New Jersey, 1963.

23. Massey, J. L., "Threshold Decoding," The M.I.T. Press, Cambridge, Massachusetts, 1963.

24. Massey, J. L., and R. W. Liu, "Application of Lyapunov's Direct Method to the Error-Propagation Effect in Convolutional Codes," *IEEE Trans. on Information Theory*, **IT-10**, pp. 248-250, July, 1964.

25. Massey, J. L., "Implementation of Burst-Correcting Convolutional Codes," *IEEE Trans. on Information Theory*, **IT-11**, pp. 416-422, July, 1965.

26. Massey, J. L., "Some Algebraic and Distance Properties of Binary Convolutional Codes," Chapter 5, *Error-Correcting Codes*, H. Mann, Ed., John Wiley, 1968.

27. Peterson, W. W., *Error-Correcting Codes*, The M.I.T. Press, Cambridge, Massachusetts, and John Wiley, New York, 1961.

28. Peterson, W. W., and E. J. Weldon, Jr., *Error-Correcting Codes*, 2nd Edition, The M.I.T. Press, Cambridge, Massachusetts, 1970.

29. Preparata, F.P., "Systematic Construction of Optimal Linear Recurrent Codes for Burst Error Correction," *Calcolo*, **2**, pp. 1-7, 1964.

30. Robinson, J. P., "An Upper Bound on the Minimum Distance of a Convolutional Code," *IEEE Trans. on Information Theory*, **IT-11**, pp. 567-571, October, 1965.

31. Robinson, J. P., and A. J. Bernstein, "A Class of Recurrent Codes with Limited Error Propagation," *IEEE Trans. on Information Theory*, **IT-13**, pp. 106-113, January, 1967.

32. Robinson, J. P., "Error Propagation and Definite Decoding of Convolutional Codes," *IEEE Trans. on Information Theory*, **IT-14**, pp. 121-128, January, 1968.

33. Sullivan, D. D., "Control of Error Propagation in Convolutional Codes," Department of Electrical Engineering, University of Notre Dame, Notre Dame, Indiana, Technical Report EE 67, 1967.

34. Viterbi, A. J., "Error Bounds for Convolutional Codes and an Asymptotically Optimum Decoding Algorithm," *IEEE Trans. on Information Theory*, **IT-13**, pp. 260-269, April, 1967.

35. Wagner, T. J., "A Gilbert Bound for Periodic Binary Convolutional Codes," *IEEE Trans. on Information Theory*, **IT-14**, pp. 752-755, September, 1968.

36. Wozencraft, J. M., and B. Reiffen, *Sequential Decoding*, The M.I.T. Press, Cambridge, Massachusetts, 1961.

37. Wozencraft, J. M., and I. M. Jacobs, *Principles of Communication Engineering*, John Wiley, New York, 1965.

38. Wyner, A. D., and R. B. Ash, "Analysis of Recurrent Codes," *IEEE Trans. on Information Theory*, **IT-9**, pp. 143-156, July, 1963.

39. Wyner, A. D., "On the Equivalence of Two Convolutional Code Definitions," *IEEE Trans. on Information Theory*, **IT-11**, pp. 600-602, October, 1965.

CHAPTER 11

RANDOM-ERROR-CORRECTING CONVOLUTIONAL CODES

In this chapter, several classes of convolutional codes which are capable of correcting random errors are presented. The single-error-correcting convolutional codes presented in Section 11.1 were discovered by Wyner and Ash.[13] These codes are analogous to the single-error-correcting Hamming (block) codes. Similar to block codes, certain classes of convolutional codes can be decoded with majority-logic decoding. The first majority-logic decoding algorithms for convolutional codes were devised by Massey.[5,6] He also constructed several classes of convolutional codes which are decodable by majority-logic decoding. Important majority-logic decodable codes are presented in Sections 11.3 and 11.4.

The majority-logic decoding algorithms for convolutional codes presented in Section 11.2 and the codes presented in Section 11.4 are taken from Massey's work.[5,6] The material in Section 11.3 is based primarily on the work of Robinson and Bernstein.[10]

11.1 SINGLE-ERROR-CORRECTING WYNER-ASH CODES

Description of Codes

Let m be a positive integer. Then any non-negative integer i less than 2^m can be uniquely expressed in the radix-2 form as

$$i = i_0 + i_1 2^1 + i_2 2^2 + \ldots + i_{m-1} 2^{m-1} ,$$

where i_ℓ is either 0 or 1. The m-tuple $(i_0, i_1, i_2, \ldots, i_{m-1})$ is the binary representation of the integer i.

Wyner and Ash[13] have shown that, for any positive integer m, there exists a single-error-correcting convolutional code with the following parameters:

$$n = 2^m$$

$$k = 2^m - 1$$

$$N = m + 1 \ .$$

The $2^m - 1$ sub-generators of this code are

$$\mathbf{g}(i,1) = (1, i_0, i_1, \ldots, i_{m-1}) \tag{11.1}$$

for $i = 1, 2, \ldots, 2^m - 1$, where $(i_0, i_1, \ldots, i_{m-1})$ is the binary representation of i. There is only one parity-check digit in each code block. This code can be encoded by an m-stage encoding circuit as shown in Fig. 10.2.

Example 11.1: For $m = 3$, the (8,7) Wyner-Ash code of constraint length 4 is specified by the following 7 sub-generators:

$$\mathbf{g}(1,1) = (1\ 1\ 0\ 0)$$

$$\mathbf{g}(2,1) = (1\ 0\ 1\ 0)$$

$$\mathbf{g}(3,1) = (1\ 1\ 1\ 0)$$

$$\mathbf{g}(4,1) = (1\ 0\ 0\ 1)$$

$$\mathbf{g}(5,1) = (1\ 1\ 0\ 1)$$

$$\mathbf{g}(6,1) = (1\ 0\ 1\ 1)$$

$$\mathbf{g}(7,1) = (1\ 1\ 1\ 1) \ .$$

Decoding

It was described in Section 10.4 that, in order to decode the 0th block of the received sequence, the decoder examines the first $N(n-k)$ syndrome digits. Based on these syndrome digits, the decoder must then determine: (1) whether or not there are errors in the 0th block of the received sequence; and (2) the locations of these errors.

To demonstrate that a Wyner-Ash $(2^m, 2^m-1)$ code is capable of correcting any single error in a span of $(m+1)2^m$ consecutive digits, we write the first $(m+1)$ syndrome digits as follows (use Eqs. (10.19) and (11.1)):

$$
\begin{aligned}
s_0(1) &= e_0(2^m) + e_0(1) + e_0(2) + \ldots + e_0(2^m-1) \\
s_1(1) &= e_1(2^m) + \sum_{i=1}^{2^m-1} e_1(i) + \sum_{i=1}^{2^m-1} e_0(i)\, i_0 \\
s_2(1) &= e_2(2^m) + \sum_{i=1}^{2^m-1} e_2(i) + \sum_{i=1}^{2^m-1} e_1(i)\, i_0 + \sum_{i=1}^{2^m-1} e_0(i)\, i_1 \\
&\vdots \\
s_m(1) &= e_m(2^m) + \sum_{i=1}^{2^m-1} e_m(i) + \sum_{i=1}^{2^m-1} e_{m-1}(i)\, i_0 + \ldots + \sum_{i=1}^{2^m-1} e_0(i)\, i_{m-1} \,.
\end{aligned}
\tag{11.2}
$$

If this single error is not in the 0th block of the received sequence, then $e_0(1) = e_0(2) = \ldots = e_0(2^m) = 0$, which implies that $s_0(1) = 0$. If this single error is in the 0th block, say at the $i^{*\text{th}}$ position, then

$$s_0(1) = e_0(i^*) = 1$$

and

$$(s_1(1), s_2(1), \ldots, s_m(1)) = (i_0^*, i_1^*, \ldots, i_{m-1}^*) \,,$$

where $(i_0^*, i_1^*, \ldots, i_{m-1}^*)$ is the binary representation of i^*. Therefore, the first syndrome digit indicates whether or not the single error is in the 0th block of the received sequence. If it is in the 0th block, then the next m syndrome digits give the exact location of the error. Thus, the 0th block of the received sequence will be decoded correctly if a single error occurs in a span of $(m+1)2^m$ consecutive received digits. There are error sequences with more than one error in a span of $(m+1)2^m$ consecutive digits which are not correctable by this code. For example, consider an error sequence with $\lambda > 1$ errors in the 0th block. If λ is odd, then, by Eq. (11.2), $s_0(1) = 1$

and $(s_1(1), s_2(1), \ldots, s_m(1))$ is a certain m-tuple. Thus, this error sequence will be treated as a certain error sequence with a single error in the span of the first $(m+1)2^m$ consecutive positions. Therefore, the 0th block will be decoded incorrectly. If λ is even, then $s_0(1) = 0$, and we will assume that the error sequence has no errors in the 0th block. Therefore, the 0th block of the received sequence will be decoded incorrectly. From the above discussion, we conclude that the Wyner-Ash $(2^m, 2^m\text{-}1)$ code is a single-error-correcting convolutional code.

A decoding circuit for the above code is shown in Fig. 11.1. The decoding procedure can be described as follows:

Step 1. For decoding the 0th block of the received sequence, the first $m+1$ syndrome bits are calculated.

Step 2. (a) If the first syndrome bit is a zero, the decoder assumes that no error has occurred and no correction is necessary. (b) If the first syndrome bit is a one, the decoder assumes that a single error has occurred in the first received block. The remaining m syndrome bits give the location of the single error. If these m bits are the binary representation of the integer i, then the ith received information digit is an erroneous digit and must be corrected.

Step 3. The $2^m\text{-}1$ received message digits of the 0th block are serialized and shifted out of the decoder one at a time. At the same time, a counter starts to count from 1. When the contents of the counter match the contents of the last m bits of the syndrome, the received message digit which was just shifted out is the erroneous digit. This digit is corrected by the output of Gate A.

Step 4. Set the syndrome to zero after the correction has been made.

Step 5. The $(m+1)^{th}$ block of the received sequence is shifted into the decoder and its corresponding syndrome bit is calculated and shifted into the leftmost stage of the syndrome register. The decoder starts to decode the 1st received block and repeats Steps 1, 2, 3, and 4.

Since the syndrome register is reset to zero after each correction, a decoding error cannot trigger additional errors in subsequent decodings; therefore, no error propagation can possibly occur.

The Wyner-Ash convolutional codes are analogous to the Hamming block codes. It has been shown by Freiman and Robinson[1] that there is

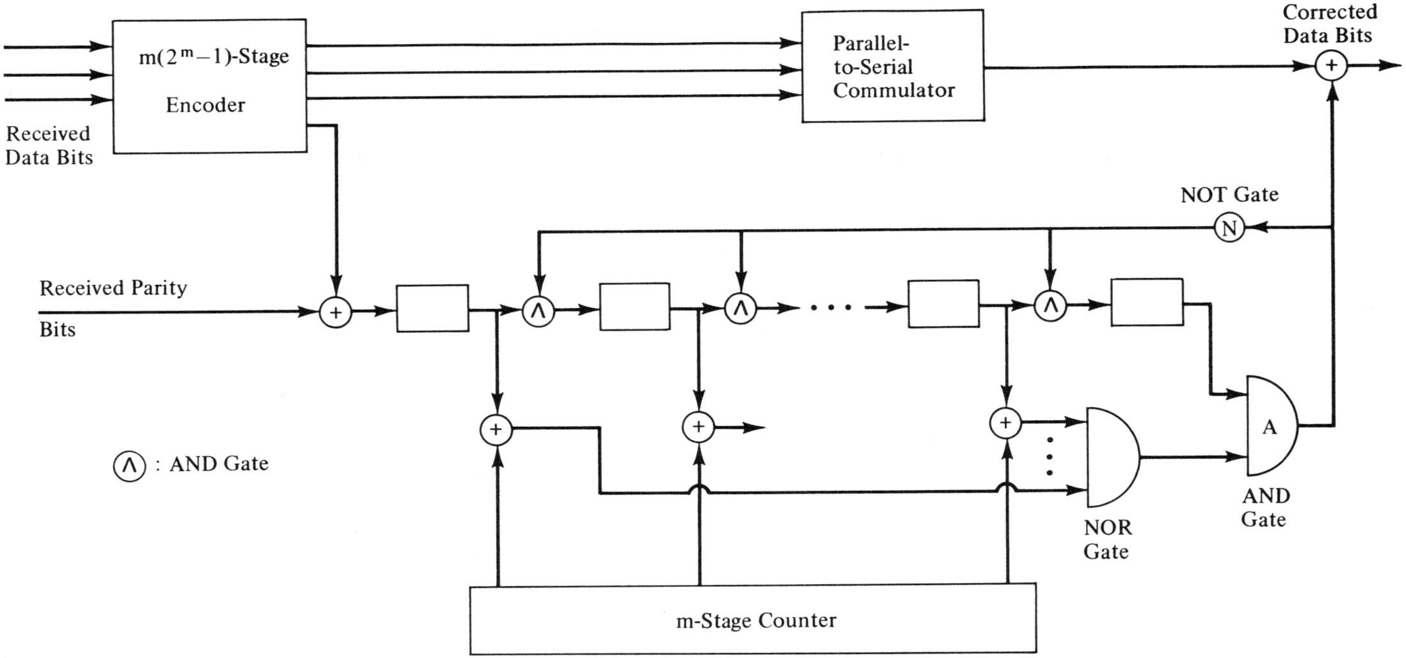

Fig. 11.1. A decoder for the Wyner-Ash code.

little difference in performance (on binary symmetric channels) between these two classes of codes.

A decoder for the (8,7) Wyner-Ash code of Example 11.1 is shown in Fig. 11.2.

11.2 MAJORITY-LOGIC DECODING FOR CONVOLUTIONAL CODES

Similar to block codes, there are convolutional codes with special structures such that they can be decoded easily by majority-logic decoding. The concept of parity-check sums orthogonal on a single error digit which was developed for block codes in Chapter 7 can be readily applied to convolutional codes. An (n,k) convolutional code of constraint length N is capable of correcting any error sequence $\mathbf{e}$ with t or fewer errors in any span of nN consecutive positions by the majority-logic decoding algorithm, provided that a set of $2t$ or more parity-check sums orthogonal on the error digit $e_0(i)$ for $i = 1, 2, \ldots, k$ can be formed from the first $N(n-k)$ syndrome digits.[6] Alternatively, if it is possible to form J parity-check sums orthogonal on $e_0(i)$ for $i = 1, 2, \ldots, k$ for an (n,k) convolutional code of constraint length N, then any error sequence with $t = [J/2]$ or fewer errors in any span of nN positions can be corrected by the majority-logic decoding algorithm. A convolutional code with minimum distance d is said to be completely orthogonalizable if and only if $J = d - 1$.[6]

A general majority-logic decoder for a t-error-correcting (n,k) convolutional code is shown in Fig. 11.3. The error correction procedure can be described as follows:

Step 1. For decoding the 0th block of the received sequence, the $N(n-k)$-bit syndrome sequence corresponding to the received sequence from the 0th block to the $(N-1)^{th}$ block is calculated.

Step 2. Form k sets $A_1, A_2, \ldots, A_k$ of orthogonal check sums from the $N(n-k)$ syndrome bits calculated in Step 1. The set A_i consists of $2t$ parity-check sums orthogonal on $e_0(i)$.

Step 3. The $2t$ check sums of the set A_i are fed into a $2t$-input majority-logic gate $\mathbf{M}_i$. If the output of $\mathbf{M}_i$ is "1," the ith received message digit of the 0th block is assumed to be an erroneous digit and

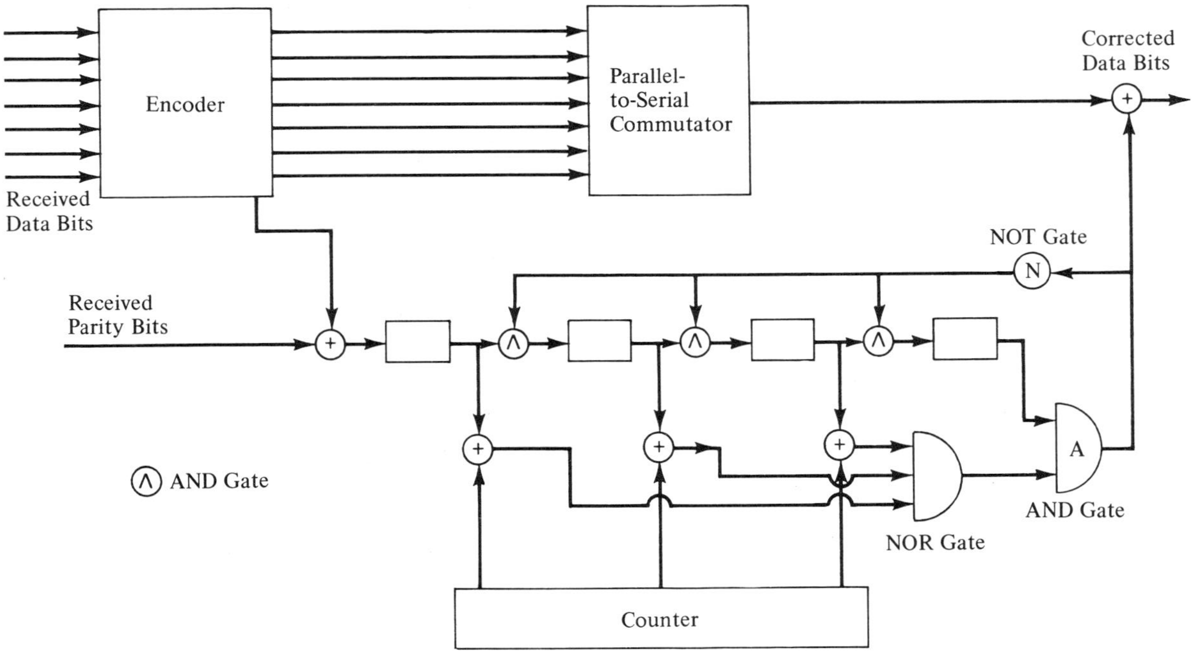

Fig. 11.2. A decoder for the (8,7) Wyner-Ash code.

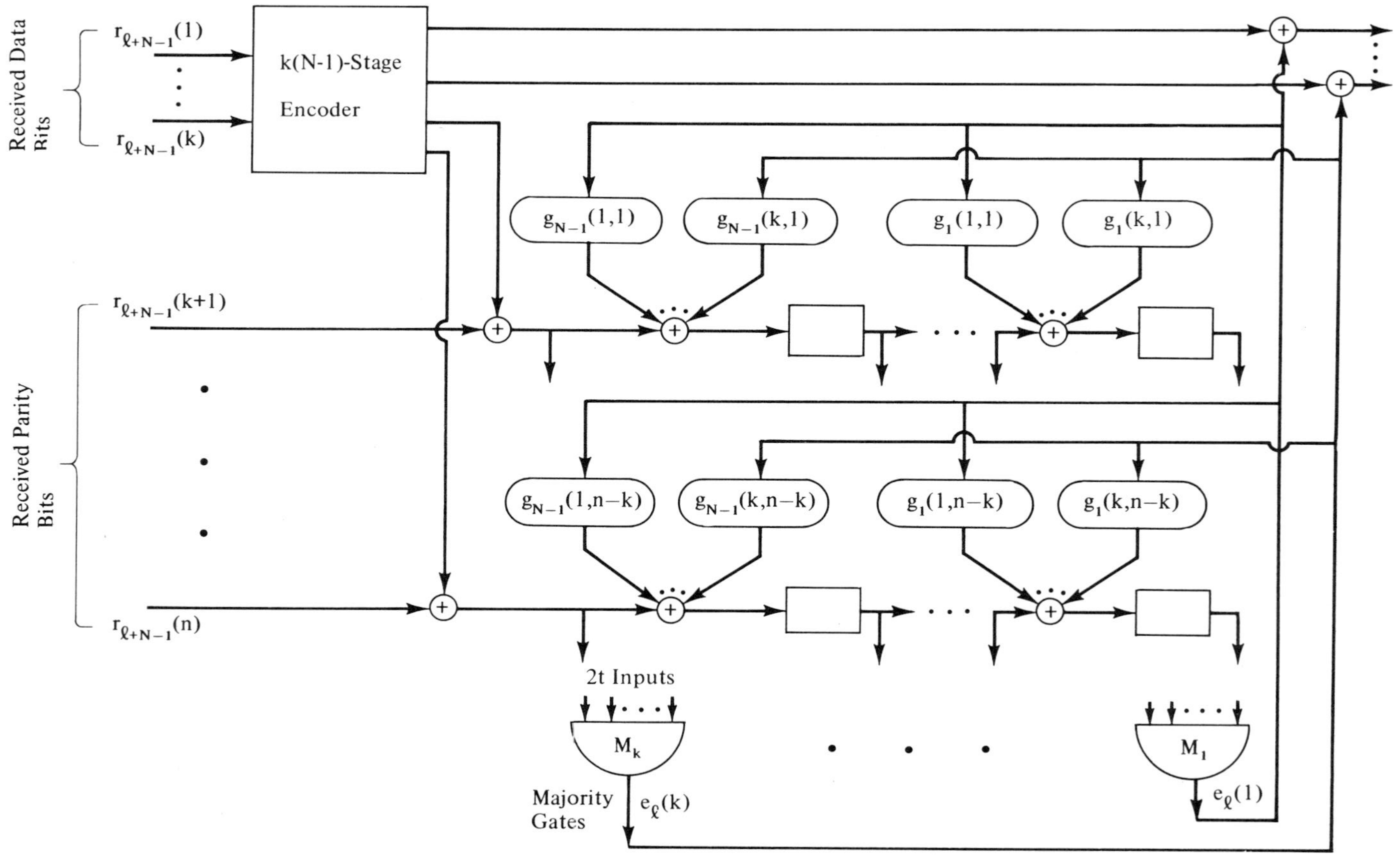

Fig. 11.3. A majority-logic decoder for an *(n,k)* convolutional code.

should be corrected. If the output of $\mathbf{M}_i$ is "0," the ith received message digit of the 0th block is assumed to be correct. The output of $\mathbf{M}_i$ is added (modulo-2) to the ith received message digit for correction. At the same time, the outputs of the k majority gates are fed back to the syndrome registers to remove their effect on the syndrome sequence (syndrome resetting).

Step 4. After all k received information digits of the 0th block have been corrected, they are shifted out to the data sink. The $n-k$ syndrome registers are shifted to the right once. At the same time, the Nth block of the received sequence is shifted into the decoder and its corresponding $n-k$ syndrome bits are calculated and shifted into the leftmost stages of the $n-k$ syndrome registers.

Step 5. Now the syndrome registers contain the modified syndrome sequence. The decoder starts to decode the 1st received block and then repeats Steps 2, 3, and 4.

The decoder described above is a one-step majority-logic decoder. Massey[6] has shown that the L-step orthogonalization process for block codes does not apply to convolutional codes.

11.3 SELF-ORTHOGONAL CONVOLUTIONAL CODES

Consider the (2,1) convolutional code of constraint length 7 which is specified by the following sub-generator,

$$\mathbf{g}(1,1) = (1\ 0\ 1\ 0\ 0\ 1\ 1) .$$

From Eq. (10.18), we obtain the first 7 syndrome digits as follows:

$$s_0(1) = e_0(1) + e_0(2)$$

$$s_1(1) = e_1(1) + e_1(2)$$

$$s_2(1) = e_0(1) + e_2(1) + e_2(2)$$

$$s_3(1) = e_1(1) + e_3(1) + e_3(2)$$

$$s_4(1) = e_2(1) + e_4(1) + e_4(2)$$

$$s_5(1) = e_0(1) + e_3(1) + e_5(1) + e_5(2)$$

$$s_6(1) = e_0(1) + e_1(1) + e_4(1) + e_6(1) + e_6(2) \quad .$$

By examining these 7 parity-check equations, we notice that the syndrome bits $s_0(1), s_2(1), s_5(1)$, and $s_6(1)$ which check $e_0(1)$ are orthogonal on $e_0(1)$. Thus, the error digit $e_0(1)$ can be estimated from $s_0(1)$, $s_2(1)$, $s_5(1)$, and $s_6(1)$ by majority vote. This code is called a *self-orthogonal code* and is capable of correcting any error sequence **e** of 2 or fewer errors in any span of 14 consecutive positions.

> **Definition 11.1:** *An (n,k) convolutional code is said to be self-orthogonal if and only if the set of J_i syndrome digits which check $e_0(i)$ are orthogonal on $e_0(i)$ for $i = 1, 2, \ldots, k$. This code is capable of correcting any error sequence with $[J/2]$ or fewer errors in a span of $N(n-k)$ consecutive positions, where J is equal to the minimum of $J_1, J_2, \ldots, J_k$.*

The self-orthogonal convolutional codes were introduced independently by Hagelbarger,[2] Macy,[4] and Massey.[5,6] The rest of this section will be devoted to discussing the properties of self-orthogonal codes.

Consider an (n,k) code which is specified by the following $k(n-k)$ sub-generators:

$$\mathbf{g}(i,j) = (g_0(i,j), g_1(i,j), g_2(i,j) \ldots g_{N-1}(i,j))$$

for $i = 1, 2, \ldots, k$ and $j = 1, 2, \ldots, n-k$. Consider four distinct components of the form

$$\begin{matrix} g_{\ell_1}(i_1,j_1) & g_{s_1}(i_2,j_1) \\ g_{\ell_2}(i_1,j_2) & g_{s_2}(i_2,j_2) \end{matrix} \qquad (11.3)$$

where $0 \leqslant \ell_1 \leqslant \ell_2 \leqslant N\text{-}1$, $0 \leqslant s_1 \leqslant s_2 \leqslant N\text{-}1$, and $\ell_2 - \ell_1 = s_2 - s_1$. These four components are said to form a *rectangle* if $g_{\ell_1}(i_1,j_1) = g_{\ell_2}(i_1,j_2) = g_{s_1}(i_2,j_1) = g_{s_2}(i_2,j_1) = 1$. It follows from Eq. (10.18) and Definition 11.1 that a necessary and sufficient condition for an (n,k) convolutional code to be self-orthogonal is that no rectangle can exist in the set of $k(n-k)$ sub-generators of the code. Thus, when constructing a self-orthogonal convolutional code, we encounter the problem of finding a set of $k(n-k)$ sub-generators which do not contain any rectangle. In the following, we shall consider the construction of certain special subclasses of self-orthogonal codes.

$(n,n\text{-}1)$ *Self-Orthogonal Convolutional Codes*

An $(n,n\text{-}1)$ code is specified by $n - 1$ sub-generators,

$$\mathbf{g}(i,1) = (g_0(i,1), g_1(i,1), g_2(i,1), \ldots, g_{N-1}(i,1)) \qquad (11.4)$$

for $i = 1, 2, \ldots, n-1$. Let $g_{\ell_1}(i,1), g_{\ell_2}(i,1), \ldots, g_{\ell_{J_i}}(i,1)$ be the non-zero components of $\mathbf{g}(i,1)$, where $\ell_1 < \ell_2 < \ldots < \ell_{J_i}$. Then, by examining Eq. (10.18), we find that $s_{\ell_1}(1), s_{\ell_2}(1), \ldots, s_{\ell_{J_i}}(1)$ are the syndrome digits which check the error bit $e_0(i)$. If the code is self-orthogonal, then these syndrome digits form J_i parity-check sums orthogonal on $e_0(i)$. Thus, $e_0(i)$ will be decoded correctly by the majority-logic decoding algorithm if there are $[J_i/2]$ or fewer errors in the span of the first nN received digits. Let J be equal to the minimum of $J_1, J_2, \ldots, J_{n-1}$. Then every error digit in the 0th block of the received sequence will be decoded correctly if $[J/2]$ or fewer errors occur in the span of the first N received blocks. Since the decoding of successive received blocks is the same as the decoding of the 0th block, the code is capable of correcting any error sequence e with $[J/2]$ or fewer errors in any span of nN consecutive positions.

In the following, we shall prove a theorem which forms the basis for constructing a class of $(n,n\text{-}1)$ convolutional codes. Before we prove this theorem, we must define the *difference triangle*[10] associated with a sub-generator. The difference triangle $\Delta(i)$ associated with $\mathbf{g}(i,1)$ is defined as the set of $J_i(J_i\text{-}1)/2$ positive differences $\ell_d - \ell_c$ for $d > c$, where ℓ_c and ℓ_d are the subscripts of the two non-zero components $g_{\ell_c}(i,1)$ and $g_{\ell_d}(i,1)$ of

$g(i,1)$. The triangle $\Delta(i)$ is said to be *full* if all the differences in $\Delta(i)$ are distinct. The triangles $\Delta(i_1)$ and $\Delta(i_2)$ are said to be *disjoint* if they do not contain any common difference. The following theorem is the basis for the construction of a class of self-orthogonal convolutional codes.

Theorem 11.1:[10] The $(n, n-1)$ code specified by the set of sub-generators of Eq. (11.4) is self-orthogonal if and only if the difference triangles $\Delta(1), \Delta(2), \ldots, \Delta(n-1)$ are full and mutually disjoint.

Proof: The proof of this theorem consists of two parts:

(1) Assume that the code is self-orthogonal; we want to show that all the difference triangles are full and disjoint. Suppose that a difference triangle $\Delta(i)$ exists which is not full. Then at least two differences in $\Delta(i)$ are equal, say $\ell_d - \ell_c = \ell_f - \ell_e$. That is, there exists a rectangle of the form

$$\begin{array}{ll} g_{\ell_c}(i,1) = 1 & g_{\ell_e}(i,1) = 1 \\ g_{\ell_d}(i,1) = 1 & g_{\ell_f}(i,1) = 1 \end{array}$$

in the sub-generators of the code. Thus, the code cannot be self-orthogonal. This contradicts the assumption that the code is self-orthogonal. Suppose two triangles $\Delta(i_1)$ and $\Delta(i_2)$ exist which are not disjoint. Then they must at least have a common difference. Let $\ell_d - \ell_c$ and $s_f - s_e$ be the common differences in $\Delta(i_1)$ and $\Delta(i_2)$ respectively. Since $\ell_d - \ell_c = s_f - s_e$, there must exist a rectangle

$$\begin{array}{ll} g_{\ell_c}(i_1,1) = 1 & g_{s_e}(i_2,1) = 1 \\ g_{\ell_d}(i_1,1) = 1 & g_{s_f}(i_2,1) = 1 \end{array}$$

in the sub-generators of the code. That is, the code cannot be self-orthogonal. However, this contradicts the assumption that the code is self-orthogonal. Therefore, we conclude that all the triangles must be full and disjoint.

(2) Assume that all the triangles are full and disjoint; we want to show that the code is self-orthogonal. Suppose that the code is not self-orthogonal. Then at least one rectangle must exist in the sub-generators of the code. This rectangle must be of the form

$$g_{\ell_c}(i_1,1) = 1 \qquad g_{s_e}(i_2,1) = 1$$

$$g_{\ell_d}(i_1,1) = 1 \qquad g_{s_f}(i_2,1) = 1$$

and $\ell_d - \ell_c = s_f - s_e$. If $i_1 = i_2 = i$, the differences $\ell_d - \ell_c$ and $s_f - s_e$ are both in $\Delta(i)$. Thus, $\Delta(i)$ cannot be full. This contradicts the assumption that $\Delta(i)$ is full. If $i_1 \neq i_2$, then $\ell_d - \ell_c$ is in $\Delta(i_1)$ and $s_f - s_e$ is in $\Delta(i_2)$. Thus, $\Delta(i_1)$ and $\Delta(i_2)$ are not disjoint. This contradicts the assumption that $\Delta(i_1)$ and $\Delta(i_2)$ are disjoint. Therefore, we conclude that the code must be self-orthogonal.

Q.E.D.

Based on the above theorem, Robinson and Bernstein[10] have developed a procedure for constructing a class of $(n, n-1)$ self-orthogonal convolutional codes.* A list of such codes of various error-correcting capabilities and constraint lengths is given in Table 11.1. In the table, the $n-1$ sub-generators are specified by $(n-1)$ sets of integers; each set specifies the locations of the non-zero components of a sub-generator. This can be best explained by an example.

Example 11.2: Consider the double-error-correcting (3,2) code with constraint length N=14 in Table 11.1b. The first generator sequence $\mathbf{g}(1,1)$ is specified by the first set of integers $(0, 8, 9, 12)^1$ as follows:

Location Number	0	1	2	3	4	5	6	7	8	9	10	11	12	13
$\mathbf{g}(1,1)$ =	(1	0	0	0	0	0	0	0	1	1	0	0	1	0) .

* The first procedure for constructing self-orthogonal codes was devised by Massey.[5] Massey's procedure generally results in codes with constraint length longer than that of the codes resulting from Robinson and Bernstein's procedure.

n	t	N	Generator Sequences
2	1	3	(0,1)[1]
	2	7	(0,2,5,6)[1]
	3	18	(0,2,7,13,16,17)[1]
	4	36	(0,7,10,16,18,30,31,35)[1]
	5	56	(0,2,14,21,29,32,45,49,54,55)[1]
	6	86	(0,2,6,24,29,40,43,55,68,75,76,85)[1]
	7	128	(0,5,28,38,41,49,50,68,75,92,107,121,123,127)[1]
	8	180	(0,6,19,40,58,67,78,83,109,132,133,162,165,169, 177,179)[1]
	9	217	(0,2,10,22,53,56,82,83,89,98,130,148,153,167,188, 192,205,216)[1]
	10	284	(0,24,30,43,55,71,75,89,104,125,127,162,167,189, 206,215,272,275,282,283)[1]
	11	359	(0,3,16,45,50,51,65,104,125,142,182,206,210,218, 228,237,289,300,326,333,356,358)[1]
	12	426	(0,22,41,57,72,93,99,139,147,153,197,200,214,253, 263,265,276,283,308,367,368,372,396,425)[1]

Table 11.1a.* (2,1) codes.

* Table 11.1 is taken from J. P. Robinson and A. J. Bernstein, "A Class of Binary Recurrent Codes with Limited Error Propagation," *IEEE Trans. on Information Theory*, IT-13, Table 1, p. 110, January, 1967, by permission.

n	t	N	Generator Sequences
3	1	3	$(0,1)^1$
	2	14	$(0,8,9,12)^1$
			$(0,6,11,13)^2$
	3	41	$(0,2,6,24,29,40)^1$
			$(0,3,15,28,35,36)^2$
	4	87	$(0,1,27,30,61,73,81,83)^1$
			$(0,18,23,37,58,62,75,86)^2$
	5	131	$(0,1,6,25,32,72,100,108,120,130)^1$
			$(0,23,39,57,60,74,101,103,112,116)^2$
	6	196	$(0,17,46,50,52,66,88,125,150,165,168,195)^1$
			$(0,26,34,47,57,58,112,121,140,181,188,193)^2$
	7	289	$(0,2,7,42,45,117,163,185,195,216,229,246,255,279)^1$
			$(0,8,12,27,28,64,113,131,154,160,208,219,233,288)^2$

Table 11.1b. (3,2) codes.

n	t	N	Generator Sequences
4	1	4	$(0,1)^1$
			$(0,2)^2$
			$(0,3)^3$
	2	20	$(0,3,15,19)^1$
			$(0,8,17,18)^2$
			$(0,6,11,13)^3$
	3	68	$(0,5,15,34,35,42)^1$
	4	130	$(0,9,33,37,38,97,122,129)^1$
			$(0,11,13,23,62,76,79,123)^2$
			$(0,19,35,50,71,77,117,125)^3$
	5	203	$(0,7,27,76,113,137,155,156,170,202)^1$
			$(0,8,38,48,59,82,111,146,150,152)^2$
			$(0,12,25,26,76,81,98,107,143,197)^3$

Table 11.1c. (4,3) codes.

n	t	N	Generator Sequences
5	1	5	$(0,1)^1$
			$(0,2)^2$
			$(0,3)^3$
			$(0,4)^4$
	2	27	$(0,16,20,21)^1$
			$(0,2,10,25)^2$
			$(0,14,17,26)^3$
			$(0,11,18,24)^4$
	3	79	$(0,5,26,51,55,69)^1$
			$(0,6,7,41,60,72)^2$
			$(0,8,11,24,44,78)^3$
			$(0,10,32,47,49,77)^4$
	4	179	$(0,19,59,68,85,88,103,141)^1$
			$(0,39,87,117,138,148,154,162)^2$
			$(0,2,13,25,96,118,168,172)^3$
			$(0,7,65,70,97,98,144,178)^4$

Table 11.1d. (5,4) codes.

The second generator sequence $\mathbf{g}(2,1)$ is specified by the second set of integers $(0, 6, 11, 13)^2$ as follows:

Location Number	0	1	2	3	4	5	6	7	8	9	10	11	12	13
$\mathbf{g}(2,1)$ =	(1	0	0	0	0	0	1	0	0	0	0	1	0	1) .

The difference triangle associated with $\mathbf{g}(1,1)$ is

$$\Delta(1) = \{3, 4, 12, 1, 9, 8\} ,$$

and the difference triangle associated with $\mathbf{g}(2,1)$ is

$$\Delta(2) = \{2, 7, 13, 5, 11, 6\} .$$

It is clear that both $\Delta(1)$ and $\Delta(2)$ are full and disjoint. Therefore, this code is self-orthogonal. According to $\mathbf{g}(1,1)$, the syndrome bits which are orthogonal on $e_0(1)$ are $s_0(1)$, $s_8(1)$, $s_9(1)$, and $s_{12}(1)$. According to $\mathbf{g}(2,1)$, the syndrome bits which are orthogonal on $e_0(2)$ are $s_0(1)$, $s_6(1)$, $s_{11}(1)$, and $s_{13}(1)$. A majority-logic decoder for this code is shown in Fig. 11.4.

$(n,1)$ *Self-Orthogonal Codes*

An $(n,1)$ convolutional code has only one message digit per block and is specified by $(n-1)$ sub-generators

$$\mathbf{h}(1,i) = (h_0(1,i), h_1(1,i), \ldots, h_{N-1}(1,i))$$

for $i = 1, 2, \ldots, n-1$. A self-orthogonal $(n,1)$ code can be obtained from a self-orthogonal $(n, n-1)$ code. Consider a t-error-correcting self-orthogonal $(n, n-1)$ code which is specified by the following sub-generators:

$$\mathbf{g}(i,1) = (g_0(i,1), g_1(i,1), \ldots, g_{N-1}(i,1))$$

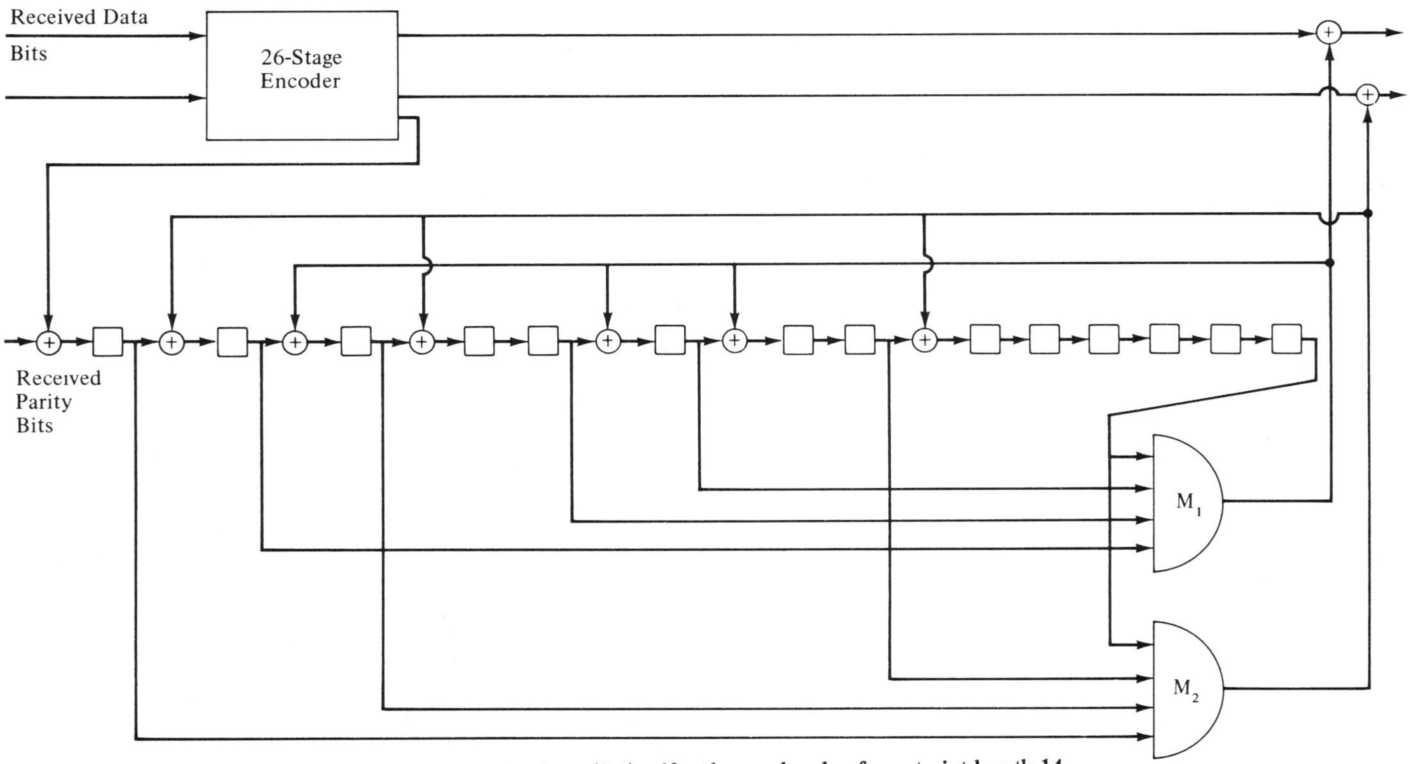

Fig. 11.4. Majority decoder for a (3,2) self-orthogonal code of constraint length 14.

for $i = 1, 2, \ldots, n-1$. A self-orthogonal $(n,1)$ code is obtained from this $(n,n-1)$ code by setting

$$\mathbf{h}(1,i) = \mathbf{g}(i,1)$$

for $i = 1, 2, \ldots, n-1$. This $(n,1)$ code is called the *dual* of the $(n,n-1)$ code or vice versa. It can be shown that no rectangle exists in $\mathbf{h}(1,1), \mathbf{h}(1,2), \ldots, \mathbf{h}(1,n-1)$. If J_i is the number of non-zero components in $\mathbf{g}(i,1)$, then there are $J^* = J_1 + J_2 + \ldots + J_{n-1}$ syndrome bits orthogonal on $e_0(1)$ for the $(n,1)$ code. Thus, the $(n,1)$ code is a $[J^*/2]$-error-correcting convolutional code.

Example 11.3: The dual of the (3,2) code considered in Example 11.2 has the following sub-generators:

$$\mathbf{h}(1,1) = (1\ 0\ 0\ 0\ 0\ 0\ 0\ 0\ 1\ 1\ 0\ 0\ 1\ 0)$$

$$\mathbf{h}(1,2) = (1\ 0\ 0\ 0\ 0\ 0\ 1\ 0\ 0\ 0\ 0\ 1\ 0\ 1)\ .$$

The syndrome bits which are orthogonal on $e_0(1)$ are $s_0(1)$, $s_0(2)$, $s_6(2)$, $s_8(1)$, $s_9(1)$, $s_{11}(2)$, $s_{12}(1)$, and $s_{13}(2)$. Thus, this code has error-correcting capability 4. A majority-logic decoder for this code is shown in Fig. 11.5.

It has been shown[10] that self-orthogonal codes have the automatic recovery property that allows the majority-logic decoder in feedback mode to recover from a decoding mistake in the absence of channel errors over a very short span of received digits. The length of this span is a few constraint lengths. It has also been shown[11] that self-orthogonal codes can be decoded by a majority-logic decoder in the definite decoding mode. If a self-orthogonal code is capable of correcting any error sequence with t or fewer errors in a span of nN consecutive positions by feedback decoding, then it is capable of correcting any error sequence with t or fewer errors in a span of $n(2N-1)$ consecutive positions by definite decoding. This indicates that the elimination of error propagation by using definite decoding can be purchased at the cost of a reduction in the error-correcting capability of the code. A definite

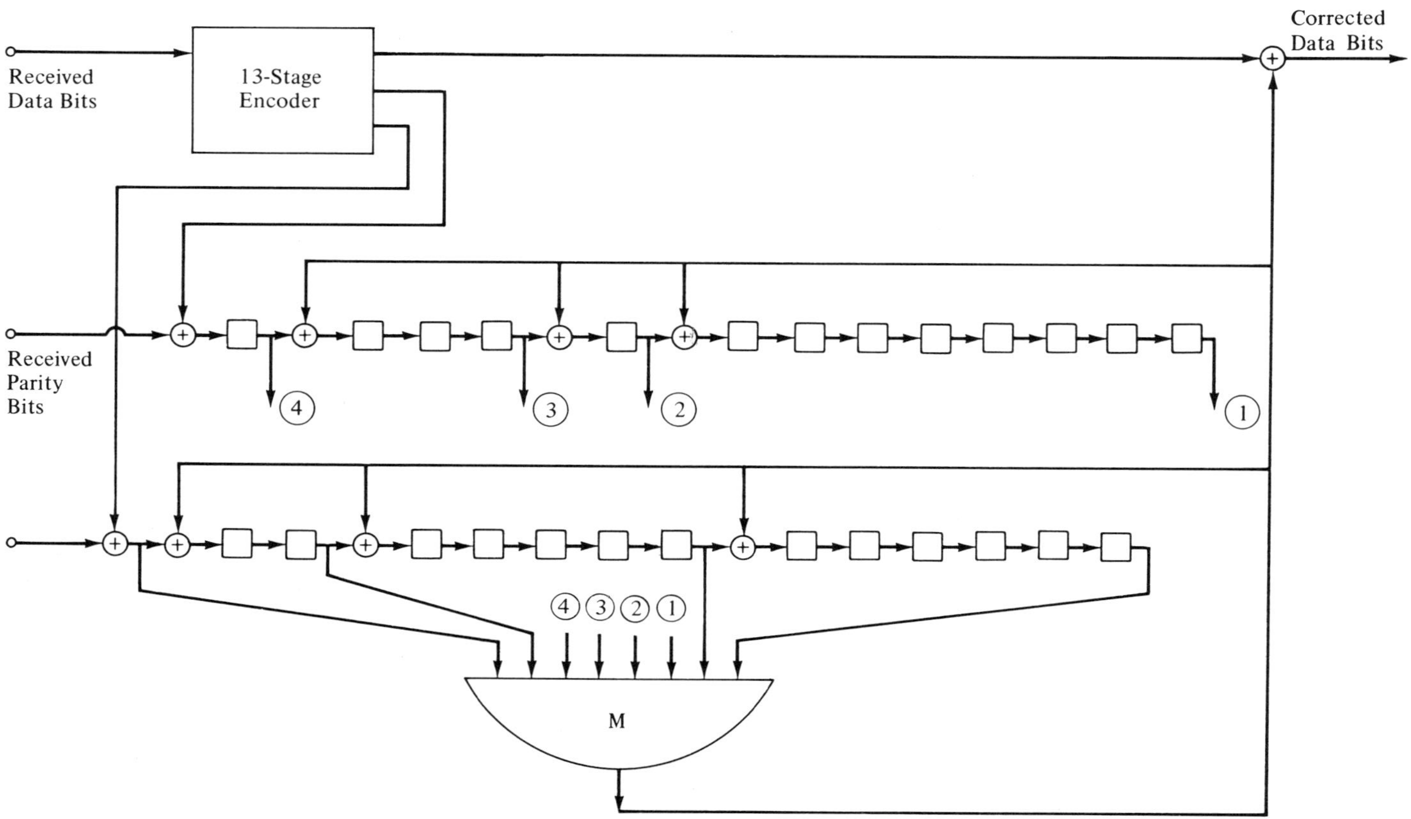

Fig. 11.5. Majority-logic decoder for a (3,1) self-orthogonal code of constraint length 14.

majority-logic decoder for a self-orthogonal code is obtained simply by disconnecting the feedback connections in a feedback majority-logic decoder.

11.4 ORTHOGONALIZABLE CONVOLUTIONAL CODES

Consider the (3,1) code of constraint length $N = 5$ which is specified by the following 2 sub-generators:

$$\mathbf{g}(1,1) = (1\ 1\ 0\ 0\ 0)$$

$$\mathbf{g}(1,2) = (1\ 0\ 1\ 1\ 1) \ .$$

To decode the 0th block of this code, we must examine the first 10 syndrome bits which are found as follows:

$$\begin{aligned}
s_0(1) &= e_0(1) + e_0(2) \\
s_0(2) &= e_0(1) + e_0(3) \\
s_1(1) &= e_0(1) + e_1(1) + e_1(2) \\
s_1(2) &= e_1(1) + e_1(3) \\
s_2(1) &= e_1(1) + e_2(1) + e_2(2) \\
s_2(2) &= e_0(1) + e_2(1) + e_2(3) \\
s_3(1) &= e_2(1) + e_3(1) + e_3(2) \\
s_3(2) &= e_0(1) + e_1(1) + e_3(1) + e_3(3) \\
s_4(1) &= e_3(1) + e_4(1) + e_4(2) \\
s_4(2) &= e_0(1) + e_1(1) + e_2(1) + e_4(1) + e_4(3) \ .
\end{aligned}$$

By taking linear sums of these syndrome bits, we obtain the following parity-check sums orthogonal on $e_0(1)$,

$$A_1 = s_0(1) = e_0(1) + e_0(2)$$

$$A_2 = s_0(2) = e_0(1) + e_0(3)$$

$$A_3 = s_1(1) = e_0(1) + e_1(1) + e_1(2)$$

$$A_4 = s_2(2) = e_0(1) + e_2(1) + e_2(3)$$

$$A_5 = s_1(2) + s_3(2) = e_0(1) + e_1(3) + e_3(1) + e_3(3)$$

$$A_6 = s_2(1) + s_4(2) = e_0(1) + e_2(2) + e_4(1) + e_4(3) \; .$$

Thus, $e_0(1)$ can be estimated from A_1, A_2, A_3, A_4, A_5, and A_6 by using majority vote. This error digit will be decoded correctly if three or fewer errors occur in the span of the first 15 received digits. Thus, this code is capable of correcting any error sequence with three or fewer errors in any span of 15 consecutive positions by the majority decoding algorithm. Based on this example, we can define a class of convolutional codes as follows.

> **Definition 13.2:** *An (n,k) convolutional code is said to be J-orthogonalizable if it is possible to form J or more parity-check sums orthogonal on $e_0(i)$ for $i = 1, 2, \ldots, k$ by taking proper linear modulo-2 sums of the first $N(n-k)$ syndrome bits. If d is the minimum distance of this code and $J = d - 1$, then this code is said to be completely orthogonalizable.*

Obviously, this code is capable of correcting any error sequence with $[J/2]$ or fewer errors in any span of nN consecutive positions by the feedback majority decoding algorithm. Orthogonalizable codes were first studied by Massey.[6]

No systematic procedure has been found for constructing orthogonalizable codes, except for some special subclasses. By the trial-and-error method, Massey[6] was able to construct a collection of orthogonalizable codes. A list of these codes is given in Table 11.2. For each code, the rules for forming the orthogonal check sums are given (Massey's notations are adopted). An example will serve to explain both the table and the method of forming orthogonal parity-check sums.

n	t	N	Generator Sequences	Rules for Forming Check Sums
2	1	2	(0,1)[1]	(0)(1)
	2	6	(0,3,4,5)[1]	(0)(3)(4)(1,5)
	3	12	(0,6,7,9,10,11)[1]	(0)(6)(7)(9)(1,3,10) (4,8,11)
	4	22	(0,11,13,16,17,19,20, 21)[1]	(0)(11)(13)(16)(17) (2,3,6,19)(4,14,20) (1,5,8,15,21)
	5	36	(0,18,19,27,28,29,30, 32,33,35)[1]	(0)(18)(19)(27)(1,9,28) (10,20,29)(11,30,31) (13,21,23,32)(14,33,34) (2,3,16,24,26,35)
	6	52	(0,26,27,39,40,41,42, 44,45,47,48,51)[1]	(0)(26)(27)(39) (1,13,40)(14,28,41) (15,42,43)(17,29,31,44) (18,45,46)(2,3,20,32,34,47) (21,35,48,49,50) (24,30,33,36,38,51)

Table 11.2a.* (2,1) codes.

* Table 11.2 is taken from J. L. Massey, *Threshold Decoding*, Table II, pp. 42-44, M.I.T. Press, 1963, by permission.

n	t	N	Generator Sequences	Rules for Forming Check Sums
3	2	3	$(0,1)^1$ $(0,2)^2$	$(0^1)\ (0^2)\ (1^1)\ (2^2)$
	3	5	$(0,1)^1$ $(0,2,3,4)^2$	$(0^1)\ (0^2)\ (1^1)\ (2^2)$ $(1^2\ 3^2)\ (2^1\ 4^2)$
	4	8	$(0,1,7)^1$ $(0,2,3,4,6)^2$	$(0^1)\ (0^2)\ (1^1)\ (2^2)$ $(1^2\ 3^2)\ (2^1\ 4^2)\ (7^1)$ $(3^1\ 5^1\ 6^1\ 6^2)$
	5	11	$(0,1,9)^1$ $(0,1,2,3,5,8,9)^2$	$(0^1)\ (0^2)\ (1^1)\ (2^1\ 2^2)$ $(9^1)\ (3^2\ 4^2)\ (3^1\ 5^1\ 5^2)$ $(1^2\ 4^1\ 6^1\ 6^2)\ (8^1\ 8^2)$ $(7^2\ 9^2\ 10^2)$
	6	18	$(0,4,5,6,7,9,12,13,$ $16)^1$ $(0,1,14,15,16)^2$	$(0^1)\ (0^2)\ (1^1\ 1^2)\ (4^1)\ (5^1)$ $(2^2\ 6^1)\ (14^2)\ (7^1\ 10^1\ 11^1\ 11^2)$ $(3^2\ 5^2\ 9^1)\ (6^2\ 8^2\ 12^1)$ $(3^2\ 16^2\ 17^2)\ (4^2\ 10^2\ 12^2\ 16^1)$
	7	23	$(0,4,5,6,7,9,12,13,$ $16,19,20,21)^1$ $(0,1,20,22)^2$	$(0^1)\ (0^2)\ (1^1\ 1^2)\ (4^1)$ $(5^1)\ (2^2\ 6^1)\ (7^1\ 10^1\ 11^1\ 11^2)$ $(3^2\ 5^2\ 9^1)\ (19^2\ 20^2)$ $(22^2)\ (6^2\ 8^2\ 12^1)$ $(4^2\ 10^2\ 12^2\ 16^1)$ $(3^1\ 7^2\ 13^2\ 15^2\ 19^1)$ $(9^2\ 13^1\ 14^2\ 18^1)\ (20^1\ 21^1\ 21^2)$
	8	36	$(0,4,5,6,7,9,12,16,$ $17,30,31)^1$ $(0,1,22,25,35)^2$	$(0^1)\ (0^2)\ (1^1\ 1^2)\ (4^1)$ $(5^1)\ (2^2\ 6^1)\ (22^2)$ $(7^1\ 10^1\ 11^1\ 11^2)\ (3^1\ 25^2)$ $(3^2\ 5^2\ 9^1)\ (6^2\ 8^2\ 12^1)$ $(7^2\ 14^1\ 17^1\ 18^1\ 18^2)$ $(9^2\ 16^1\ 19^1\ 20^1\ 20^2)$ $(14^2\ 15^2\ 35^2)$ $(12^2\ 21^2\ 28^1\ 31^1\ 32^1)$ $(10^2\ 13^2\ 19^2\ 26^2\ 29^2\ 30^1)$

Table 11.2b. (3,1) codes.

n	t	N	Generator Sequences	Rules for Forming Check Sums
5	3	2	$(0,1)^1$ $(0,1)^2\ (0)^3\ (0)^4$	$(0^1)\ (0^2)\ (0^3)\ (0^4)$ $(1^1\ 1^3)\ (1^2\ 1^4)$
	4	3	$(0,1,2)^1$ $(0,1)^2\ (0,2)^3\ (0)^4$	$(0^1)\ (0^2)\ (0^3)\ (0^4)$ $(1^1\ 1^3)\ (1^2\ 1^4)\ (2^1\ 2^2)$ $(2^3\ 2^4)$
	5	4	$(0,1,2,3)^1$ $(0,1)^2\ (0,2)^3$ $(0,3)^4$	$(0^1)\ (0^2)\ (0^3)\ (0^4)$ $(1^1\ 1^3)\ (1^2\ 1^4)\ (2^1\ 2^2)$ $(2^3\ 2^4)\ (3^4)\ (3^1\ 3^2)$
	6	6	$(0,1,2,3,4)^1\ (0,1)^2$ $(0,2,5)^3\ (0,3,5)^4$	$(0^1)\ (0^2)\ (0^3)\ (0^4)$ $(1^1\ 1^3)\ (1^2\ 1^4)\ (2^1\ 2^2)$ $(2^3\ 2^4)\ (3^4)\ (3^1\ 3^2)$ $(3^3\ 4^1\ 4^3)\ (5^4)\ (4^2\ 5^2\ 5^3)$
	7	7	$(0,1,2,3,4)^1\ (0,1)^2$ $(0,2,5,6)^3\ (0,3,5)^4$	$(0^1)\ (0^2)\ (0^3)\ (0^4)$ $(1^1\ 1^3)\ (1^2\ 1^4)\ (2^1\ 2^2)$ $(2^3\ 2^4)\ (3^4)\ (3^1\ 3^2)$ $(3^3\ 4^1\ 4^3)\ (5^4)\ (4^2\ 5^2\ 5^3)$ $(4^4\ 6^3)$
	8	9	$(0,1,2,3,4)^1$ $(0,1,8)^2$ $(0,2,5,6,7)^3$ $(0,3,5)^4$	$(0^1)\ (0^2)\ (0^3)\ (0^4)$ $(1^1\ 1^3)\ (1^2\ 1^4)\ (2^1\ 2^2)$ $(2^3\ 2^4)\ (3^4)\ (3^1\ 3^2)$ $(3^3\ 4^1\ 4^3)\ (5^4)\ (4^2\ 5^2\ 5^3)$ $(4^4\ 6^3)\ (8^2)\ (5^1\ 6^2\ 7^1\ 7^3)$
	9	11	$(0,1,2,3,5,6,8,10)^1$ $(0,3,5,6,8)^2\ (0,1)^3$ $(0,2,10)^4$	$(0^1)\ (0^2)\ (0^3)\ (0^4)\ (1^1)$ $(2^1\ 2^3)\ (3^2)\ (1^3\ 1^4)$ $(2^2\ 2^4)\ (3^1\ 4^1)\ (3^3\ 5^1\ 5^3)$ $(9^3\ 10^1\ 10^2)\ (5^2)\ (3^4\ 6^2)$ $(10^4)\ (1^2\ 4^3\ 6^1\ 6^3)$ $(7^1\ 7^3\ 8^1\ 9^1)$ $(4^2\ 5^4\ 7^2\ 8^2\ 8^3)$
	10	13	$(0,1,2,3,5,6,8,10)^1$ $(0,3,5,6,8)^2\ (0,1,10)^3$ $(0,2,10,12)^4$	Above rules plus $(6^4\ 9^4\ 12^2)$ $(10^3\ 11^4\ 12^3\ 12^4)$

Table 11.2c. (5,1) codes.

Example 11.4: Consider the triple-error-correcting (3,1) code of constraint length 5 given in Table 11.2b. The two sub-generators are specified by two sets of integers $(0, 1)^1$ and $(0, 2, 3, 4)^2$. The first set $(0, 1)^1$ gives the locations of the non-zero components of $\mathbf{g}(1,1)$ as follows:

$$g_0(1,1) = g_1(1,1) = 1 \quad .$$

The second set $(0, 2, 3, 4)^2$ gives the locations of the non-zero components of $\mathbf{g}(1,2)$ as follows:

$$g_0(1,2) = g_2(1,2) = g_3(1,2) = g_4(1,2) = 1 \quad .$$

Thus, the two sub-generators are

$$\begin{aligned} \mathbf{g}(1,1) &= (1\ 1\ 0\ 0\ 0) \\ \mathbf{g}(1,2) &= (1\ 0\ 1\ 1\ 1) \quad . \end{aligned}$$

The rule for forming $J = 6$ parity-check sums orthogonal on $e_0(1)$ is given by the set

$$\{0^1, 0^2, 1^1, 2^2, (1^2\ 3^2), (2^1\ 4^2)\} \quad ,$$

where the notation ℓ^i indicates that the syndrome bit $s_\ell(i)$ forms a parity-check sum orthogonal on $e_0(1)$ and the notation $(\ell^i\ m^j)$ indicates that the sum $s_\ell(i) + s_m(j)$ forms a parity-check sum orthogonal on $e_0(1)$. Thus, the 6 parity-check sums orthogonal on $e_0(1)$ are $s_0(1)$, $s_0(2)$, $s_1(1)$, $s_2(2)$, $s_1(2) + s_3(2)$, and $s_2(1) + s_4(2)$. This is the code considered at the beginning of this section. The feedback majority-logic decoder for this code is shown in Fig. 11.6.

For given n, k, and N, a trial-and-error orthogonalizable code has larger error-correcting capability than a self-orthogonal code. The major disadvantage of trial-and-error codes is that they do not have the automatic

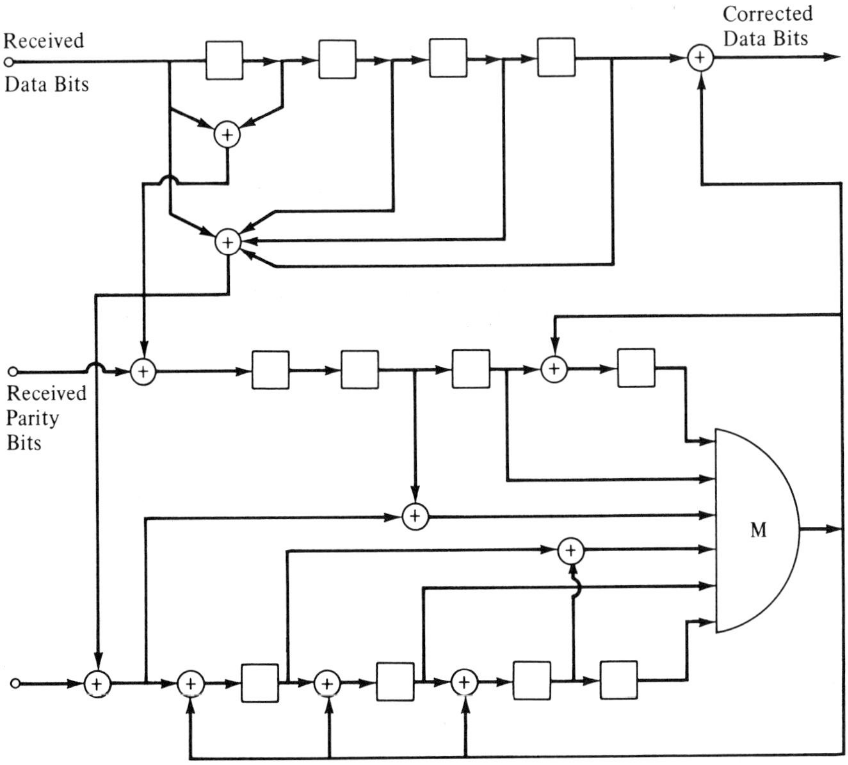

Fig. 11.6. Majority-logic decoder for a (3,1) orthogonalizable code with $N = 5$.

recovery property that limits error propagation. Definite majority decoding is not suitable for decoding because it will result in a large loss of error-correcting capability. The performance of trial-and-error orthogonalizable codes on the binary symmetric channel has been studied by Massey.[6] He has shown that there is little difference in performance between the short trial-and-error orthogonalizable codes and the corresponding *BCH* codes (or shortened *BCH* codes).

Besides the trial-and-error orthogonalizable codes, Massey[6] also constructed analytically two other classes of orthogonalizable convolutional codes, the *uniform codes* and the *Reed-Muller-like codes*. Both of these two classes of codes have very low rate $R = k/n$. In the following, a subclass of uniform codes (which is also a subclass of Reed-Muller-like codes) is considered. This subclass of uniform codes is related to the class of single-error-correcting Wyner-Ash codes.

For any positive integer m, there exists a $(2^m,1)$ uniform code of constraint length $N = m + 1$ which is specified by the following $2^m - 1$ sub-generators:

$$g(1,i) = (1, i_0, i_1, \ldots, i_{m-1}) \tag{11.5}$$

for $i = 1, 2, \ldots, 2^m - 1$, where $(i_0, i_1, \ldots, i_{m-1})$ is the binary representation of i. Comparing Eq. (11.5) with Eq. (11.1), we notice that a $(2^m,1)$ uniform code is the dual of a $(2^m, 2^m\text{-}1)$ Wyner-Ash single-error-correcting code. Massey has proved that a $(2^m,1)$ uniform code has minimum distance $d = (m+2)\,2^{m-1}$ and is completely orthogonalizable such that

$$J = (m+2)\,2^{m-1} - 1$$

parity-check sums orthogonal on $e_0(1)$ can be formed. Thus, this code is capable of correcting any error sequence with $(m+2)\,2^{m-2}\text{-}1$ or fewer errors in any span of $(m+1)\,2^m$ consecutive positions by feedback majority decoding. It has been shown[12] that error propagation is not a serious problem for uniform codes with feedback majority decoding. Uniform codes have been proven to be decodable by definite majority decoding with only a slight reduction in performance. When a uniform code is decoded by definite majority decoding, it is capable of correcting any error sequence with $(m+2)\,2^{m-2}\text{-}1$ or fewer errors in any span of $(m+2)\,2^m\text{-}1$ consecutive positions.

PROBLEMS

11.1. Find the sub-generators for the Wyner-Ash code with $m = 2$. Construct a decoder for this code.

11.2. Consider the triple-error-correcting self-orthogonal (2,1) code in Table 11.1a.

(a) Form the parity-check sums which are orthogonal on the error bit $e_0(1)$.

(b) Construct a majority-logic decoder for this code.

11.3. Consider the double-error-correcting orthogonalizable (2,1) code in Table 11.2a.

(a) Form the parity-check sums which are orthogonal on $e_0(1)$.

(b) Construct a majority-logic decoder for this code.

11.4. The (2,1) convolutional code which is generated by the following sub-generator.

$$g(1,1) = (1\ 1\ 0\ 1\ 0\ 1)$$

has minimum distance 5. Is this code self-orthogonal? If not, is this code completely orthogonalizable?

11.5. Construct a double-error-correcting self-orthogonal (2,1) code which is different from the double-error-correcting code in Table 11.1a.

11.6. Find the sub-generators for the $(2^m,1)$ uniform code with $m = 2$.

(a) Construct the code tree of 3 branches for this code. Show that this code has minimum distance 8.

(b) Form the parity-check sums orthogonal on $e_0(1)$. Show that this code is completely orthogonalizable.

(c) Construct a majority-logic decoder for this code.

REFERENCES

1. Freiman, C. V., and J. P. Robinson, "A Comparison of Block and Recurrent Codes for the Correction of Independent Errors," *IEEE Trans. on Information Theory*, **IT-11**, pp. 445-449, July, 1965.

2. Gallager, R. G., *Information Theory and Reliable Communication*, John Wiley, New York, 1968.

3. Hagelbarger, D. W., "Recurrent Codes for the Binary Symmetric Channel," lecture notes from the University of Michigan Summer Conference on Coding Theory, 1962.

4. Macy, J. R., "Theory of Serial Codes," Ph.D. Thesis, Stevens Institute of Technology, Hoboken, New Jersey, 1963.

5. Massey, J. L., "Threshold Decoding," Ph.D. Thesis, Massachusetts Institute of Technology, Cambridge, Massachusetts, 1962.

6. Massey, J. L., *Threshold Decoding*, The M.I.T. Press, Cambridge, Massachusetts, 1963.

7. Massey, J. L., "Uniform Codes," *IEEE Trans. on Information Theory*, **IT-12**, pp. 132-134, April, 1966.

8. Massey, J. L., *Advances in Threshold Decoding*, in "Advances in Communications Systems," 2, A. V. Balakrishnan, Ed., Academic Press, Inc., New York, 1968.

9. Peterson, W. W., and E. J. Weldon, Jr., *Error-Correcting Codes*, 2nd Edition, The M.I.T. Press, Cambridge, Massachusetts, 1970.

10. Robinson, J. P., and A. J. Bernsein, "A Class of Binary Recurrent Codes with Limited Error Propagation," *IEEE Trans. on Information Theory*, **IT-13**, pp. 106-113, January, 1967.

11. Robinson, J. P., "Error Propagation and Definite Decoding of Convolutional Codes," *IEEE Trans. on Information Theory*, **IT-14**, pp. 121-128, January, 1968.

12. Sullivan, D. D., "Error-Propagation Properties of Uniform Codes," *IEEE Trans. on Information Theory*, **IT-15**, pp. 152-161, January, 1969.

13. Wyner, A. D., and R. B. Ash, "Analysis of Recurrent Codes," *IEEE Trans. on Information Theory*, **IT-9**, pp. 143-156, July, 1963.

CHAPTER 12

BURST-ERROR-CORRECTING CONVOLUTIONAL CODES

12.1 INTRODUCTION

The study of convolutional codes for correcting burst errors falls into two categories, Type 1 burst-error-correcting codes (Type-B1 codes) and Type 2 burst-error-correcting codes (Type-B2 codes). The following definitions of these two types of codes are due to Wyner and Ash.[30]

Definition 12.1: *An (n,k) convolutional code of constraint length N is said to be a Type-B1 convolutional code with burst-error-correcting capability ℓ if, by some decoding algorithm, it is capable of correcting any error sequence* **e**, *provided that the non-zero digits of any nN consecutive digits of* **e** *are confined to a burst of ℓ consecutive digits.*

From the above definition, it is clear that any two successive bursts in **e** must be separated by an *error-free zone* of $nN-1$ digits. This error-free zone is called the *guard space* g of the code.

Definition 12.2: *An (n,k) convolutional code of constraint length N is said to be a Type-B2 code with phased-burst-error-correcting capability $\ell = \lambda n$ if, for some decoding algorithm, it is capable of correcting any error sequence* **e**, *provided that the non-zero digits of any nN consecutive digits of* **e** *are confined to λ consecutive blocks.*

It can be easily seen that the guard space of a Type-B2 code is $n(N-1)$. Since a burst of length $(\lambda-1)n+1$, no matter where it starts, can at most affect λ consecutive blocks, a Type-B2 code with phased-error-correcting capability $\ell = \lambda n$ can be used as a Type-B1 code to correct all burst errors of length $(\lambda-1)n+1$ or less.

On a channel where burst errors occur frequently, it is highly desirable to minimize the guard space of a code for a fixed burst-error-correcting capability ℓ. For fixed ℓ, minimizing the guard space of a code is equivalent to minimizing the constraint length of a code. A lower bound on the constraint length N of a Type-B2 (n,k) code with phased-error-correcting capability $\ell = \lambda n$ has been derived by Wyner and Ash.[30] This bound states that, for such a Type-B2 code, the constraint length N must satisfy the following inequality:

$$N \geqslant \left(\frac{n+k}{n-k}\right)\lambda + 1 \quad . \tag{12.1}$$

A Type-B2 code with constraint length equal to the Wyner-Ash bound is said to be *optimal*. Since a Type-B1 code with burst-error-correcting capability ℓ is also a Type-B2 code with phased-error-correcting capability $\ell' = \lambda n$ $(\lambda = [\ell/n])$, the above lower bound is applicable to Type-B1 codes.

The first class of Type-B1 codes was devised by Hagelbarger in 1959.[12] Hagelbarger's work was later refined by Peterson in 1961.[25] The disadvantage of Hagelbarger codes is the requirement of long guard space. Recently, Iwadare[15] discovered two classes of Type-B1 codes which require much shorter guard space than the corresponding Hagelbarger codes. Type-B2 codes were first studied by Wyner and Ash in 1963.[30] They also found optimal Type-B2 $(n,n\text{-}1)$ codes for $n = 2$, 3, and 4. Based on Wyner and Ash's work, Berlekamp[2] formulated a general procedure to construct optimal Type-B2 $(n, n-1)$ codes for any n. (Preparata[27] discovered the same class of codes independently at about the same time.) In 1965, Massey[23] devised a decoding procedure for the Berlekamp-Preparata codes. When the Berlekamp-Preparata codes are used for Type-B1 burst-error correction, they also require much shorter guard space than the corresponding Hagelbarger codes. Comparing the Iwadare codes to the Berlekamp-Preparata codes, the Iwadare codes, in general, require slightly longer guard space. However, the simple structures of the Iwadare codes result in much simpler decoding implementation. For this reason, the Iwadare Type-B1 codes are more useful in practical applications. In the following, we shall only present Iwadare codes. Other Type-B1 codes can be found in References 8, 14, 20, and 30. For details of Type-B2 codes, the reader is referred to References 2, 23, 27, and 30.

In the last section of this chapter, we shall discuss various techniques for correcting combinations of burst errors and random errors.

12.2 THE FIRST CLASS OF IWADARE CODES

For any n, there exists an $(n, n-1)$ burst-error-correcting convolutional code with the following parameters:

Constraint Length:	$N = (\lambda+1)(2n-1) - 1$
Burst-Correcting Capability:	$\ell = \lambda n$
Guard Space:	$g = nN - 1$

where λ is any positive integer. This code is generated by a set of $n-1$ subgenerators of the following form:

$$\mathbf{g}(i,1) = (0\,0 \ldots 0\,\underset{\substack{\uparrow \\ g_a(i,1)}}{1}\,0\,0 \ldots 0\,\underset{\substack{\uparrow \\ g_b(i,1)}}{1}\,0\,0 \ldots 0) \tag{12.2}$$

for $i = 1, 2, \ldots, n-1$ where $a = [(\lambda+1)(n-i)-1]$ and $b = [(\lambda+1)(2n-i)+i-3]$. For economic reasons, the circuit of Fig. 10.2 should be used for encoding. Since $k = n-1$, there is only one shift-register chain of $N-1$ stages.

The codes defined above are simple in structure and can be decoded in a simple way. The decoding of this class of codes can be best explained by an example. Consider the (3,2) code with $\lambda = 3$, which is capable of correcting any error-burst of length 9 or less. According to Eq. (12.2), the two subgenerators of this code are

$$\mathbf{g}(1,1) = (0\,0\,0\,0\,0\,0\,0\,1\,0\,0\,0\,0\,0\,0\,0\,0\,0\,0\,1)$$

$$\mathbf{g}(2,1) = (0\,0\,0\,1\,0\,0\,0\,0\,0\,0\,0\,0\,0\,0\,0\,1\,0\,0\,0) \;.$$

First we assume that an error-burst of length 9 starts at the first digit of the 0th block. This error-burst is of the following form:

$$\mathbf{e} = (e_0(1)\,e_0(2)\,e_0(3)\,e_1(1)\,e_1(2)\,e_1(3)\,e_2(1)\,e_2(2)\,e_2(3)\;0\,0\,0 \ldots) \;.$$

It follows from Eq. (10.18) that the syndrome sequence of $\mathbf{e}$ is

$$\begin{aligned}\mathbf{s} &= (s_0\ s_1\ s_2\ \ldots\ s_{20}\ \ldots) \\ &= (e_0(3)\ e_1(3)\ e_2(3)\ e_0(2)\ e_1(2)\ e_2(2)\ 0\ e_0(1)\ e_1(1)\ e_2(1) \\ &\qquad 0\ 0\ 0\ 0\ 0\ e_0(2)\ e_1(2)\ e_2(2)\ e_0(1)\ e_1(1)\ e_2(1)\ 0\ 0\ 0\ \ldots)\ .\end{aligned}$$

We notice that each message error bit $e_\ell(i)$ for $i = 1, 2$ and $\ell = 0, 1, 2$ appears twice in the syndrome sequence $\mathbf{s}$, and error bits in each block appear in a reverse order (that is, $e_\ell(2)$ appears in $\mathbf{s}$ before $e_\ell(1)$). The number of digits between the two occurrences of $e_\ell(i)$ is $9+i$, which will be called the *recurrence distance* of $e_\ell(i)$. The recurrence distance of $e_\ell(1)$ is 10, and the recurrence distance of $e_\ell(2)$ is 11. Therefore, the two message error bits of each block have distinct recurrence distances. The above facts will be utilized for detecting errors in each block.

The results are essentially the same if the burst starts at the second or third digit of the 0th block. If the burst starts at the second digit of the 0th block, then the error sequence is

$$\mathbf{e}' = (0\ e_0(2)\ e_0(3)\ e_1(1)\ e_1(2)\ e_1(3)\ e_2(1)\ e_2(2)\ e_2(3)\ e_3(1)\ 0\ 0\ 0\ \ldots)$$

whose syndrome sequence is

$$\begin{aligned}\mathbf{s}' &= (s_0\ s_1\ s_2\ \ldots\ s_{20}\ s_{21}\ \ldots) \\ &= (e_0(3)\ e_1(3)\ e_2(3)\ e_0(2)\ e_1(2)\ e_2(2)\ 0\ 0\ e_1(1)\ e_2(1)\ e_3(1) \\ &\qquad 0\ 0\ 0\ 0\ e_0(2)\ e_1(2)\ e_2(2)\ 0\ e_1(1)\ e_2(1)\ e_3(1)\ 0\ 0\ 0\ \ldots)\ .\end{aligned}$$

If the burst starts at the third digit of the 0th block, then the error sequence is

$$\mathbf{e}'' = (0\ 0\ e_0(3)\ e_1(1)\ e_1(2)\ e_1(3)\ e_2(1)\ e_2(2)\ e_2(3)\ e_3(1)\ e_3(2)\ 0\ 0\ 0\ 0\ldots)$$

whose syndrome sequence is

$$\begin{aligned} \mathbf{s}'' &= (s_0\ s_1\ s_2\ \ldots\ s_{20}\ s_{21}\ \ldots) \\ &= (e_0(3)\ e_1(3)\ e_2(3)\ 0\ e_1(2)\ e_2(2)\ e_3(2)\ 0\ e_1(1)\ e_2(1)\ e_3(1) \\ &\quad\ 0\ 0\ 0\ 0\ 0\ e_1(2)\ e_2(2)\ e_3(2)\ e_1(1)\ e_2(1)\ e_3(1)\ 0\ 0\ 0\ \ldots) \ . \end{aligned}$$

By examining $\mathbf{s}'$ and $\mathbf{s}''$, we can see that each message error bit still appears twice, and the recurrence distance of $e_\ell(i)$ is still $9+i$.

A decoder for the above code is shown in Fig. 12.1. It consists of a re-encoder for syndrome calculation and a decoding algorithm circuit. The circuit of Fig. 10.3 is used for syndrome calculation. There are 2 shift-register chains. Each register chain of the re-encoder consists of N-1 = 18 stages. The correction procedure of this decoder is described as follows. The syndrome bits are formed and shifted into the syndrome register one at a time. The two inputs of AND gate $\mathbf{A}_2$ are spaced 11 bits (the recurrence distance of $e_\ell(2)$) apart. Two of the inputs of AND gate $\mathbf{A}_1$ are spaced 10 bits (the recurrence distance of $e_\ell(1)$) apart. At each time unit, at most one of the two AND gates is activated. $\mathbf{A}_2$ is not activated until the error bit $e_0(2)$ appears at both inputs of $\mathbf{A}_2$. Then the output of $\mathbf{A}_2$ is the correct value of $e_0(2)$. At this moment, the received message digit $r_0(2)$ which is to be corrected is about to come out of the 15th stage of the second shift register chain of the re-encoder. The output of $\mathbf{A}_2$ is added to $r_0(2)$ for correction by a modulo-2 adder. The output of $\mathbf{A}_2$ is also fed back to the syndrome register for syndrome resetting. Having decoded $e_0(2)$, the syndrome register is shifted once to the right. Now $e_1(2)$ appears at two inputs of $\mathbf{A}_2$. Therefore, the output of $\mathbf{A}_2$ is the correct value of $e_1(2)$ which is then used to correct the received message digit $r_1(2)$ about to come out of the 15th stage of the second register chain of the re-encoder. The syndrome is reset again. In exactly the same manner, the decoder decodes $e_2(2)$. During the corrections of $e_0(2)$, $e_1(2)$, and $e_2(2)$, the output of $\mathbf{A}_1$ is inhibited by the output of the rightmost stage of the syndrome register in order to prevent $\mathbf{A}_1$ from making any erroneous corrections. For example, when $e_0(2)$ appears at the two inputs of $\mathbf{A}_2$, the first $e_1(2)$ in $\mathbf{s}$ and the second $e_0(2)$ in $\mathbf{s}$ appear at the two of the inputs of $\mathbf{A}_1$. If the inhibited input $\mathbf{I}$ is not provided and if

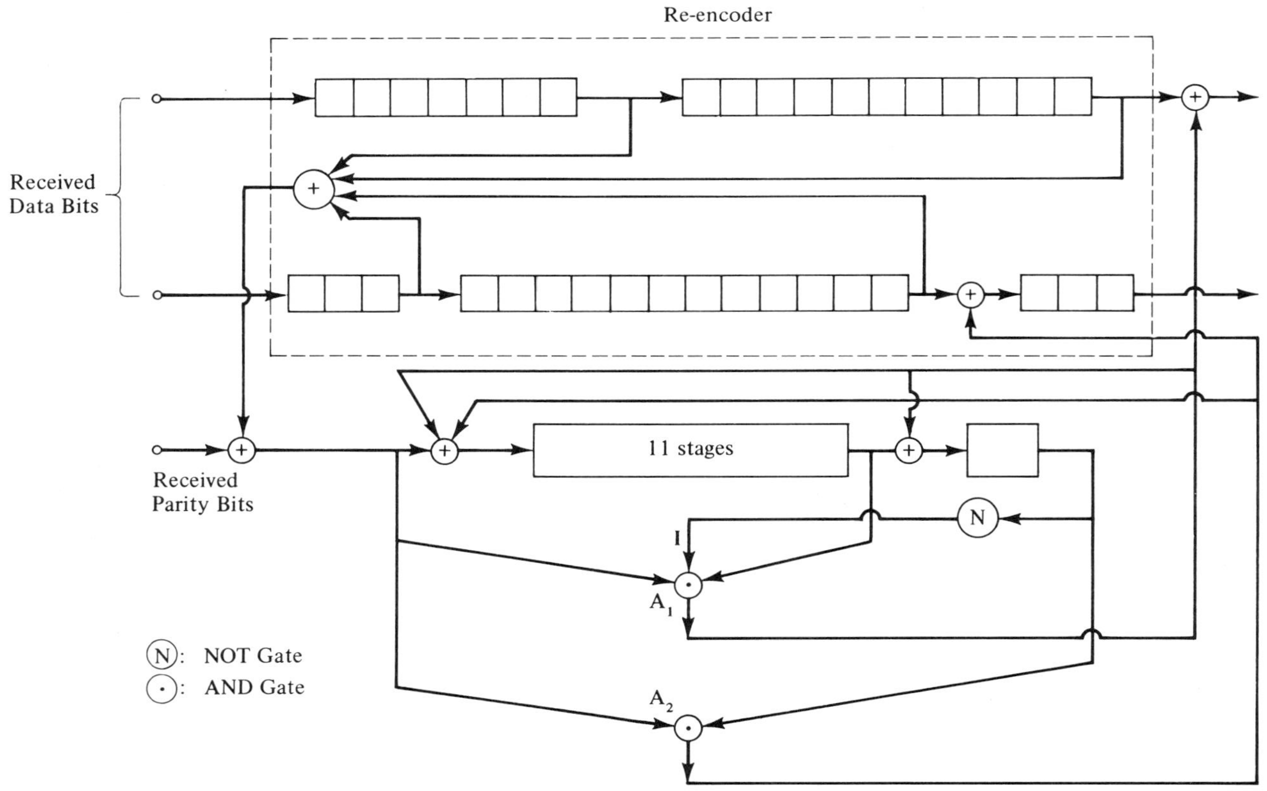

Fig. 12.1. A decoder for the 9-burst-error-correcting (3,2) Iwadare code.

$e_0(2) = e_1(2) = 1$, then the output of $\mathbf{A}_1$ will be "1," which would cause an erroneous correction at the output of the first register chain of the re-encoder.

Having decoded $e_2(2)$, the syndrome register is shifted once. Now $e_0(1)$ appears at two inputs of $\mathbf{A}_1$. Since the rightmost stage of the syndrome register contains "0," the inhibited input $\mathbf{I}$ of $\mathbf{A}_1$ is "1." Therefore, the output of $\mathbf{A}_1$ gives the correct value of $e_0(1)$. At this time, the received message digit $r_0(1)$ is about to come out of the rightmost stage of the first register chain of the re-encoder, and it will be corrected by $e_0(1)$. The error bit $e_0(1)$ is fed back to the syndrome register for syndrome resetting. After the decoding of $e_0(1)$, the syndrome register is shifted to the right once. Since $e_0(1)$ has been fed back for resetting the syndrome, the rightmost stage of the syndrome register contains "0" again. Now the inputs of $\mathbf{A}_1$ are 1, $e_1(1)$, and $e_1(1)$. Thus, the output of $\mathbf{A}_1$ is the correct value of $e_1(1)$. The decoder then proceeds to decode $e_2(1)$ in exactly the same manner as it decoded $e_1(1)$. After the decoding of $e_2(1)$, the syndrome register contains all zeros, and the decoder is ready to decode the next incoming burst.

The ideas of decoding illustrated in the above example can be easily extended to any code defined by Eq. (12.2). Consider the $(n, n\text{-}1)$ code which corrects any error-burst of length λn or less. Assume that a burst of length λn starts at the first digit of the 0th block. The error sequence is of the form

$$\begin{aligned}\mathbf{e} \;=\; &(e_0(1)\, e_0(2) \ldots e_0(n)\; e_1(1)\, e_1(2) \ldots e_1(n) \ldots \\ &e_{\lambda\text{-}1}(1)\, e_{\lambda\text{-}1}(2) \ldots e_{\lambda\text{-}1}(n)\; 0\,0\,0 \ldots) \;.\end{aligned}$$

The syndrome sequence corresponding to $\mathbf{e}$ is found to be

$$\begin{aligned}\mathbf{s} &= (s_0\; s_1\; s_2 \ldots s_{N+\lambda\text{-}2} \ldots) \\ &= (e_0(n)\, e_1(n) \ldots e_{\lambda\text{-}1}(n) \mid e_0(n\text{-}1)\, e_1(n\text{-}1) \ldots e_{\lambda\text{-}1}(n\text{-}1) \mid 0 \mid \\ &\quad e_0(n\text{-}2)\, e_1(n\text{-}2) \ldots e_{\lambda\text{-}1}(n\text{-}2) \mid 0 \mid \ldots \mid 0 \mid e_0(1)\, e_1(1) \ldots e_{\lambda\text{-}1}(1) \\ &\quad \mid \underbrace{0\,0 \ldots 0}_{n+\lambda\text{-}1} \mid e_0(n\text{-}1)\, e_1(n\text{-}1) \ldots e_{\lambda\text{-}1}(n\text{-}1) \mid e_0(n\text{-}2)\, e_1(n\text{-}2) \ldots \\ &\quad e_{\lambda\text{-}1}(n\text{-}2) \mid \ldots \mid e_0(1)\, e_1(1) \ldots e_{\lambda\text{-}1}(1) \mid 0\,0\,0 \ldots) \;.\end{aligned}$$

Each error $e_\ell(i)$, for $i = 1, 2, \ldots, n-1$ and $\ell = 0, 1, 2, \ldots, \lambda-1$, appears twice in the syndrome at the $[(\lambda+1)(n-i)+\ell-1]^{\text{th}}$ bit position and the $[(\lambda+1)(2n-i)+\ell+i-3]^{\text{th}}$ bit position. The recurrence distance of $e_\ell(i)$ is $(\lambda+1)n+i-3$. Therefore, no two errors in the same block have the same recurrence distance. This fact is the basis for error detecting. If the distance between two non-zero syndrome bits which do not correspond to the same error digit is equal to the recurrence distance of a certain error digit, erroneous decoding operations may occur. In order to prevent erroneous operations, inhibiting rules must be provided.

If the burst starts at the jth digit of the 0th block, then the syndrome sequence is

$$\begin{aligned}
\mathbf{s}' &= (s_0\ s_1\ s_2 \ldots s_{N+\lambda-2}\ s_{N+\lambda-1} \ldots) \\
&= (e_0(n)\, e_1(n) \ldots e_{\lambda-1}(n) \mid e_0(n-1)\ e_1(n-1) \ldots e_{\lambda-1}(n-1) \mid 0 \mid e_0(n-2)\ e_1(n-2) \\
&\quad \ldots e_{\lambda-1}(n-2) \mid 0 \mid \ldots \mid 0 \mid e_0(j)\ e_1(j) \ldots e_{\lambda-1}(j) \mid 0\ 0 \mid e_1(j-1) \\
&\quad e_2(j-1) \ldots e_\lambda(j-1) \mid 0 \mid \ldots \mid 0 \mid e_1(1)\ e_2(1) \ldots e_\lambda(1) \mid \underbrace{0\ 0 \ldots 0}_{n+\lambda-2} \mid \\
&\quad e_0(n-1)\ e_1(n-1) \ldots e_{\lambda-1}(n-1) \mid e_0(n-2)\ e_1(n-2) \ldots e_{\lambda-1}(n-2) \mid \ldots \\
&\quad \mid e_0(j)\ e_1(j) \ldots e_{\lambda-1}(j) \mid 0 \mid e_1(j-1)\ e_2(j-1) \ldots e_\lambda(j-1) \mid e_1(j-2) \\
&\quad e_2(j-2) \ldots e_\lambda(j-2) \mid \ldots \mid e_1(1)\, e_2(1) \ldots e_{\lambda-1}(1)\, e_\lambda(1) \mid 0\ 0 \ldots)
\end{aligned}$$

where the $(N+\lambda-1)^{\text{th}}$ syndrome bit $s_{N+\lambda-1}$ is equal to the second $e_\lambda(1)$. By examining $\mathbf{s}'$, we find that each message error digit still appears twice, and the recurrence distance of $e_\ell(i)$ is still equal to $(\lambda+1)n+i-3$. A decoder for this code is shown in Fig. 12.2. The AND gates $\mathbf{A}_{n-2}, \mathbf{A}_{n-3}, \ldots, \mathbf{A}_1$ are inhibited in order to prevent any erroneous decoding operation. This decoder is called the *forward acting decoder.*[15]

An alternative decoder for the λn-burst-error-correcting code is shown in Fig. 12.3. This decoder is called the *backward acting decoder* [15] and is slightly different from the forward acting decoder. Error propagation is not a serious problem with the first class of Iwadare codes. If a decoding error is followed by an error-free zone of $n[N+(\lambda+2)n-2]-1$ digits, the syndrome

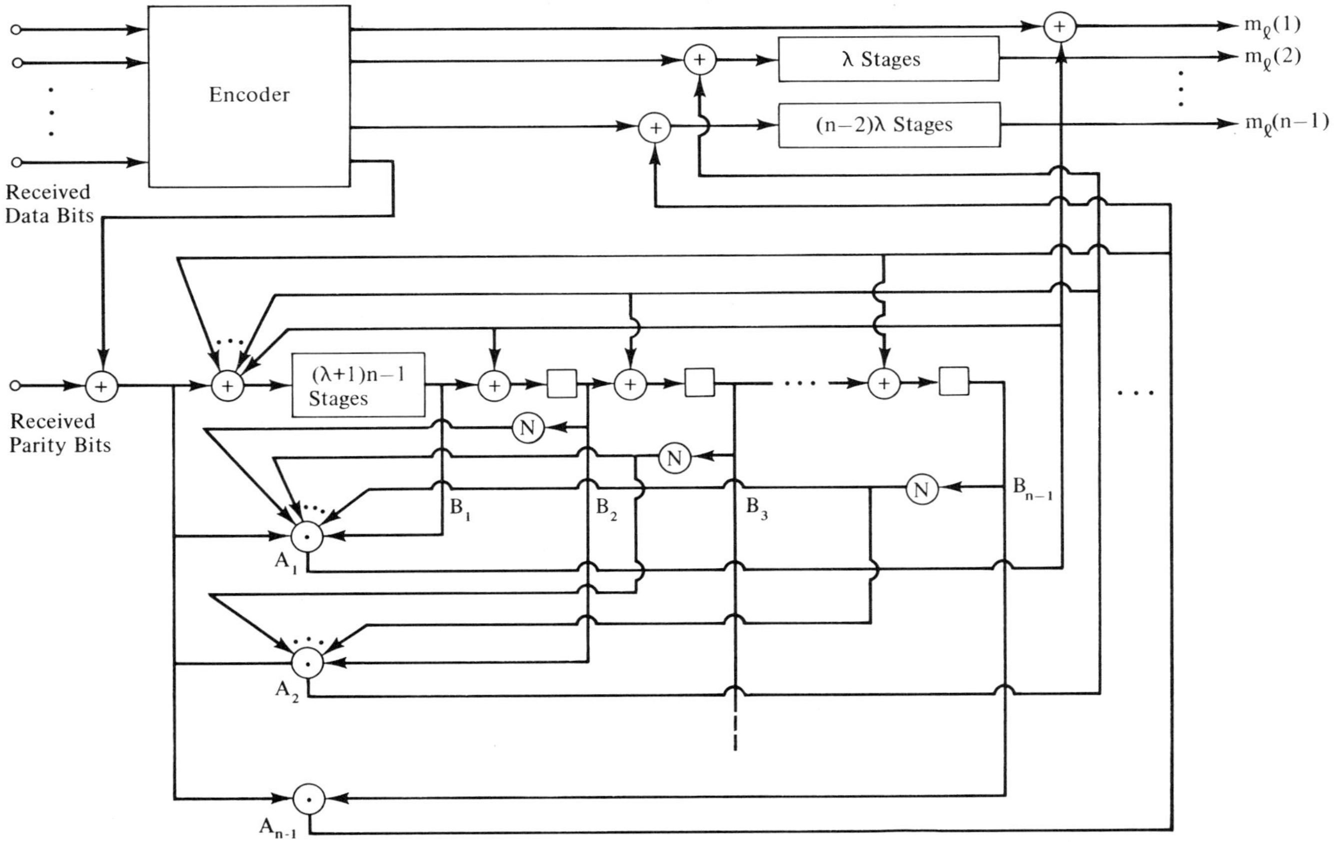

Fig. 12.2. A general forward acting decoder for the first class of Iwadare codes. (From Y. Iwadare, "On Type B1 Burst-Error-Correcting Convolutional Codes," *IEEE Trans. on Information Theory*, **IT-14**, Fig. 5, p. 580, July, 1968. Redrawn by permission.)

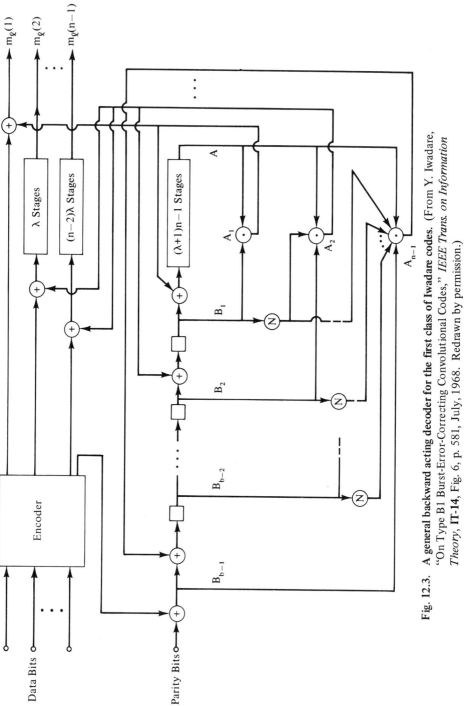

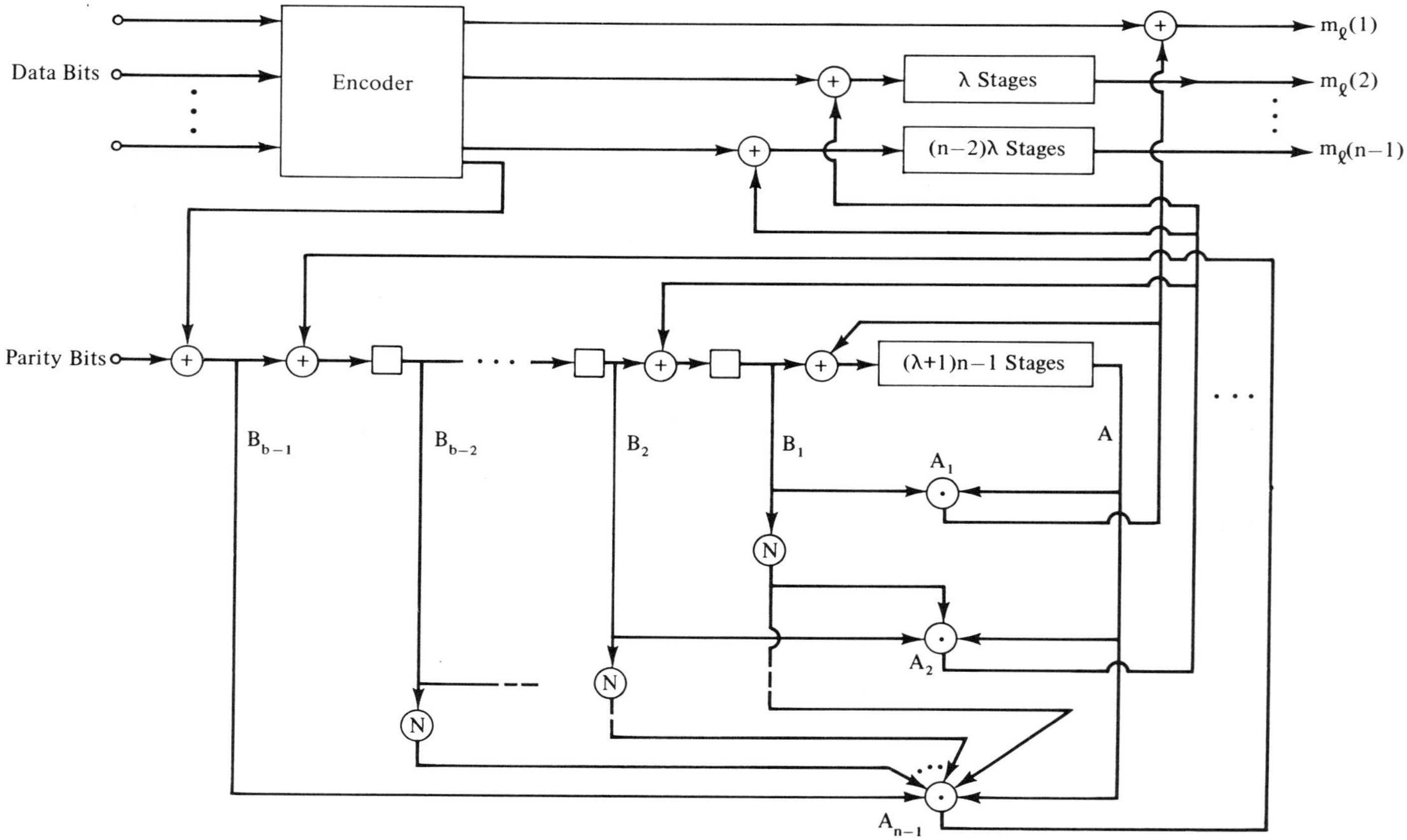

Fig. 12.3. A general backward acting decoder for the first class of Iwadare codes. (From Y. Iwadare, "On Type B1 Burst-Error-Correcting Convolutional Codes," *IEEE Trans. on Information Theory*, **IT-14**, Fig. 6, p. 581, July, 1968. Redrawn by permission.)

register will be cleared and error propagation will be terminated.

For $k = n - 1$, the Wyner-Ash bound on N given by Eq. (12.1) is reduced to

$$N \geqslant (2n - 1)\lambda + 1 \quad . \tag{12.3}$$

The difference between the constraint length N of an Iwadare code with burst-error-correcting capability $\ell = \lambda n$ and the lower bound given by Eq. (12.3) is $2n - 3$. Therefore, for small n, Iwadare codes are very efficient.

12.3 THE SECOND CLASS OF IWADARE CODES

This is another class of $(n, n-1)$ codes designed for burst-error correction. For any positive integer λ, a code in this class is specified by the following $(n-1)$ sub-generators:

$$\mathrm{g}(i,1) \;=\; (0\,0\,\ldots\,0\,\underset{\substack{\uparrow \\ g_a(i,1)}}{1}\,0\,0\,\ldots\,0\,\underset{\substack{\uparrow \\ g_b(i,1)}}{1}\,0\,0\,\ldots\,0) \tag{12.4}$$

for $i = 1, 2, \ldots, n-1$, where $a = \tfrac{1}{2}(n-i)(4\lambda+n-i-3)+n-1$ and $b = \tfrac{1}{2}(n-i)(4\lambda+n-i-1)+n+\lambda-2$. This code has the following parameters:

$$N = \lambda(2n-1) + \tfrac{1}{2}n(n-1)$$

$$\ell = \lambda n$$

$$g = nN - 1 \quad .$$

Example 12.1: For $n = 3$ and $\lambda = 3$, the (3,2) code which corrects bursts of length 9 or less is specified by

$$\mathrm{g}(1,1) = (0\,0\,0\,0\,0\,0\,0\,0\,0\,0\,0\,0\,0\,0\,0\,1\,0\,0\,0\,1)$$

$$\mathrm{g}(2,1) = (0\,0\,0\,0\,0\,0\,0\,1\,0\,0\,1\,0\,0\,0\,0\,0\,0\,0) \quad .$$

Consider the syndrome sequence which corresponds to an error sequence **e** with a burst of length λn starting at the first digit of the 0th block,

$$\mathbf{s} = (e_0(n)\, e_1(n) \ldots e_{\lambda-1}(n) \mid \underbrace{0\, 0 \ldots 0}_{n+\lambda-2} \mid$$

$$\mid e_0(n-1)\, e_1(n-1) \ldots e_{\lambda-1}(n-1)\; e_0(n-1)\, e_1(n-1) \ldots e_{\lambda-1}(n-1) \mid$$

$$\mid e_0(n-2)\, e_1(n-2) \ldots e_{\lambda-1}(n-1)\; 0\; e_0(n-1)\, e_1(n-1) \ldots e_{\lambda-1}(n-2) \mid$$

$$\vdots$$

$$\mid e_0(1)\, e_1(1) \ldots e_{\lambda-1}(1)\; \underbrace{0\, 0\, 0 \ldots 0}_{n-2}\; e_0(1)\, e_1(1) \ldots e_{\lambda-1}(1) \mid$$

$$0\, 0\, 0 \ldots) \; . \tag{12.5}$$

Each error $e_\ell(i)$ for $i = 1, 2, \ldots, n-1$, and $\ell = 0, 1, 2, \ldots, \lambda-1$, appears twice in the syndrome sequence. The recurrence distance of $e_\ell(i)$ is $\lambda+n-i-2$. No two error digits in the same block have the same recurrence distance. The results are the same for the burst starting at any digit of the 0th block other than the first digit. The decoding of this class of codes is similar to the decoding of the first class of codes. Inhibiting rules must be provided in the decoder to prevent erroneous decoding operations. A general forward-acting decoder for the second class of Iwadare codes is given in Fig. 12.4, where $\ell_{n-i} = (n-i-1)(4\lambda+n+i-2)/2$ for $i = 1, 2, \ldots, n-1$. A decoder for the 9-burst-error-correcting (3,2) code of Example 12.1 is shown in Fig. 12.5. Again, error propagation is not a serious problem. It can be shown that an error-free zone of $n[N+\lambda+n-1]-1$ digits is sufficient for terminating any error propagation after a decoding failure.

Except for $n = 2$ and 3, a code in the first class requires a shorter guard space than the corresponding code in the second class. For large n $(n \geqslant 4)$ and small λ, the number of register stages required for implementing a code in the first class is smaller than the number required for implementing the corresponding code in the second class. But, for large λ $(\lambda \geqslant n)$, the second class of codes results in more economical encoding and decoding

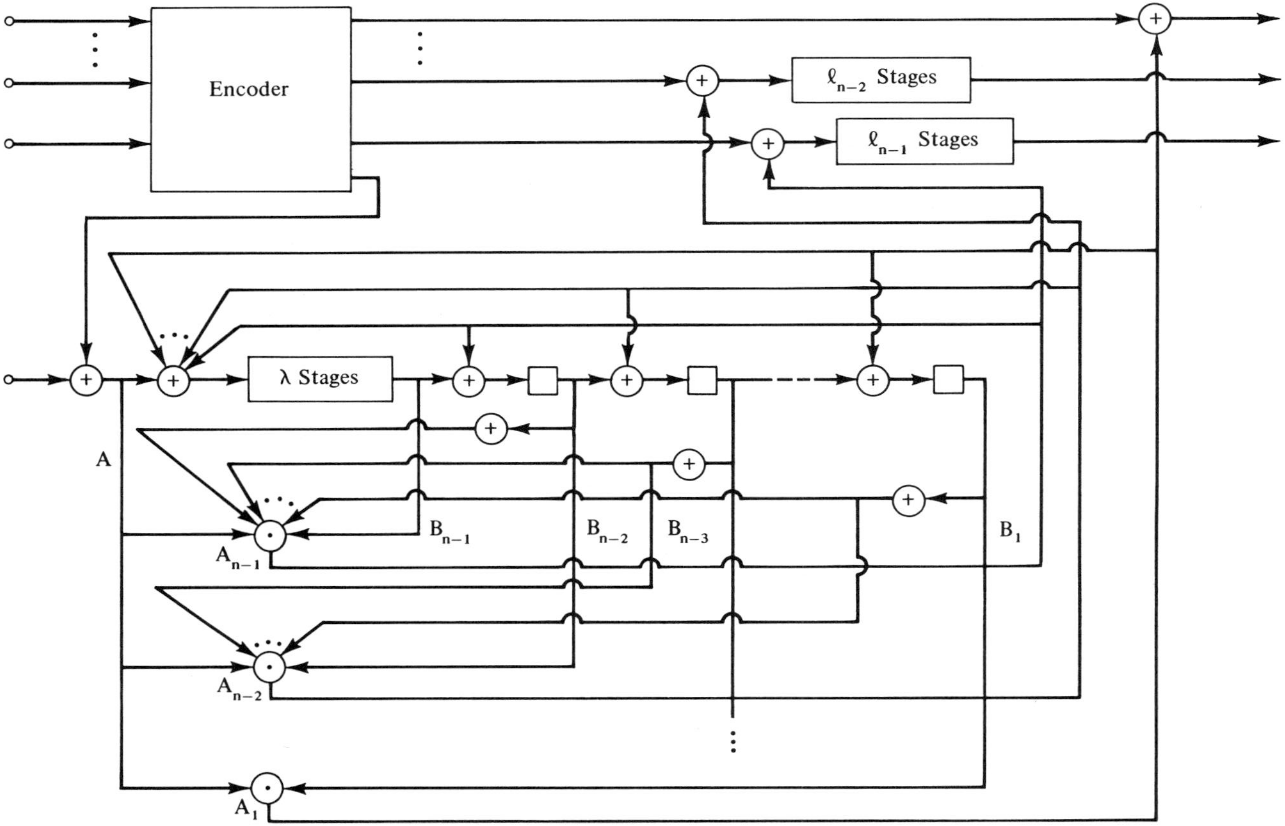

Fig. 12.4. A general forward acting decoder for the second class of Iwadare codes. (From Y. Iwadare, "On Type B1 Burst-Error-Correcting Convolutional Codes," *IEEE Trans. on Information Theory*, **IT-14**, Fig. 9, p. 582, July, 1968. Redrawn by permission.)

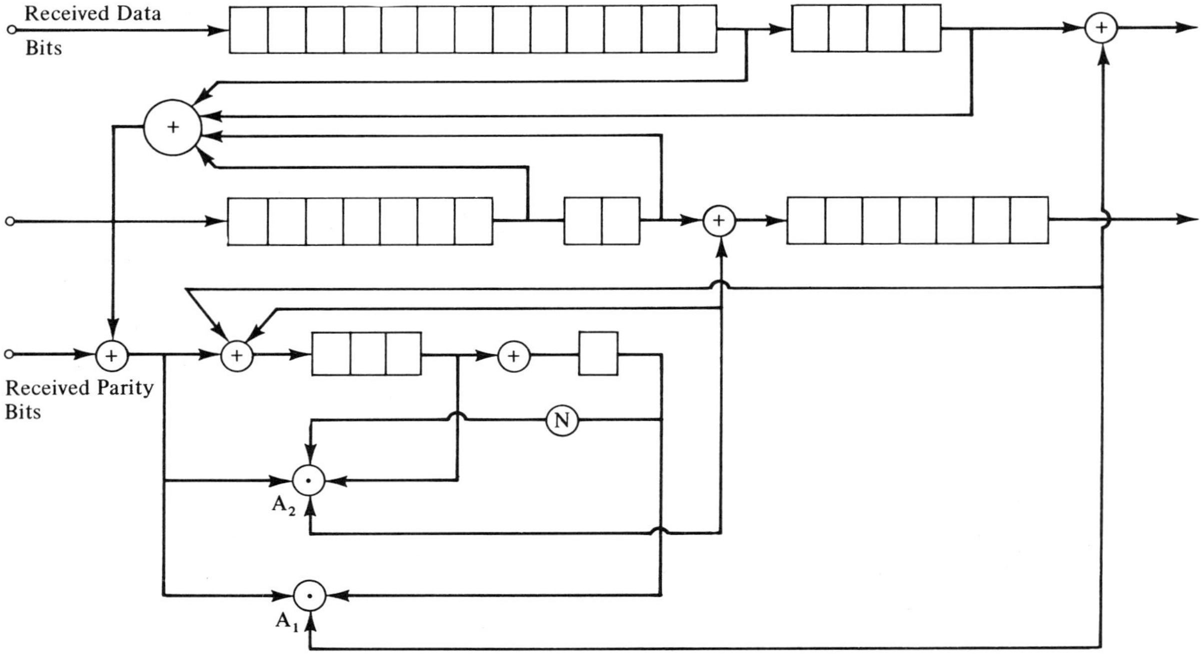

Fig. 12.5. The forward acting decoder for the 9-burst-error-correcting (3,2) code of Example 12.1.

circuits than the first class of codes.

12.4 CONVOLUTIONAL CODES FOR CORRECTING BURST ERRORS AND RANDOM ERRORS

In this section, we shall consider various techniques for correcting combinations of burst errors and random errors with convolutional codes.

Block Interlacing[12]

Consider an (n,k) convolutional code $\mathbf{C}$ with constraint length N which is specified by the following $k(n-k)$ sub-generators:

$$\mathbf{g}(i,j) = (g_0(i,j)\ g_1(i,j)\ g_2(i,j) \ldots g_{N-1}(i,j)) \tag{12.6}$$

for $i = 1, 2, \ldots, k$ and $j = 1, 2, \ldots, n-k$. Now we construct a new (n,k) code $\mathbf{C}_I$ with sub-generators

$$\mathbf{g}'(i,j)$$

for $i = 1, 2, \ldots, k$ and $j = 1, 2, \ldots, n-k$, where $\mathbf{g}'(i,j)$ is obtained from $\mathbf{g}(i,j)$ by inserting $\lambda-1$ zeros (λ is any positive integer) between every two consecutive components, i.e.,

$$\begin{aligned}\mathbf{g}'(i,j) = (g_0(i,j)\ \overbrace{0\,0 \ldots 0}^{\lambda-1}\ g_1(i,j)\ 0\,0 \ldots 0\ g_2(i,j)\ 0\,0 \ldots 0 \\ \ldots g_{N-2}(i,j)\ 0\,0 \ldots 0\ g_{N-1}(i,j))\ .\end{aligned} \tag{12.7}$$

It is clear that the constraint length of $\mathbf{C}_I$ is

$$N' = (N-1)\lambda + 1\ .$$

The k generator sequences of $\mathbf{C}_I$ are of the following form:

$$\begin{bmatrix} \mathbf{g}'(1) \\ \mathbf{g}'(2) \\ \vdots \\ \mathbf{g}'(k) \end{bmatrix} = [\,\mathbf{I}_k\mathbf{P}_0 \;\; \mathbf{Z}\;\mathbf{Z}\,\ldots\,\mathbf{Z}\;\;\mathbf{O}\mathbf{P}_1\;\;\mathbf{Z}\;\mathbf{Z}\,\ldots\,\mathbf{Z}\;\;\mathbf{O}\mathbf{P}_2 \;\ldots\; \mathbf{O}\mathbf{P}_{N-2}\;\;\mathbf{Z}\;\mathbf{Z}\,\ldots\,\mathbf{Z}\;\;\mathbf{O}\mathbf{P}_{N-1}\,] \tag{12.8}$$

where $\mathbf{P}_\ell$ is given in Eq. (10.3) and $\mathbf{Z}$ is a k-by-n zero matrix. Therefore, the generator matrix of $\mathbf{C}_I$ is

$$\mathbf{G}'_\infty = \begin{bmatrix} \mathbf{I}_k\mathbf{P}_0 & \mathbf{Z} & \mathbf{Z}\ldots\mathbf{Z} & \mathbf{O}\mathbf{P}_1 & \mathbf{Z} & \mathbf{Z} & \ldots\mathbf{Z}\ldots & & \\ & \mathbf{I}_k\mathbf{P}_0 & \mathbf{Z} & \mathbf{Z}\ldots\mathbf{Z} & \mathbf{O}\mathbf{P}_1 & \mathbf{Z} & \mathbf{Z}\ldots\mathbf{Z}\ldots & & \\ & & \mathbf{I}_k\mathbf{P}_0 & \mathbf{Z} & \mathbf{Z}\ldots\mathbf{Z} & \mathbf{O}\mathbf{P}_1 & \mathbf{Z}\ldots\mathbf{Z}\ldots & & \\ & & & & \infty & & & & \end{bmatrix} \tag{12.9}$$

Let $\mathbf{m} = \underline{\mathbf{m}}_0\,\underline{\mathbf{m}}_1\,\underline{\mathbf{m}}_2\ldots$ be the message sequence to be encoded in accordance with code $\mathbf{C}_I$, where $\underline{\mathbf{m}}_\ell$ is a block of k message digits,

$$\underline{\mathbf{m}}_\ell = m_\ell(1)\,m_\ell(2)\ldots m_\ell(k) \;.$$

Then the corresponding code sequence is

$$\mathbf{c} = (\underline{\mathbf{c}}_0\;\underline{\mathbf{c}}_1\;\underline{\mathbf{c}}_2\;\ldots)\;,$$

where $\underline{\mathbf{c}}_\ell$ is a block of n code digits,

$$\underline{\mathbf{c}}_\ell = c_\ell(1)\,c_\ell(2)\ldots c_\ell(n) \;.$$

Separate the code sequence $\mathbf{c}$ into λ sub-code sequences as follows:

$$
\begin{aligned}
\mathbf{c}^{(0)} &= (\underline{\mathbf{c}}_0 \; \underline{\mathbf{c}}_\lambda \; \underline{\mathbf{c}}_{2\lambda} \; \ldots) \\
\mathbf{c}^{(1)} &= (\underline{\mathbf{c}}_1 \; \underline{\mathbf{c}}_{\lambda+1} \; \underline{\mathbf{c}}_{2\lambda+1} \ldots) \\
&\vdots \\
\mathbf{c}^{(\lambda-1)} &= (\underline{\mathbf{c}}_{\lambda-1} \; \underline{\mathbf{c}}_{2\lambda-1} \; \underline{\mathbf{c}}_{3\lambda-1} \ldots) \quad .
\end{aligned}
\qquad (12.10)
$$

By examining Eq. (12.8) and Eq. (12.9), it can be seen that the sub-code sequence $\mathbf{c}^{(q)}$ for $0 \leqslant q \leqslant \lambda\text{-}1$ is the code sequence obtained by encoding the sub-message sequence

$$
\mathbf{m}^{(q)} = (\underline{\mathbf{m}}_q \; \underline{\mathbf{m}}_{\lambda+q} \; \underline{\mathbf{m}}_{2\lambda+q} \; \ldots)
$$

in accordance with the original code $\mathbf{C}$. That is, each code sequence of code $\mathbf{C}_I$ is obtained by interlacing the blocks of λ code sequences of the original code $\mathbf{C}$. Because of this fact, $\mathbf{C}$ is called a *basic code* and $\mathbf{C}_I$ is called an *interlaced code of degree* λ.

The error-correcting capability of an interlaced code is based upon the error-correcting capability of the given basic code. Suppose that the basic code is a burst-error-correcting code which is capable of correcting any burst of length $\ell = \sigma n$ or less. It can be seen easily that a burst of length $\lambda\ell$ or less, no matter where it starts in $\mathbf{c}$, affects no more than ℓ consecutive digits in each sub-code sequence $\mathbf{c}^{(q)}$. Thus, the interlaced code is capable of correcting any burst of length $\lambda\ell$ or less (within a constraint length of N' blocks) by decoding the sub-code sequences separately. Suppose that the basic code is a random-error-correcting code which is capable of correcting any combination of t or fewer errors. Let $\mu = [t/n]$. If there are μ bursts of length λn or less in $\mathbf{c}$ within a constraint length of N' blocks, then no sub-code sequence is affected at more than t places. Thus, the interlaced code is capable of correcting any combination of μ bursts of length λn or less by decoding each sub-code sequence separately.

Let $\mathbf{r} = (\underline{\mathbf{r}}_0 \; \underline{\mathbf{r}}_1 \; \underline{\mathbf{r}}_2 \ldots)$ be the received sequence and let $\mathbf{s} = (\underline{\mathbf{s}}_0 \; \underline{\mathbf{s}}_1 \; \underline{\mathbf{s}}_2 \ldots)$ be the corresponding syndrome sequence. Then the sub-syndrome sequence

$$\mathbf{s}^{(q)} = (\underline{\mathbf{s}}_q \ \underline{\mathbf{s}}_{\lambda+q} \ \underline{\mathbf{s}}_{2\lambda+q} \cdots)$$

is used for decoding the sub-received sequence

$$\mathbf{r}^{(q)} = (\underline{\mathbf{r}}_q \ \underline{\mathbf{r}}_{\lambda+q} \ \underline{\mathbf{r}}_{2\lambda+q} \cdots) \ .$$

From the above discussions, it is clear that the encoder and the decoder of an interlaced code can be derived from the basic code simply by replacing each register stage by λ stages without changing the other connections. Therefore, the complexity of implementing an interlaced code is about λ times the complexity of implementing the basic code.

Bit Interlacing

Given a basic (n,k) code of constraint length N as described by Eq. (12.6), it is possible to construct a $(\lambda n, \lambda k)$ code $\mathbf{C}_{II}$ with $\lambda^2 k(n-k)$ sub-generators $\mathbf{g}'(i',j')$. These $\lambda^2 k(n-k)$ sub-generators $\mathbf{g}'(i',j')$ are obtained from the sub-generators $\mathbf{g}(i,j)$ of the given basic code as follows:

(1) $\mathbf{g}'(i',j') = \mathbf{g}(i,j)$ for $i' = (i-1)\lambda + \rho$ and $j' = (j-1)\lambda + \rho$ where $i = 1, 2, \ldots, k$, $j = 1, 2, \ldots, n-k$, and $\rho = 1, 2, \ldots, \lambda$.

(2) $\mathbf{g}'(i',j') = \mathbf{o}$ for other i' and j', where $\mathbf{o}$ is an all-zero vector.

Obviously, the constraint length of code $\mathbf{C}_{II}$ is equal to the constraint length N of the given basic code. The λk generators of $\mathbf{C}_{II}$ are of the form

$$\begin{bmatrix} \mathbf{g}'(1) \\ \mathbf{g}'(2) \\ \vdots \\ \mathbf{g}'(\lambda k) \end{bmatrix} = [\, \mathbf{I}_{\lambda k}\, \mathbf{P}'_0 \ \ \mathbf{O}\,\mathbf{P}'_1 \ \ \mathbf{O}\,\mathbf{P}'_2 \ \ldots \ \mathbf{O}\,\mathbf{P}'_{N-1} \,] \qquad (12.11)$$

where (1) $\mathbf{I}_{\lambda k}$ is a λk-by-λk identity matrix,

(2) $\mathbf{O}$ is a λk-by-λk zero matrix, and

(3)

$$\mathbf{P}'_\ell = \begin{bmatrix} \mathbf{D}_{11} & \mathbf{D}_{12} & \cdots & \mathbf{D}_{1,n-k} \\ \mathbf{D}_{21} & \mathbf{D}_{22} & \cdots & \mathbf{D}_{2,n-k} \\ \vdots & & & \\ \mathbf{D}_{k1} & \mathbf{D}_{k2} & \cdots & \mathbf{D}_{k,n-k} \end{bmatrix}$$

with $\mathbf{D}_{ij}$ as a diagonal λ-by-λ matrix

$$\mathbf{D}_{ij} = \begin{bmatrix} g_\ell(i,j) & 0 & 0 & \cdots & 0 \\ 0 & g_\ell(i,j) & 0 & \cdots & 0 \\ 0 & 0 & g_\ell(i,j) & \cdots & 0 \\ \vdots & \vdots & \vdots & & \\ 0 & 0 & 0 & \cdots & g_\ell(i,j) \end{bmatrix} .$$

Let $\mathbf{m} = (m_0(1)\ m_0(2)\ \ldots\ m_0(\lambda k)\ m_1(1)\ m_1(2)\ \ldots\ m_1(\lambda k)\ \ldots)$ be the message sequence to be encoded in accordance with $\mathbf{C}_{II}$ and let

$$\mathbf{c} = (c_0(1)\ c_0(2) \ldots c_0(\lambda n)\ c_1(1)\ c_1(2) \ldots c_1(\lambda n) \ldots)$$

be the corresponding code sequence. This code sequence can be separated into λ sub-code sequences as follows:

$$\mathbf{c}^{(0)} = (c_0(1)\ c_0(\lambda+1) \ldots c_0(\overline{n-1}\lambda+1)^*\ c_1(1)\ c_1(\lambda+1) \ldots c_1(\overline{n-1}\lambda+1) \ldots)$$

$$\mathbf{c}^{(1)} = (c_0(2)\ c_0(\lambda+2) \ldots c_0(\overline{n-1}\lambda+2)\ \ c_1(2)\ c_1(\lambda+2) \ldots c_1(\overline{n-1}\lambda+1) \ldots)$$

$$\vdots$$

$$\mathbf{c}^{(\lambda-1)} = (c_0(\lambda)\ c_0(2\lambda)\ \ldots c_0(n\lambda)\qquad c_1(\lambda)\ c_2(2\lambda)\ \ldots c_1(n\lambda)\qquad \ldots) .$$

* Note that $\overline{n-1} = (n-1)$.

By examining Eq. (12.11) carefully, it can be seen that the sub-code sequence $\mathbf{c}^{(q)}$ is the code sequence obtained by encoding the sub-message sequence

$$\mathbf{m}^{(q)} = (m_0(q)\, m_0(\lambda+q) \ldots m_0(\overline{n-1}\lambda+q)\, m_1(q)\, m_1(\lambda+q) \ldots m_1(\overline{n-1}\lambda+q) \ldots)$$

in accordance with the given basic code. Therefore, a code sequence in $\mathbf{C}_{II}$ is obtained by interlacing the bits of λ code sequences from the basic code. Thus, $\mathbf{C}_{II}$ is also an interlaced code.

If there is a burst of length λ, no matter where it starts it will affect no more than one bit in each sub-code sequence $\mathbf{c}^{(q)}$. Thus, if the basic code corrects single errors, the interlaced code corrects single bursts of length λ or less. Similarly, if the basic code corrects all combinations of t or fewer errors, the interlaced code $\mathbf{C}_{II}$ will correct any combination of t bursts of length λ or less. If the basic code corrects any burst of length ℓ (not necessarily a multiple of n) or less, the interlaced code will correct any burst of length $\lambda\ell$ or less. Thus, the bit-interlacing technique results in a code which has more flexibility to deal with a combination of bursts and random errors.

Let

$$\mathbf{r} = (r_0(1)\, r_0(2) \ldots r_0(\lambda n)\, r_1(1)\, r_1(2) \ldots r_1(\lambda n) \ldots)$$

be the received sequence and

$$\mathbf{s} = (s_0(1)\, s_0(2) \ldots s_0(\overline{n-k}\lambda)\, s_1(1)\, s_1(2) \ldots s_1(\overline{n-k}\lambda) \ldots)$$

be the corresponding syndrome sequence. Then the sub-syndrome sequence

$$\mathbf{s}^{(q)} = (s_0(q)\, s_0(\lambda+q) \ldots s_0(\overline{n-k-1}\lambda+q)\, s_1(q)\, s_1(\lambda+q) \ldots s_1(\overline{n-k-1}\lambda+q) \ldots)$$

is used for decoding the received sub-sequence

$$\mathbf{r}^{(q)} = (r_0(q)\, r_0(\lambda+q) \ldots r_0(\overline{n-1}\lambda+q)\, r_1(q)\, r_1(\lambda+q) \ldots$$
$$r_1(\overline{n-1}\lambda+q) \ldots) \quad ,$$

where $q = 1, 2, \ldots, \lambda$. It can be shown that the complexity of implementing $\mathbf{C}_{II}$ is the same as the complexity of implementing $\mathbf{C}_I$ with the same λ.

Diffuse Codes

Consider a self-orthogonal or orthogonalizable (n,k) convolutional code such that $J = 2t$ parity-check sums orthogonal on $e_0(i)$ can be formed for $i = 1, 2, \ldots, k$. This code is said to be an *ℓ-diffuse code*[17, 24] if, for each i, the J parity-check sums orthogonal on $e_0(i)$ have the properties that (1) excluding $e_0(i)$, error bits from a burst of length ℓ which starts before or at the ith position of the 0th block are checked by no more than t-1 of these check sums, (2) error bits from a burst which starts at any position after the ith one of the 0th block are checked by no more than t of these check sums. Obviously, an ℓ-diffuse code is capable of correcting any t or fewer random errors within any N consecutive blocks by majority-logic decoding. In addition to this random-error-correcting capability, this code has burst-error-correcting capability ℓ. This can be seen as follows. Suppose that a burst of length ℓ or less has occurred. If $e_0(i)$ is within the burst and $e_0(i) = 1$, then it follows the first property that at least $t+1$ check sums are equal to $e_0(i) = 1$. Thus, $e_0(i) = 1$ will be estimated correctly by majority decoding. If $e_0(i) = 0$, either $e_0(i)$ is within the burst or outside the burst. In either case, there are at least t check sums which are equal to $e_0(i) = 0$. Thus, by the rule of majority decoding, $e_0(i) = 0$ will be decoded correctly.

Example 12.2: Consider the double-error-correcting self-orthogonal (2,1) code with constraint $N = 10$ which is specified by the following sub-generator:

$$\mathbf{g}(1,1) = (1\,0\,0\,1\,0\,0\,0\,0\,1\,0\,1) \quad .$$

It follows from Eq. (10.18) that we obtain the first 10 syndrome bits,

$$
\begin{aligned}
s_0(1) &= e_0(1) + e_0(2) \\
s_1(1) &= e_1(1) + e_1(2) \\
s_2(1) &= e_2(1) + e_2(2) \\
s_3(1) &= e_0(1) + e_3(1) + e_3(2) \\
s_4(1) &= e_1(1) + e_4(1) + e_4(2) \\
s_5(1) &= e_2(1) + e_5(1) + e_5(2) \\
s_6(1) &= e_3(1) + e_6(1) + e_6(2) \\
s_7(1) &= e_0(1) + e_4(1) + e_7(1) + e_7(2) \\
s_8(1) &= e_1(1) + e_5(1) + e_8(1) + e_8(2) \\
s_9(1) &= e_0(1) + e_2(1) + e_6(1) + e_9(1) + e_9(2) \quad .
\end{aligned}
$$

The four parity-check sums orthogonal on $e_0(1)$ are

$$
\begin{aligned}
s_0(1) &= e_0(1) + e_0(2) \\
s_3(1) &= e_0(1) + e_3(1) + e_3(2) \\
s_7(1) &= e_0(1) + e_4(1) + e_7(1) + e_7(2) \\
s_9(1) &= e_0(1) + e_2(1) + e_6(1) + e_9(1) + e_9(2) \quad .
\end{aligned}
$$

By examining these four parity-check sums, we can see that the code is a 4-diffuse code. Thus, this code is capable of correcting any two or fewer random errors, or any burst error of length ℓ or less within nN consecutive digits. For correcting burst errors, this code requires a guard space of 18 bits.

Let $\ell = 2m$, where m is any positive integer greater than 1. Another example of an ℓ-diffuse code is the (2,1) code whose sub-generator $\mathbf{g}(1,1)$ has the following four non-zero components:

$$g_0(1,1) = g_m(1,1) = g_{2m}(1,1) = g_{3m+1}(1,1) = 1. \qquad (12.12)$$

The constraint length of this code is $N = 3m + 2$. Four parity-check sums orthogonal on $e_0(1)$ can be formed as follows:

$$\begin{aligned} s_0(1) &= e_0(1) + e_0(2) \\ s_m(1) &= e_0(1) + e_m(1) + e_m(2) \\ s_{2m}(1) + s_{3m}(1) &= e_0(1) + e_{2m}(2) + e_{3m}(1) + e_{3m}(2) \\ s_{3m+1}(1) &= e_0(1) + e_{m+1}(1) + e_{2m+1}(1) + e_{3m+1}(1) + e_{3m+1}(2) \ . \end{aligned} \qquad (12.13)$$

It can be checked easily that these four parity-check sums satisfy the conditions required for an ℓ-diffuse code. Thus, this code is capable of correcting any two or fewer random errors, or any burst error of length $\ell = 2m$ or less. The guard space required for this code is $6m + 2$. This code was devised by the Codex Corporation. The performance of this code over telephone lines, HF radio, and troposcatter channels has been evaluated by Brayer,[3] Kohlenberg and Forney,[19] and Cohn et al.[6] They have shown that, when properly used, this code can provide a significant reduction in error rate. Kohlenberg and Forney have also shown that the majority-logic decoder for this code does not propagate decoding errors.

Procedures for constructing diffuse codes have been proposed by Tong[29] and Iwadare.[16]

Gallager Coding Technique[10]

This is another effective technique for correcting random errors and burst errors with convolutional codes. For the ease of explanation, we consider a Gallager coding system with rate $R = ½$ (i.e., $n = 2$ and $k = 1$). Let

$$\mathbf{g}(1) = (g_0(1,1)\, g_1(1,1)\, g_2(1,1) \ldots g_{N\text{-}1}(1,1)) \tag{12.14}$$

be the sub-generator of a (2,1) convolutional code which is suitable for random-error correction and detection (for example, an orthogonalizable code). Based on the given code, we construct a new (2,1) convolutional code whose sub-generator is of the following form:

$$\mathbf{g}'(1,1) = (g_0(1,1)\, g_1(1,1) \ldots g_{N\text{-}1}(1,1)\, \overbrace{0\,0 \ldots 0}^{L-1}\, 1) \tag{12.15}$$

where $L \gg N$. This new code has constraint length $N' = N + L$ and is called a *Gallager code*. The original code is called a *basic code*. An encoder for the Gallager code specified by Eq. (12.15) is shown in Fig. 12.6 (a Type II encoding circuit is used here). This encoder consists of two parts: (1) Part **E** is an encoder for the basic code specified by Eq. (12.15). (2) Part **D** is a shift register of L stages with its rightmost stage connected to the parity-check adder **P**.

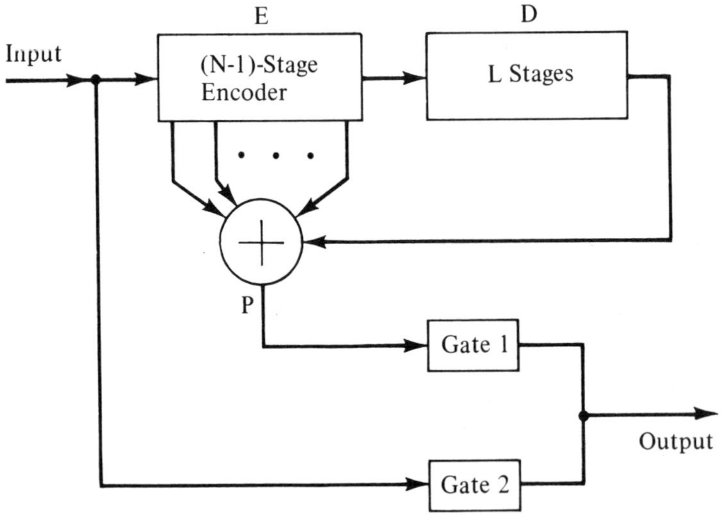

Fig. 12.6. An encoder for a half-rate Gallager code.

Gallager has devised an *adaptive* decoding scheme for this code such that it is capable of correcting random errors (within the capability of the basic code) as well as burst errors. The Gallager decoder for this code is shown in Fig. 12.7. The decoder has two decoding modes, the random-error-correcting mode and the burst-error-correcting mode. Normally, the decoder is in the random-error-correcting mode. It corrects random errors according to the basic code. The syndrome bits in the register $\mathbf{S}_2$ are used for the decoding of the received message bit in the rightmost stage of register $\mathbf{D}_1$. If the basic code is an orthogonalizable code, the random-error corrector is a majority-logic gate as described in Chapter 11. The decoded message bits are stored in register $\mathbf{D}_2$ for M time units before they are shifted out of the decoder. If there are no decoding mistakes, $\mathbf{D}_2$ will be filled with correct message bits. When these correct message bits are shifted out of the decoder, they do not affect the syndrome bits formed at parity-check adder **P** since only errors are involved in the calculation of syndrome bits (see Eq. (10.18)). As long as the random errors are within the error-correcting capability of the basic code, the decoder operates smoothly.

If an error pattern with errors beyond the error-correcting capability of the basic code (such as a long and dense burst error) occurs and if this error pattern is detected by the decoder, then the decoder switches to the burst-error-correcting mode. The burst-error correction is performed at the output of register $\mathbf{D}_2$. The correction is based on the following fact. If, at any time unit, the input bits (the received message and parity bits) to the encoder and the bits in the re-encoder **E** are error-free, then the syndrome bit formed at the output of the parity adder **P** is "1" when and only when the bit in the rightmost stage of $\mathbf{D}_2$ is incorrect. Therefore, this incorrect message bit can be corrected by the syndrome bit formed at the output of **P**. If a burst of length $2(L-M)$ bits is detected and if this burst is followed by an error-free zone (guard space) of $2(L+N)-1$ bits, then the burst will be corrected by the decoder. Actually, it can be shown that, for a burst of length $b \leqslant 2(L-M)$, the guard space required is about equal to $b+2N$. Since, in general, the parameter N is small, the guard space is approximately equal to the length of the burst. The decoder stays in the burst-error-correcting mode until all the syndrome bits in the register $\mathbf{S}_2$ and $\mathbf{S}_3$ are zero. At this point, the burst has passed out of the decoder and the decoder returns to the random-error-correcting mode.

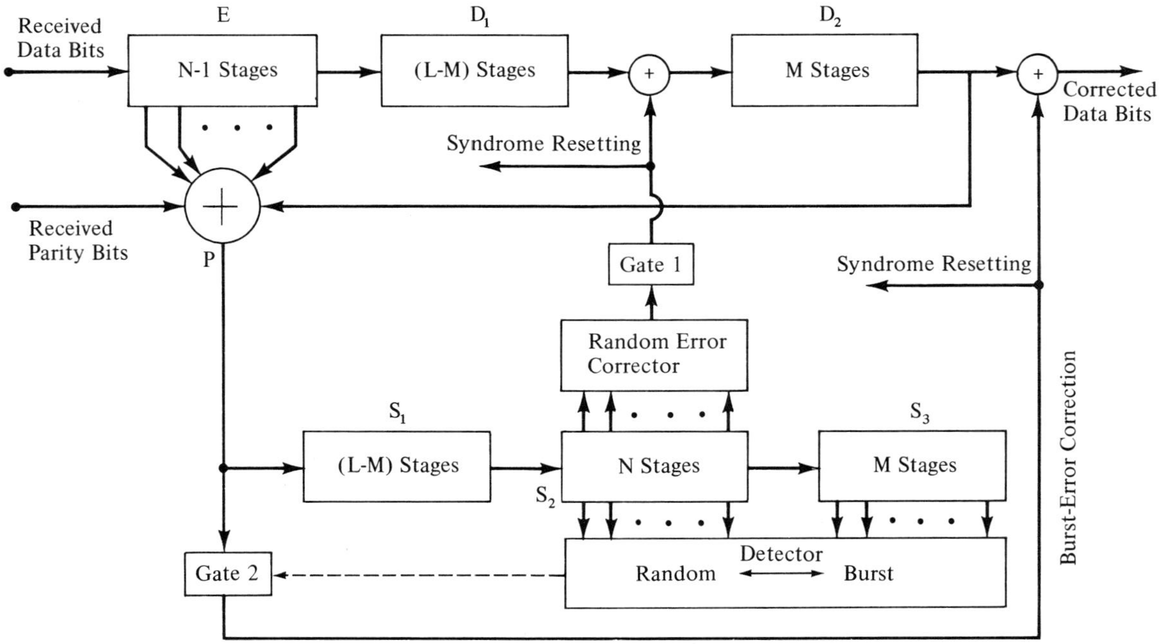

Fig. 12.7. A decoder for a half-rate Gallager code.

With the above decoding scheme, not all the bursts of length $2(L-M)$ or less can be corrected since some of these bursts are not detectable by the decoder. If a suitable error-detecting criterion is used, the number of undetected bursts will become insignificant. The error-correcting capability t of the basic code and the numbers N, L, and M are designed parameters which should be chosen in accordance with the channel characteristics and the system requirements.

The above rate $R = \frac{1}{2}$ Gallager coding system can be generalized to other rates. The performance of a Gallager coding system over HF and troposcatter channels have been evaluated in References 4, 5, 18, and 19.

PROBLEMS

12.1. Consider the Iwadare (2,1) code (first class) with $\lambda = 4$.

(a) Find the sub-generator of this code.

(b) Construct the Type I encoder for this code.

(c) What is the recurrence distance of the error bit $e_0(1)$?

(d) Construct a forward-acting decoder for this code.

12.2. Find the sub-generators for the Iwadare (3,2) code (second class) with $\lambda = 4$. Construct a forward-acting decoder for this code.

12.3. Consider a (2,1) code whose sub-generator is

$$g(1,1) = (1\ 0\ 1\ 0\ 0\ 1\ 0\ 0\ 0\ 1) .$$

(a) Is this code self-orthogonal? What is the random-error-correcting capability of this code?

(b) Is this code a diffuse code? What is its burst-error-correcting capability?

(c) Construct a decoder for this code.

REFERENCES

1. Berlekamp, E. R., "A Class of Convolutional Codes," *Information and Control*, **6**, pp. 1-13, March, 1963.

2. Berlekamp, E. R., "Note on Recurrent Codes," *IEEE Trans. on Information Theory*, **IT-10**, pp. 257-258, July, 1964.

3. Brayer, K., "The Performance of a Simulated Convolutional Decoder on Measured HF and Tropospheric Data Channels," A.F. ESD-TR-67-423, January, 1968.

4. Brayer, K., "Performance Evaluation of the Codex Gallager Decoder on a Measured HF Channel," A.F. ESD-TR-67-365, February, 1968.

5. Brayer, K., "Performance Evaluation of the Codex Gallager Decoder on Measured HF and Troposcatter Channels," A.F. ESD-TR-67-398, March, 1968.

6. Cohn, D. L., A. H. Levesque, J. H. Meyn, and A. W. Pierce, "Performance of Selected Block and Convolutional Codes on a Fading HF Channel," *IEEE Trans. on Information Theory*, **IT-14**, pp. 627-640, September, 1968.

7. Ebert, P. M., and S. Y. Tong, "A Family of Character Error Correcting Convolutional Codes," Proceedings of the IEEE International Conference on Communication, Minneapolis, Minnesota, 1967.

8. Epley, A. W., and L. Lin, "On the Burst-Error Correcting Recurrent Codes," Air Force Cambridge Research Center Report 10, AF19(628)-4379, Bedford, Massachusetts, 1966.

9. Freiman, C. V., J. P. Robinson, and A. D. Wyner, "Error Control through Coding, Vol. 2: Recurrent Burst-Error-Correcting Codes," Rome Air Dev. Ct. Tech. Rept. RADC-TDR-64-149, DOC. AD609467, Rome, New York, 1964.

10. Gallager, R. G., "Lower Bounds on the Tails of Probability Distributions," M.I.T. Research Lab. of Electronics, QPR77, pp. 277-291, 1965.

11. Gallager, R. G., *Information Theory and Reliable Communications*, McGraw-Hill, New York, 1968.

12. Hagelbarger, D. W., "Recurrent Codes: Easily Mechanized, Burst-Correcting, Binary Codes," *Bell Systems Tech. J.*, **38**, pp. 969-984, July, 1959.

13. Hagelbarger, D. W., "Recurrent Codes for the Binary Symmetric Channel," lecture notes from the University of Michigan Summer Conference on Coding Theory, 1962.

14. Hsu, H. T., "A New Class of Recurrent Codes," *IEEE Trans. on Information Theory*, **IT-15**, pp. 592-597, September, 1969.

15. Iwadare, Y., "On Type B1 Burst-Error-Correcting Convolutional Codes," *IEEE Trans. on Information Theory*, **IT-14**, pp. 577-583, July, 1968.

16. Iwadare, Y., "Burst and Random Error Correction by Means of Threshold Decoding," Tech. Report, Central Research Labs., Nippon Electric Co., Ltd., Japan, 1968.

17. Kohlenberg, A., "Random and Burst Error Control," Proceedings of the First IEEE Annual Communications Convention, pp. 55-56, June, 1965.

18. Kohlenberg, A., and A. S. Berner, "An Experimental Comparison of Coding vs. Frequency Diversity for HF Telegraphy Transmission," *IEEE Trans. on Communication Technology*, **COM-14**, pp. 532-533, August, 1966.

19. Kohlenberg, A., and G. D. Forney, Jr., "Convolutional Coding for Channels with Memory," *IEEE Trans. on Information Theory*, **IT-14**, pp. 618-626, September, 1968.

20. Kilmer, W. L., "Some Results on Best Recurrent-Type Binary-Error-Correcting Codes," IRE Conv. Rec., pt. 4, pp. 135-147, 1960.

21. Lucky, R. W., J. Salz, and E. J. Weldon, Jr., *Principles of Data Communication*, McGraw-Hill, New York, 1968.

22. Massey, J. L., *Threshold Decoding*, The M.I.T. Press, Cambridge, Massachusetts, 1963.

23. Massey, J. L., "Implementation of Burst-Correcting Convolutional Codes," *IEEE Trans. on Information Theory*, **IT-11**, pp. 416-422, July, 1965.

24. Massey, J. L., *Advances in Threshold Decoding—Advances in Communication Systems*, **2**, A. V. Balakrishnan, Ed., Academic Press, Inc., 1968.

25. Peterson, W. W., *Error-Correcting Codes*, The M.I.T. Press, Cambridge, Massachusetts, 1961.

26. Peterson, W. W., and E. J. Weldon, Jr., *Error-Correcting Codes*, 2nd Edition, The M.I.T. Press, Cambridge, Massachusetts, 1970.

27. Preparata, F. P., "Systematic Construction of Optimal Linear Recurrent Codes for Burst Error Correction," *Calcolo*, **2**, pp. 1-7, 1964.

28. Tong, S. Y., "Burst Trapping Techniques for a Compound Channel," presented at the IEEE International Symposium on Information Theory, Ellenville, New York, 1969.

29. Tong, S. Y., "Systematic Construction of Self-Orthogonal Diffuse Codes," *IEEE Trans. on Information Theory*, in press.

30. Wyner, A. D., and R. B. Ash, "Analysis of Recurrent Codes," *IEEE Trans. on Information Theory*, **IT-9**, pp. 143-156, July, 1963.

31. Wyner, A. D., "Some Results on Burst-Correcting Recurrent Codes," IEEE International Convention Record, part 4, pp. 139-152, 1963.

CHAPTER 13

SEQUENTIAL DECODING FOR CONVOLUTIONAL CODES

In the previous three chapters, we considered convolutional codes whose decodings are based entirely on their algebraic structures. There exist other decoding methods for convolutional codes which utilize the statistics of a channel in such ways that the probability of a decoding error can be made arbitrarily small by increasing the constraint length. These decoding methods are referred to as *probabilistic decodings*. One such probabilistic decoding, known as *sequential decoding*, was first devised by Wozencraft.[30] It has been shown that with this decoding method arbitrarily small error probabilities can be achieved by employing almost any code of sufficiently long constraint length. Moreover, sequential decoding can be implemented at a modest cost. Another probabilistic decoding method for convolutional codes which is becoming increasingly important is Viterbi's maximum likelihood decoding scheme.[28] For codes with short constraint lengths, Viterbi's decoding method is very effective and has several advantages over sequential decoding. However, for codes with large constraint lengths, the complexity of the Viterbi decoder becomes impractical.

In this chapter, only a brief description of sequential decoding over the binary symmetric channel (*BSC*) is given. This description is intended to serve an an introduction to the subject. References 5, 8, 23, and 34 contain excellent expositions of sequential decoding. Viterbi's decoding algorithm will not be discussed here. The interested reader is referred to Reference 28.

13.1 BASIC CONCEPTS

As described in Chapter 10, an (n, k) convolutional code can be represented topologically by an infinite code tree with nodes and branches. There are 2^k branches stemming from each node, and each branch is n digits long. A code sequence is a path through the tree. The encoding operation can be viewed as a process in which the encoder traces a particular path through the code tree according to the instructions of the input message blocks. Conversely, the decoding operation may be regarded as a process in which the decoder, based on the received sequence and the channel statistics, attempts to retrace the transmitted path through the code tree. With little thought, one would adopt a simple strategy as follows. Starting from the initial node of the tree, the decoder compares the 0th block of the received sequence with the 2^k branches stemming from the initial node and accepts the nearest branch (in Hamming distance). Then the decoder prints out the message block which corresponds to the accepted branch. By doing so, the decoder has moved to a first order node. At this node, the decoder compares the 1st block of the received sequence with all the 2^k branches stemming from the node and accepts the nearest branch. Then the decoder prints out the message block which corresponds to this second accepted branch; the decoder is now at a second order node. Proceeding in this way, the decoder will eventually trace a path through the tree in a simple and rapid manner. When the channel is quiet, each accepted branch would be a correct branch and the path traced by the decoder would be the actual transmitted path. This can be best demonstrated by an example. Consider the code tree in Fig. 13.1. Suppose that the all-zero path (the top-most path in the tree) was transmitted and that the sequence $\mathbf{r}_1$ = (001 010 000 100 000 . . .) is received, where each block of $\mathbf{r}_1$ contains either one error or no error. According to the above branch-by-branch search strategy, the decoder would accept the all-zero branch as it moves from one node to the next node, and the path traced by the decoder would be the all-zero transmitted path. Problems arise, however, when the density of errors increases momentarily. Suppose that the ℓth received block is the first block with a high density of errors. When the decoder compares this received block with the 2^k branches stemming from the previously accepted $(\ell-1)^{th}$-order node, it might find an incorrect branch which is closer to the ℓth received block than the correct branch. The decoder would then accept this incorrect branch and subsequently follow an incorrect path. Once the decoder is on an incorrect path, branch-by-branch search cannot possibly return the decoder to the correct path. The node at which the decoder made its first incorrect branch choice is called the *node of separation*. The decodings after this node would be unreliable. Consider the same code tree that we considered previously. Suppose that an all-zero path was transmitted and that the sequence $\mathbf{r}_2$ = (000 000 011 000 000 . . .) is received, with no errors other than two errors in the 2nd received block. According to the branch-by-branch search strategy, the decoder follows the correct path to

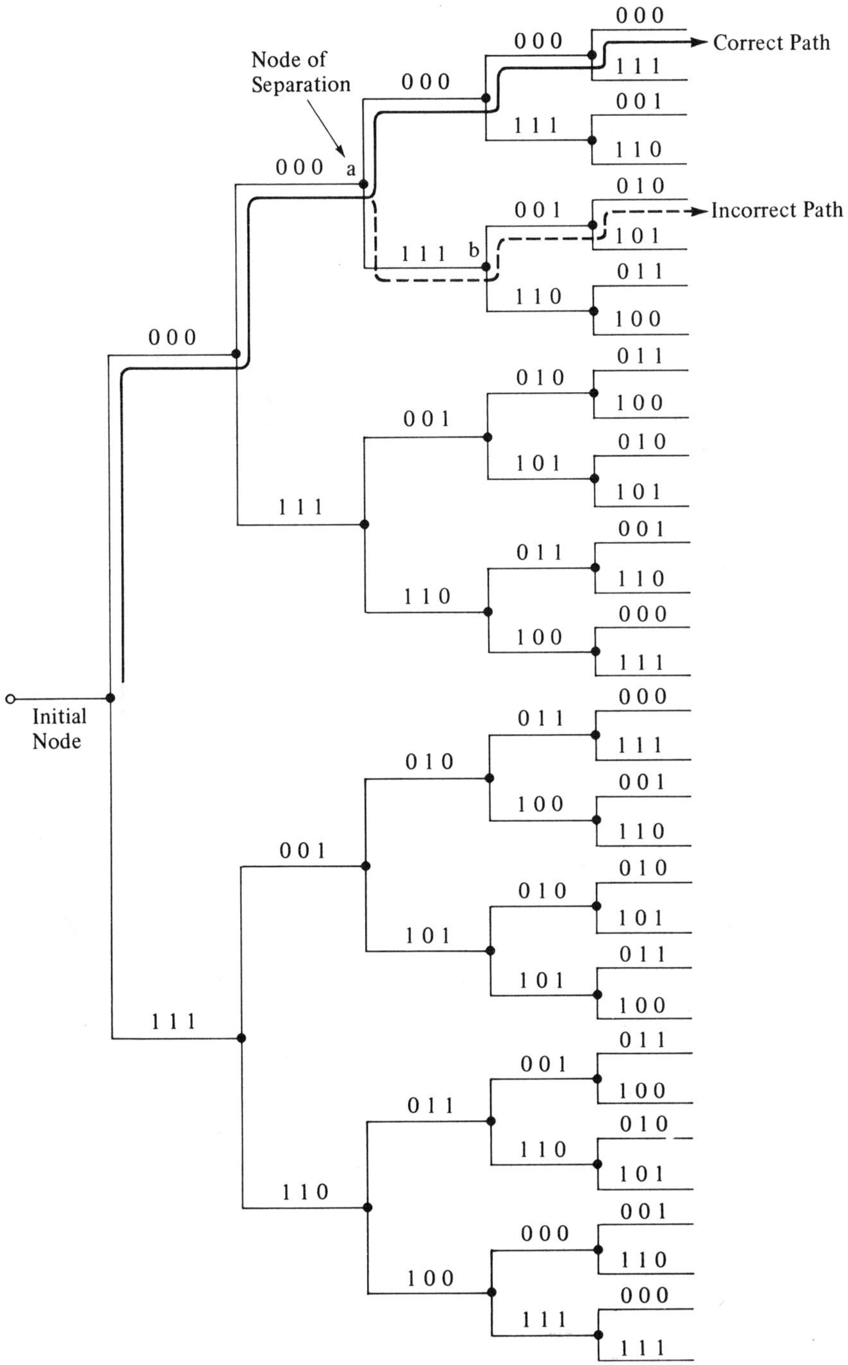

Fig. 13.1. Code tree for a (3,1) convolutional code.

node **a** and then makes an incorrect choice of branch 111 to node **b**. The path traced by the decoder will be

$$\begin{array}{c} \text{Node of Separation} \\ \downarrow \\ 000\ 000\ 111\ 001\ 010\ldots \\ \vdash\!\!\longrightarrow \text{Incorrect Path} \end{array}$$

Thus, **a** is the node of separation and the path traced by the decoder after node **a** is incorrect. From the previous example, we notice that the branch-by-branch search would result in an incorrect path (even though the total number of errors in the second received sequence $\mathbf{r}_2$ is much less than the number of errors in the 1st received sequence $\mathbf{r}_1$). Therefore, the simple branch-by-branch search is insufficient to provide a reliable decoding process. Thus, a set of rules called a decoding algorithm is required in addition to the branch-by-branch search. To be successful, a decoding algorithm must have the following properties: (1) It must be able to detect with high probability the fact that an incorrect path has been followed by the decoder. (2) It must provide strategies with a high probability of returning to the correct path, once the fact of incorrect choice is detected. (3) It must not require an excessive amount of effort to make a decoding decision.

The first decoding algorithm called *sequential decoding* was introduced by Wozencraft in 1957.[30] Wozencraft and Reiffen[33] showed that, with such an algorithm: (1) the average effort (number of computations) required to decode a received block is proportional to a small power of the code constraint length for information transmission rate below a rate called R_{comp}; and (2) the probability of a decoding error decreases exponentially with the code constraint length. In 1963, Fano[3] proposed another sequential decoding algorithm which was an improved version of Wozencraft's. Since then, Fano's algorithm has been studied and experimented on extensively. It has been proved that, with Fano's algorithm, the average effort of decoding a received block is independent of the code constraint length at a rate below R_{comp}.[3, 26] It has also been shown that Fano's algorithm can be more easily implemented than Wozencraft's. In the rest of this chapter, we shall give a brief discussion of Fano's algorithm. No analysis will be covered.

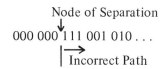

13.2 THE FANO DECODING ALGORITHM

Let $\mathbf{c}(\ell) = (\underline{c}_0, \underline{c}_1, \underline{c}_2, \ldots, \underline{c}_{\ell-1})$ be an ℓ-branch path stemming from the initial node of the code tree and let $\mathbf{r}(\ell) = (\underline{r}_0, \underline{r}_1, \underline{r}_2, \ldots, \underline{r}_{\ell-1})$ be the first ℓ-block segment of the received sequence $\mathbf{r}$. Let $d[\mathbf{c}(\ell), \mathbf{r}(\ell)]$ denote the Hamming distance between $\mathbf{c}(\ell)$ and $\mathbf{r}(\ell)$. Consider the *tilted distance* between $\mathbf{c}(\ell)$ and $\mathbf{r}(\ell)$,

$$\lambda(\ell) = pn\ell - d[\mathbf{c}(\ell), \mathbf{r}(\ell)] \quad , \tag{13.1}$$

where p is a design parameter chosen between the channel (BSC) transition probability p_0 and ½, i.e., $p_0 < p < ½$. If $\mathbf{c}(\ell)$ is the transmitted path, $d[\mathbf{c}(\ell), \mathbf{r}(\ell)]$ is approximately equal to $p_0 n\ell$ for considerably large ℓ. Thus, the tilted distance $\lambda(\ell)$ will be approximately $(p-p_0)n\ell$, which is positive and increases as ℓ increases. However, if $\mathbf{c}(\ell)$ is an incorrect path which branches off from the correct path at some node (the node of separation), then $d[\mathbf{c}(\ell), \mathbf{r}(\ell)]$ typically starts to increase beyond the node of separation. For a considerably large number of branches beyond the node of separation, $d[\mathbf{c}(\ell), \mathbf{r}(\ell)]$ will be approximately equal to $½n\ell$, and the tilted distance $\lambda(\ell)$ will be approximately equal to $(p-½)n\ell$, which is negative and decreases as ℓ increases. The typical behavior of $\lambda(\ell)$ for correct path and incorrect paths is shown in Fig. 13.2. This behavior of $\lambda(\ell)$ will be used to indicate whether the decoder is tracing the correct path or an incorrect path. As the decoder traces a path $\mathbf{c}(\ell)$ through the code tree one branch at a time, it computes the tilted distance $\lambda(\ell)$ of $\mathbf{c}(\ell)$. When $\lambda(\ell)$ increases as ℓ increases, $\mathbf{c}(\ell)$ is presumably the correct path. However, when $\lambda(\ell)$ starts to decrease with increasing ℓ, the decoder is presumably tracing an incorrect path. In this event, a search for the node of separation (the node where an incorrect path branches off from the correct path) begins. Fano's decoding algorithm is a set of rules by which the decoder is able to do the following two things: (1) to recognize (with high probability) whether it is tracing the correct path or an incorrect path; and (2) to initiate a systematic search for the node of separation when the decoder senses the possibility that it is tracing an incorrect path.

For any integer ℓ, there are $(2^k)^\ell$ ℓ^{th}-order nodes in the code tree. To each of these nodes we assign a λ-value which is equal to the tilted distance

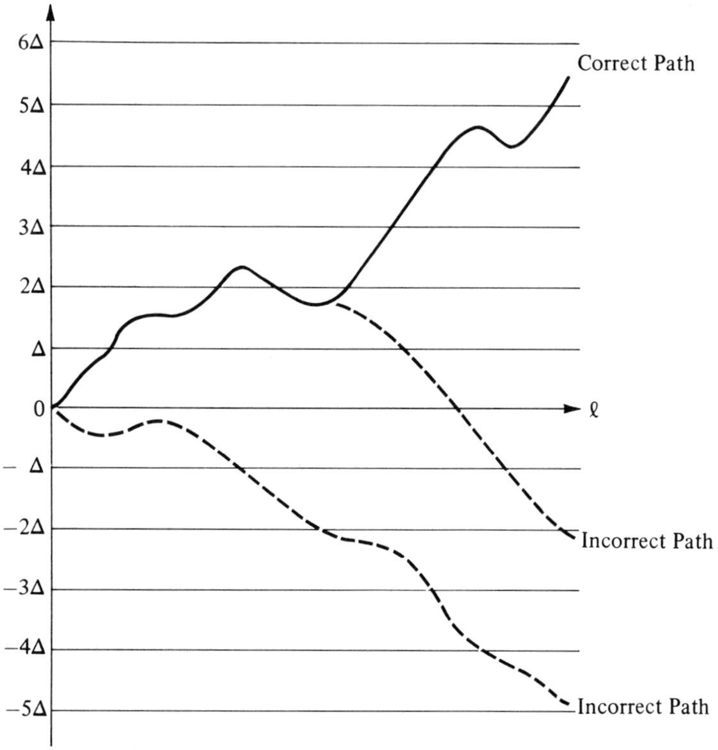

Fig. 13.2. Typical behavior of tilted distance $\lambda(\ell)$ for correct path and incorrect paths.

$\lambda(\ell)$ of the path leading to the node. Obviously, the λ-value of the initial node is zero. Before we describe Fano's decoding algorithm, we must first order the 2^k branches stemming from an ℓth-order node in accordance with their Hamming distances to the ℓth block of the received sequence; the branch which is nearest to the ℓth received block is called the *first branch*; the branch which is next nearest to the ℓth received block is called the *second branch*; and so on. The last branch is farthest from the ℓth received block. The essential features of Fano's decoding algorithm are described as follows:

(1) The decoder begins searching for the correct path from the initial node of the code tree. It moves one branch at a time.

(2) Suppose that the decoder has traced a path $\mathbf{c}(\ell)$ up to an ℓth-order node, say node **A** as shown in Fig. 13.3. From node **A**, the

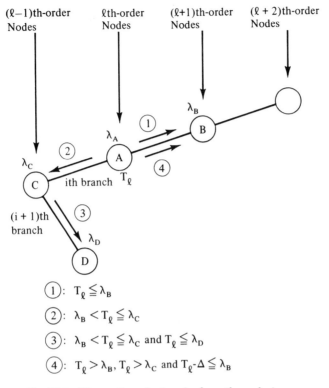

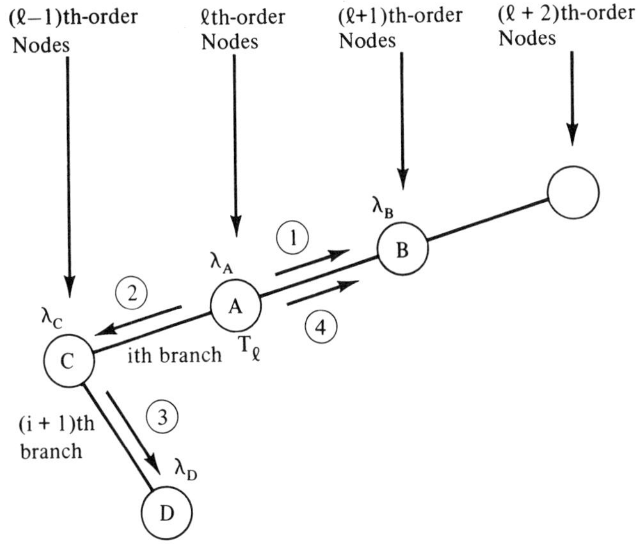

① : $T_\ell \leqq \lambda_B$

② : $\lambda_B < T_\ell \leqq \lambda_C$

③ : $\lambda_B < T_\ell \leqq \lambda_C$ and $T_\ell \leqq \lambda_D$

④ : $T_\ell > \lambda_B$, $T_\ell > \lambda_C$ and $T_\ell - \Delta \leqq \lambda_B$

Fig. 13.3. The motion of a decoder from the node A.

decoder either moves along a branch forward to an $(\ell+1)^{th}$-order node **B** or steps back to the $(\ell-1)^{th}$-order node **C** which was accepted previously.

(3) As the decoder moves from one node to another, it maintains a running threshold $T = k\Delta$, where k is an integer and Δ is a design parameter. The running threshold at the initial node is set to zero.

(4) Suppose that the decoder is at an ℓth-order node **A** and the current running threshold is T_ℓ. First, the decoder attempts to make a forward movement. It considers the $(\ell+1)^{th}$-order node **B** which is connected to node **A** by the first branch stemming from node **A**. The λ-value of node **B**, denoted λ_B, is computed

and compared with the current running threshold T_ℓ. If $\lambda_B \geqslant T_\ell$, the decoder *steps forward* and accepts node **B**. If this is the first time that the decoder has ever reached node **B**, the running threshold is raised to $T_{\ell+1} = T_\ell + \mu\Delta$, where μ is the integer such that $T_\ell + \mu\Delta \leqslant \lambda_B < T + (\mu+1)\Delta$. By doing so, we say that the running threshold is *tightened*. In the same manner, the decoder attempts to move forward to an $(\ell+2)^{th}$-order node from node **B**. If $\lambda_B < T_\ell$, the decoder looks back from node **A** to the $(\ell-1)^{th}$-order node **C** from which the decoder moved to **A** in a previous forward movement. The λ-value of node **C**, λ_C, is compared to T_ℓ. If $\lambda_C > T_\ell$, the decoder moves back to node **C**. From node **C**, the decoder looks forward to the ℓth-order node **D** which is connected to **C** by a branch whose order is one higher than the order of the branch which connects node **A** to node **C**. If $\lambda_D > T_\ell$, the decoder accepts node **D**. From node **D**, the decoder attempts to move forward again. If both λ_B and λ_C are less than the current running threshold T_ℓ at node **A**, the decoder can neither move forward nor backward. In this event, the running threshold T_ℓ is reduced by Δ. Thus, the running threshold at node **A** becomes $T_\ell^{(1)} = T_\ell - \Delta$. With this reduced running threshold, the decoder looks forward to node **B** again.

(5) The running threshold is tightened when and only when the decoder moves forward to a node which has never been examined before. The running threshold is never tightened during backward motion. The running threshold is reduced when and only when the decoder is trapped at a node (i.e., the decoder can move neither forward nor backward).

The detailed movement of the decoder is illustrated by the flow chart shown in Fig. 13.4.

When the channel is quiet, the decoder, under the guidance of the above rules, moves forward branch-by-branch smoothly along the correct path. In the event that the channel becomes noisy, the decoder may branch off from the correct path. As soon as the decoder senses the possibility that it is tracing an incorrect path, a search for the node of separation is then initiated. It is clear that the number of movements (backward and forward)

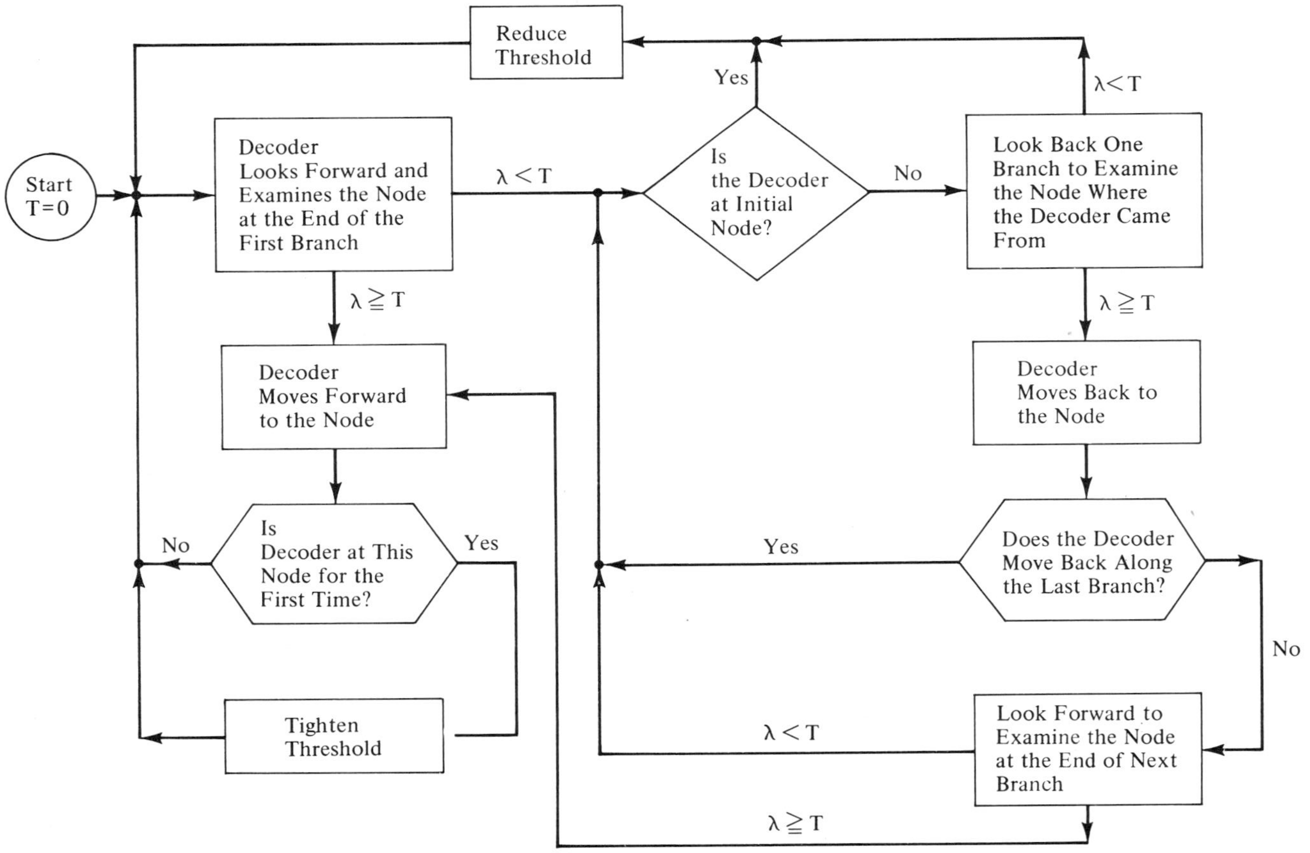

Fig. 13.4. Flow chart for the Fano decoding algorithm.

that the decoder has to make before it moves back to the correct path depends on the channel noise. This number is small when the noise level is low, and is large when the noise is severe.

13.3 DECODER

A block diagram of Fano's sequential decoder[1,13,23,34] is shown in Fig. 13.5. The decoder consists of four major parts:

(1) A buffer **B** of n parallel L-stage shift registers for storing received blocks (L is much longer than the code constraint length N).

(2) A buffer **D** of k parallel $(L+\rho N)$-stage shift registers for storing tentatively decoded message blocks, where ρ is an integer (usually 2 or 3).

(3) A replica of an encoder for generating the code tree.

(4) A decoder logic for directing the path search.

The incoming received sequence **r** is read into the buffer **B** one block at a time. Whenever a newly received block is shifted into **B**, the received block in the rightmost stage of **B** is shifted out and dumped. As the received sequence is shifted through the buffer **B**, the decoder logic directs the decoder to search for the correct path (the transmitted path) through the code tree generated by the replica of the encoder. Whenever the decoder accepts a branch according to the search algorithm, the message block which corresponds to this accepted branch is decoded and stored in the buffer **D** at the position under the corresponding received block. For example, the message block $\underline{\mathbf{m}}_{\ell+i} = (m_{\ell+i}(1), m_{\ell+i}(2), \ldots, m_{\ell+i}(k))$ is the tentatively decoded message block corresponding to $\underline{\mathbf{r}}_{\ell+i} = (r_{\ell+i}(1), r_{\ell+i}(2), \ldots, r_{\ell+i}(n))$. However, when the decoder backs up one branch, the message block corresponding to this branch is removed from buffer **D**. At the same time that the received block $\underline{\mathbf{r}}_{\ell}$ at the rightmost stage of **B** is read out and dumped, the corresponding message block $\underline{\mathbf{m}}_{\ell}$ under it is shifted into the safety zone, and the message block $\underline{\mathbf{m}}_{\ell-\rho N}$ at the rightmost stage of the safety zone is released to the user. Once a message block is released from the safety zone, it becomes a permanently decoded message block. A decoding error is made whenever the released message block is incorrect. It has been proven that the probability

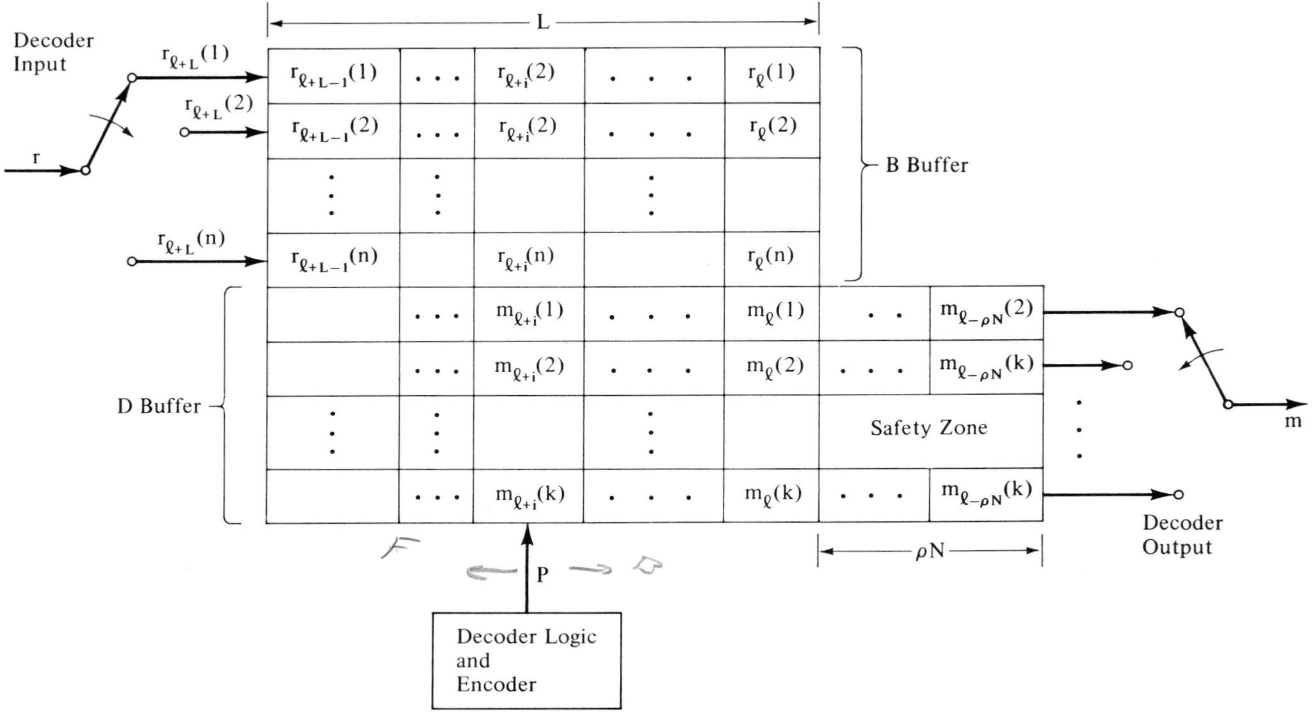

Fig. 13.5. Block diagram of the Fano decoder.

of decoding error per received block decreases exponentially with the increasing constraint length N for transmission rate R below R_{comp}. Thus, the probability of decoding error can be made as small as we desire by increasing the code constraint length.

The arrow **P** indicates the location of the decoder in the code tree. As the decoder moves forward along a path, the arrow **P** moves to the left; as the decoder moves backward to search for the node of separation, the arrow **P** moves to the right. The stages of buffer **D** to the right of arrow **P** are filled with tentatively decoded message blocks; those stages to the left of **P** are empty. When the channel is relatively quiet, the arrow **P** hovers near the input end of buffer **B** and the decoder waits for new received blocks. When the channel is very noisy, the decoder is forced to do a large amount of searching, and the arrow **P** is dragged to the input end of the safety zone. When the oldest received block is read out of buffer **B** and the decoder is unable to find an acceptable branch to match it, the decoder will stop searching and the decoding process will be halted. This event is called *buffer overflow*. Let ζ be the decoder speed factor which is defined as the number of branches the decoder can search for in the time allotted to the transmission of each branch. It has been shown that the probability of buffer overflow, P_{BF}, decreases algebraically with the product of the buffer size L and the decoder speed factor ζ as follows:

$$P_{BF} \cong K(\zeta L)^{-\beta}$$

where K is a positive constant and β, a positive function of the data transmission rate R, increases as R decreases.[20,21,22] Buffer overflow is of primary concern in the design of a sequential decoder; its probability should be kept as small as possible. There is no known method to prevent the occurrence of this event. However, once it occurs, it can be terminated by employing periodic resynchronization as described in Chapter 10. Buffer overflow is detectable by the decoder. When its occurrence is detected, the message blocks in the safety zone of buffer **M** are unreliable and will not be released to the user. Thus, the purpose of adding a safety zone of few constraint lengths is to hold the tentatively decoded message bits until they prove to be reliable.

Besides the probability of decoding error and the problem of buffer overflow, the number of computations required for decoding a message block (the number of branches searched per decoded message block) is also of primary concern in the design of a sequential decoder. This number of computations, C, is a function of the channel noise as well as the data transmission rate R. It is small when the channel is relatively quiet, and large when the channel is noisy. It has been proven that, for data transmission rate R below R_{comp}, the average number of computations, C_{ave}, is bounded from above by a constant which is independent of the code constraint length N.[3,26,36] However, for $R \geqslant R_{comp}$, C_{ave} increases exponentially with N.

Sequential decoding has been shown to be a very powerful and practical decoding technique for channels which closely approximate a memoryless channel (or a channel with independent errors). A sequential decoder can be either built as a special purpose computer or programmed on a general purpose computer. Several sequential decoders have actually been built.[11,12,14,16] As the cost of digital hardware is decreasing rapidly, sequential decoding will be increasingly widely applied to practical error-control situations.

REFERENCES

1. Bluestein, G., and K. L. Jordan, "An Investigation of the Fano Sequential Decoding Algorithm by Computer Simulation," Group Report 62G-5, M.I.T.-Lincoln Laboratory, 1963.

2. Falconer, D.D., "A Hybrid Sequential and Algebraic Decoding Scheme," M.I.T. Doctoral Thesis, Cambridge, Massachusetts, September, 1966.

3. Fano, R. M., "A Heuristic Discussion of Probabilistic Decoding," *IEEE Trans. on Information Theory*, **IT-9**, pp. 64-74, April, 1963.

4. Gallager, R. G., "Sequential Decoding for Binary Channels with Noise and Synchronization Errors," Group Report 25-6-2, M.I.T.-Lincoln Laboratory, October 27, 1961.

5. Gallager, R. G., *Information Theory and Reliable Communication*, John Wiley, New York, 1968.

6. Horstein, M., "An Experimental Study of Sequential Decoding for the Binary Symmetric Channel," Group Report 34-74, M.I.T.-Lincoln Laboratory, November 20, 1958.

7. Jacobs, I. M., and E. R. Berlekamp, "A Lower Bound to the Distribution of Computation for Sequential Decoding," *IEEE Trans. on Information Theory*, **IT-13**, pp. 167-174, April, 1967.

8. Jelinek, F., *Probabilistic Information Theory*, McGraw-Hill, New York, 1968.

9. Jelinek, F., "An Upper Bound on Moments of Sequential Decoding Effort," *IEEE Trans. on Information Theory*, **IT-15**, pp. 140-149, January, 1969.

10. Jones, D. M., W. R. Wadden, and J. J. Bussgang, "A Comparative Evaluation of Sequential Decoding Algorithms," IRE Wescon Convention Record, August 21-24, 1963.

11. Jordan, K. L., Jr., "The Performance of Sequential Decoding in Conjunction with Efficient Modulation," *IEEE Trans. on Communication Technology*, **COM-14**, pp. 283-296, June, 1966.

12. Lebow, I. L., et al., "Application of Sequential Decoding to High-Rate Data Communication on a Telephone Line," *IEEE Trans. on Information Theory*, **IT-9**, p. 124, April, 1963.

13. Lebow, I. L., "A Quantitative Description of Sequential Decoding," Group Report 62G-4, M.I.T.-Lincoln Laboratory, July 12, 1963.

14. Lebow, I. L., "Sequential Decoding for Efficient Channel Utilization," First IEEE Annual Communications Convention Record, pp. 47-49, June, 1965.

15. Omura, J. K., "On the Viterbi Decoding Algorithm," *IEEE Trans. on Information Theory*, **IT-15**, pp. 177-179, January, 1969.

16. Perry, K. M., and J. M. Wozencraft, "Seco: A Self-Regulating Error Correcting Coder-Decoder," *IRE Trans. on Information Theory*, **IT-8**, pp. 128-135, September, 1962.

17. Pinsker, M. S., "Complexity of the Decoding Process," *Probl. Peredachi Informatsii*, **1**, pp. 113-116, 1965.

18. Reiffen, B., "Sequential Decoding for Discrete Input Memoryless Channels," *IEEE Trans. on Information Theory*, **IT-8**, April, 1962.

19. Reiffen, B., and R. Wiggert, "Some Experimental Results for a Sequential Decoding Algorithm Applied to an Asymmetric Channel," Group Report 25G-17, M.I.T.-Lincoln Laboratory, February 21, 1963.

20. Savage, J. E., "The Computation Problem with Sequential Decoding," M.I.T. Research Laboratory of Electronics, Technical Report 439 (also M.I.T.-Lincoln Laboratory Technical Report 371), 1965.

21. Savage, J. E., "Sequential Decoding – The Computation Problem," *Bell Systems Tech. J.*, **XLV**, pp. 149-175, January, 1966.

22. Savage, J. E., "The Distribution of the Sequential Decoding Computation Time," *IEEE Trans. on Information Theory*, **IT-12**, pp. 143-147, April, 1966.

23. Savage, J. E., "Progress in Sequential Decoding," *Advances in Communications Systems*, edited by A. V. Balakrishnan, **Vol. 3**, Academic Press, New York, 1968.

24. Savage, J. E., "Minimum Distance Estimates of the Performance of Sequential Decoding," *IEEE Trans. on Information Theory*, **IT-15**, pp. 128-140, January, 1969.

25. Shannon, C. E., R. G. Gallager, and E. R. Berlekamp, "Lower Bounds to Error Probability for Coding on Discrete Memoryless Channels," *Information and Control*, **10**, pp 65-103 (Part 1), January, 1967, and pp. 522-552 (Part 2), April, 1967.

26. Stiglitz, I. G., "Sequential Decoding with Feedback," Ph.D. Thesis, M.I.T. Department of Electrical Engineering, August, 1963.

27. Stiglitz, I. G., "Iterative Sequential Decoding," *IEEE Trans. on Information Theory*, **IT-15**, pp. 715-721, November, 1969.

28. Viterbi, A. J., "Error Bounds for Convolutional Codes and an Asymptotically Optimum Decoding Algorithm," *IEEE Trans. on Information Theory*, **IT-13**, pp. 260-269, January, 1967.

29. Wadden, W. R., D. M. Jones, and J. Pennypacker, "An Investigation of Sequential Decoding," RCA Review, pp. 522-542, September, 1961.

30. Wozencraft, J. M., "Sequential Decoding for Reliable Communication," 1957 National IRE Convention Record, **5**, Part 2, pp. 11-25; also, M.I.T. Research Laboratory of Electronics Technical Report 325, Cambridge, Massachusetts, 1957.

31. Wozencraft, J. M., and M. Horstein, "Coding for Two-Way Channels," published in *Information Theory*, edited by Colin Cherry, Butterworth and Co., London, 1960.

32. Wozencraft, J. M., and M. Horstein, "Coding for Two-Way Channels," M.I.T. Research Laboratory of Electronics Technical Report 383, Cambridge, Massachusetts, 1961.

33. Wozencraft, J. M., and B. Reiffen, *Sequential Decoding*, The M.I.T. Press, Cambridge, Massachusetts, and John Wiley, New York, 1961.

34. Wozencraft, J. M., and I. M. Jacobs, *Principles of Communication Engineering*, John Wiley, New York, 1965.

35. Wozencraft, J. M., and R. S. Kennedy, "Modulation and Demodulation for Probabilistic Coding," *IEEE Trans. on Information Theory*, **IT-12**, July, 1966.

36. Yudkin, H. L., "Channel State Testing in Information Decoding," Ph.D. Thesis, M.I.T. Department of Electrical Engineering, September, 1964.

37. Ziv, J., "Successive Decoding Scheme for Memoryless Channels," *IEEE Trans. on Information Theory*, **IT-9**, pp. 97-104, April, 1963.

INDEX